NEGOTIATING NATIONAL IDENTITY

"Negotiating

National Identity "

Immigrants, Minorities, and the Struggle for Ethnicity in Brazil

Jeffrey "Lesser"

Duke University Press   Durham & London   1999

© 1999 Duke University Press
All rights reserved
Printed in the United States of America on acid-free paper ⊗
Typeset in Stone by Tseng Information Systems, Inc.
Library of Congress Cataloging-in-Publication Data
appear on the last printed page of this book.

Dedicated to the memories of
my father, William Morris Lesser, ז״ל
and my mentor, Warren Dean, two
people whom I think of every day.

Contents

Preface

In 1935 Margarida Gloria da Faria, a teacher at Rio de Janeiro's Escola General Trompowsky, discovered that one of her students was a "descendant of Arabs." As a faculty member at an institution known for its modern approaches, Faria decided to use the child's presence as a "point of departure" for a study of "the man of the desert." In addition, the teacher decided to make three other groups part of that year's social studies curriculum: Brazilian Indians, Japanese, and Chinese.[1] Why did Margarida Gloria da Faria link these groups? Was it to integrate them into Brazilian society or to guarantee their rejection? Perhaps even she was unsure.

Non-European immigrants have been generally ignored in the historiography, surprising lacunae, given the millions of people involved. Yet research on Middle Easterners and Asians often takes place out of the mainstream of archives, and in these unseen but omnipresent Brazilian worlds terms like "foreigner" and "Brazilian" may be synonyms. For many Brazilians multiple identities were common long before airplanes made international travel a matter of hours rather than weeks or months. This book examines how non-European immigrants and their descendants negotiated their public identities as Brazilians.

Acknowledgments

This book could not have been written without the generosity of many people who gave me places to research and who read the manuscript as it slowly was transformed into a book. Professors Susumu Miyao and Kazunori Wakisaka of the Centro de Estudos Nipo-Brasileiros invited me to spend a year as a fellow, as did Thomas Skidmore at the Thomas Watson Institute's Center for Latin American Studies at Brown University. In Brazil, Roney Cytrynowicz, Samy Katz, Marcos Chor Maio, Koichi Mori, Margareth Rago, Alfredo Tolmasquim, and Celso Zilbovicius provided me with constant intellectual stimulation, as did Walter J. J. Dávila, Marc Forster, and Kerry Smith in the United States.

Roney Cytrynowicz, Walter J. J. Dávila, Marc Forster, Leo Spitzer, Gail Triner, and Barbara Weinstein read the entire manuscript in various forms, and anything good in this work stems from their excellent and provocative criticisms, comments, and suggestions. Valerie Milholland of the Duke University Press has been an ideal editor, and her support for and interest in this project have been invaluable. I am additionally grateful to Beth Wilson for her fine copyediting.

Many people took me into their homes, gave me advice and help, or read large parts of the manuscript. Each, in his or her own way, has improved this book greatly. Many thanks thus go to Anita Allen, George Reid Andrews, Laura Barnebey, Ilana Blaj, Gabriel and Clelia Bolaffi, Dain Borges, Adriana Brodsky, Heloisa Buarque, Sueann Caufield, Doug Cope, Maria Celia da Costa, Todd Diacon, Anani Dzidzienyo, Boris Fausto, Ronald Florence, the late Dr. Guido Fonseca, Gina Foster, Rene Gertz, Ilton and Ana Gitz, Monica Grin, Roberto Grün, Shuhei Hosokawa, Gilbert Joseph,

Harold Julie,Todd Kelly, Ignacio Klich, Robert Lee, Robert Levine, Bryan D. McCann, José Carlos Sebe bom Meihy, Laurie Mengel, Michael Molasky, Sandra Murayama, Mieko Nishida, Anita Novinsky, Fred Paxton, Patricia Pessar, Todd Porterfield, Ronald Rathier, Aron Rodrigue, Jorge Sáfady, Célia Sakurai, Marjorie Salvodon, Thomas Skidmore, Shawn Smallman, David Sorkin, Ilana Strozenberg, Shigeru Suzuki, Ayumi Takenaka, Alfredo and Patricia Tolmasquim, Oswaldo Truzzi, Daryle Williams, Joel Wolfe, Susane Worcman, and Xun Zhou. Many others who helped me with specific questions are thanked in the endnotes.

Many of my ideas were refined or modified after seminar presentations. My deep appreciation goes to John Coatsworth and the members of the Harvard University Latin American History Workshop; John French and the Duke University Center for Latin American Studies; Sander Gilman, Milton Shain, and the Kaplan Centre for Jewish Studies at the University of Capetown; K. David Jackson and the Yale University Lecture Series on Latin America; and Raanan Rein and the Tel Aviv University Department of History for giving me opportunities to engage in serious discussions. In Brazil, colleagues at universities in Campinas, Curitiba, Florianópolis, Porto Alegre, Rio de Janeiro, and São Paulo gave me numerous opportunities to present my work. Particular thanks go to my students, who have never failed to ask me the hard questions that constantly inspire me.

A number of foundations were extraordinarily generous in providing the funds needed to conduct research and to write over the past few years. To those organizations committed to encouraging scholarly research go my thanks: the American Council of Learned Societies, the J. William Fulbright Commission,the Fulbright-Hays Commission, the Lucius N. Littauer Foundation, the National Endowment for the Humanities, and the North–South Center. Connecticut College aided the project through the R. Francis Johnson Faculty Development Fund. Marco Antonio Rocha and Eva Reichman from the Brazilian Fulbright Commission were always helpful and kind as I did my research.

Brazil has experienced a remarkable transformation in access to its libraries and archives in the last decade, and my thanks go to the staffs of the Arquivo Nacional in Rio de Janeiro, the Itamaraty Archives (especially its director, Dona Lucia Monte Alto Silva), the Centro de Pesquisa e Documentação de História Contemporânea at Rio de Janeiro's Fundação Getúlio Vargas, Lucia at the São Francisco Law School Library, the Museu de Imigração in São Paulo and its director, Midori Kimura Figuti, and the staff of the Museu de Imigração Japonesa in São Paulo. Subscribers to the international electronic mail services H-LatAm and H-Ethnic were kind and quick in responding to queries. At Connecticut College my colleagues Beth Hansen, Ashley Hanson, Jeff Kosokoff, James McDonald, Marian Shilstone, and Erie Taniuchi provided bibliographical and technical help with great humor. To those many people who opened their homes and their private papers, this brief note does not adequately express my gratitude.

My scholarly work is ultimately the result of the support of my family and friends. To the Lesser, Friedlander, and Shavitt families goes my great love. Yet most important was the love of my wife, Eliana Shavitt Lesser, and our sons, Gabriel and Aron. They are what life is all about.

Abbreviations

ACENB-SP	Arquivo do Centro de Estudos Nipo-Brasileiros (Archive of the Center for Japanese-Brazilian Studies, São Paulo)
AESP	Archive do Estado de São Paulo (São Paulo State Archive)
AHI-R	Arquivo Histórico Itamaraty, Rio de Janeiro (Archive of the Brazilian Foreign Ministry)
AN-R	Arquivo Nacional, Rio de Janeiro (Brazilian National Archive)
APE-RJ	Arquivo Público do Estado do Rio de Janeiro (Public Archive of the State of Rio de Janeiro)
APP,SJ	Arquivos das Polícias Politícas, Setor Japonês (Archives of the Political Police, Japanese Section)
BN-R	Biblioteca Nacional, Rio de Janeiro (National Library)
BRATAC	Brasil Takushoku Kumiai (Brazil Colonization Corporation)
CIC	Conselho de Imigração e Colonização (Immigration and Colonization Council)
CPDOC-R	Centro de Pesquisa e Documentação de História Contemporânea do Brasil, Fundação Getúlio Vargas, Rio de Janeiro (Center for Research and Documentation on the Contemporary History of Brazil)
DEOPS	Departamento Estadual de Ordem Pública e Segurança (State Department of Public Order and Security)
DNI	Departamento Nacional de Imigração (National Department of Immigration)

DNP	Departamento Nacional de Povoamento (National Department of Colonization)
DTCI	Directória de Terras, Colonização e Imigração (Land, Colonization, and Immigration Directorate)
IHGB-R	Instituto Histórico e Geográfico Brasileiro, Rio de Janeiro (Brazilian Historical and Geographical Institute)
JMFA-MT	Japanese Ministry of Foreign Affairs, Tokyo (1868–1945, Meiji–Taisho). Microfilmed for the Library of Congress, 1949–1951
KKKK	Kaigai Kogyo Kabushiki Kaisha (Overseas Development Company or Kaiko)
NARC-W	National Archives and Record Center, Washington, D.C.
PRO-L	Public Records Office, London
RIC	*Revista de Imigração e Colonização* (Journal of Immigration and Colonization)
SEPS/CHI-SP	Secretaria do Estado da Promoção Social-Centro Histórico do Imigrante (Archives of the Center for Immigrant History, São Paulo)
SL-UF	Department of Special Collections, George A. Smathers Libraries, University of Florida

The Hidden Hyphen

Portuguese, Japanese, Spanish, Italians, Arabs—

Don't Miss The Most Brazilian Soap Opera

on Television

—*Advertisement for the Bandeirantes Television Network*

telenovela Os imigrantes *(1981)*[1]

At the end of an escalator that only goes up, I have a vision of Brazil's ethnic world. The escalator is in a nondescript building in São Paulo's traditional immigrant neighborhood of Bom Retiro. On the ground floor are tiny storefronts, one after another, selling clothes, cloth, handbags, and belts. Pushing through this teeming gallery, I reach the escalator. As I step off, there is a crowd negotiating their identities as Brazilians. In front of me is the little *lanchonete* serving "typical" Brazilian bar food like *esfiha* or *kibe* that might be recognized in the Middle East, or the suggestively named "Beirute" sandwich that would not. To the right is Malcha's, a falafel shop, owned by a woman who left Yemen to settle first in Israel and then in Brazil. Her menu reveals her clientele: it is written in Portuguese, Hebrew, and Korean. On the left side are a group of tiny Korean restaurants that share the rest of the floor with sweatshops that I glimpse through cracked boards. A peek inside suggests that most of the laborers are Bolivian and that most of the owners are Korean. The lingua franca is Portuguese, and home is a Brazil where shared culture revolves around social and economic opportunity.

Bom Retiro has long been viewed as an "ethnic" neighborhood. When Italians and Portuguese settled there in the nineteenth century, they saw the luxurious country homes that dominated the neighborhood along with the nearby Jardim da Luz, founded as São Paulo's botanical garden. Later, as Greeks and East European Jews entered, they mixed uncomfortably with students from elite educational institutions like the Escola Politécnica and Escola de Farmácia e Odontologia, both later incorporated into the University of São Paulo. Immigrants may then have seen the world of the elite up close, but it was still far away. Recently, however, things have changed. Today, every corner in Bom Retiro has a newsstand full of glossy magazines with titles like *Japão Aqui* (Japan Here) and *Raça Negra* (Black Race).[2] The ostensibly African religion of *candomblé* has exploded while practice of the syncretic *umbanda* has diminished noticeably. The music shops sell compact discs by the *sertanejo* group Nissei/Sansei, who proclaim that Brazilian country-western music, when sung in Japanese, achieves a "particularly artistic melody." To the consternation of some Jewish residents, Bom Retiro's Renascença school has a number of Brazilian children of Korean immigrants who do not seem to mind studying Hebrew as part of their educational program.[3]

Ethnicity, it seems, has become a popular motif in modern Brazil. While such open expressions may be new, ethnicity has been critical to the negotiation of Brazilian national identity over the last 150 years. This haggling undoubtedly happened at all levels of society, but my focus is on how and why immigrants and their descendants entered into public discussion with Brazil's political and intellectual leaders. These real-life strangers were, as Zygmunt Bauman has argued, "relevant whether . . . friend or foe."[4] They were *diferente* in a country where the popular definition of the word describes something that straddles the border between acceptable and unacceptable. What the newcomers understood, however, was that an apparently static elite discourse was in fact ambiguous. Unlike Eric Hobsbawn's peasants who "work[ed] the system . . . to their minimum disadvantage," these immigrants both manipulated and changed the system, rapidly becoming an integral part of the modern Brazilian nation even as they challenged how that nation would be imagined and constructed.[5]

The sense of being different yet similar was particularly noticeable among the non-Europeans who stood to gain the most by embracing *both* an imagined uniform Brazilian nationality and their new postmigratory ethnicities. These identities were multiple and often contradictory, and the symbols available to draw upon and rework were in constant flux. Throughout the twentieth century, members of a growing immigrant elite (university students, directors of farming colonies, small and large business owners, journalists, and intellectuals) engaged actively in a public discourse about what it meant to be Brazilian—via newspapers, books, the political arena, and frequently in mass action—with influential state and federal politicians, intellectuals, and business leaders. They created written and oral genres where ethnic distinction was reformulated to appropriate Brazilian identity. Some insisted that they were "white" and thus fit neatly into a traditional society that ran along a bipolar black/white continuum. Others, however, refused to categorize themselves with those terms. These immigrants (and their descendants) insisted that new hyphenated categories be created under the rubric "Brazilian." This was not an easy or smooth process, and attempts to legislate or enforce *brasilidade* (Brazilianness) were never successful. As the millennium approaches, Brazil remains a country where hyphenated ethnicity is predominant yet unacknowledged.

What does it mean to be a public "Brazilian," and how is "Brazilianness" contested? From the mid-nineteenth century on, both terms, and the notions behind them, were increasingly arbitrary, creating the space needed by newcomers to insert themselves into, or to change, paradigms about national identity. A single or static national identity never existed: the very fluidity of the concept made it open to pushes and pulls from below and above. While a relatively coherent elite discourse asserting ethnicity as treasonous was intended to constrain and coerce new residents into accepting a Europeanized and homogeneous national identity, this should not be confused with the actual ways in which it was perceived at either the elite or the popular level. Indeed, immigrants and their descendants developed sophisticated and successful ways of becoming Brazilian by altering the notion of nation as proposed by those in dominant positions. The thesis that elite conceptions of national identity were predicated on the elimination of ethnic distinctions thus must be modified to include the challenges progressively incorporated into notions of Brazilianness.[6]

The shifting sands of nationality and ethnicity were frequently revealed in discussions over the desirability of certain immigrant groups. Much of the language stemmed from Lamarckian eugenics, which theorized that traits, and thus culture, were acquired via local human and climatic environments. The eugenic proposition that a single "national race" was biologically possible provided a convenient ideological scaffold for national and immigrant elite support of policies to promote the entry of "desirable" immigrants who would "whiten" the country.[7] Eugenics-influenced policy initially favored the entry of German, Portuguese, Spanish, and Italian workers as *braços para a lavoura* (agricultural labor). Yet a fear of social and labor activism, and concerns about whether even Central Europeans would assimilate (Sílvio Romero's 1906 attack on the "dangers [of] Germanism" was the most famous) encouraged a look at non-European groups.[8] This necessitated a modification in the language that linked desirability to Europeanness. The elite craving to make immigrants "white," regardless of their ostensible biological race, matched neatly with immigrant hopes to be included in the desirable category. "Whiteness" remained one important component for inclusion in the Brazilian "race," but what it meant to be "white" shifted markedly between 1850 and 1950.

The experiences of Syrian, Lebanese, and Japanese immigrants and their descendants (known respectively as "Syrian-Lebanese" and *nikkei*) shows the transformation of whiteness as a cultural category. Three very flexible strategies emerged that, while at some times in competition and at others intertwined, crossed group, spatial, and temporal lines. Some immigrant elites argued that their own group was ethnically "white," proposing to render their premigratory identities harmless in return for inclusion in the pantheon of traditionally desirable groups. Others proposed that "whiteness" was not a necessary component of Brazilianness. Instead, they promoted the idea that Brazil would improve by becoming more "Japanese" or "Arab," terms constructed to mean "economically productive" and/or "supernationalist." These immigrants sought to interpret class status as a marker of Brazilian identity, allowing ethnicity to be maintained even as its importance was dismissed. They also proposed that a presumed blind loyalty to rulers prior to migration would be turned into modern Brazilian nationalism. Finally, many immigrants and their descendants seemed to reject all forms of inclusion by creating ultranationalist groups that, at least on the surface, sought to maintain political and cultural loyalty to the countries of origin.

The subjects of this book constructed and used multiple ethnicities that operated in both parallel and intersecting planes. Assimilation (in which a person's premigratory culture disappears entirely) was a rare phenomenon while acculturation (the modification of one culture as the result of contact with another) was common, even among those who ostensibly rejected majority society by remaining in closed communities. While the "special sorrow" (to borrow Matthew Frye Jacobson's term) of immigrants and their descendants was to create a vision of an unreal national past, hyphenated Brazilians incorporated many elements of majority culture even as they endured as distinct. Acculturation, not surprisingly, often went unrecognized by both outsiders and insiders.[9]

Members of the Brazilian elite were as bewildered as immigrants about the relationship between ethnicity and national identity. Some saw desirability as geographically based and urged prohibitions on immigrants from Asia and the Middle East. Others saw the granting of the full legal and social rights of citizenship to Syrian-Lebanese and nikkei as a reasonable price for economic growth. Still others wavered, wondering if the Brazilian state might insist on the disappearance of immigrant ethnicity *and* garner the benefits of immigrant labor. My analysis of these disparate positions suggests that *mestiçagem*, which many scholars have taken to mean the emergence of a new and uniform Brazilian "race" out of the mixing of peoples, was often understood as a joining (rather than mixing) of different identities, as the creation of a multiplicity of hyphenated Brazilians rather than a single, uniform one.

I have constructed a research model that explores public immigrant ethnicity as expressed in the language of the majority. While much of this discourse has been ignored by scholars both in Brazil and abroad, this is not a story of "hidden transcripts."[10] Rather, the written, oral, and visual texts I have used were openly expressed and understood by immigrants, their descendants, and members of the majority society whose public positions reveal much about private strategies of inclusion and cultural maintenance. Much of the documentation was created in Portuguese, and I have had the good fortune to find translations of materials ranging from Arabic-language poetry to Japanese-language haiku and government documents. Taken together, this material shows how attitudes about ethnicity are both constructed by, and construct, notions of national identity.

As private identities were interpreted for the public sphere, a tug-of-war took place between the leaders of non-European immigrant communities seeking to define social spaces, and politicians, intellectuals, and the press attempting to create the boundaries of Brazilianness. The tension was often expressed as racism, but this is not exclusively a study of bigotry. Rather, prejudice and the stereotypes that emerge from it were one way that identity was contested as negotiating positions were expounded and then revised as different publics responded. This cultural, economic, and political bargaining left neither side unchanged, keeping Brazilian majority society and postmigratory identities in a constant state of flux. In the end, a homogenization of national or cultural identity simply never took place.

* * *

Since the mid-nineteenth century, the world of non-European immigrant ethnicity could be found in large and small cities throughout Brazil, from Porto Alegre in the south to Belém near the mouth of the Amazon. It could be found in agricultural colonies in São Paulo, Paraná, and Rio Grande do Sul. It could be found in the hinterlands of Goiás and Minas Gerais. While non-European immigrants came from the Middle East and Asia, they were not of any single national, racial, or religious group. Tying them together was social and economic opportunity in a country so consumed with notions of race and ethnicity that even *futebol* players were believed to have the "qualities" of a "people," and the scoring of four goals in one game by seventeen-year-old Pelé made him "racially perfect." [11]

The relationship between race and Brazilian identity, however, is not one of color alone. Indeed, the concept of race is far more complex, and perhaps debased, than the fifteenth- and sixteenth-century European dictionary definition of a "population . . . of human beings who through inheritance possessed common characteristics." [12] Cultural presumptions about racial hierarchy and categories formalized in the seventeenth and eighteenth centuries reflected and promoted a sense of European superiority, and many Brazilian thinkers were monogenesists who saw race as biologically and environmentally linked. The German anatomist and naturalist Johann Friedrich Blumenbach, author of the influential *De generis humani varietate nativa* (1775/1776), was one of the most frequently cited of the early scientific racialists. He believed that the area around the Caucasus Mountains produced "the most beautiful race of men," and he placed the "Caucasian race" at the top of his racial hierarchy. [13] Such ideas touched the core of Brazil's elite, desperate to derive legitimacy through tentative connections to distant places and cultures. By asserting that geography (i.e., nature) was the basis of race, "white" immigrants *in* Brazil would create a European-like national identity that would smother the native and African populations with its superiority. Even the word *raça* was fluid: it could refer to people (the human race) or animals (breeds) or, even more generally, species.[14] The same words could describe a person's cultural identity or dehumanize him/her as a "half-breed." Race was an elusive category, and the language of race shows a visceral concern with defining the "other."

Nothing allowed social chemists to see their country as a "racial laboratory"—that ubiquitous metaphor for Brazil—more than immigrants. Immigration played a central role in policy from at least 1850, when it became clear that slavery would not exist long into the future. Although most elites did not seek to use immigrants as a replacement for an eliminated native population (as was the case in Argentina), they did assume a high correlation between immigrant entry and social change. An influential nineteenth-century book on colonization viewed immigrants as the "seed" of municipal life from which would spring the "powerful force of homogeneity and cohesion that will pull together and assimilate" the population at large.[15] In 1888, the literary critic Sílvio Romero used the language of chemistry in asserting that immigration was a social reagent to be handled with the greatest of care since Brazil had "a singular ethnic composition."[16] In the 1930s the anthropologist and Brazilian National Museum director Edgard Roquette-Pinto made the same point as he tried to distinguish between those who "created" wealth and those who "consumed" it.[17] More recently both Brazilian scholars and international observers have looked to Brazilian culture for its "unique" power of assimilation.[18] Ethnicity, then, was never only about social culture, it was about economic culture as well.

Immigrants challenged simplistic notions of race by adding a new element—ethnicity—to the mix. All of the 4.55 million immigrants who entered Brazil between 1872 and 1949 brought premigratory culture with them and created new ethnic identities. Yet it was the 400,000 Asians, Arabs, and Jews, deemed both nonwhite and nonblack, who most challenged elite notions of national identity.[19] Double assimilation was the key to creating a clear national identity: as colonists became Brazilian, Brazil would become European. Thus, as ideology metamorphosed into policy, who was denied entry became as important as who entered. Words like *imigrante* and *brasileiro* came to have much of the same fluidity as "raça," applicable to present residents or potential ones, to those born inside and outside of Brazil.

The ethnicities that these immigrants brought and constructed were situational rather than "immutable primordial indentit[ies]."[20] At various

Table 1. Immigrants Entering Brazil, 1880–1969, by Decade

	Portuguese	Italian	Spanish	German	Japanese	Middle Easterners	Others
1880–1889	104,690	277,124	30,066	18,901	——	——	17,841
1890–1899	219,353	690,365	164,293	17,084	——	4,215	103,017
1900–1909	195,586	221,394	113,232	13,848	861	26,846	50,640
1910–1919	318,481	138,168	181,651	25,902	27,432	38,407	85,412
1920–1929	301,915	106,835	81,931	75,801	58,284	40,695	181,186
1930–1939	102,743	22,170	12,746	27,497	99,222	5,549	62,841
1940–1949	45,604	15,819	4,702	6,807	2,828	3,351	34,974
1950–1959	241,579	91,931	94,693	16,643	33,593	16,996	87,633
1960–1969	74,129	12,414	28,397	5,659	25,092	4,405	47,491
Total	1,604,080	1,576,220	711,711	208,142	247,312	140,464	671,035
	31%	30%	14%	4%	5%	3%	13%

Sources: Brazil, Serviço de Estatística Econômica e Financeira do Tesouro Nacional, Ministério da Fazenda, Quadros estatísticos, resumo anual de estatísticas econômicas, 1932–1939 (Rio de Janeiro: Imprensa Nacional, 1941), pp. 80–82; Brazil, "Discriminação por nacionalidade dos imigrantes entrando no Brasil no período 1884–1939," Revista de Imigração e Colonização 1, no. 3 (July 1940): 617–642; Armin K. Ludwig, Brazil: A Handbook of Historical Statistics (Boston: G. K. Hall, 1985), pp. 104–106; Maria Stella Ferreira Levy, "O papel da migração internacional na evolução da população brasileira (1872 a 1972)," Revista de Saúde Pública supp., 8 (1974): 71–73.

Note: The Middle Eastern category is made up of many different national immigrant groups. Until 1903 the only groups to appear in official statistics were Syrians and Turks. In 1908 Egyptians and Moroccans were added. Later additions were Algerians, Armenians, Iraqis, Palestinians, and Persians. In 1926 the Lebanese category first appeared, and almost immediately thereafter the numbers of people entering as Turks dropped significantly. In 1954 the categories Iranian, Israeli, Jordanian, and Turk/Arab were added.

moments, immigrants and their descendants could embrace their "Japaneseness" or "Lebaneseness" as easily as their "Brazilianness." Ethnicity often intersected with nationalism (Brazilian and otherwise), making identity extremely pliant.[21] The Brazilian case thus suggests two immediate comparisons, one similar and one different. The former emerges from Mexico, where the ideology of a "Cosmic Race" suggests a social and cultural equality of which few Mexicans, especially those of clearly indigenous descent, are aware.[22] A contrary example comes from the United States, where seemingly inflexible categories of both race and ethnicity put power and "Americanness," but surely not "whiteness," up for grabs among those of non-European descent.

While the dominant forces in Brazil, Mexico, the United States, and other nations continue, in their own ways, to insist falsely that all citizens are members of the larger nation, the mask of nondiscrimination is removed when discussing immigration. During the Mexican Revolution, Chinese and Jewish immigrants found themselves attacked both physically and in the press as being unable to integrate to what was ostensibly an all-encompassing Mexican race.[23] In the United States the melting pot rhetoric did not prevent the establishment of immigration quotas or the denial of naturalization rights to Asians.

Brazil shows some similarities to the cases mentioned above. *Official* discrimination with regard to potential residents was common from the seventeenth century through at least 1942, and immigration policies were explicitly and unapologetically bigoted. During Brazil's colonial era, heretics (the code word for Jews and Muslims) were banned from entering, even though the New Christian (recent converts to Christianity) and Marrano (the derogatory term used to describe New Christians who secretly maintained their non-Christian religion) population of the colony was significant.[24] Independence from Portugal in 1822 led the new Brazilian imperial government to allow the practice of non-Catholic Christianity, but "the native population [showed] a great jealousy and dislike for foreigners."[25] In 1889 a republic was declared, and the government's first immigration decree banned the entry of Asians and Africans. Thirty years later the government imposed these prohibitions on anyone it judged "African" or "Asian," including those who had never been to Africa or Asia.[26] Immigration *was* the construction of national identity.

Asking questions about the public construction of immigrant ethnicity opens many windows to Brazilian national identity. Nineteenth-century debates over Chinese entry took place within the context of abolition of slavery and the creation of a republican regime. The arrival of tens of thousands of Japanese immigrants came during a radicalization of Brazilian politics in the 1920s. The rejection of Catholic immigrants from Iraq came in the aftermath of the Revolution of 1930 and the triumphs of fascism and Nazism. In spite of the structures created to manipulate ethnic hierarchies

Table 2. Percent of Immigrants Entering Brazil, 1900–1939, by Nationality and Decade

	1900–1909	1910–1919	1920–1929	1930–1939
Portuguese	32% (195,586)	39% (318,481)	35% (301,915)	31% (102,743)
Italian	36% (221,394)	17% (138,168)	13% (106,835)	7% (22,170)
Spanish	18% (113,232)	22% (181,651)	10% (81,931)	4% (12,746)
German	2% (13,848)	3% (25,902)	9% (75,801)	8% (27,497)
Japanese	.01% (861)	3% (27,432)	7% (58,284)	30% (99,222)
Middle Easterners	4% (26,846)	5% (38,407)	5% (40,695)	2% (5,549)
Others	8% (50,640)	11% (85,412)	21% (181,186)	18% (62,841)
	100% (622,407)	100% (815,453)	100% (846,647)	100% (332,768)

Sources: Brazil, Serviço de Estatística Econômica e Financeira do Tesouro Nacional, Ministério da Fazenda, Quadros estatísticos, resumo anual de estatísticas econômicas, 1932–1939 (Rio de Janeiro: Imprensa Nacional, 1941), pp. 80–82; Brazil, "Discriminação por nacionalidade dos imigrantes entrando no Brasil no período 1884–1939," Revista de Imigração e Colonização 1, no. 3 (July 1940): 617–642; Armin K. Ludwig, Brazil: A Handbook of Historical Statistics (Boston: G. K. Hall, 1985), pp. 104–106; Maria Stella Ferreira Levy, "O papel da migração internacional na evolução da população brasileira (1872 a 1972)," Revista de Saúde Pública supp., 8 (1974): 71–73.

Note: The Middle Eastern category is made up of many different national immigrant groups. Until 1903 the only groups to appear in official statistics were Syrians and Turks. In 1908 Egyptians and Moroccans were added. Later additions were Algerians, Armenians, Iraqis, Palestinians, and Persians. In 1926 the Lebanese category first appeared, and almost immediately thereafter the numbers of people entering as Turks dropped significantly. In 1954 the categories Iranian, Israeli, Jordanian, and Turk/Arab were added.

through the control of discourse and policy, immigrants often stood firm, creating dialectical spaces where serious negotiations about national identity took place. Probing the intersection of ethnicity and national identity allows a picture to emerge of how immigrants and elites reacted when confronted with a changing world that demanded new responses to cultural questions. It helps explain curious outcomes, such as when "dominant" elites and "subordinate" immigrants came to agree that Brazil was engaged in a mythic search for a "national race."[27]

My discussion of ethnicity and its relation to national identity should not suggest that race can be dismissed as a factor in understanding Brazil. In the nineteenth century some powerful intellectuals and politicians

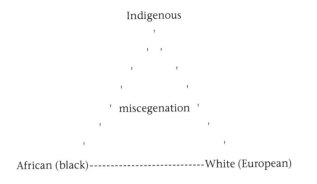

Figure 1

sought "pure" European immigrants who would re-create the Old World in the New. Others argued that the reality of miscegenation underneath the fiction of racial democracy prevented Brazil from achieving its rightful place among elite nations.[28] Since "racial purity," from both a biological and a cultural standpoint, was (and is) necessarily an illusion, a product of nostalgia for an imaginary era of harmony and homogeneity, the mixing of conceptual categories like "nation" and "ethnicity" was often described with racial language. This has led many scholars to subscribe to what might be called the triangle theory of Brazilian society: a "civilization" created from the "collision of three races": Africans (blacks), whites (Europeans), and Indians (indigenous), where the mixture of peoples found within the area enclosed by the borders of the triangle created infinite genetic possibilities.[29]

Disease combined with the often murderous policies of the various Brazilian colonial, imperial, and republican governments to remove indigenous peoples almost entirely from the equation. This compressed the triangle into a continuum that combined ethnicity and skin color by placing Africans (blacks) at one end and whites (Europeans) on the other. Thus, according to the traditional paradigm, Brazil is a country struggling with an identity that always exists at some point along the continuum, and many academics have presumed or implied that anyone without African or indigenous ancestry is, by definition, in the "white" category.[30] A number of studies make this point in their titles: Roger Bastide and Florestan Fernandes's *Brancos e negros em São Paulo*, Thomas Skidmore's *Black into White*, Carl Degler's *Neither Black nor White*, Lilia M. Schwarcz's *Retrato em branco*

African (black)--------------------------White (European)

[Brazilian society]

Figure 2

e negro, Célia Maria Marinho de Azevedo's *Onda negra, medo branco,* and George Reid Andrews's *Blacks and Whites in São Paulo Brazil, 1888–1988* are just a few of the better-known examples.[31]

Although Brazil's ethnic world of immigrant nonwhites and nonblacks often intersects traditional black/white society, it parallels it as well. Cursory readings of anything from nineteenth-century rural slave-owner reports to mid-twentieth-century diplomatic correspondence show that it was the rare person who believed that a Tupí was a Guaraní, a Portuguese Catholic was a German Protestant, or a Hausa Muslim was a Yoruba *orisha* cultist. By exploring outside of the black/white continuum, we can better analyze how cultural meetings spawned new hyphenated ethnicities, all of which had in common their Brazilianness.[32]

How non-European immigrants sought to define their place within Brazilian national identity, and the reaction to these attempts, are the focus of this book. Chapter 2 examines elite discourse on non-European ethnicity in the nineteenth century and suggests that the debates over Chinese immigrant labor created the overarching paradigm against which all other non-European groups would struggle. Chapter 3 investigates how Syrian and Lebanese immigrants manipulated elite discourses on ethnicity to create a hyphenated space for themselves and how, in response, the state and press sought to redefine one Christian Arab group hoping to immigrate to Brazil as "Muslims" and "fanatics" in order to prohibit their entry. The next three chapters analyze how ethnicity and economics came together in the twentieth century to redefine what it meant to be Brazilian, focusing on the massive immigration of Japanese that began in 1908.

The story, however, begins in the early nineteenth century as nervous planters began to search for replacements for slaves. European workers, perhaps from Switzerland or Prussia, captured the Brazilian imagination. There was a problem, though. European wage laborers were neither economically cheap nor socially servile. Soon a perfect new group was discovered. They came from faraway Asia, a place few had been but everyone knew.

2

Chinese Labor and the Debate
over Ethnic Integration

Through the mysterious correlation by which
costume influences character, I already felt myself
imbued with Chinese ideas and instincts [after
putting on a mandarin's robes]: the love of
meticulous ceremonial, respect for bureaucratic
formula, a tinge of cultivated skepticism. At the
same time I was filled with abject terror of the
Emperor, abject hatred of foreigners, devotion to
the cult of ancestor worship, fanaticism for
tradition, and a consuming passion for sweets.

—*Eça de Queiroz describing his protagonist's mysterious*
transformation from European to Chinese in
The Mandarin *(1880)*[1]

The physical presence of Asians was never necessary for images of Chinese to float like an omnipresent specter through discussions of ethnicity in Brazil. Nineteenth-century policy makers would argue for decades over whether and how Chinese laborers might fit into Brazilian society, and analyses of the cultural and physical traits of the "Mongolian type" could be found in numerous intellectual treatises. While elites were quite evenly divided over the utility of Chinese labor, they uniformly accepted Blumenbach's racial/physical beauty scale that placed Asians far below Europeans and well above Africans.[2] All believed in the cultural basis of labor utility and all reinterpreted European discourses on ethnicity for the Brazilian context. The belief that skin pigmentation and culture were related thus coexisted with an understanding that nationality and ethnicity (usually described with words like "culture" or "race") were not always synonymous.[3]

Brazilian fascination with Asia emerged from Portugal, which in 1511 became the first European maritime power to establish direct relations with the Chinese empire. The relationship even affected language, and the word "mandarin," flowing from its etymological roots in *mandar* (to send or to order), was introduced to describe members of the Chinese elite. Asians, according to both Portuguese and Brazilian intellectuals, were exotics who "differed essentially" from Africans because of their superior position in the racial hierarchy.[4] As other empires grew on the backs of "coolie" labor, a work/culture discussion emerged over whether Chinese workers would enrich Brazil economically or harm its culture by transforming it from "European" to "Asian."[5] Chinese entry could never be disentangled from ideas about Brazil's future.

As both domestic and international pressure to abolish slavery increased, plantation owners and the politicians they supported began to understand that the Central Europeans they so highly desired would not immigrate in large numbers. Equally disturbing was the realization that the large population of African descent, seen as both culturally degenerate and unproductive, would not quickly disappear from Brazilian society.[6] Chinese labor provided a perfect solution to the dual problem: a servile yet nonslave class could be created that would help de-Africanize Brazil. A further advantage was advanced by Chinese and Brazilian intellectuals who claimed that Asians were of the same "racial stock" as the native populations of the Americas.[7] The biological connection of Chinese to Brazilian "Indians" had ramifications beyond assimilation and touched deeply on what Doris Sommer has called "Brazil's two-faced indigenism," the notion that "Indianness" was a crucial part of the national identity of a nation "founded on Indian removal." By placing Chinese in the same category as indigenous populations who would disappear in the face of "Brazilian" expansion, planters like João Maurício Wanderley (Baron Cotegipe) could easily propose that Chinese ethnicity also would be left behind as a new Brazilian "race" was created.[8]

Embedded in the disputes over Chinese labor were deep divisions about how the entry of a new ethnic group would affect Brazilian national identity. Those in favor of introduction focused on an increase in economic production, while opponents feared social "pollution." Important intellectuals, planters, and politicians such as Quintino Bocayuva (future leader of Rio de Janeiro's Republican party), Senator Alfredo d'Escragnolle Taunay (who would later become one of the leaders of the Sociedade Central de Imigração, the Central Immigration Society), the progressive entrepreneur and industrialist Irineu Evangelista de Sousa (Baron Mauá), Liberal politician and president of the Province of Rio de Janeiro João Lins Vieira Cansanção de Sinimbú (who was later appointed prime minister), and the abolitionist politicians André Rebouças and Joaquim Nabuco, to name just a few, spoke frequently and fervently about "the Chinese question." The positions these politicians took were not always consistent with their Liberal or Conservative affiliations, and bizarre political alliances were the rule. The "anti" group brought together fervent nationalists/racists who asserted that Chinese were biologically degenerate, abolitionists who believed that Chinese laborers would form a neoslave class, and a few large landowners who were convinced that only Africans were biologically suited for backbreaking plantation work. The other side included a combination of plantation owners who wanted to replace African slaves with a cheaper and more docile group, other planters who believed that Chinese workers were biologically suited for agricultural labor and would help make Brazil more competitive in the world market, and abolitionists convinced that Chinese contract labor would be a step forward on the path to full wage labor. What everyone agreed was that Chinese workers were little more than merchandise.

* * *

Brazilian interest in Chinese labor can be found as early as 1807. An economist and member of the high court of Salvador, Bahia, Judge João Rodrigues de Brito, encouraged the entry of Chinese and East Indians in his influential *Cartas econômico-políticas sobre a agricultura, e commércio da Bahia,* noting that they were "not only hard workers but . . . active, industrious and skilled in arts and agriculture."[9] Portugal's foreign minister-in-exile in Rio de Janeiro (in 1808 the Portuguese court fled Napoleon), the count of Linhares, agreed. He considered bringing in two million Chinese as a means of skirting the English suppression of the slave trade and satisfying King Dom João's desire to make tea a major export commodity.[10] The plan was implemented in 1810 when several hundred Chinese tea growers began work on the imperial government's plantation in Rio de Janeiro (known later as the Royal Botanical Garden) and Niterói's Fazenda Imperial de Santa Cruz (Santa Cruz Imperial Estate). Two years later, four hundred or five hundred more tea cultivators arrived, and the Chinese word for tea, *chá,* gained wide usage in popular and elite language.[11]

In spite of eagerness on both sides—in 1814 and 1815 Chinese diplomats were housed at the residence of the minister of war and foreign affairs, who later contracted a group from Macao for the Royal Naval Arsenal—Chinese tea cultivation was generally viewed as a failure.[12] Wilhelm L. von Eschwege, a German baron who spent eleven years in Brazil as a colonel in the Royal Engineering Corps and intendant general of mines, pointed out the unhappiness of the Chinese, who were frustrated that "all the attempts to bring women were in vain." Charles Darwin visited the Royal Botanical Garden in 1832 and complained that the 164 acres of "an insignificant little [tea] bush[es] . . . scarcely possessed the proper tea flavor." John Luccock, a British merchant who spent some ten years in Brazil beginning in 1808, put the onus on the Chinese workers in a different way. He claimed that they were overpaid and too "diligent, . . . too precise, and [too] slow in their modes of culture" even though they had a "rapidity of comprehension which surpassed whatever I have observed of the kind in any other race."[13]

The Chinese workers appear to have been equally ambivalent about their lives in Brazil. This stemmed in part from traditional notions that South America contained "the States of the Beasts," populated by peoples "more barbarous" than others.[14] These premigratory stereotypes appear to have been confirmed by two specific incidents. When some Chinese fled the Royal Botanical Garden, Dom João's son hunted them with horses and dogs. Furthermore, the director of the Botanical Garden treated the workers harshly, suspecting that they had intentionally failed to reveal their most sophisticated tea-processing techniques. Warren Dean has

"Plantation chinoise de thé dans le Jardim boutanique de Rio de Janeiro." From Johann Moritz Rugendas, *Malerische Reise in Brasilien von Moritz Rugendas* (Paris: Engelmann, 1835). Courtesy of Biblioteca Nacional, Rio de Janeiro.

pointed out, however, that the Chinese drank their tea green and may simply not have known Euro-Brazilian tastes.[15]

Chinese workers did not accept poor treatment passively. Many fled, settling in Rio de Janeiro, where they worked as peddlers and cooks.[16] Those who remained on the imperial estate complained openly, and in 1819 they proposed that a worker who spoke Portuguese (he may have learned it in the Macao area) be assigned as official interpreter for the group and be paid a special wage by the royal court.[17] While there is no evidence of a reply, the German traveler Johann Moritz Rugendas did find three hundred Chinese still working on the estate in 1835. While labor conditions may have improved, tea cultivation was viewed as a failure. Imperial elites blamed this on the "Chinese race," and in 1843 the Chamber of Deputies refused Lord Aberdeen's offer to negotiate the importation of sixty thousand Chinese.[18]

It was the 1845 passage of the Aberdeen Act, which allowed the British navy to treat slave vessels as pirate ships, that motivated a number of Brazilian merchants to consider mass Chinese migration.[19] Further encouragement came with reports of Chinese participation in the expansion of the Peruvian and Cuban economies. Finally, in late 1854 the imperial government ordered its legation in London to bring six thousand Chinese laborers to Brazil, and hired the Boston firm of Sampson and Tappan to transport them. The labor contracts offered by the Brazilian government are worth considering, since they provide clues to presumptions about labor and ethnicity. A common stereotype, that all Chinese were opium addicts, was rejected in one clause while another demanded that sugarcane cultivators come from different areas than tea growers, implying that nurture rather than nature was critical to agricultural success. In an attempt to prevent miscegenation, all workers were to be married (or engaged) with the right to bring fiancées, wives, and children under twelve years old.[20]

Sampson and Tappan brought few Chinese to Brazil, but the announcement of the contract regenerated the debate. A memorandum to the imperial government on "Chinese Emigration and What We Know of Its Results in Various Countries" dismissed fears by insisting that the "Chinaman is not like the black who only works enough to sustain himself" while assuring politicians that "they do not establish themselves and . . . they do not colonize."[21] A different report expressed a contrary sentiment, claiming that the Chinese would neither "increase the sum of our agricultural knowledge nor improve our morality and civilization!"[22] Adadus Calpe, an Argentine who had spent five years in the United States and another two in Brazil, agreed. In a study presented to the marquis of Abrantes, Calpe condemned "the organic configuration of the Chinaman" as "retrograde by nature." Playing on fears that miscegenation would darken rather than whiten the population, Calpe asked, "What would stop the joining of the Chinese and the black?," and argued that the Chinese did not work hard, in part because they "were not Christian." As if this were not enough, Calpe believed that any emigrating Chinese was by definition "the most sordid that the Celestial Empire has to offer, [he is] the most obtuse and ignorant, the most uncouth, the least useful, the most unprofitable of that retrograde race. . . . The Chinaman is not as strong as the black and is not as patient or constant as the European."[23]

The most influential early attack on Chinese immigration came from Luiz Peixoto de Lacerda Werneck, a coffee planter who believed that only small holdings would attract immigrants and that slavery could never be replaced by immigrant wage labor.[24] His two law degrees (from the Paris Academy and the University of Rome) and his prestigious academic memberships provided him the status to present his ideas in frequent editorials in the Rio de Janeiro newspaper *Jornal do Comércio*.[25] Werneck thought social hierarchies were determined by a combination of place, culture, and biology; thus all Protestant Germans were "moral, peaceful and hard-working," and all Chinese were "animal-men" whose "character . . . is seen by all travelers in unfavorable and terrible colors . . . their vile egoism, their pride, their barbarous insensitivity fed by the practice of child abandonment and decapitation . . . are the general vices of China."[26] To the planter the Chinese were "stationary, from a doubtful civilization, inert from progress, [that] must cede its place and be exterminated by the nations of Europe and America who are obeying a providential mission, marching, armed like evangelical gladiators with the light of civilization."[27] Even so, Brazil's race-in-formation was not powerful enough to overcome millions of inferior Asians. Chinese culture would thus "degenerate" Brazil's population, which had already suffered "the deformity of the indigenous and the African."[28]

Werneck's ideas were widely distributed and influential. A planter from Maranhão cited Werneck in his argument that Chinese labor was "so stationary, so alien to human progress, so superstitious and badly educated . . . [that we should] establish once and for all the predominance of the Caucasian race—smarter, more industrious and progressive than all others."[29] Twenty years later Werneck's ideas bubbled up during debates on Chinese immigration in the Bahian Provincial Assembly, while in Rio de Janeiro medical student José de Souza Pereira de Cruz Junior claimed that the "colonization fever" had led to a Brazil covered with "tattered Chinese, broken by their sickness, begging in our streets."[30] Another half-century later, Joaquim da Silva Rocha, head of the Directorate of the Brazilian Colonization Service, cited Werneck in his three-volume *História da colonização do Brasil* (1919).[31]

While Brazilians engaged in ferocious debates about Asian immigration, international legal disputes over the "coolie trade" made Chinese labor contracts difficult to sign. In the 1850s and 1860s there were fewer than one thousand Chinese in Brazil, yet even this small number caused an outcry. In 1858, when the United States prohibited its citizens from transporting Chinese workers to any country, the director of the Imperial Public Lands Office (Repartição Geral das Terras Públicas) hailed the news, exclaiming that "the experiment with Chinese workers led to terrible results . . . and now we are free of such people who certainly will not be received by anyone else."[32] The abolitionist Agostinho Marques Perdigão Malheiro linked the low status of Brazil's indigenous communities to "racially defective" Chinese immigration, claiming that "coolies are the Indians of Asia; however we also have Indians and their descendants—the experiment with Chinese [here in Brazil] is already completed."[33]

Powerful antislavery, pro-immigration (and pro-Chinese) voices responded, with the Alagoan abolitionist and federal deputy Aureliano Candido Tavares Bastos (1839–1875) leading the way. Like many intellectuals, Tavares Bastos, who had a doctorate from the São Paulo Law School and in 1866 helped found the Sociedade Internacional da Imigração, linked the end of slavery in Brazil with the development of free labor and spontaneous immigration.[34] Since "racial mixture in all peoples will create a new population . . . vigorous, intelligent and able," Tavares Bastos wondered in the society's 1867 Annual Report if Brazilian culture, which already had "the imagination of the African and the reflection of the white," should include Chinese as well.[35] His answer was a resounding yes! Pointing to economic growth in the United States and the English Caribbean, Tavares Bastos insisted that the Chinese, as a result of their "sobriety, perseverance and aptitude for commerce," were an intermediate step between unintelligent and depraved (although imaginative) African labor, and European immigrants, who were too smart to go to Brazil's hinterlands.[36]

Tavares Bastos's support of Chinese labor should not be understood as respect for Chinese culture. In the aggressively titled pamphlet *Os males do presente e esperanças do futuro* (Present Evils and Future Hopes, 1861), Tavares Bastos complained that the same "Asian" attributes that had ruined Portugal had infected Brazilian decision makers.[37] The government's refusal to open the Amazon region "to the flags of all nations" as a means of attracting European and North American immigrants thus became both "the Chinese policy" and "the Japanese policy" because it "separates them from the world." Brazil's "Asian" approach, claimed Tavares Bastos, would lead the country to disappear in the face of the "invincible Occidental armada [of] . . . civilization . . . Christianity, truth and equality."[38]

How could someone who so despised Chinese and Japanese culture favor Chinese entry? Tavares Bastos himself was not sure, and in 1869 reversed his position completely. Convinced that the seed of Asia had germinated in Brazil, he wrote in the semiofficial newspaper *Reforma* (Rio de Janeiro), and again in his book *A província* (1870), that Chinese entry was a new form of slave trafficking, that those who had entered Brazil came from the "mud pits of China and India" and were "even more disgusting spiritually than they were repugnant physically."[39]

At about the same time that Tavares Bastos was shifting his position, the future Republican leader Quintino Bocayuva began agitating in favor of Chinese immigration. Half of Bocayuva's eighty-page pamphlet *A crise da lavoura* (1868) was devoted to the importation of Chinese or Indian "coolies," since "to wait and only count on European colonization, appears to me an error." By linking abolition with Chinese immigration, Bocayuva could provide a "race with an aptitude for agricultural work" while ensuring that Chinese would "deflect all [attempts at] assimilation." He even proposed that negative aspects of Chinese culture were positive for Brazil. A "passion for gambling . . . a naturally perverted moral [character] and a tendency to emigrate alone, without women, [leading to] vile and harmful acts . . . leads them to be inward looking. Their soul is permanently [in China] and they work for the money to return to their country."[40] Chinese laborers would bring economic growth and, best of all, would leave Brazil after completing their tasks.[41]

Bocayuva and his allies persuaded the imperial government that Chinese workers would ameliorate Brazil's labor crisis, and in July 1870 a ten-year labor importation plan was enacted.[42] The announcement resonated most notably in the halls of the semiofficial Sociedade Auxiliadora da Indústria Nacional, which witnessed no less than six long lectures on Chinese labor during 1870. I. C. Galvão, Miguel Calmon Menezes de Macedo, and Thomaz Deschamps de Montmorency of the group's Colonization Section published a *parecer* (opinion) on the question "Is the Importation of Chinese Colonists Suitable for Brazil?" While the topic was Chinese labor, the subject was national identity. Expressing the view that any *immigrant* willing to do servile labor would *not* be capable of improving society, the three argued that short-term Chinese labor in a "state of incomplete civilization" could help Brazil "pass the diverse gradations of imperfection" on the way to the "perfect state of free labor."[43] Chinese workers, while neither immigrants nor human, were climatically adaptable, docile, sober, and willing to work for low pay. There were other advantages as well. Chinese lacked the "developed sense of equality and independence" found among European immigrants, making them easier to control. Like Bocayuva, the group insisted that the Chinese had "no ambitions to become landowners and . . . only one aspiration, to return to their homeland."[44] To Galvão et al. the Chinese were perfect non-European migrants—they worked quietly, and at the end of their contract they left Brazil.

Other members of the Sociedade Auxiliadora took a contrary position. Nicolão Moreira of the Agricultural Section placed social value over labor utility complaining that Chinese would "not remain in the country and will not miscegenate with our population," doing nothing to help Brazil improve itself.[45] Second Vice President Joaquim Antonio d'Azevedo agreed, suggesting that Brazil needed immigrants who would set up colonies and stay permanently.[46] Now the Sociedade Auxiliadora was consumed by the Chinese question. Menezes de Macedo opined that Brazil's economy would wither without Chinese workers. "The stupid and impotent Negro resists or dies: the [European] colonist abandons his patron in search of better luck . . . the importation of Chinese is of urgent necessity."[47] I. C. Galvão concurred, arguing that "If the Chinese are not convenient [you are] admitting that England, France, the United States, Spain, Peru and all the planters of all the colonies are in complete error and are rapidly wasting their money." Quoting sources ranging from the *Encyclopedia Britannica* to Edouard Du Hailly's five-part series in the influential French Positivist journal *Revue des Deux Mondes,* Galvão insisted that culture was not genetic. Problems with Chinese would disappear in Brazil, since "Under a better government the Chinese would be without a doubt a better people."[48]

Perhaps the most explicit linkage of Brazilian national identity and immigrant ethnicity came in a speech before the Sociedade Auxiliadora in late 1870. José Ricardo Moniz mocked his colleagues for suggesting that "Koolies" would not be part of the "population question—the question of the State." His "scientific" approach—the published version of the speech cited thirty-four authors ranging from the famous (Fichte, Kant, Locke, Confucius, Hegel, Voltaire) to the obscure (Gortz, Dubosch, Ponsielgue, Trèves)—led him to view geography as more critical than biological "race." In the same way that others had connected Chinese and Amazon indigenes, Moniz insisted that "the Chinaman is the Azorean" and that Germans and East Asians shared an "Aryan gene."[49] He asked opponents if they did "not want the Mongoloid race because the yellow color does not please you?" and insisted that selecting laborers was as simple as going to mountain cities, where "all . . . [are] strong and robust," rather than to Canton (Guangzhou), which was "peopled with the feces of other provinces."[50]

An important subtext to all discussions involved Brazil's future as an equal partner among the world's most powerful nations. Brazilian elites thus reinterpreted reports of Chinese labor in other countries to fit their own political positions.[51] Two books frequently thrown into the muddle were Alfred Legoyt's *L'Émigration européenne, son importance, ses causes, ses effets, avec un appendice sur l'Émigration africaine, hindoue et chinoise* (1861) and Leonard Wray's *The Practical Sugar Planter* (1848). While Legoyt's comments on Asians were buried in a ten-page appendix, his work appealed to those interested in immigration as a means of modifying culture. It also had the double cachet of being published in France *and* analyzing why Brazil's economic potential had not led to mass immigration from Europe. While my reading of Legoyt shows that he had no strong feelings on Chinese labor—his major thesis was that introduction of meat into Asian diets would have a positive cultural effect—both the anti-Chinese Agostinho Marques Perdigão Malheiro and the pro-Chinese I. C. Galvão interpreted Legoyt to their own advantage.[52]

Those who treated the Chinese question primarily as a labor issue found *The Practical Sugar Planter* appealing, and all members of the Sociedade Auxiliadora da Indústria hailed it.[53] Leonard Wray spent sixteen years managing sugar plantations in Jamaica, India, and Southeast Asia, and saw a distinction between the "trash" from India and the "intelligent, industrious and enterprising Chinese: the best class of emigrants under heaven."[54] *The Practical Sugar Planter* became widely known among Brazil's elites after the president of the province of Rio de Janeiro ordered a Portuguese translation for distribution to planters. Members of the Bahian Assembly also received copies to remedy a "lack of information and education," and they approved (without financing) an importation plan in spite of one representative's claim that Chinese "only serve to catch shrimp in the lakes and sell them in the city."[55]

The ebb and flow of the Brazilian discussion operated independently of Chinese and British plans to dismantle the "coolie trade." Thus growing Brazilian support came as Chinese emigration diminished. In 1873, the Chinese government prohibited all but clearly voluntary emigration and the British banned exit from Hong Kong, except to British colonies. A rupture in diplomatic relations between China and Portugal led to a ban on emigration from Macao, and Peru, with a Chinese labor force of some ninety thousand, banned entry.[56] In spite of this, a thousand Chinese workers from Macao were smuggled by boat to Brazil in early 1874; later in the year the Japanese navy confiscated a Brazilian ship with two thousand uncontracted Chinese.[57] Other attempts to bring Chinese workers via California and France also failed when new Chinese laws prohibited subjects from signing contracts outside of the country.[58]

British and Chinese prohibitions led planters to demand that the Brazilian government take charge of arranging official labor contracts. This proposition markedly changed the ways that the Brazilian state related to immigration and immigrants. Now government operatives, rather than businesspeople, were charged with finding and selecting immigrants while state-sponsored immigration agencies received the task of constructing an ideal society filled with industrious, content, and culturally appropriate workers. A growing stream of diplomats and merchants began to spend long periods in Asia, and their contact with real Chinese and Japanese workers and elites changed ideas about the relationship of immigrant ethnicity to Brazilian national identity.

Alagoan senator João Lins Vieira Cansanção de Sinimbú was instrumental in making Chinese labor a national political issue. In 1875 he convinced Minister of Agriculture Coelho de Almeida to ask Nicolão Joaquim Moreira, a member of the Sociedade Auxiliadora and of the Brazilian delegation to the 1876 Philadelphia Centennial Exposition, to examine the role of immigration in the United States.[59] Moreira's report was detailed, and his prior anti-Chinese position was not modified by firsthand experience. In a scathing denunciation, Moreira insisted that Brazil needed "a sedentary and moral population," and that "the importation of Chinese or coolies in identical conditions, if not worse than the African slaves, [will lead] to the impoverishment of our civil and political education."[60]

Moreira's widely distributed comments, along with other reports from Brazilians in the United States, filtered quickly through the elite.[61] The Rio de Janeiro monthly *Mephistópheles* attacked Chinese colonization in a full-page, eight-section editorial cartoon, claiming that Minister of Agriculture Coelho de Almeida loved "sardines and fried shrimp," and that tea would become a competitor of Brazilian coffee in the domestic and world markets.[62] Yet the comical aspects of the *Mephistópheles* cartoon did not overshadow its ugly racism. One section portrayed a devious-looking Chinese vendor selling a Brazilian priest sardines "at the price of gold," and another showed a boat steaming into Rio de Janeiro overflowing with an indistinguishable mass of Asians. The text explained that Brazilians would have to guard their chickens at night, and in the final section an emaciated, pigtailed, sneering Chinese man was dressed in a Brazilian military uniform. The caption read, "Our race will be the most perfect, and we can perhaps count Sr. Tcham-tchim-Bum . . . da Silva among our most important politicians."

The fear of economic competition and ethnic mixing made easy approval of a treaty mission to China impossible.[63] Colonization companies and a number of powerful planters increased the pressure, culminating in Pedro Dias Gordilho Paes Leme's open letter of 1877 to politicians and planters, entitled "A nossa lavoura." Paes Leme, like virtually all his educated contemporaries, believed that it would be "a grave error to introduce and establish an inferior race in our country," but his travels to Calfornia, Cuba, Martinique, and Guadeloupe convinced him of the utility of Chinese labor.[64] Such sentiment led Sinimbú, now president of the Imperial Council and minister of agriculture, commerce, and public works, to convoke a conference of large landowners as an elite referendum on Chinese labor.[65] His opening speech at the Congresso Agrícola argued that European immigrants were more interested in being landowners than salaried workers, and that the success of English, French, and Spanish colonies was based on Chinese labor. Even the United States was filled with Chinese workers in spite of North Americans being "so jealous about the purity of Saxonic blood."[66]

Sinimbú's desires, and his introduction of Paes Leme's "A nossa lavoura" as a discussion guide, did not lead to any consensus.[67] The positions expressed at the Congresso Agrícola, however, are worth exploring for their discourse on Brazilian society. Many representatives, for example, used biological metaphors that constructed national identity as a living organism. When one representative spoke of his fears that Brazil was "injecting into its veins a poor and degenerate blood, toxic and noxious to the great laws of race mixing," he portrayed a weak country teetering on the edge of a collapse of national identity.[68] João José Carneiro da Silva, a representative from Rio de Janeiro province, disagreed. He posited that if "the white race produced so many mulattos of distinction, why can't we do the same for the Chinese, a race incontestably superior to the African."[69] Such far-reaching differences meant that Sinimbú was able to convince planters to approve only a weak resolution that encouraged the "acquisition of workers of other peoples from races or civilizations inferior to ours," including free Africans and "well chosen coolies and not those who live on the water or packed (literally *formigueiros,* "anthills") in the large cities."[70]

The public reaction to the Congresso Agrícola was far from enthusias-

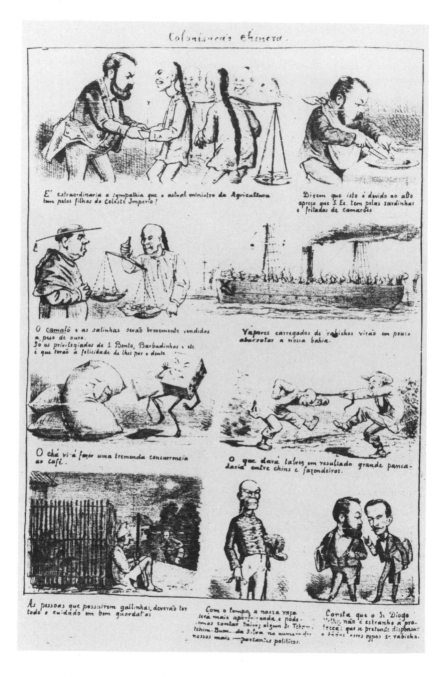

Chinese Colonization. *Mephistópheles* 2:60 (August 1875). Courtesy of Biblioteca Nacional, Rio de Janeiro.

tic. The immensely popular *Revista Illustrada,* which Joaquim Nabuco once characterized as the "Bible of abolition for those who cannot read," denounced Sinimbú as an "apologist," complaining, "As if we have not had enough of the black, [now] we will have the yellow!"[71] Another assault came from Domingos José Nogueira Jaguaribe Filho, a slave-owning, pro-abolition (he claimed the slaves belonged to his wife!!!) planter from Rio Claro (São Paulo). The son of a senator, Jaguaribe had attended the Congresso Agrícola but made only one short speech. Thus his *Reflexões sobre a colonização no Brasil* (1878), a self-labeled "cry of indignation that I give in the name of Brazilian youth against the stingy and despotic system of Portuguese colonization," came as a surprise.[72] The text stemmed from Jaguaribe's 1874 Imperial Academy of Medicine thesis, "The Acclimatization of Races from the Point of View of Colonization in Relation to Brazil," an attack on Chinese immigration and its supporters in the Sociedade Auxiliadora.[73] *Reflexões* mixed Brazilian and European pseudo-scientific theories of race and culture, and was based on the Darwinian idea that although all humans were part of the same "family," ethnic mixing had created superior "peoples."[74] Citing scores of European and Brazilian authors who argued that climate created ethnic hierarchies, Jaguaribe insisted that an ostensible absence of racism justified a Brazilian prohibition on the entry of nonwhite immigrants.

Jaguaribe contended that Chinese were dangerous if they stayed and unpatriotic if they left, a position repeated in the 1920s and 1930s with regard to Japanese immigrants, and more recently in reference to Koreans. This convoluted position emerged from the previously discussed theories on why indigenous people would vanish from Brazil. Jaguaribe believed that the disappearance of the "Jews of Asia" would be slowed by a "more civilized" Brazilian meat diet, leading to the "crime, indolence . . . and a propensity for robbery" so common to the local "degraded" indigenous peoples.[75] Interracial sexual relations reinforced the problems, since the "natural repugnance" that white Brazilian women had for Africans would be less with regard to "intermediate" races such as Asians.

Introducing sexuality and blaming women for social sickness were important in the conceptualization of nonblack/nonwhite immigrants in Brazil. Some elites saw national identity as male-produced, and proposed that uniformly unattractive "yellow" men presented a physical danger to Brazilian women and would produce large numbers of illegitimate and inferior "Mongoloid" children. Others, however, presumed that culture flowed from the womb, and when Brazilian men had relations with Chinese women, the result was also "Mongoloid" children. As Chinese men destroyed Brazilian womanhood, so weak, vulnerable, and promiscuous Chinese women destroyed Brazilian civilization. Musing about a future Brazil filled with Asians, a member of Bahia's Legislative Assembly complained that Chinese were "deformed both physically and morally; use opium, kill their children, are disloyal, egotistical and are given to begging; their only virtue is patience."[76] Jaguaribe gazed north to Mexico, whose indigenized society was exactly what Brazil's elite feared most. The root of Mexico's weakness, according to Jaguaribe, was a group of Chinese sailors who had been blown off course in 1281 during an attempted raid on Japan, and whose genes now polluted the national race.[77] Not surprisingly the word *china* came to be used in some parts of Brazil as a term for prostitute or mistress, and the verb *chinear* (to "Chinese" oneself) meant to live among prostitutes.[78]

Widespread anti-Chinese sentiment was countered by the political ascension of João Lins Vieira Cansanção de Sinimbú, appointed prime minister (*ministro do conselho*) in 1879. One of his first acts was to order the pro-Chinese consul-general in the United States, Salvador de Mendonça, to prepare a report on Chinese immigration (later published as a book).[79] Sinimbú used the report as an excuse for financing a treaty mission to Asia, since "exploratory voyages" did not need House or Senate approval. As General Arthur Silveira da Motta, Baron Jaceguai, led a "naval mission" charged with the task of arranging diplomatic relations with China, a Brazilian delegation was sent to London to discuss labor issues with China's diplomats.[80] Although opposition to Sinimbú's deviousness sprang up immediately, the Senate could muster only a halfhearted debate on the budget issue.[81] The House took a more aggressive stance as Joaquim Nabuco used the language of war to "combat" the "yellow immigration" that he insisted would create a new slave class. Nabuco's ostensible humanitarian position did little to disguise his bigotry: "Ethnologically, why create a racial conflict and degrade what exists in the country . . . morally, why introduce into our society this addictive leprosy that infests all the cities where Chinese immigration is established?" Positing a tenuous Brazilian civilization, and hearkening back to Jaguaribe's blaming of women for social problems, Nabuco contended that Chinese men would inevitably mix with Brazilian women, creating a degenerate new race: "World history is the proof that the more intelligent and brilliant race, when put into contact with inferior races, is often beaten and succumbs. It is not the level of civilization that perpetuates the race." [82]

While the opposition could do nothing to stop the Silveira da Motta mission, Nabuco's comments were well circulated in the United Kingdom. The British and Foreign Anti-Slavery Society approached China's envoy extraordinary and minister plenipotentiary to the Court of St. James, the Marquis Tseng Chi-ce [Zeng Ji-ze], to suggest that it "has been confirmed not only by history but by their own experience that in any country in which slavery exists neither treaty provisions nor laws will prevent imported and contracted labour from becoming a virtual slavery, and therefore any treaty between China and Brazil . . . must infallibly result in the virtual enslavement of the unfortunate immigrant." [83] The pro-British, English-language *Rio News* agreed, publishing advance sheets from London's *Anti-Slavery Reporter,* bulletins from the Anti-Slavery Society, and editorializing that Sinimbú desired "a servile element of labor [to] bolster up the decaying great proprietorships of Brazil . . . that will bring unmeasured disaster to the prosperity of the country." [84]

In early November 1879 a representative of the Marquis Tseng rejected the overtures after British and Brazilian abolitionists sent him transcripts of House and Senate debates, the published proceedings of the Congresso Agrícola, and Salvador de Mendonça's official report. [85] Brazil's elites reacted as if slapped in the face, unable to believe that "Even the Chinese . . . want nothing to do with [us]." The *Gazeta de Notícias* complained that the imperial government "in its zeal to improve our race by giving it certain yellow touches, suffers a tremendous censure [since] our country is not judged unfavorably by the European alone . . . What is the government waiting for? To overcome the opposition of the Chinese representative by bestowing on him the Order of Christ, free of duties? Labor cannot remain uncertain as to whether it is to have or not have Chinese in order to progress." [86] Sinimbú, however, was unfazed. In September 1880, Brazil signed a broad treaty of "Friendship, Commerce and Navigation" with China, but the Qing government refused to allow contract labor, understanding that landowners saw "the Asiatic and the free black African . . . as machines or as cheap labor" rather than as colonists. [87]

Sinimbú continued to push, and in 1880 the São Paulo Provincial Legislature debated a budget to bring one thousand Chinese who were "intelligent . . . and until today have no rivals [for labor], and cannot in any way be compared to the brute Hottentot, the Zulu, or any other African people." [88]

While the federal Ministry of Agriculture, Commerce, and Public Works attempted to establish shipping lines to Asia, a group of São Paulo planters decided to circumvent the Qing government by sending Dr. José Custodio Alves de Lima, a graduate of Syracuse University, to contract three thousand Chinese laborers residing in the United States.[89] While none of the plans achieved any results, high hopes remained, and in 1882 the Companhia de Comércio e Imigração Chineza (CCIC) was founded with active government assistance to bring twenty-one thousand workers to Brazil.[90] The first group of one hundred was sent by the CCIC to Minas Gerais to work for the British-owned St. John d'el Rey Mining Company, owners of South America's largest mine, Morro Velho. This group confirmed the Chinese government's worst fears: over half refused to set foot in the mine, and those who did, fled soon after.[91]

The Companhia de Comércio e Imigração Chineza was a spectacular failure, yet emerging from its annals is a fascinating story of ethnicity and national identity. The tale begins in 1880 when the Brazilian diplomat Eduardo Callado, eager to send Chinese workers to Brazil and to fill the returning ships with coffee, tobacco, and timber, contacted G. C. Butler, a U.S. citizen living in Shanghai who was a former adviser to the Marquis Tseng.[92] Butler was now the executive secretary to a wealthy Cantonese entrepreneur, T'ang T'ing-shu, known to foreigners and referred to in most of the Brazilian documents as Tong King-sing. The T'ang clan dominated shrimp sauce production and sales around Macao and had long contacts with Portuguese traders; many clan members entered the Chinese government. Tong King-sing, however, took a different route. He attended missionary school and learned English, first working as an interpreter in the Hong Kong police court and the Shanghai customs house, and later becoming the top comprador at Jardine, Matheson and Company, the leading British opium merchants on the China coast. His high income allowed him to invest in everything from pawnshops to banks to newspapers, and soon he was able to purchase a degree and official title.[93]

Concurrent with Tong's rise to prominence, Li Hung-chang (1823–1901), imperial governor general at Tientsin, became Peking's de facto foreign minister. Li, known as the "Bismarck of the East," was one of the few powerful officials in late-nineteenth-century China who favored Western-style economic development. In 1873 he founded the Chao Shang Chü (China Merchants' Steam Navigation Company), a commercial steam fleet aimed at displacing Jardine, Matheson and Company from the rice tribute and trade monopoly. Li asked Tong to oversee both the Navigation Company and the Kaiping coal mines that fueled the steamships. The Chao Shang Chü soon became a successful enterprise.[94]

By 1880 the company had forty-five ships plying the waters between China and Liverpool, but profits were small. Migrant labor attracted Li's attention, and Brazil became a focus in part because of a desire to expand China's tea trade to South America. While Tong King-sing's long contact with the Portuguese in Macao seems to have convinced him that the idea was unworkable, Li and G. C. Butler favored the plan. Soon Butler began quiet meetings with Eduardo Callado to explore bringing hundreds of thousands of Chinese to Brazil.[95] While Callado was in China, Tong and Butler met with him a number of times, making it clear that they expected Brazilian government aid would allow a minimal investment by the Chao Shang Chü to be turned into a rapid profit. Tong emphasized that Brazil was a "distant and partly unknown foreign country," that only decent wages would attract good workers, and that attempts to begin "immigration based upon the vicious contract system which proved to be detrimental to the interests of Chinese laborers in South America and Cuba" would not be tolerated. Any contract would have to state explicitly that "Chinese immigrants [would be] treated with the same regard and on the same footing as other favored nations."[96]

In mid-1882 Callado agreed to the terms set out by the China Merchants' Steam Navigation Company, which included a subsidy of 100,000 Mexican dollars for three years, privileges equal to those of the English Royal Mail Company in Brazil, the possibility of a 25 percent reduction in the subsidy if the company was able to arrange a similar deal with Cuba, and a guarantee of six round trips per year with a thousand to twelve hundred passengers on each trip. Workers would receive free room and board as well as a monthly salary in Mexican dollars. "In order to avoid . . . appearance of continuation of [the] old [contract] system," passage costs would go directly to the China Merchants' Steam Navigation Company rather than the Brazilian government or employers.[97] With a draft agreement in order, Tong King-sing and G. C. Butler set out to visit Brazil.

When Tong and Butler arrived in October 1883, they created a stir of some proportion that provided numerous opportunities for public definitions of Brazilian national identity. Appearing before reporters at São Paulo's Grande Hotel wearing traditional Chinese clothing and complimenting Brazil and its people in English, Tong endlessly challenged stereotypes. The *Correio Paulistano* saw Tong as an eccentric exotic, noting that "he conserves, in spite of his European affinities, his national costume, the silk tunic, the little gold buttons, the shoes with fleece soles and the black beret with a red top, insignia of the educated class."[98] While Tong was remade into an acceptable quasi-European, G. C. Butler, who was an African American, seemed to shock observers by being "intelligent" and having "all the refinement of Parisian elegance."[99] Carl von Koseritz, a founder of the Sociedade Central de Imigração, dismissed Tong as a seller of "Mongolian meat" but was impressed by the "Negro from California, resplendent with diamonds." We can only squirm with pleasure imagining the "positive and cold" Tong and the "audacious" Butler sitting in the drawing rooms of Brazil's *fazendeiros,* a point not lost on the abolitionist Koseritz, who noted the irony in plantation owners being "forced to receive a representative of that despised race in their golden salons—and having to fete him."[100]

While planters seemed impressed with Tong and Butler, there are indications that the pair were horrified by Brazilian slavery. Henrique Lisboa, secretary to Brazil's special mission to China, reported that an audience with Emperor Dom Pedro II left Tong convinced that anti-Chinese sentiment was common.[101] The emperor informed Tong that the travel and housing subventions would come from the planters, not the government —in effect creating a contract system. An outraged Tong reportedly told Dom Pedro that "this scheme must fall through; I will be no party to bringing Chinamen here except as free immigrants."[102] Dom Pedro seems to have had similar feelings, exclaiming after the meeting, "I am sure that the ethnic influence of these peoples will aggravate even further the heterogeneous aspects of our people."[103]

The excitement surrounding Tong and Butler's visit to Brazil vanished when, without explanation, the two suddenly left for London. Henrique Lisboa attributed the departure to a failure of the negotiations with Dom Pedro. Others blamed the Chinaphobic press and politicians and their British allies, who all put pressure on Tong to resist any temptation to sign contracts with members of Brazil's slavocracy.[104] The British Anti-Slavery Society took the public credit, claiming to the *Anti-Slavery Reporter* that they had "obtained a promise . . . that [Tong] would not be a party to any contract for forced labor."[105] Abolitionist pressure aside, Tong and Butler appear to have been genuinely outraged by the palpable bigotry they encountered. In a letter to the Companhia de Comércio e Imigração Chineza,

Tong wrote of his "astonishment at the prejudice entertained by your government and by the enlightened classes of your nation against Chinese labor," sentiments echoed by Butler in a letter sent to an English friend in Rio de Janeiro.[106] While Tong and Butler must be applauded for their rejection of Brazilian racism, their sudden departure from Brazil may have been unrelated to those attitudes. It seems they were called back to China following an outbreak of hostilities with France instigated by none other than Li Hung-chang, Tong King-sing's political and commercial patron.[107]

The Companhia de Comércio e Imigração Chineza was dissolved in late 1883, but its failure did not remove Chinese workers as both a best hope and a worst nightmare. Imperial and provincial debates in late 1888 were almost verbatim repeats of the charges and countercharges that had floated around Brazil since midcentury.[108] Senator Alfredo d'Escragnolle Taunay, vice president of the Sociedade Central de Imigração, led a virulent and Chinaphobic "anti" side. His political positions were reinforced when the society's monthly newspaper, A Immigração, ran regular stories against the "weak bastard race, filled with hedonistic vices, without a doubt inferior to the ethnic elements we have." One article charged that Chinese would be "a terrible competitor to national workers," and another insisted that the "atrophied and corrupt race [was] incapable of collaborating efficiently with this neo-Latin people." [109] At one point the society even sent a group to Europe to discourage Chinese diplomats from considering Brazil as an emigration site. When Taunay was accused by fellow senator Viriato de Medeiros of confusing "the good Chinese with the bad Chinese," the response was clear: "The bad Chinese, they come from China. How is it possible to make a distinction?" [110]

Taunay's anti-Chinese discourse contained two components that would soon become official Brazilian social policy. The first was a ban on all Chinese entry, codified in 1890 as a prohibition on the entry of all Asians and Africans without congressional approval.[111] The second posited that immigrants need not speak Portuguese or follow Brazilian religious norms to be useful to development. Of course Taunay had Germans, not Chinese, in mind, but such policies would create spaces, however unintended, for other non-European groups (like Arabs and Japanese) just a few decades later.[112] These principles were quickly embedded in Brazil's political culture. Abolition, which was followed by the establishment of the Republic on 15 November 1889, did nothing to lessen the discussion of the social aspects of Chinese labor. The press was deeply involved in the story, in part because José do Patrocinio, director of the fervently abolitionist *Cidade do Rio,* joined Taunay in leading the anti-Chinese campaign. Typically, an anti-Chinese article might be born in the *Ceylon Observer,* reach adolescence in Rio de Janeiro's *Jornal do Comércio,* and finally die in *O Estado de S. Paulo. O Estado,* proud of its report (or perhaps proud of the *Jornal do Comércio* article . . . or maybe the original one from Ceylon!!) would print the story again a few days later.[113]

Press reports did little to convince planters outside of São Paulo state that European immigrants would replace slaves. For them, Chinese labor remained a best hope. Landowners in Juiz de Fora, one of Minas Gerais's most important cities, created a commission to promote Asian immigration and published their findings in the Juiz de Fora newspaper *O Pharol* as well as in a book. While the commission members accepted the Chinaphobic fear of "Mongolization," they also argued that if the numbers were limited to one hundred thousand, the migrants would find themselves Brazilianized: "If the Chinaman is inferior to our race, will we see, for the first time, the absorption of the superior race, ten times more numerous, by the inferior race? [I]f we are superior to the Chinaman, why won't we win? If we are inferior, what will we lose?"[114] A different group from the Amazon region supposed that "lock[ing our] doors to Asians or free Africans . . . is antihumanitarian since it negates the benefits of catechism and civilization" while positing that Chinese workers would not harm Brazilian society because "dead or alive, [they] always return to China."[115]

During the First Republic not all concern over immigrant integration focused on the Chinese as elites demanded workers who were subservient *and* would help to transform Brazilian identity. One São Paulo state deputy complained that the Italian immigrants flowing into Brazil had not assimilated, had "anarchized labor," and were "bad" for São Paulo.[116] Fourteen city governments in the state agreed, demanding legal changes that would allow them to employ Chinese workers rather than European ones.[117] Another deputy dismissed European labor altogether, proposing that the entry of fifty thousand Puerto Ricans "will more or less serve perfectly" because of their "race, their language and other assimilative conditions."[118] The African background of many Puerto Ricans quashed that plan, and yet again the Chinese rose to the top of the servile worker ladder.

Once again the federal government was forced to take the offensive. In early 1892 the official Imprensa Nacional translated General Tcheng-Ki-Tong's *Meu paiz: A China contemporânea* (My Country: Contemporary

China), an ecstatic vision of Chinese life and society. Soon after, the Senate approved funds for diplomatic missions in China and Japan, and passed a law permitting Chinese and Japanese immigration.[119] Rio de Janeiro's Senate hoped to bring members of the "Hakka and Punti races" (two Cantonese ethnic groups whose eleven-year conflict took one hundred thousand lives) to areas where the climate and latitude were "equal" to China's by paying 30 to 50 percent of the passage costs.[120] The state Legislative Assembly followed suit with a different plan to introduce five hundred Asian and fifteen thousand European colonists into the state.[121] In Minas Gerais, Secretary of Agriculture David Moretzsohn Campista conducted a labor survey of sixty-four municipal and district politicians and large landowners in 1893. Chinese workers were among the most desirable, and he reported that the "introduction of the Asiatic worker whose labor is reputed to be indispensable, is urgent."[122] Campista's sentiments were echoed in the state Senate, which sent representatives to Europe and Asia to find immigrants. Even so, the two groups were not seen as equals: different reception centers (hospedarias) were established for each group.[123]

The firm federal commitment encouraged ambitious businesspeople to form companies to transport Chinese laborers to Brazil. The São Paulo office of Wertheimer and Co. hoped to bring five hundred thousand workers, and competitor Mutualidade Agrícola appointed João Lins Vieira Cansanção de Sinimbú as its president.[124] Sinimbú's name led, expectedly, to negative press, and the Correio Paulistano published an eight-part series of anti-Chinese articles just as the Mutualidade was purchasing space to announce its formation. Each Mutualidade advertisement was surrounded by an article suggesting that Chinese workers would harm Brazilian society. On the day the Mutualidade was formed, a story implied that Chinese backwardness had led to over one hundred deaths after a ship sank while traveling between Shanghai and Hong Kong. Another story, headlined "CHINESE SUPERSTITION," questioned Chinese moral values: "A Chinese, even less if he is a pirate, will never save a drowning man." Why? According to the tale, because the Chinese believed that a drowning person's evil spirit rises to the surface to find a new body, and anyone nearby would be possessed.[125]

Sinimbú's entry into the Chinese labor business led numerous other companies to open, attack their competitors, and fail on a regular basis.[126] Soon thereafter, in late 1893, Baron Ladario, José de Costa Azevedo, was sent to Beijing to negotiate a new trade and immigration treaty with the Chinese emperor and Li Hung-chang. The *Hong Kong Daily Telegraph* mocked the mission openly, and English officials in Hong Kong wondered if Ladario was trying to renew the slave trade. The baron, however, was in no hurry to sign the treaty, considering Chinese labor "undesirable" and "hugely inconvenient," in comparison with the Japanese.[127] The Qing government was as uninterested in Brazil as Costa Azevedo was in China. As *The China Mail* noted, "It will take all the persuasiveness of which the Brazilian Mission is capable to induce the Chinese Authorities to withdraw the embargo preventing coolies from leaving China for Brazil or any of the other South American countries." [128]

The exception that proved the rule was Júlio Benavides's scandalous Companhia Metropolitania, set up at the direction of Rio de Janeiro's governor. The story began in August 1893, when Brazil's consul in Macao reported that Benavides had chartered the German steamship *Tetartos* to bring Chinese immigrants to Brazil. The voyage had been a torturous one as the boat traveled from Singapore to Bangkok for a load of rice and then to Hong Kong for provisions. This was the first of Benavides's many mistakes: British law did not permit ships bringing emigrants from Macao or Canton to stop in Hong Kong, and thus the *Tetartos* was forced to remain in port under British guard. Eventually, after numerous pleas to the British-run Hong Kong Tribunal, the *Tetartos* was allowed to continue its voyage.[129]

Benavides, apparently unconcerned about the Chinese prohibition on labor emigration to Brazil, began posting placards around Macao offering free transport in exchange for five-year labor contracts. This put Benavides on the wrong side of Portuguese law, but neither he nor the Brazilian consul, Baron Asumpção, was troubled by the juridical issues, especially when there was money to be made.[130] Indeed, the baron tried to extort a "special fee" for each labor visa he issued, and while Benavides's local lawyer negotiated a revised "document fee," 375 Chinese passengers (or 474, or 475, depending on the source) were boarded and sent on their way.[131] With the passengers already at sea, the baron bought Benavides's argument for a reduced fee, or perhaps Benavides bought the baron. While the Foreign Ministry never formally reprimanded the baron for his actions, the consul-general in Hong Kong was told explicitly that he was not to approve any more emigration visas.[132]

While Benavides's stunt succeeded brilliantly in getting Chinese laborers to Brazil, British and Portuguese colonial authorities were outraged. The governors of Hong Kong and Macao sniped at each other in the press, and in a series of furious interviews the commissioner of the Kowloon Customs Office emphasized that "coolie emigration to Brazil is not permitted."[133] Chinese authorities were equally angry, and demanded that those on the *Tetartos* be repatriated.[134] When Brazilian officials responded that the group had entered freely and were hard at work in Rio de Janeiro, the Chinese superintendent of trade withdrew the right from all German ships (like the *Tetartos*) to carry any Chinese passengers, noting that "if in the future crafty and nefarious traders and brokers attempt to act as accomplices and inveigle Chinese laborers abroad, when arrested they will be punished to the fullest extent of the law without mercy. Let each one carefully obey this proclamation."[135]

Chinese, British, and Portuguese anger was matched by Brazilian delight. The governor of Rio de Janeiro called the new arrivals the "best" workers in the state.[136] The *Jornal do Comércio* was equally excited about the arrival of "sallow-complexioned coolies . . . forced by the power of fate . . . to change the rice and chopsticks of China for the manioc of Brazil."[137] Within a week, the Chinese had been remade into ideal Brazilians. They were clean ("They saw . . . the rushing stream of water—an indispensable element to them—in which they bathe twice a day."), intelligent ("[They] know how to read and write in their native language—a fact that favors to a great extent Chinese civilization."), and desirable ("These 475 men do not in the least resemble the Chinese we have been accustomed to seeing hawking fish on the streets . . . [where] it was not an uncommon sight to see them being arrested for chicken stealing.").[138]

Positive assessments also came from the planters who contracted Chinese from the *Tetartos*. In a survey conducted by Henrique Lisboa, most agreed with Augusto Jordão, who thought his thirty workers were good. Ambrosio Leitão da Cunha was equally pleased until "the day when thirteen [of fifteen] became misguided and fled."[139] A long article in Rio de Janeiro's *Gazeta de Notícias* about Pedro Cunha's suggestively named Monte Hymalaia plantation was written by a family friend, Amelia Gomes de Azevedo.[140] She found the Chinese "organisms" "extremely scrupulous" and "obedient." They "observed all the rules of hygiene . . . and know much about roots and use aromatic medicines that they brought from China." In physical terms "they were not disgusting," in part because only three of the twenty-five were "of the real Chinese type, that is those with the oblique characteristic of the eyes; others are like our *caboclo* with strong and well-developed muscles." Only one thing disturbed Amelia Gomes de Azevedo.

Contrary to popular wisdom, no one seemed to be saving money to return home. Few Chinese had come to Brazil, but they had come to stay.[141]

* * *

The debates over Chinese labor were important to the ways in which ethnicity would intersect with questions of national identity. For the first time elites began to expand the panorama of what Brazil might become by considering the impact of migrants who were neither black nor white. This led to an important new role for the diplomatic corps, now charged with choosing immigrants, and thus Brazil's future. No longer was the social question linked to the disappearance of Africans, rejuvenating the debate over whether economic growth was worth the cost of a non-European Brazil.

The answer to the social/economic conundrum remained in the realm of the theoretical for most of the nineteenth century because so few Chinese workers actually settled in Brazil. Yet this immigration that never was, created the parameters for the place of ethnicity in Brazil in much the same way as mass Chinese immigration did for the United States, which banned entry in 1882. In both countries Asians were no longer lumped together in a single group, and Japan, beginning its transformation into a capitalist world power following the Meiji Restoration, began to hold a new interest. In both countries, discussion of the relationship between immigrants and their descendants became a key to defining national identity. While local birth made one a legal citizen in Brazil and the United States, most policy makers and intellectuals in the late-nineteenth-century United States defined the hundreds of thousands of Asian-(United States) Americans as a third "racial" group, essentially different from both "blacks" and "whites."[142] In Brazil the story was markedly different: the lack of actual Chinese immigrants led to a complex and divisive discourse that often revolved around whether non-European/non-Africans could be white. As new groups not prohibited under the constitutional ban on Africans and Asians arrived, the language of both inclusion and exclusion was in place.

And what of the few Chinese who remained in Brazil? Other than the comments of the famed essayist João do Rio in the Gazeta de Notícias (Rio de Janeiro), we have little information. Visiting an opium den in Rio de Janeiro in 1905, he found the descendants of that "famous immigration . . . sell[ing] fish on the beach" in addition to making addicts of "Romanian nihilists, miserable Russian professors, Spanish anarchists,

[and] debauched gypsies." Like Eça de Queiroz's hero at the beginning of the chapter, João do Rio found that the simple presence of these "Westernized Chinese" could physically take him from Brazil to "the streets of Tien-Tsin . . . persecuted by imperial guards; I see myself in the bodegas of Singapore, with the bodies of the celestials dragged by rickshaws, between crazed Malays brandishing assassinating kriss." The presence of the Chinese was like a death knell: "Get out or I will die," shouted João, unaware that hundreds of thousands of non-Europeans were preparing to enter, each ready to fight for a niche within the Brazilian nation.[143]

3

Constructing Ethnic Space

A popular saying in Brazil is that when a person
from the Middle East first arrives, s/he is a *turco*.
After getting a first steady job, s/he becomes a *sirio*.
If a shop or factory is purchased, s/he is transformed
into a *libanese*. But I always ask, when do they
become Brazilian?

It was the arrival of a diplomat in 1810 that gave Brazilians the opportunity
to see "a Persian for the first time." This act of seeing, however, should not
suggest that some Brazilians did not "know" the Middle East. The diplomat's presence led one contemporary to observe that Arabs were "as sacred
as they were profane," a position repeated more than one hundred years
later by novelist Jorge Amado, whose character Nacib in *Gabriela, Clove
and Cinnamon* was "a Brazilian from the Arabies."[1] Iberia's conquest by the
Moors, the thrill of European reconquest and the excesses of the Inqui-
sition, and the clear Arabic influence on the Portuguese language placed
Middle Easterners in a special place, as both friend and enemy, as exoti-
cally different yet somehow familiar.

Challenges to the stereotypes of Arabs came from the tens of thousands of Syrians and Lebanese who began entering Brazil quietly in the
late nineteenth century. Whether these non-European, non-African immigrants could become Brazilian was the focus of much discussion among

elites whose discursive model emerged from the vehement political and economic debates over Chinese entry. Yet unlike the few Chinese residents, Middle Easterners and their descendants actively engaged in a wide-ranging negotiation about how "Arab" ethnicity might change Brazil's cultural, economic, and social identity.

Arabs were simultaneously insiders (the majority were Christians) and outsiders (they were not considered "black," "white," or "yellow"). Physically indistinguishable from other "Brazilians," they were imagined to be exotic and different. Arabs met elite goals by succeeding economically while infuriating them by often remaining uninterested in wholly accepting Euro-Brazilian culture. These dualities were not lost on Syrian and Lebanese immigrants who used the contradictions to create a hyphenated ethnicity that included an implicit notion of Brazilianness. By the early twentieth century a new ethnic group had been formed, the Syrian-Lebanese, a designation that purposely concealed the social hierarchies implied by "national" terms like "turco," "sirio," and "libanese."[2]

Images of Arabs were common in Brazil. Portuguese travelers to the Middle East, like the young Eça de Queiroz, who traveled to Egypt in 1869, found an audience for their Orientalist musings among Brazil's elite. Representations, both textual and visual, of feminized men abounded, and suppressed "chaste" women behind veils kept their "lasciviousness . . . hidden behind the mask" and "loose" women in harems sat naked, waiting for sex.[3] Francisco Antonio de Almeida, a former Brazilian diplomat, was impressed by two things during a visit to Cairo in 1874: the "sensual" dances of the women and the festivals surrounding the circumcision of young men. Eduardo Prado's (1860–1901) visit to Egypt in early 1885 was presented in a similarly Orientalist form: The only people he came to know were foreigners, and both humans and pyramids became tourist sites.[4] In 1930, the well-known hygienist Afrânio Peixoto wrote passionately of his visit to a Cairo brothel, and more than a decade later a Lebanese-born resident of São Paulo illustrated his Portuguese-language autobiography with photos of naked female "masseuses," "slaves," and "beauties."[5]

Images of the Middle East could be found in discussions of everything from politics to ethnicity. A planter from São Paulo complained in 1857 that Brazil's monopolistic economic legislation "excluded Germans from black [African] work [like] the exclusion today of Christians and Jews from property in Turkey." Some seventy years later the nationalist Cezar Magalhaens, a professor at the Academia Brasileira de Ciências Econômicas,

Políticas, e Sociais, blamed Brazil's "backwardness" on the "Muslim passivity" it had inherited from the Portuguese.[6] Teófilo Braga's influential *A pátria portugueza: O território e a raça* reformulated a Portuguese theory that focused on the Mozarabs (*musta 'rabun*), Christians who adopted Muslim clothes and spoke Arabic in Al-Andalus. To Braga the Mozarabs were a uniquely Iberian "race" that flowed out of the miscegenation between the indigenous Roman-Goth population and Arabs who had "instinctively" made Spain a "fatherland [because it] reminded them of Yemen with its freshness and fecundity."[7] Apparently based on the commutative property, Braga's analysis insisted that an Arab biological affinity for Iberia proved that Brazil's Portuguese colonizers were themselves Arabized. Braga (and others) combined this Mozarab ethnic construction with Friedrich Max Müller's theory that a "Turanian" language/cultural group (which included all languages in Asia and Europe that were neither Semitic nor Aryan, except Chinese) linked the Tartars and American Indians. This created a biologically determined bond between Portuguese colonizers, presumed to be of Mozarabic descent, and Tupí tribes, believed to be of Asian origin.[8] Although these ideas may appear to represent the extremes of pseudoscientific racial babble, they were widespread and widely discussed. In the end Arabs were European, Asian, and indigenous to Brazil.[9]

The Arab-Portuguese-Mozarab-Tupí-Brazilian link settled deeply into the psyches of learned Brazilians. In the twentieth century those who looked to Portugal for self-understanding, like Gilberto Freyre and Luís da Câmara Cascudo, searched for traces of a "Moorish presence" in their own Lusified identities.[10] Others mixed the Turanian/Mozarab notions with French crackpot theories suggesting that King Solomon ("ancestor of the Syrians") had sailed the Amazon River and that the Quechua and Portuguese languages were offshoots of ancient Hebrew.[11] In the decades after World War I, the leader of the fascistic Ação Integralista Brasileira, the nativist Plínio Salgado, filled his novel *O estrangeiro* (The Foreigner, 1926) with examples of interethnic marriage between Syrians and Brazilians. He also conflated Brazilian and Middle Eastern identities in his diary of a 1930 trip to the Middle East (which was published in 1954). Salgado's description of his arrival in Lebanon was constructed so that it became a return to Brazil: "I hear, coming from one of the boats . . . [in] the guttural accent of the Asiatics, the roguish [carnival] music of Brazil. At the far limits of the Mediterranean, with its indescribable flavor. We are in Beirut."[12] In a revised version of his diary included in a published homage to the Syrian-

Lebanese community, Salgado, apparently consumed by his own stereotypes that the only Arab-Brazilians who could (or were allowed) to read were males, felt compelled to add the misogynist samba lyric that he left out of the original—"This woman has provoked me for a long time; give it to her! give it to her!" [13]

The idea of a special relationship between Arabs and Brazilians was heartily endorsed by leading members of the Arab-Brazilian community, who often used an exaggerated Orientalism to define their own ethnic difference within a Brazilian national (and nationalist) identity. The prize-winning poet, author, and commentator Salomão Jorge was known best for his program "1001 Nights" on the extremely popular São Paulo Rádio Tupi. In "The Arab in Brazilian Civilization," Jorge awkwardly mimicked the national raison d'être of Brazil's elite ("Brazil—The Country of the Future") by citing Gilberto Freyre's miscegenationist ideas about Moors and Portuguese. At the same time he suggested that the Turanian/Mozarab link created a colonial Brazilian culture more Middle Eastern than European, thus transforming Arab immigrants into "original" Brazilians. [14]

Jorge's ideas represented a typical pattern by which Arab-Brazilian intellectuals struggled to assert their Syrian-Lebanese ethnicity. Another way was through privately published books in which multiple identities provide the narrative subtext. They generally begin with a photograph of the author's father in European dress, and the title page usually has a Brazilianized family name printed above the Arabic name given at birth. References to the *pátria* are not identifiable as either to Brazil or Lebanon (or Syria). The common theme is that Brazil has assimilated to an "older" Middle Eastern culture as much as the Middle Eastern immigrants have acculturated to Brazil.

Tanus Jorge Bastani's *O Líbano e os libanêses no Brasil* is illustrative. Bastani's father Jorge (Giries) emigrated from Sarba, Lebanon in 1895; Tanus's dedicatory photograph and comments equally glorify Brazil and Lebanon through references to Jorge's help in creating "the greatness of the Fatherland of his sons." Some 70 percent of *O Líbano e os libanêses* focuses on Lebanese history, while the section on Brazil speaks of a "traditional Luso-Lebanese friendship that dates from the Crusades." This friendship, according to Bastani, led to a shared culture where everything from the *bombachas* (leggings) used by gaúchos to churrasco (the famous Brazilian meat grill) became of Lebanese origin. [15] At the same time, the frequent ingestion of other foods widely considered "Arab" (like kibbe or kabobs) was evidence that Lebanon and Brazil were "very united [and] . . . dedicated to sincere and reciprocal friendship." Bastani's final words quote the song "Líbano! Brasil!," whose lyrics characterize Brazil and Lebanon as "brothers." Brothers come from the same biological stock, and thus Lebanese are Brazilians and vice versa.

> Familial Fatherlands! Only one noble and pure sentiment!
> Together in the defense of sacred liberty!
> Brazil! Proudly singing the song of the future!
> Lebanon! Sadly singing the song of yearning![16]

* * *

In the nineteenth century large numbers of immigrants from both the Levant (Mashriq) and French- and Spanish-speaking North Africa (Maghrib) began to make Brazil one of the centers of the *mahjar* (literally "countries" of emigration," but taken to mean the Arab diaspora).[17] Unlike the waves of Italian, Spanish, and Portuguese immigrants who were actively pursued by those seeking to change Brazil's social composition, Syrians and Lebanese came quietly on their own. Thus, when Brazil's elite "discovered" Arabs in their midst, the first reaction was to contact diplomats in the Middle East for information. These consuls and attachés found the idea of Arabs settling in their homeland distasteful, viewing the Middle East as "incredibly backward, lacking in culture, with neither administration nor organized workforces."[18] This made Brazil's diplomatic compounds the beacons of civilization among an irreparably godless people, and it was exactly this grandiose view that led many potential emigrants to view Brazil as a hospitable nation for relocation. The more Brazil's diplomats insisted on their cultural and national superiority, the more the stream of emigrants from the Middle East grew.

Brazilian surprise at an expanding Middle Eastern population turned to shock when it became apparent that the earliest large group of Arab immigrants to Brazil was neither Muslim nor Christian. Indeed, the North African community that began settling at the mouth of the Amazon in the first decades of the nineteenth century was exclusively Jewish. Little is known about these early settlers in Belém do Pará, but an old man once told me a story that hearkened back to that time.

> When the Jews arrived, they came without women or rabbis. Many began relationships with indigenous women and wanted to marry,

but there was no rabbi among the immigrants to conduct conversion ceremonies. The leader of the immigrants appointed the most learned member of the group to teach all the fiancées about Judaism, emphasizing one principle—that Hashem [the traditional term used by the informant to replace the word "God"] was the one and only G-d. The day of the marriage, the bride-to-be was brought into a room blindfolded, and told that a spoonful of molten gold would be put in her mouth. If she really believed that Hashem was the one and only G-d, the gold would taste as sweet as honey. And every woman believed, and the gold always tasted like honey.[19]

As the nineteenth century progressed, regular letters and some return migration led hundreds of Moroccan (or Maghribi) Jewish families to move to Brazil, where they settled in Rio de Janeiro and Belém. The Spanish-Moroccan War (1859–1860) may have been the catalyst for their flight, but deeper issues also propelled the migrants.[20] Historically, Jews had worked as business agents for the sultan, occasionally receiving the title *tujjar al-sultan* (the sultan's merchants). Yet living in a Muslim world gave Jews a profound sense of minority status while their multilingualism—Arabic and Spanish were used for business; French and Hebrew were studied at the Alliance Israélite Universelle (AIU) schools that had been set up in Tangier, Tetouan, and other large towns; and Haquitia was spoken at home—gave them a transnational perspective.[21] As Moroccan economic opportunity diminished, Muslim merchants became increasingly xenophobic and resentful of the economic ties many Jewish merchants had to the French. Jews thus began to emigrate, some leaving for Egypt and Algeria, while many of those educated at the AIU schools exited the region altogether. According to a report from one of the AIU's directors, by the 1880s 95 percent of the boys completing an Alliance education migrated to South America.[22]

By 1890 more than one thousand Maghribi Jews had migrated to Pará. The rubber economy was booming, and Belém was filled with peddlers and small merchants.[23] Many Jews settled in small towns along the Amazon, where they traded city products like clothes, medicine, tobacco, and cachaça (a sugarcane-based liquor) for fish, Brazil nuts, rubber, and copaiba oil.[24] Prosperity, however, was only one of the attractions for Morocco's Jews: they soon discovered they could easily obtain Brazilian naturalization certificates. This placed Maghribi Jews in much the same category as the protégés, wealthy Jews who used foreign papers as a means of economic and social protection. Becoming Brazilian gave return to Morocco new meaning. Now it potentially included both a significant sum of money and a sense of security. The leap in economic and national status did not go unnoticed, and there are reports that Jewish men who had not migrated experienced a decrease in their marriage prospects.[25]

Mimom Elbás was typical in many ways. He emigrated to Belém in 1892 and after a year moved to Rio de Janeiro. Six months later he was naturalized, and returned to Morocco as a Brazilian citizen.[26] Elbás learned little Portuguese, infuriating the consul in Tangier, José Daniel Colaco, who was sure that there was something wrong with a Brazilian who "does not know how to speak any language but Arabic."[27] Colaco feared the introduction of a new, and potentially dangerous, ethnic stream into Brazil, but there was little he could do. Moroccan Jews were not desirable Europeans and North Americans, but they were not banned as undesirable Africans and Asians.

Diplomats urged the Ministry of Justice to be more careful in granting naturalization certificates, but no one took the necessary measures.[28] In the first years of the twentieth century there were over six hundred naturalized Brazilians living in Morocco, all of whom looked to Brazil for protection, especially in times of crisis. Simão (or Simon) Nahmias moved to Pará in 1879, when he was twenty-three years old. Three years later he requested a naturalization certificate, based on his "firm intention to continue residing in the Empire and to adopt it as my fatherland."[29] The process took about a month. Some years later Nahmias returned to Tangier to set up an importing business, Brazilian citizenship papers in hand. In 1901 he became engaged in a land rights battle with a local Muslim merchant and found himself arguing his case before the Shraa Tribunal (Native High Court). He lost the case and was held in contempt of court, an offense punishable by prison. As police arrived at Nahmias's house, he raised the Brazilian flag, but to no avail.[30]

Nahmias immediately contacted the Brazilian consul, A. Mauritz de Calinerio, for help. Calinerio was less than excited about helping the "Hebrew," but feared that if he did not, the "semi-barbarous" Moroccan political system would be perceived as having defeated the Brazilian "spirit of Justice."[31] Strong measures were needed, and the consul's threat to break Brazilian/Moroccan relations if Nahmias was not released made international headlines.[32] While there is no evidence that the publicity was effective, Calinerio's "private representations," probably in the form of cash, led to Nahmias's release. Yet the situation was just one of many. Time after time naturalized citizens demanded, and received, the help of the consulate in Tangier. This so angered the Brazilian government that in 1900 it decided only Moroccans naturalized before 1880 would be considered citizens. The Moroccan government, which had cordial relations with Brazil "in everything and for everything as long as it is not related to the Hebrew Moroccans, naturalized Brazilians," was equally upset.[33] Indeed, the positive relations "in everything and for everything" meant little because Brazilian-Moroccan diplomatic relations seem to have revolved almost exclusively around questions of how to treat Brazilian Jews of Moroccan birth. On 4 March 1903, a solution was found: Brazil closed its diplomatic offices and turned the problem over to the Portuguese.[34]

The traditional images of Moors that collided with new ideas about Arab Jews with Brazilian citizenship were put to a further test by the some 107,000 Middle Easterners, mainly Greek (Melkite) and Maronite Catholics and Orthodox, who entered Brazil between 1884 and 1939. A few settled in Rio de Janeiro and São Paulo in the 1860s; the first substantial group arrived in the Amazon region in the 1880s, and they quickly established themselves in trading and commerce.[35] The overwhelming majority (almost 91 percent) came from today's Syria and Lebanon between 1904 and 1930. Syrian entry alone rose from over eleven hundred between 1914 and 1923 to over fourteen thousand between 1924 and 1933.[36] (See table 3.) French consular reports during the 1920s suggest that there were about 130,000 Syrian and Lebanese immigrants in São Paulo and Santos, twenty thousand in Pará, fifteen thousand in Rio de Janeiro, fourteen thousand in Rio Grande do Sul, and over twelve thousand in Bahia.[37]

The motives for emigration were as varied as the reasons for the choice of Brazil over the more popular United States.[38] An internal migration from the northern mountain valleys to the more economically viable southern Shuf created new population pressures that combined with the religious and political persecution that dominates the collective memories of Christian Arabs.[39] Family pressure, and the presence of emigration agents or brokers (simsars) who traveled throughout the region, encouraged many (one scholar suggests one quarter of Lebanon's population by 1915) young men to leave.[40] From the mid-nineteenth century, steamships regularly plied the waters between the Middle East and Brazil (with stops in Europe), making it easy, and decreasingly expensive, to migrate. Although statistics on religious background are incomplete, Lebanese and Syrians entering Brazil through the port of Santos between 1908 and 1941 were generally

Table 3. Middle Eastern Immigration to Brazil, 1884–1939

	1884–1893	1894–1903	1904–1913	1914–1923	1924–1933	1934–1939	Total 1884–1939
Algerians	*	*	*	*	1	0	1
Armenians	*		*	1	821	4	826
Egyptians	*	51	42	190	335	27	645
Iranians	*	*	*	12	107	10	129
Iraqis	*	*	*	*	10	0	10
Lebanese	*	*	*	*	3,853	1,321	5,174
Moroccans	*	192	31	35	47	23	328
Palestinians	*	*	*	*	611	66	677
Persians	*	*	*	*	374	9	383
Syrians	93	602	3,826	1,145	14,264	577	20,507
Turks	3	6,522	42,177	19,255	10,227	271	78,455
Total	96	7,367	46,076	20,638	30,650	2,308	107,135

Source: "Discriminação por nacionalidade dos imigrantes entrando no Brasil no período 1884–1939," Revista de Imigração e Colonização 1, no. 3 (July 1940): 617–638.

*Data not available.

Catholic (65 percent) or Greek Orthodox (20 percent); the rest (15 percent) were Muslim.[41]

Arab immigrants challenged Brazil's elite by placing long-held ideas within a context of contact with real immigrants.[42] While Syrian and Lebanese residents generally accepted Brazil's de facto state religion, they were highly visible, often residing and laboring in specific urban neighborhoods or wandering through the interior regions as peddlers. It was this prominence that led elites to ask an easy question with a very hard answer: What would Arab immigrants in Brazil be called? Initial sentiment favored the term "turco" (Turk) because most who entered before World War I had Ottoman passports. For those fleeing the Ottoman Empire, however, the usage was fraught with negative meaning, and their self-definition was as Lebanese or Syrian.[43] Soon, in a neat twist on the slippery nature of racial identification in Brazil, both Arabs and Brazilians began to joke that while newly arrived immigrants were "turcos," a first steady job transformed them into "Syrians," and shop or factory ownership remade them into "Lebanese." Regional terms frequently placed Middle Easterners in still other ethnic categories. In Pará, Arabs were frequently referred to as "Jews," and in Ceará they were deemed *galegos,* a deprecative term for those from the Iberian peninsula.[44]

The image of the "turco" runs deeply through Brazilian popular culture, in large part as the result of peddling, the prototype of Arab economic integration in Brazil. Known popularly as *mascates,* Arab peddlers often supplied household and dry goods to workers on the coffee *fazendas* (plantations) or to urban dwellers in the lower socioeconomic classes—a tertiary sector of retail trade and consumer credit was virtually nonexistent outside of a few cities. As coffee brought new prosperity, Syrian and Lebanese peddlers could be found throughout the country, often moving along new rail lines. From Minas Gerais to Goiás, the words "mascate" and "turco" were synonymous.[45]

Peddling was important to the construction of Arab-Brazilian ethnicity. The Feres family, from Syria's Akar region, sold their wares in the "Mineiro Triangle" in Minas Gerais state's Guaxupé and Teófilo Otoni regions. After the elder Feres was robbed and killed, his son, the poet Assis Feres, wrote "O mascate" (The Peddler) in his honor: "When we came from the East, God's sacred land, we found the newborn land. . . . How sad, this dubious path, carpeted with pain!"[46] Arab-Brazilian ethnicity was also constructed out of peddling in the following story, "The Legend of Marataize," quoted here in one of several versions I heard.

> There once was a group of peddlers who sold their wares in the interior of Espírito Santo, going from place to place by mule. One of the peddlers was named Aziz, and his wife [*marat,* in colloquial Arabic] was considered the leader of the women who stayed behind while the men went out to sell their goods. These women washed their clothes in a place called the "Turkish bath," and over time, the town that grew up around the place came to be called Marataize in honor of the wife of Aziz.[47]

Brazil was a fertile ground for peddling. Wadih Safady, who emigrated from Lebanon in 1922, recalls "hordes" of Arab peddlers in his memoirs.[48] Syrian and Lebanese store or factory owners (about 10 percent of the Middle Eastern immigrant population) sold piece goods or housewares on credit to the newcomers, often choosing agents who were relatives or from their cities of origin. While Middle Easterners were not Brazil's first im-migrant peddlers (for much of the nineteenth century, Portuguese immi-grants were associated with the trade), the use of ethnicity to construct wholesale-retail linkages provided new economies of scale. Personal re-lationships allowed Syrian and Lebanese peddlers to establish credit that they then extended to clients, a radical innovation in a country that had only recently moved from slave to wage labor.

Peddlers generally carried their goods on mules and "habitually traveled in groups of two, in part to reduce danger but also to help business."[49] Salt, cloth, and hats made up much of the stock, and given the lack of available capital, product rather than cash trade was common. Items were often re-sold in urban areas, allowing Syrian and Lebanese peddlers to gross twice the average daily wage; soon they began to invest in the urban manufac-turing sector. The early decades of the twentieth century saw settlement shift from rural to urban, and the number of Syrian-Lebanese companies inscribed in the São Paulo commercial almanac rose from six in 1895 to five hundred in 1901.[50] Syrian and Lebanese immigrants often grouped their shops together in inexpensive neighborhoods, living on the upper floors of the buildings they owned or rented for shops or factories.[51] These areas tended to be strategically located between markets and the railroad stations, so that shoppers had to pass through them when returning home from work.[52]

The growing Arab presence did not go unnoticed. An angry 1888 edi-torial in the newspaper *Mariannense* (Mariana, Minas Gerais) complained that "throngs" of "Turkish vagabonds" treated their children in an inhu-mane manner and retarded Brazil's economic growth through the use of outdated agricultural methods. The solution was simple: "Lock the doors so that they do not infiltrate our organism, [bringing] instead of strong blood, the evil virus of an indolent people." While the Sociedade Cen-tral da Imigração's newspaper clarified for its more "sophisticated" read-ership that "these Turks [are really] Syrians and Maronites or Catholics from Lebanon," it did agree with the *Mariannense* article, complimenting its own Alfredo d'Escragnolle Taunay for an anti-Arab speech in the Senate that argued for legislation to "impede the entrance of people whose only habits are vagrancy and laziness."[53] Residents of Rio Preto (state of São Paulo) agreed, complaining in 1898 that eight of the twelve commercial establishments in the thousand-inhabitant city were owned by Arabs. Less than a decade later a local alderman led a movement to erase all traces of "foreign interference in public life," proposing that all "turco" and "árabe" businesses be obligated to have a "Brazilian" accountant or face a hefty fine. Those who spoke Arabic near a Brazilian were to be fined a more modest amount on the spot. The suggestion was formally distributed to Rio Preto's Justice Commission, but was so "violent and absurd" that it was never even discussed."[54]

The police also harped on the entry of Arabs, emphasizing that foreign prison residents outnumbered Brazilian ones by a substantial margin. The "Árabe," "Turco-asiático" or "Turco" category appeared frequently in police reports, and in 1897 more than 10 percent (30 of 271) of the foreigners incarcerated in the São Paulo city prison were "turcos," the second largest group after Italians.[55] These widely circulated statistics, and U.S. Senator Justin Morrill's 1887 attempt to restrict immigration to the United States, led the Sociedade Central da Imigração to demand that Arabs be prevented from embarking for Brazil, which they feared would become home to immigrants that "other countries reject." Showing a keen awareness of policies elsewhere, the society claimed that it was cheaper for steamship companies to pay the fare from the United States to Brazil for "Turkish" passengers than to pay the fines that would be levied for trying to sneak them into the United States![56]

Middle Easterners in Brazil reacted to the agitation in two related ways. Some insisted publicly that Arab-Brazilian ethnicity was a positive development, while others sought to minimize public recognition of their identity. Those who took the latter approach often changed their names, ostensibly to make them easier to pronounce. Yet the reasoning behind name changing was more complex than pronunciation. First, modification often took place with names that contained only vowels and consonants found in Portuguese, suggesting that fear of recognition, rather than ease of rendition, was a critical factor. Even so, it was common to create Brazilian names that had hidden linkages to original names. This communally understood coding meant Taufik became Teófilo, Fauzi became Fausto, and Mohamad became Manuel. A particularly illustrative case is that of a dentist in Goiás who changed his name from Abdulmajid Dáu to Hermenegildo da Luz because "Hermenegildo sounded like Abdulmajid, and Dáu means light [luz]."[57]

These attempts at integration rarely changed bigoted attitudes. One author accused Syrians of taking "Brazilian" names to mask their presence in prosperous urban areas, and the famed anthropologist Edgard Roquette-

Pinto viewed Arab immigrants as a regressive "germ" attacking the "heart" of Brazil.[58]

> In the heart of Mato-Grosso, Amazonia, Minas Gerais, in the Capital of the Republic, live enormous masses of turco vendors. Although, as a result of the conditions of their habitual occupation, they are obliged to enter into relations with Brazilians, they in fact live completely segregated within their race, within their norms, within their character. No one knows for sure what they are called, where they are from, what religion they profess. They live within themselves, virtually ignored by the Brazilians. Where there is one who is richer, more intelligent or more learned, they congregate around him; and when this "leader" has a certain influence in the country, he begins to direct the nucleus of his compatriots.
>
> It would be unjust to negate the elementary services that these peddlers give to the people of the interior. It is an immigration that complies, at this moment, with a utilitarian mission; they have not brought, however, a germ of progress.

Elite concerns about the relationship between ethnicity and economic expansion led to new laws meant to control immigrant entrepreneurial activity. Ironically, the result was immigrant concentration in cities. Legislation forcing peddlers to buy or lease stalls in government-constructed markets, for example, helped spur individual economic growth while segregating Syrians and Lebanese in certain economic sectors. As immigrants sent for family members to help expand and consolidate their businesses, new wealth helped new communal institutions and organizations to spring up. One of the most important was the Arabic-language press, which had a dual, and contradictory, function. While the use of Arabic helped maintain premigratory culture, articles on how to negotiate life in a new setting (by providing aid in finding jobs and housing) helped Middle Easterners acculturate. Brazil's first Arabic newspaper, *Al-Faiāh* (Al-Fayha), was founded in the city of Campinas in November 1895, and *Al-Brasil* was founded less than six months later in Santos. The two papers merged a year later in São Paulo, and by 1902 there were three Arabic-language newspapers in São Paulo and two more in Rio de Janeiro. In 1914, fourteen Arabic-language newspapers circulated, and even the immigrants were surprised that "the collectivity could sustain such a high number."[59]

Arabic-language culture flourished in Brazil, and the São Paulo literary circle, Al-'Usba al-Andalusiyya (Brazilian New Andalusian League), published an internationally renowned monthly that placed Brazil in the center of *mahjar* literature. Seventeen-year-old Ilyās Farhāt (1893–1976) followed his brother from Lebanon to Brazil in 1910. While working as a peddler, Farhāt helped found the literary review *Al-Jadīd,* which published for a decade (1919–1929). Rashīd Salīm Khūrī (better known as al-Shafir al-Qarawi, "the village poet") migrated from Lebanon in 1913. Arabic-language newspapers throughout the world published his writings, which were often used to raise money for famine victims in the Middle East.[60] The al-Ma'lūf brothers, Fauzī (1899–1930) and Shafīq (1905–1976), came from a distinguished Lebanese family from Zahle. In São Paulo they prospered as textile manufacturers and wrote poetry in Arabic that would eventually be translated into Portuguese, Spanish, French, Russian, German, and Italian.[61]

By the early 1920s Syrian and Lebanese immigrants and their descendants were heavily concentrated in small-scale textile sales and the dry goods trade in most major Brazilian cities. This allowed many to save the equivalent of 2,000–4,000 French francs a year, a staggering amount, considering that a one-way ticket from Syria to South America cost only 250 francs.[62] How the surplus was used shows the deep division among those who saw Brazil as a new home and those who looked at it as a way station. While some immigrants, especially those with large sums, reinvested in the Brazilian economy, the majority, whose means were more modest, remitted significant amounts of money. Philip Hitti reports that 41 percent of Lebanon's total income in the early 1900s came from foreign transfers, and that by the 1950s virtually every village had "a red-tile roofed house built by money from abroad."[63] Money was followed by people, and statistics from Santos show a stunning out-migration rate of almost 46 percent for Middle Easterners (43,596 entries and 19,951 exits of "Turcos" and "Syrios").[64]

Return to Lebanon and Syria (as well as non-Middle Eastern destinations) was an important aspect of the Arab experience in Brazil. The Beirut neighborhood of Al-Sufi had its own Avenida Brasil and was known as the "bairro dos brasileiros." In mid-1925, Father José de Castro visited the Lebanese cities of Beirut and Zahle, and reported meeting Portuguese-speakers throughout the country. In one place the Brazilian national anthem was sung spontaneously in his honor.[65] The journalist Paulo Torres visited the region in 1926, and a lecture he presented after his return to

São Paulo was "overflowing [and] often interrupted by altercations among the audience." He reported that the *jogo do bicho* (a game of chance) was so popular that the Rio de Janeiro results were wired to Beirut each evening.[66] In the mid-1930s some 70 percent of the inhabitants of Zahle spoke Portuguese, and the main thoroughfare's name, Avenida Brazil, was painted in enormous letters on the pavement.[67] The transmission of Brazilian culture to the Middle East did little to impress Júlio de Revorêdo, an official of São Paulo's Department of Labor, who attacked "turcos" as dangerous for entering Brazil and as anti-Brazilian for leaving![68]

It was economic wealth that became the most important means of constructing Syrian-Lebanese ethnic space, frequently through the establishment of communal organizations whose actions could be interpreted as "Brazilian."[69] Ceará's Maronite Sociedade a Mão Branca, for example, raised funds for local disease victims. Syrian-Lebanese donations led São Paulo's House of Deputies to pass motions of appreciation in 1917 and 1918, and a public "thanks" from the Brazilian Boy Scouts is reported to have drawn fifteen thousand people.[70] While immigrants may have thought of themselves as Syrian or Lebanese (or, more specifically, as from Aleppo or Damascus or Zahle or Beirut) in the private sphere, they sought to create a single Syrian-Lebanese identity for the public sphere.

The 1922 centennial of Brazilian independence provided one of the best openings for the public participation of Syrian-Lebanese. For elites the decade-long celebration was an opportunity to show the world that Brazil had arrived as a "modern" nation. At home, nationalism was reinforced through massive public ceremonies following the construction of new buildings, bridges, roads, and monuments. Understanding the ethnic discursive space that nationalist rhetoric provided, leaders of the Syrian-Lebanese community established a Commission for Syrian-Lebanese Homage on the Centennial of the Independence of Brazil, under the leadership of the wealthy industrialist Basilio Jafet. Immediately the group commissioned Ettore Ximenes, a world-renowned Italian sculptor, to create a monument to the Syrian-Lebanese community in Brazil.[71] The choice of Ximenes, whose work was associated with Brazilian nationalism, and the monument's placement in the Parque Dom Pedro II as part of the centennial celebration, were intended to show that Syrian and Lebanese immigrants had become desirable Brazilians.

The monument, *Amizade sírio-libanesa* (Syrian-Lebanese Friendship), was a fifty-foot tower of bronze and granite. The base was divided into

Amizade sírio-libanesa.
Full Shot. Monument by
Ettore Ximenes, São Paulo,
1928. Photographs by Eliana
Shavitt Lesser.

"The Phoenicians." *Amizade
sírio-libanesa.* Monument by
Ettore Ximenes, São Paulo,
1928. Photograph by
Eliana Shavitt Lesser.

"The Brazilian Republic, the Indigenous Warrior, and the Pure Syrian Maiden." *Amizade sírio-libanesa.* Monument by Ettore Ximenes, São Paulo, 1928. Photograph by Eliana Shavitt Lesser.

four sections. Each of three sides contained reliefs representing "Syrian" contributions to world culture: the Phoenicians as pioneers of navigation, Haitam I's discovery of the Canary Islands, and the teaching of the alphabet. The fourth side was the "symbol of Syrian penetration in Brazil," represented by the "the commerce [that has led to] great prosperity." The top of the monument was composed of three life-size figures. At the back stood a female figure representing the Brazilian Republic, "whose glory is the glory of the Brazilian fatherland." In front of her a "pure Syrian maiden" offers a gift to her "Brazilian brother," an indigenous warrior, "with the same love with which she was welcomed upon arriving in this land blessed by God."[72]

If the reliefs in *Amizade sírio-libanesa* are imagined as a story that begins from the base, the message is clear: ancient Syrian greatness changed the world, allowing Brazil to be "discovered" and then to prosper. By suggesting that Arabs were part of the colonization of Brazil, and asserting that the three figures at the top of the monument were "brothers," the Syrian-Lebanese community became biologically Brazilian. The symbolism, however, should not be read as assimilationist. The dedicatory plaque, which reads "To the Brazilian Nation on the Hundredth Anniversary of its Independence. In admiration and recognition from the Syrian-Lebanese Colony," is repeated fully in Arabic, making a clear statement of a hyphenated identity.

The public dedication of *Amizade sírio-libanesa* took place in the Parque Dom Pedro II in 1928. Photographs published in *O Estado de S. Paulo* show that it was a huge event. The ceremony celebrated "the traditional friendship that unites the hardworking Syrian community to the Brazilian people," and included a parade by over two thousand soldiers and speeches by the mayor and city councilmen. Basilio Jafet, president of the commission that raised funds for the statue, was given the honor of opening the ceremony in the name of the president of Brazil. A military band played the national anthems of Brazil, Syria, and Lebanon. In a remarkable display of collective ahistorical memory, the "Syrians and Brazilians" in the crowd "exchanged expressions of the ancient friendship that unites them."[73]

Nagib Jafet, vice-president of the monument commission, gave a keynote speech that interpreted *Amizade sírio-libanesa* in a number of interesting ways. By reminding the audience that the monument had been forged in São Paulo's Lyceu de Artes e Ofícios ("the pride of Brazilian industry") and that the Phoenicians were "the father of the colonizers who came later, the Greek, the Roman, the Portuguese, the Spaniard and the English," Jafet remade Syrian and Lebanese immigrants and their descendants into Brazil's colonizers. This gave the community a "Syrian-Brazilian soul."[74] An interesting footnote suggests how ideas about hyphenated ethnicity have changed in Brazil. In 1988 the monument was moved from the Parque Dom Pedro II. The new location, which appears to have been chosen and funded by the large Ragueb Chohfi Textile Company, was a park at the entrance to 25 de Março Street, the area associated most strongly with

Syrian-Lebanese commerce in São Paulo. In a half-century the assertion of Syrian-Lebanese ethnicity saw a spatial shift—from the Brazilian nation (Parque Dom Pedro II) to its own ethnic neighborhood.

One of the most fascinating events surrounding the dedication of *Amizade sírio-libanesa* was a poetry contest whose simple rule was to describe the immigrant experience in Brazil. The winner was Ilyās Farhāt, whose Arabic-language poem suggested that Lebanese ethnicity was not related to place but to person, thus allowing Lebanese immigrants to be easily incorporated into Brazilian national identity. The poem asserted that while Lebanese immigrants were indebted to Brazil for allowing them to settle, the Lebanese presence had increased Brazil's presence as a "Christian nation" because Arabs, regardless of the religion they practiced, were at the heart of Christianity.

> If we cut all the cedars in Lebanon
> —and the cedars are the base of our inspiration;
> and with them we built a temple
> whose towers crossed the clouds;
> if we snatched from Baalbeck and Palmyra
> the vestiges of our glorious past;
> if we plucked Saladin's Tomb from Damascus
> and the Sepulcher of the Savior from Jerusalem;
> if we brought all of these treasures
> to this great independent nation
> and its glorious children
> we would still feel that
> we had not paid our debt
> to Brazil and the Brazilians.[75]

The themes in Farhāt's poem were far from unique. In 1929, the Muslim Beneficent Society began raising funds to build a large mosque in Rio de Janeiro, defining Brazil as "our second Andalusia."[76] A few years later Sadallah Amin Ghanem evoked a similar image in a speech demanding that Lebanese ethnicity be accepted as one component of Brazilian nationality: "I hear the eternal voice of the martyrs, sons of an elevated and heroic nationality. I hear the mysterious murmurs of our cedars. Save Brazil! Save Lebanon!"[77] Leaders of the twenty-five thousand-member Armenian community, formed in the late nineteenth century, defined their place even more aggressively by seeking to separate themselves from "Arab" immigrants. They insisted that Armenians were white, and a "legitimate and heroically Occidental ethnicity."[78]

Assertions of Syrian-Lebanese (or Armenian) ethnicity as a legitimate component of Brazilian national identity came during the economic dislocations and assimilationist theories that marked the pre-Depression years. The press, policy makers, and academics frequently commented on immigrants who seemed to adapt profitably to Brazil's economic climate while refusing to embrace Euro-Brazilian culture wholeheartedly. Brazil's minister of agriculture complained in a 1926 interview with the *New York Herald Tribune* of the "influx into the towns of Levantines, who mostly go under the name of 'Syrios' although some of them are Mohammedans. These visitors carry themselves to the towns and cities where they open small shops and sell inferior goods at high prices."[79] Guilherme de Almeida, a well-known vanguard poet who had participated in the 1922 Modern Art Movement and would flee Brazil after joining the São Paulo Constitutionalist Revolt of 1932, was more ambiguous. In 1929 he wrote eight satirical articles on his "impressions of our diverse foreign neighborhoods" for the mass circulation newspaper *O Estado de S. Paulo*. "The More Than Near East" poked fun at Orientalism by making Arabs not people but "mustaches, only mustaches. Contemplative mustaches . . . hopeful mustaches . . . smoky mustaches . . . sonorous mustaches. Mustaches." A street of Syrian-Lebanese owned shops became a space where "wholesalers sell giant bundles from giant plantations, with giant men with giant mustaches." The nearby residential neighborhood had "Mustaches, only mustaches." He even mocked the wide differences in the community, using an image straight from Euro-Brazilian bar culture: "What's the recipe for 'a Turk'? Take the 25 de Março Street cocktail shaker and put in a Syrian, an Arab, an Armenian, a Persian, an Egyptian, a Kurd. Shake it up really well and—boom—out comes a Turk."[80]

Plínio Salgado, leader of the green-shirted Brazilian fascist movement, also had mixed feelings about Middle Eastern immigrants. During his travels to the Middle East in the late 1920s, he frequently "saw" Brazil. He marveled at the "complex of races superimposed, mixed and coexisting," and after he met three Syrian businessmen from Minas Gerais returning to their country of birth, "There were hours of strong Brazilianness in which we played recordings of Rio de Janeiro sambas and the nostalgic songs of the country folk."[81] For Almeida and Salgado, Brazilian national identity might include Arabs: Almeida's "turcos" were both dark and blond, while

Salgado's Syrians were full of the "Brazilianness" that was the backbone of his nativist ideology.

The new views of who might fit into the Brazilian nation were not uniformly accepted. A consular officer in Alexandria, Egypt, suggested that Armenian immigrants be prohibited (a position later adopted) because they were "opium producers" who would provide a "perpetual temptation" to "yellow" immigrants already in Brazil.[82] J. Rodrigues Valle, an economist and law professor at the University of Brazil Law School in Rio de Janeiro, agreed. In a wide-ranging attack on immigrants and Afro-Brazilians, he complained that "backward" Arabs, Turks, and Syrians were "drug traffickers" who remained "segregated from other Brazilian populations. . . . They rarely marry outside of their own. They retain, almost intact, their nationality."[83] Also instructive was a 1925 survey on immigration by the Sociedade Nacional de Agricultura that included responses from influential politicians along with doctors, lawyers, and agricultural workers. Most were heavily pro-immigrant, especially on the question of Japanese labor. Yet with regard to Arabs, the anti-immigrant Rodrigues Valle and the pro-immigrant respondents to the survey were of one mind. Twenty-five separate groups were referred to as desirably "white," but none came from the Middle East. The Sociedade Pastoril Agrícola Industrial of Jaguarão in Rio Grande do Sul argued that Arabs should be avoided because "They are never farmworkers and are always peddlers when they are not gamblers or smugglers." Others described Syrian and "Semitic" immigrants with words like "parasitic," "exploitative," and "conmen."[84]

Sentiments such as these would find strong policy backing following the Revolution of 1930, led by Getúlio Vargas.[85] The Vargas coup was nationalist in action and nativist in tone, and provided the political bureaucracy with license to express prejudice openly. It was decreed that "one of the causes of unemployment is found in the free entry of foreigners . . . [who] frequently contribute to an increase in economic disorder and social insecurity." The commercial attaché in Egypt agreed, complaining that Syrians "are populating Brazil and forming our race with all that is the most repugnant in the universe."[86] Syrian and Lebanese immigrants soon found themselves assailed for their urban concentration and their lack of formal schooling. Entry statistics from the port of Santos between 1908 and 1936 show that the agricultural rates of "Turcos" were the lowest among all immigrant groups, 11 percent, and Syrians were under 30 percent. "Turcos" over seven years of age had the highest level of illiteracy (almost 58 percent), while Syrians were somewhere in the middle (about 30 percent). Another issue was the frequent entry of unmarried males who then settled in cities. According to Getúlio Vargas, Brazil was interested only in "true rural agricultural workers who come in constituted families," and questions of morality similar to those that had arisen during discussions of Chinese immigration were common.[87] Yet again the future of the Brazilian nation seemed to emanate from men, and Arab men posed a particular threat to Brazilian women, who might be attracted by their lack of "blackness."

An important response to the attacks on Arab immigrants can be found among those who became actively involved in the struggles for Lebanese and Syrian nationhood (which were consummated in 1943 and 1946, respectively). For many Syrian and Lebanese immigrants who arrived as children, stories of political persecution helped create an ethnic framework in which national independence became a collective goal.[88] Public hangings in Damascus and Beirut ordered by the Turkish military governor during World War I encouraged such sentiment, and a widely shared memory of colonial discrimination and hardship intertwined easily with real discrimination in Brazil. At the same time, regional identification among immigrants dissipated with the growth of more general "Arab" organizations. In the cultural realm, poetry in Arabic produced in Brazil became among the most important in the mahjar.[89] Together these factors helped encourage Syrian and Lebanese nationalism among immigrants.

The life of Antun Sa'adih, born into a family of Greek Orthodox intellectuals in Lebanon in 1904, provides a fine illustration. Just before World War I, Antun's father, Dr. Khalil Sa'adih (a physician best known for editing the first English-Arabic dictionary, in 1911), moved to Egypt and from there to Brazil, where he published Al-Jarida, a newspaper, and the monthly Al-Majallah. Antun joined his father in São Paulo in 1920 and began writing articles proposing a Syrian state. Following the "Great Revolt" in Syria against the French mandate, Antun founded a number of semisecret societies, including the short-lived Syrian Patriotic Association and the longer-lasting Free Syrian Party. At the same time he taught Arabic language and literature at the Syrian-Brazilian School in São Paulo, and began to further define the notion of an ethnic and spatial Syrian nation. The idea took hold among many Arab émigrés in South America, and much of Sa'adih's ideology was tested and reinforced in Brazil. In 1929 Sa'adih returned to the Middle East, and in 1932 he secretly founded the Syrian Social Nationalist Party (SSNP), formalizing it publicly two years later with a reissuing of *Al-Majallah*. In Brazil other Arab immigrants began organizing sections of the SSNP, and in 1938 Sa'adih traveled to Brazil and Argentina to meet with and raise funds from those who now defined themselves as "Syrian." During this trip Sa'adih was exiled, and while in Brazil he founded *Souria al-Jadida* (The New Syria), a newspaper later banned by Vargas. This led to a two-month detention by the Vargas regime as a foreign agent, and in 1939 he left for Argentina, where he remained until his return to Syria in 1947.[90] Two years later Sa'adih was dead, executed following a military coup.

Syrian-Lebanese poets such as Shkr Allāh al-Jurr and Ilyās Farhāt were enamored of the new nationalism and began to commemorate even losing battles as important moments. Farhāt's ode to the battle of Maysalun was published in Brazil before reaching the rest of the Arab diaspora.

> He who dies for high principles lives
> and his enemy is dead, even though he remained unhurt.
> The ones you slaughtered are remembered
> the more as years pass by.
> The glory of Syria in Maysalun
> was first a sapling which they nursed with their blood.
> Soon you will see its shade spread over Arab and non-Arab.[91]

Arab nationalist movements and economic success made "turcos" a focal point of nativist anger. One manifestation was the suggestion that Arab commercial achievement was biologically determined. The nationalist Vivaldo Coaracy published a series of articles in 1929 on "National Problems" in *O Estado de S. Paulo,* and he took the following position on "Syrians, Lebanese, Armenians and Copts": "It is the Semitic current of bent-nosed Levantines whose essential activity is to buy and sell and not produce. . . . But there is not only the economic aspect to consider. These individuals bring an Eastern mentality, sinuous and strange when compared with our habits, our traditions and our Western education. They bring ways of thinking and ways of doing that come from the Near East, tortuous and sinister, the picturesque East perhaps, but always dangerous . . . the East that all civilized peoples hope to avoid."[92] Pierre Deffontaines, a professor at the Universidade do Distrito Federal in Rio De Janeiro, agreed, arguing that when Arabs "discovered Brazil, their penchant for peddling precipitated [the arrival] of a multitude. Thanks to their hereditary qualities . . . they easily supplanted the earlier peddlers."[93] Plínio Salgado's vision was similar: the rewritten portion of "Oriente (impressões de viagens) 1930" printed in an homage to the Syrian-Lebanese community edited by Salomão Jorge included a discussion of commerce as the Arab "pátria."[94]

Of all the commentators, it was Alfredo Ellis Júnior, a descendant of Confederate soldiers who had settled in Brazil after the U.S. Civil War, a politician (and son of a politician), and an essayist, who was most fascinated with the various "populations" that made up multicultural São Paulo. Ellis was both enamored of pseudoscience (he called his mix of eugenics and climatology "anthroposocial psychology") and convinced of the God-given superiority of Brazil's society of the future. His first book, Raça de gigantes (1926), looked at the traditional components of São Paulo's population (Iberian, Indian, and African). Soon thereafter Ellis became enthralled by the new immigrants pouring into the state, and he was especially interested in determining what groups would become "Brazilians" and which ones would form "[ethnic] cysts."[95] Arabs occupied much of Ellis's attention, and he used the pseudoscientific terms "brachycephalo syrioide" and "syrio-armenioide" to explain points of similarity and difference between Syrian-Lebanese and Armenians. During his "scientific investigations" Ellis observed a puzzling contradiction: while the Arab "body type" was similar to the Brazilian one and a "few blond-haired and blue-eyed elements" seemed to represent an appealing "current of Nordic blood," most Arab immigrants seemed interested in maintaining their premigratory culture.[96] In 1930, Ellis set out to complete more research for a multipart series in the Correio Paulistano, but the Revolution of 1930 stopped the process: as Vargas's troops marched through São Paulo, they destroyed the paper. In 1934 the study was finally released in book form under the title Populações paulistas, a volume of the Companhia Editora Nacional's highly regarded "nationalist culture" Brasiliana series, whose goal was to help "Brazilians discover Brazil, making it increasingly better known and thus making it increasingly loved."[97]

Populações paulistas provides a perfect example of how intellectuals struggled to discuss the ethnic cultures they observed within a discourse on national identity and Brazilianness. Ellis believed Syrian culture had maintained itself over time and space because the group "lived for many centuries, as an ethnic minority, under the heavy Muslim yoke." Long-term minority status thus transformed culture into a biological reality, making Arab immigrants "businessmen congenitally and by heredity . . .

[who] since the ancient times . . . [are] capable of selling [their] own life, swearing that [they are] making nothing on the deal." Yet Ellis's interpretation of "economic biology" was counteracted by his sense of an admirable warlike character. Since "many Syrians" had fought on the side of São Paulo during its 1932 rebellion against the federal government, Ellis extolled the "inheritors of the legendary traditions of the Phoenicians [who are] a polymorphic composite of a great mass of races." In spite of the "Levantine customs [and] impossible language" that led them to marry among themselves, the varied racial background of Syrians paved the path for easy entrance into Brazil's "ethnic democracy" for later generations. For Ellis, Syrian immigrants would improve Brazilian national identity, which would in turn help to ensure that Syrians would be transformed into "Brazilians."[98]

As the debate over the relationship between ethnicity and national identity raged, a new challenge arrived from the Middle East, this time settling in the state of Paraná. In 1932 the League of Nations, in conjunction with the Nansen International Office for Refugees, decided to expend considerable energy in helping twenty thousand Assyrian refugees leave Iraq. The Assyrians were Chaldean members of the Nestorian Church who lived in a legally separate and semiautonomous community within the Ottoman Empire.[99] Two British-led Assyrian battalions had fought Iraqi nationalists, and upon Iraq's independence in 1932, the new Muslim-dominated regime refused citizenship to the Assyrians, making them refugees within their own country.[100] In October 1932, Paraná Plantations, Ltd., a British colonization company, proposed "a scheme which opens up adequate possibilities for [settling] the whole of the Assyrian population" on an enormous plot of land in Paraná, some sixty kilometers from Londrina in an area of Austrian, Czechoslovak, German, Italian, Japanese, and Polish colonization.[101] In spite of earlier refusals by the government to aid any refugees, the League of Nations hoped Brazil would become a destination in the resettlement process.[102]

The Vargas regime identified a number of advantages to accepting the Assyrian refugees. The group's settlement would help to populate a relatively deserted area in Paraná where rail lines were being laid. The Assyrians, religiously devout and arriving in family groups, also seemed to fit with the regime's desire to return to a more traditional Catholic society.[103] Raúl do Rio Branco of Brazil's delegation in Geneva emphasized that they "are all Catholics . . . headed by a patriarch recognized by the Holy See," mimicking similar comments by the British, who boasted that the Assyrians had maintained their Christian religion in spite of "the fact that they have lived among somewhat lawless and turbulent people of an alien religion." Indeed, Rio Branco drew a sharp distinction between the "Christian" Assyrians and the majority of "Muslim fanatic[s]."[104] Arthur Thomas, representative of both Paraná Plantations and the São Paulo-Paraná Railroad Company, went even farther. In a petition to the Brazilian Ministry of Labor, he portrayed the group as "an Aryan race, without any Semitic or Arabic characteristics."[105]

In the aftermath of the Revolution of 1930, immigration policy fell under the purviews of the ministers of labor and of foreign affairs. Itamaraty (the name by which the Ministry of Foreign Affairs is known) chief José Carlos de Macedo Soares favored the Assyrian plan, perhaps because he owned land bordering the Paraná Plantation estate that would rise in value when the area was settled.[106] Minister of Labor Joaquim Salgado Filho agreed, pointing out in a letter to Porto Alegre's *Correio do Povo* that the Assyrians "can only bring benefits."[107] On 3 January 1934, the Ministry of Labor informed the League of Nations that the Assyrians would be permitted to enter under the following conditions: (1) Brazil would have no financial responsibility; (2) they were all farmers; (3) the Assyrians would come in groups of five hundred families and each group had to be settled prior to the arrival of the next; and (4) the League of Nations and Paraná Plantations would assume responsibility for repatriation if the colony was not a success.[108] Notably absent was any reference to ethnicity, religion, or race. In official parlance, the Assyrians were desirable immigrants.

The conditions set out by the Brazilian government were easy to meet. Most Assyrians were farmers, and Iraq was "ready to make [a] generous [financial] contribution" as long as it would have no future legal responsibilities. The British also offered to help pay for the scheme. In early 1934, a League of Nations official reported that Brazil had "intimated" it was prepared to admit the refugees, and the plan was released to the British press.[109] A month later, when preparations seemed to be stalled, the League of Nations again went to the press, this time expressing its "profound gratitude to the Brazilian Government for its generous offer to throw open its territory."[110]

When the British news reports arrived in Brazil, there was an uproar "of unusual violence."[111] The Vargas regime, which saw the scheme as a way of populating a frontier area at virtually no cost, now became the target of nativists who claimed that the Assyrians were unassimilable "nomads and Mohammedans," and that humanitarian efforts should be aimed at the drought-stricken Rio São Francisco Valley.[112] Major Frederico A. Rondón, who spent many years mapping Brazil's central regions, exclaimed that "Brazil is no longer the country of immigration that it was just a century ago" and that "an exotic race [like the Assyrians] . . . [should not be] accepted without any conditions."[113] News reports on the topic inflamed passions through the use of provocative headlines like "A Grave Danger to Remove: You Only Have Peace with an Assyrian After He Dies" and "An Undesirable Immigration."[114] The *Jornal do Brasil* appealed to an urban working class hit hard by the Depression and angry at the economic success associated with Arabs by suggesting that the Assyrians were "future peddlers."[115] One *A Nação* article favored the plan, claiming that only "strong and healthy farmers" would be included. Yet careful readers of that paper were probably confused a few weeks later when another extremely positive report received the headline "An Attempt to Exploit the Humanitarian Sentiments of the Brazilian People."[116] The press widely reported claims by Paulo Vageler, the German head of the Ministry of Agriculture's Institute of Chemistry, that the Assyrians were "racial[ly] inconvenien[t]" because they were not the Christians "of Ancient History."[117] São Paulo's *Platéa* dismissed the refugees as part of an "irritating question," and Rio de Janeiro's *Diário Carioca* concluded that Brazil's immigration policy was "immoral."[118] The *Diário de Notícias* concurred, judging the plan "absurd . . . incoherent . . . and reveal[ing] the basic official ignorance of the true economic, racial and moral imperatives needed for a homogeneous Brazil."[119]

The League of Nations responded with a special committee whose goal was to generate positive publicity in Brazil. Headed by John Gilbert Browne, a British general who had worked with the Assyrians in Iraq, the committee included Charles Redard, a counselor of the Swiss legation in Rio de Janeiro, and Major T. F. Johnson, secretary-general of the Nansen Office for Refugees. Recognizing that Brazilian nativism contained a great deal of anti-British sentiment, Browne was instructed by the British ambassador to emphasize that his appointment came about only "because you have had contact with Assyrians" and that "you are astonished that anyone could question their excellent qualities."[120] Browne's smooth manner did little to soothe the situation: after his arrival in Rio de Janeiro, the League of Nations became a regular target of the press, which highlighted

British interest: "If the English are so interested in finding a refuge for the Assyrians, they could be placed in the millions of square kilometers that make up the [British] Empire."[121]

All of Browne's skills came into play as he tried to assuage the fears of Brazilian politicians after the Mar Shimoun (the twenty-six-year-old Assyrian patriarch) demanded special "national minority rights" status and suggested that Assyrians should not be obligated to serve in the military.[122] Browne's meetings with bureaucrats in Labor and Foreign Affairs did produce some points of agreement: the Assyrians would be allowed to set up their own schools as long as Portuguese was taught, and Brazil's constitutional commitment to religious freedom insured that Assyrian Catholicism would be permitted.[123] Even so, the discussions sat poorly in a climate where the relationship between national identity and ethnicity was a fundamental component of elite debate. Both Brazil and Great Britain insisted that the Assyrians "must become Brazilians," and that it would not "be enough to allow this to occur by ordinary processes of naturalization of the growing up of a new generation."[124] The relationship of assimilation to citizenship was particularly difficult to negotiate. One League of Nations official believed the Brazilians would accept the Assyrians only if they traveled with Iraqi papers and could be deported if trouble arose.[125] The British government disagreed, and suggested that the Assyrians take Brazilian citizenship upon arrival because they "will sooner or later have to accept assimilation . . . [and] if national status is left indeterminate they may regard the scheme as purely temporary and cling to dangerous ideas of separate national enclave."[126]

Concerns about "national minority status" were not nearly as frequent as the claims, regularly expressed in the press and Parliament during the years of relatively open political debate from 1932 to 1936, that the Assyrians were "semibarbarians who will only disturb order and cause the Brazilian race to degenerate."[127] British officials reinforced the accusations by judging the Assyrians "a very difficult people with a genius for irritating even sympathetic persons having to deal with them."[128] Leading members of the Syrian-Lebanese community, rightly fearing that attacks on the Assyrians would carry over to all of Middle Eastern descent, confirmed the charges in Arabic-language newspapers with reports "of a rather lurid description."[129] Even the official Itamaraty label changed from the positive "Assyrian immigrants" to the much less desirable "Immigration of Refugees from Iraq" or "Assyrian Refugees from Iraq."[130] The wording was critical: Brazilian policy was pro-immigrant yet antirefugee, and proponents of the plan had gone to great pains to distinguish between Iraqis ("fanatic Muslims") and Assyrians ("a Christian people"). As Assyrian Christian *immigrants* were transformed into Iraqi (Muslim) *refugees,* they lost their desirability.

The most ardent attacks on the Assyrians emanated from the Society of the Friends of Alberto Torres, whose membership was filled with nativist intellectuals, diplomats, and politicians, including Integralist leader Plínio Salgado, Agriculture Minister Juarez Távora, and Nicolão José Debané, a former diplomat.[131] The Friends were closely tied to the press, notably former Foreign Minister Felix Pacheco, owner and editor in chief of Rio de Janeiro's influential *Jornal do Comércio.* Pacheco offered the group free space in his newspaper for "attacks on the Japanese, the League of Nations, or any other non-nationalistic element which at the time may figure in the news."[132] Full-page assaults on the Assyrians were common, and one missive demanded a "campaign against British imperialism that seems to impose on Brazil the immigration of Bedouins"; another argued that "Owing to ethnological, cultural, social and economic differences, no elements of the tribes of Iraq are suitable."[133] When the Friends castigated Itamaraty for approving the Assyrian plan, it begged forgiveness, claiming it was "a mere intermediary between the League of Nations, foreign governments and the Ministry of Labor."[134] Foreigners were less apologetic: the British ambassador dismissed "the ignorance" of the Friends with the simple explanation that Alberto Torres, for whom the group was named, "was a philosopher, who is suspected of having also been a lunatic."[135]

Articles in the Brazilian press were often written by lobbying groups who purchased space. This, and the fact that small and regional newspapers frequently reprinted stories from large, metropolitan papers, led to prominent coverage of the Assyrian issue. Ten Rio newspapers ran more than one negative story on the issue in the first quarter of 1934, as did newspapers in São Paulo, Santos, Florianópolis, Joinville, Bahia and Porto Alegre. From January to April 1934, the story was constantly in the news, and the *Correio da Manhã,* the *Jornal do Brasil,* and the *Diário Carioca* each printed at least two stories a week. The *Correio da Manhã* and *Diário Carioca,* the two papers most ardently opposed to Assyrian entry, frequently ran more than one article on the same day.[136]

The coverage played on the nationalist and nativist sentiments among economically struggling city dwellers. Nationalists rightly portrayed England as suggesting Brazil accept a refugee group that the British themselves would not admit.[137] Yet the concerns about imperialism were uniformly tinged with racist images. The columnist Belmonte opposed the Assyrians' entry on nationalist grounds, portraying them as a warlike horde: "If England has the right to raffle off its inconvenient occupants, we also have the right not to settle them here, giving them a home, food, clean clothes, drinking water and electric trolleys. Brazil still belongs to Brazilians and [only] we can say if this *invasion* is convenient or not."[138] Raúl de Paula, a member of the Society of the Friends of Alberto Torres, complained in the *Jornal do Comércio* that "we try to do everything for the foreigner in our country. With Germans, Japanese, Poles and now with Assyrians," erroneously claiming that the British were sending twenty thousand *families* to Brazil.[139] Seemingly insistent on providing evidence of their imperialist position, the British unsuccessfully demanded that the Brazilian government censor all reports on the topic.[140]

The Assyrian plan had the misfortune of coming to public attention during the debates over a new constitution. In the Constitutional Assembly, nationalist arguments melded easily with nativist ones, and in one nonbinding vote two-thirds of the politicians approved a prohibition on immigrants of any single nationality from settling in large concentrations.[141] Eventually an immigration quota was fixed at 2 percent of the number from each nation who had arrived in the previous fifty years, and the federal government gained the authority "to guarantee the ethnic integration and physical and civic capacity of the immigrant."[142] The spirited debates split Paulista landowners, who ardently supported the entry of Japanese laborers, from urban politicians, who argued that foreign residents were a cause of Brazil's post-1930 economic problems. Vargas, while realizing the domestic appeal of opposing immigration, feared that offending the Japanese government might lead to a prohibition on emigration to Brazil, a reduction in trade, or, more ominously, disturbances among the large resident Japanese population.[143] Discussing immigration by focusing on Assyrians held no such liability.

The most ardent Assyriophobes in the Constitutional Assembly were the three leaders of the anti-Japanese movement: Antônio Xavier de Oliveira, Miguel Couto, and Arthur Neiva (whose friends, ironically, had thrown him a welcome home party after his return from Japan in 1921 at Rio de Janeiro's exclusive Restaurant Assyrio).[144] All believed that the entry of nonwhites would disrupt Brazil's social progress, and all conflated the immigration debate with a broader discussion of whether Syrian and Lebanese residents had integrated "properly" into Brazilian society. Both Neiva and Xavier de Oliveira had unsuccessfully proposed that all nonwhite immigrants be banned—the latter took the more extreme position.[145] Xavier de Oliveira insisted that immigrants be "those elements judged preferable, the civilized whites of Central and Northern Europe," and thus rejected all "Arabs" in terms of both race (they were not white) and geography (not from Central or Northern Europe).[146] Pedro Aurélio de Góis Monteiro, a delegate later appointed war minister by Vargas, concurred. He asserted that "it is an error to presume that immigration brings civilization," and that "disparate and nonassimilable races" should be prohibited.[147] Morais de Andrade, a delegate from São Paulo who was also a lawyer for the Japanese-owned Brazilian Colonization Corporation, was certainly thinking of Arabs when he complained of those who "only go to the state capital cities to form neighborhoods of disorder and crime." He worked hard to differentiate widely accepted anti-Arab prejudice from the hotly debated anti-Asian sentiment, arguing that politicians should not let their "anti-Nipponic prejudices make the Japanese the *"cabeça de turco"* [scapegoat; literally Turk's head] for the extremely justified opposition to Iraq."[148]

As if the linkage of Assyrians and Japanese was not complicated enough, in 1933 and 1934 the League of Nations high commissioner for refugees was in Brazil seeking spaces for German Jews. Assyrians, Japanese, and Jews were presented as omnipresent invaders, and a Society of the Friends of Alberto Torres editorial asserted that the three formed a united military enemy that would defeat Brazil culturally if allowed to penetrate its borders.

> The threat that hovers over Brazil of an invasion of the inhabitants of Iraq, which England wished to place in Paraná, was a signal of alarm that awakened our people and warned them against certain currents of immigration that have been coming our way. We refer in particular to the Japanese and the Jews, who for good reasons are undesirable immigrants rejected today by all nations that are in need of foreign labor.[149]

While nativists sought to link Arabs to Japanese and Jews, the federal government saw the Assyrian issue as a way to resolve the disparate positions on Japanese immigration. Any prohibition on Japanese entry, while satisfying to some influential members of the political elite, would certainly anger others. Barring the Assyrians, however, had no such price. Politicians could point to their refusal to settle the Assyrians as evidence of their nativism. São Paulo elites could barter a ban on the Assyrians for the continued entry of Japanese farmworkers. For Vargas, prohibiting the Assyrians had few international ramifications because no other country was willing to settle the group.

During the Constitutional Assembly a rumor began to circulate that the regime had approved the Assyrians' settlement, leading delegates to demand a formal investigation of the "noxious people in our midst."[150] Paraná's Federação Operária asked delegates to "revoke permission for the entry of these intrusive undesirables," and the Instituto da Ordem de Advogados do Paraná (Institute of the Order of Lawyers of Paraná) mounted a public campaign in the media against the "wave of Assyrian inhabitants from Iraq in the middle of Asia."[151] The institute considered the "Campaign Against Assyrian Immigration" its major event in 1934, even giving that title to its annual publication. One counselor argued that the entry of "more active and better prepared," but socially undesirable, immigrants created a "cosmic crisis" among Brazil's population, who were "without cohesion, without their own ethnic type."[152] Another complained that the English wanted to take the Assyrians ("a decadent race that does not preserve any vestiges of its ancestral civilization, a race without useful initiative, dirty and criminal nomads") out of Iraq so that "petroleum mines" could be exploited.[153]

Anti-Assyrian comments were often tinged with a significant dose of anti-Vargas sentiment. Getúlio Vargas therefore refused to meet League of Nations representative Browne because he "dare not offend . . . what seems to be unanimous public opinion," and appointed a special commission to examine the question.[154] The commission was headed by Francisco José Oliveira Vianna, a conservative intellectual and "respected servant" of the Vargas regime who was a historian and professor at the Law Faculty in Rio de Janeiro, as well as the legal counselor to the Ministry of Labor.[155] Vianna's "scholarship" openly mimicked European racists like Gobineau and Le Bon by applauding the "new Aryan centers" of southern Brazil.[156] The committee also included the anthropologist Roquette-Pinto (who had attacked "turcos" in a 1917 book); Raúl de Paula, appointed to represent the Society of the Friends of Alberto Torres; and Nicolão Debané, another Friend noted for his fervent xenophobia and experience as a diplomat in the Middle East. Dulphe Pinheiro Machado and Renato Kehl rounded out the special commission. Machado was director general of the National Population Department (DNP), the agency in charge of colonization, and often complained of "parasitic elements that constitute ethnic minorities and that upset the tranquillity of the nations where they live."[157] Kehl was founder of the *Boletim de Eugenia* (Bulletin of Eugenics) and the Central Brazilian Commission of Eugenics, which he modeled on the German Society for Race Hygiene. With Xavier de Oliveira he had proposed during the First Brazilian Eugenics Congress (1929) that Brazil should restrict the entry of non-Europeans, a motion that was only narrowly defeated.

The composition of the special commission guaranteed a negative evaluation of the Assyrian plan. Vianna, for example, asked the Brazilian diplomats in the United States to report on Assyrian residents. When the responses labeled the group "peaceful and hard-workers," the Vianna Commission dismissed them with "the same objections as existed against the entrance of Asians."[158] Another report condemning Assyrian and Asian immigration that Raúl de Paula had written as secretary-general of the Friends was introduced as evidence. This report included statements from Agriculture Minister Távora, Navy Minister Protógenes Guimarães, and newly appointed War Minister Pedro Aurélio de Góis Monteiro, and was presented personally to President Vargas.[159]

By May the Assyrians had been transformed from peaceful Christian immigrant farmers into a warlike refugee group that would bring social and economic danger to Brazil. An official decree banning the entry of "Gypsies and nomads" was promulgated with great fanfare on 9 May 1934; it was quietly taken off the books a week later.[160] A report from the British Embassy in Rio de Janeiro noted that Brazilians felt that Brazil was "the dumping ground for the undesirables of all the people in the world" and that "Every patriotic Brazilian must wish to prevent . . . the arrival of new bad blood."[161] The *Correio da Manhã* suggested that "the Christianity of this group . . . is a pretext for rebellion and disorder," and that "they live in perpetual religious discussion."[162] João Carlos Muniz, a diplomat in Brazil's Geneva embassy who later, as head of the Conselho de Imigração e Colonização, encouraged a secret prohibition on the entry of Jews fleeing Nazism, cast virtually every attribute of the Assyrians into doubt. He argued that the group was not really Catholic and was descended from one "that flourished in the last millennium before Christ," making Muslims their "brothers." For Muniz, religion was only part of the problem because the Assyrians were "naturally independent and not inclined to discipline." They were "difficult to govern, truculent and extremely unreliable." Furthermore, in a classic case of blaming the victim, Muniz argued that "the long period for which they have been refugees will have certainly reinforced their defects."[163]

The League of Nations continued to insist that the Assyrians would go to Brazil while Vargas asserted that he had never authorized such action.[164] The confusion allowed the president to twist the issue to his advantage. Meeting with the leaders of the Society of the Friends of Alberto Torres, Vargas claimed "Geneva" (the headquarters of the League of Nations) had told him that the Assyrians were "a group of only 3,000 farmers," but his personal examinations showed that they were "a great mass."[165] Such comments show Vargas at his manipulative best, appealing to nationalists by attacking the League of Nations and England, appealing to nativists by rejecting the Assyrian "masses," appearing to support the three thousand-person/nation limit on immigration popular in the Constitutional Assembly, and soothing large landowners and nativist urban dwellers by favoring rural immigration. In April 1934, the League of Nations abandoned the scheme, wondering if the plan might have worked better if Brazilian authorities had been bribed outright.[166] Newspapers hailed the decision, which left "all of America free of the Iraqi nomads." Lindolfo Pessôa, president of the Instituto da Ordem de Advogados do Paraná, was equally pleased, announcing in a radio address that the anti-Assyrian campaign was "without racial prejudice" and that his group would "always be alert . . . against the evils that threaten Brazil."[167]

Swirling around the debate over Assyrian settlement was the presence of the tens of thousands of Middle Easterners who already resided in Brazil. Many were economically successful urban dwellers who had worked hard to establish their Syrian-Lebanese ethnicity, even if it was not exactly the Europeanized one that the elite had desired. Paulo Cursino de Moura suggested that simply "pronouncing" the name of Rua 25 de Março "mentally" conjured up images of the "turco type," sentiments echoed more recently by Manuel Diégues Júnior, who wrote in what is the standard work on minority communities in Brazil that "when a 'turco' arrives on a street to conduct some commercial activity, the street takes on another color, an ethnic color . . . soon the street is given a Syrian or Lebanese physiognomic character."[168] The ethnologist R. Paulo Souza whined that "[t]hey stick together," and Oscar Egídio de Araújo, a statistician from the Free School of Sociology and Politics of São Paulo, complained about the "invasion of

25 de Março Street by the Syrians and Lebanese . . . [who] speak more in foreign languages than in the language of the country." [169] He claimed that Arab immigrants had "low assimilation rates," and termed one neighborhood "frankly Syrian" although his own census statistics indicated that Arab immigrants were not in the majority.

Such sentiments led a number of influential academics to see commercial success and urban settlement patterns as something to be battled in a holy war for an authentic Brazil. Pierre Deffontaines complained that the city of Baurú's "richest block is inhabited in large part by Syrians," and that the preferred place of residence in São Paulo, on Avenida Paulista, was filled with "nouveaux riche blocks with extravagant and exaggerated homes." Oscar Egídio de Araújo drew a sharp distinction between the few Syrian and Lebanese farmers and the 98 percent of Japanese immigrants who worked the land. A. Tavares de Almeida used the language of sport and war when he characterized Arabs as "defeating the national competition with ease," and Paulo Cursino de Moura wrote that the Syrians had "conquered" São Paulo.[170]

Perhaps the most outrageous display of stereotyping, both positive and negative, came in 1935 when Salomão Jorge, a poet and intellectual of Syrian descent, began a public debate with Herbert Levy, a perhaps surprisingly named non-Jewish journalist and author (and later a federal deputy from São Paulo). The topic was whether Brazil should promote or discourage Syrian and/or German Jewish immigration, and both writers adopted an ethnic (i.e., culturally mutable) position rather than a racial (biologically immutable) one. Each quoted Oliveira Vianna, melting pot theory, and fusibility indexes (even those that showed that Jews and Arabs did *not* assimilate) as they insisted that "their" immigrant group would improve Brazil's culture and economy.

The gloves first came off in late 1934 when Herbert Levy suggested in his *Problemas actuaes da economia brasileira* that German Jewish refugees gave Brazil "the opportunity to receive . . . the best in the arts, in the sciences, in economics, in . . . letters [and] in all areas of cultural activity." Levy believed Arabs, and especially Syrians, should be prohibited from entering Brazil because they were "dedicated to commerce and speculation . . . [were] difficult to assimilate . . . [and had] unsatisfactory racial and hygienic qualities." [171] In other words, Levy attacked Syrian immigrants by applying to them a series of negative stereotypes traditionally used in Brazil against both Arabs and Jews.[172]

Salomão Jorge responded by suggesting that Levy's "unmeasured praise of Israelite immigration" came about because "by [Levy's] own name I conclude that he is a Jew or the descendant of one."[173] Assumption in hand, Jorge decided to turn the tables and suggest that it was Levy, and not Syrian immigrants, who had not really assimilated. "Where does Mr. Levy live?" asked Jorge. "Is it in Bessarabia or Brazil?" Why would Levy "insult his Syrian brothers"? Jorge noted that what Levy saw as positive about Jewish immigration was almost exactly what he had attacked in Syrians: "not all Jews are scientists, physicians and philosophers. A great part are businesspeople, bankers, economists and capitalists. . . . Peddling is almost a Jewish institution. . . . If the Jews present optimal racial qualities, why don't the Syrians present them as well?"[174]

Firing back, Levy claimed that "I don't hold any spirit of hostility toward any race" while insisting that urban immigrants who engaged in speculative activity were "not convenient to our country." Furthermore, Jorge did not understand that opening Brazil's doors to Jews should be done "only in the particular case of . . . persecuted German Jews who are born of the German culture."[175] In other words, Levy saw Jews as generally undesirable but modified this notion for those who had lost their negative qualities by becoming German.

The debate continued. Levy attacked Syrian immigrants as polygamous Muslims while Jorge explained that they were monogamous Christians. Levy quoted meaningless statistics and Jorge responded in kind. Strangest of all, Levy pointed out that the racist Society of the Friends of Alberto Torres was opposed to Syrian immigration, without ever mentioning its regular attacks on Jews, while supporters of Jorge cited Integralist chief Plínio Salgado's positive comments on his trip to the Middle East (see above) without ever mentioning his nativist, anti-immigrant stance.[176]

That culture was not biologically determined was critical to the Jorge/Levy debate. Both hailed ethnic identity, claiming it did not inherently prevent immigrants from becoming Brazilian, and others who joined in the fray took similar positions. The Syrian-Lebanese industrialist Eduardo Jafet, clearly confident of his status as "Brazilian," wrote of a visit to Lebanon, where "we, the children of Lebanese [immigrants] . . . involve ourselves in filial veneration of intense fervor."[177] Júnior Amarilio collected all the published materials surrounding the Jorge-Levy debate under the title *As vantagens da immigração syria no Brasil,* dedicating the book to the poets Nami Jafet and Fauzī al-Ma'lūf as "Names that honor the distant pátria

and Brazil," and to all Syrian and Lebanese immigrants who "gave to Brazil, [the] life of your life and the blood of your blood." [178] A decade later the
sociologist Alfredo Romario Martins wrote about "new ethnic factors" in
the state of Paraná, finding that Syrian immigrants had "gotten rid of their
[Muslim] fanaticism, changing it for practical activities that allowed them
to work harder, but happier, and this permitted them to rise intellectually
in our [Brazilian] social milieu." [179]

* * *

Large-scale pre-World War II Arab immigration to Brazil ended in the years
after the Assyrian scandal as part of general decrease in emigration from
the Middle East. Even so, the place of Arabs within the Brazilian nation remained paradoxical. The Vargas regime banned all foreign-language newspapers in 1941, just as Syrian nationalists were beginning to believe their
struggle would be successful. While the hopes would be frustrated for
another six years, Brazil would play a critical role in the establishment of
an independent Syria. In 1947 Antun Sa'adih was given permission to enter
Brazil with temporary French papers, allowing him to obtain the Lebanese
passport he needed to return to the Middle East.

Syrian nationalism led many Syrian-Lebanese to take increasingly public postures. In 1945, George Lian, a Brazilian journalist of Syrian descent
writing for São Paulo's business community, suggested that Arab immigrants were notable for "mixing themselves with other races already here,"
in part because "ancient Arab culture infiltrated itself in Brazil via the Portuguese and Spanish." [180] The poet and literary critic Manoelito de Ornellas
gave a regionalized reading of Gilberto Freyre's thesis on the Moorish presence in Brazil in his *Gaúchos e beduinos: A origem étnica e a formação social
do Rio Grande do Sul* (1948), claiming that the roots of the modern residents
of southern Brazil could be found in North Africa.[181]

Even the famed French Brazilianist Roger Bastide, who helped create the
University of São Paulo's sociology department before accepting a chair at
the Sorbonne, asserted a deep connection between Arabs and Brazilians.
In his ground-breaking *Brésil: Terre des contrastes* (1957), Bastide lumped
Arabs and Japanese (along with Germans) into the "marginal category"
but still asserted that the Brazilian and Arab "civilizations" had converged.
"The Syrian-Lebanese family was patriarchal like the Brazilian one, with
the same authority of the father; the same secret and submissive life of
the wife . . . the same respectful obedience of the children; the same soli-

darity between relatives." [182] The North American Clark Knowlton's study of Syrians and Lebanese in São Paulo, completed in the late 1950s, took an equally "Brazilianized" approach. He focused only on commerce and politics, incorrectly equating high levels of immigrant illiteracy with a notion that "the interest in literature, poetry and in the arts so characteristic of many Arab groups in the Middle East is not part of the culture of the Syrio-Lebanese colony in São Paulo." In fact, by 1945 the Syrian-Lebanese community had produced 97 newspapers and magazines along with over 150 books, but like so many commentators in the 1920s, 1930s, and 1940s, Knowlton saw those of Arab descent as dangerously foreign, speaking of their "infiltration" into Brazil.[183]

Syrian-Lebanese ethnicity never had a single location within the broad idea of Brazilian identity. The evidence suggests that endeavors to render Arabs ethnically harmless by whitening were often matched by Syrian-Lebanese attempts to create a space for Arab ethnicity within a Brazilian context. This was done either by expanding the notion of "whiteness" to include the Middle East or by raising the Middle East to an equal, yet still separate, level with Europe.

The strategies at play, while easy to identify, do not follow simple patterns. In the most general sense it was in Brazil's largest cities, with large Syrian-Lebanese communities, that whitening was least noticeable. Thus, it comes as little surprise that in Rio de Janeiro, Syrian-Lebanese merchants working in a relatively unmodernized zone of small shops and narrow streets decided to name their association Sociedade de Amigos da Alfándega e Ruas Adjacentes (SAARA). While few if any of these merchants or their immigrant predecessors were actually from the Sahara region, using the name of a respected "Arab" locale was meant to transform the image of the neighborhood from a negative to a positive one. Outside of the urban centers, however, the struggle to include ethnicity within national identity was more difficult. As a prize-winning Brazilian author boasted in his 1988 book on the Syrian experience in Juiz de Fora (state of Minas Gerais), the "Syrian youth, born in Brazil, have effectively permutated with Brazilians through marriage, forming a healthy race." [184]

Most Syrian and Lebanese immigrants and their descendants had a choice. Their physiognomy allowed them to become instant Brazilians simply by a name change. Yet this did not take place as frequently as it might have, and the new Syrian-Lebanese ethnicity that emerged was a fully Brazilian one. For immigrants from Asia the story had another dimension. Speaking Portuguese, going to an elite university, and serving in the government never changed their appearance. For Japanese immigrants, arriving in large numbers in the years when eugenics represented sophisticated thought, the struggle for ethnicity would be doubly complicated.

4

Searching for a Hyphen

A large float representing the *Kasato-Maru,* the ship
that brought the first Japanese immigrants to Brazil,
is preceded by a smaller one topped by a fifteen-
foot-high bottle of Sakura soy sauce with giant
plastic sushi and sashimi revolving around it. On
top is the sushi man, a Caucasian painted to "look"
Japanese. The dancers are dressed as carnivalized
samurais and geishas.

"Burajiru, Meu Japão Brasileiro"
(My Brazilian Japan)
. . . Geishas with patterned kimonos,
taught to serve and seduce with love.
Monks, warriors, samurai,
the Buddha is the religious image,
and in judo my Brazil is champion.
From the country of soccer to the Empire of the Rising Sun,
I mix sake with samba to make our people happy.
I mix sake with samba to make our carnival happy.

—*Sociedade Educativa e Recreativa Escola de Samba,*
Unidos do Cabuçu, Rio de Janeiro Carnival, 1994

It all began when the special immigration envoy steamed into Santos harbor, interested in getting the Chrysanthemum Throne's subjects out of the Land of the Rising Sun. Sho Nemoto's arrival during the last week of September 1894 led him to confront a Brazil both eager for, and frightened of, immigrants. Since the 1870s planters had encouraged the federal and state governments to seek Europeans as replacements for slaves, and the state of São Paulo, with its massive coffee economy, was the center of activity. By 1888 thousands of immigrants were pouring into São Paulo every month. Italians, the largest single national group, were first hailed for their help in transforming Brazil from "black" to "white." Yet an inability to move out of impoverishment, and regular immigrant-led protests against labor and social conditions, convinced many in the elite that a mistake had been made. By the time Nemoto stepped off the steamer, a few Italians had already been deported for their "anarchism" and the search for a more docile group had begun.[1]

The hunt for submissive labor meshed well with Sho Nemoto's not-so-subtle proposition that the Japanese were the "whites" of Asia. Unlike Tong King-sing, who had awed and perhaps frightened the Paulista planters with his long silk robes and his African-American secretary, Nemoto disembarked in a Western-style suit. He flattered Brazilian elites with a front-page article in the *Correio Paulistano* in which he wrote of his "enchantment" with a country where Japanese "immigrants could be perfectly settled" and "we can improve our standard of living, buy property, educate our children, and live happily."[2] Building on his homeland's remarkable economic growth in the latter decades of the nineteenth century, Nemoto sold Japanese immigrants as everything Europeans were not: quiet, hard-working, and eager to become Brazilian.

Nemoto, and all of the diplomats who would follow him in the next fifty years, built the bridge over which Japanese immigrants would cross. The Meiji government's interest in emigration was motivated by a growing rural population that had become increasingly hungry and restless. Emigration was a "persistent . . . theme in discussions of Japan's economic situation and its place in the world" because it was aimed at relieving pressure on the land while creating colonies that would grow food for export back to Japan.[3] Brazilian planters, disappointed with their European replacements for slaves, were in the midst of a supposed labor shortage and saw Japanese immigration as a ready solution. Both countries hoped that immigration would lead to an increase in trade.

Nemoto left Brazil without a colonization contract—the lack of a treaty between the two countries made such formal deals impossible—but it took less than fifteen years to solve the bureaucratic problems.[4] Between 1908 and 1941 some 189,000 Japanese immigrants would settle in Brazil, almost all with some sort of subsidy. These high numbers are not surprising, given the "modernization" of Japan that had taken place with the Meiji Revolution. In 1882 Eduardo Callado and Arthur Silveira da Motta, ministers plenipotentiary in Beijing, visited Tokyo to explore immigration issues and were favorably impressed. A letter from Motta to Joaquim Nabuco noted the fact that human history was filled with "race-mixing" and that while "thirty years ago Western geographers and publicists considered the Japanese a despicable race, [now] this people is amazing us with their power to assimilate everything from European civilization in letters, in science, in art, in industry and even in political institutions."[5] A newspaper report in Minas Gerais was equally emphatic, noting that the success of Japanese settlement was assured because of their "intelligent and energetic forces."[6] Positive images of Japan even found their way into the world of marketing. A large drawing and text advertisement for "Iris du Japon Parfum Esquis" in São Paulo's *Correio Paulistano* shows an Asian woman coquettishly fanning herself while lying on a hammock with mountains and junks in the background. In the foreground a large bird leers at her, suggesting the unique sexual appeal, and quality, of a "Japanese" perfume.[7]

In 1892 the Brazilian government decided to promote immigration from China and Japan by establishing embassies and consulates. A year later José de Costa Azevedo sabotaged his own treaty mission to China in order to focus on Japan.[8] His comments extolling the ability of the Japanese "to receive the civilization and customs of civilized people . . . [since they] have, in general and naturally, qualities never considered in the Chinese," and a later declaration that he was "firmly in favor of Japanese immigration," so annoyed the Chinese that he was never even allowed to present his credentials.[9] Henrique Lisboa, secretary to that mission, was equally enamored of the Japanese, writing that everything from the sound of the language to the introduction of Christianity made the country a perfect source of immigrants: "When I think of the delicious fatherland of 'Mme. Chrysanthemum,' my imagination can only see it covered with colored and sweet flowers and inundated with happy rays of sunshine."[10] Over the next years there was continued pressure to establish diplomatic relations as favorable reports about Japanese workers poured in from Brazilians in the

United States.[11] When the cruiser *Almirante Barroso* docked in Yokohama, one of the passengers was Prince Augusto, grandson of Dom Pedro II, emperor of Brazil. Wasaburo Ōtake, a seventeen-year-old student who spoke some French and English, visited the ship, and may well have had an affair with Augusto, described as a "very intimate" friend. Ōtake traveled to Brazil with Augusto, and spent a number of years at the Rio de Janeiro Naval School; later he published a Japanese-Portuguese dictionary that made him a well-known figure in both Japan and Brazil.[12]

In 1895 the first Brazil-Japan treaty was signed, and the next five years saw a rapid growth of official discussions of Japanese labor.[13] Two years later Brazil opened a legation in Tokyo and a consulate in Yokohama, appointing Henrique Lisboa as minister plenipotentiary. Thrilled that "Japanese chancelleries function in the European style" and that "In Japan there are no Macaus or Hong-Kongs," Lisboa began to agitate for increased commercial and cultural relations.[14] Writing to the minister of foreign relations, Lisboa could barely contain his excitement over Japanese scientific, economic, and cultural advancement: "During the two months I have been here, I am already convinced of the positive results that would come to Brazil by establishing a Japanese emigration stream and direct commercial relations . . . the character of these people is unbeatable in terms of the desire to do perfect work . . . the Japanese possess initiative and a spirit of invention and adaptation."[15] Such high hopes led to the establishment of a consulate in Kobe, a major port, and in 1897 the São Paulo secretary of agriculture gave his blessing to Japanese immigration and the Japanese government decided that emigration passports for Hawaii were valid for Brazil as well.[16]

In spite of the efforts—in 1901 São Paulo sent an agent to contract six hundred Japanese families—the plans were never realized because of opposition in both Brazil and Japan. Brazil's minister plenipotentiary in Tokyo, Manuel de Oliveira Lima, believed that it would be a "danger to . . . mix inferior races in our population."[17] An agent from the Morioka Makoto Immigration Company, a major player in the transportation and settlement of Japanese workers in Hawaii, had visited Brazil in 1898 and was left with a poor impression. According to a report in *The Japan Times,* Brazil's plantations were crowded with Italians "who are given to all sorts of disreputable habits," and plantation owners were "not infrequently unpunctual" in wage payments.[18] In late 1905 Japan's minister in Brazil, Fukashi Suguimura, investigated sending Japanese workers to the Morro Velho gold mine in Minas Gerais, but after seeing the conditions, he refused to pursue the project.[19]

Official concerns did not prevent an image of Brazilian wealth from spreading among the Japanese peasantry. In late 1906 a village headman in Gumma prefecture wrote to the Japanese Foreign Ministry that in São Paulo "the government and the populace are enthusiastic about receiving foreign immigrants. If Japanese subjects want to emigrate to work, what are the procedures?"[20] While a few spontaneous immigrants did settle in São Paulo, a plan to establish colonies in the Amazon valley was scuttled after Viscount Shuzo Aoki of the Foreign Ministry called it "the worst region in Brazil."[21] Attitudes changed quickly, however, when the United States banned most Japanese entry in December 1907. Immediately the directors of a group of Japanese emigration companies set out to convince their own government that in Brazil "our emigrants could go and develop themselves without causing diplomatic troubles."[22] In early 1908 Ryu Mizuno, director of the Tokyo-based Kōkoku Shokumin Kaisha (Empire Emigration Company), returned from Brazil and reported that "the country is healthy, except Bahia." More important, wages would be "the same as for European laborers," a critical point among Japanese officials, who insisted on being treated as equals in the international sphere.[23] A report in Tokyo's *Japan Times,* which was denied by all parties, even hailed Japanese "racial" equality by claiming that "the statesmen of Brazil are looking for some force to counteract the supremacy of the Kaiser's people."[24]

Many influential Brazilians began to reevaluate Japanese labor after the Italian government prohibited its citizens from accepting subsidized transportation to Brazil in 1902. Sensing that their needs were equally urgent, São Paulo's secretary of agriculture and Japan's minister plenipotentiary began to work both sides of the aisle. While Fukashi Suguimura insisted that "our colonists will find in the state of São Paulo a rare happiness and a true paradise," Carlos Botelho, in an act of inspired desperation, sent his immigration commissioner to Argentina, Chile, and the United States to study Japanese colonies.[25] The final report was enthusiastic, and in 1907 Botelho arranged a contract for three thousand Japanese laborers. Following the São Paulo lead, the government of Rio de Janeiro decided to create a series of Japanese immigrant colonies in the abandoned Baixada Fluminense area, where "they will produce in rice a richness equal, if not superior, to that of coffee in São Paulo."[26]

On the morning of 18 June 1908, the *Kasato-Maru* completed its fifty-one-day, 12,500-mile journey from Japan, docking in Santos and bringing to Brazil's shores the first 781 members of what would become the largest Japanese community outside of Japan.[27] Like most migrants, those on the *Kasato-Maru* did not expect to remain in Brazil permanently. Music composed during the voyage was return-oriented, and the propaganda proffered by Japanese emigration companies led most to believe that Brazil was so rich that in five years they would return home wealthy.[28] Even those in the middle class saw Brazil as a land of opportunity; the 1910 diary of Nakano Makiko, the wife of a Kyoto merchant, reports the emigration of "[brave] modern men" with a wide range of professional backgrounds.[29]

Japanese immigrants, unlike Chinese and Arabs, carried with them the weight of world power. The Brazilian discourse on Japanese immigration thus combined a social fear of "Mongolization" with a desire to mirror Japan's economic and social development. Antonio Coutinho Gomes Pereira, captain of the floating school *Benjamin Constant,* was enthralled by the sophistication of the Japanese Navy, but Alcino Santos Silva, the consul in Yokohama, worried that the "ugly and short" Japanese were not ready "to conform to Western customs."[30] These types of competing images are found in a series of letters that Luiz Guimarães, the second secretary of the legation in Tokyo, wrote to Brazil's minister of foreign affairs after accompanying a group of Japanese diplomats to Brazil in 1907. Guimarães had a degree in philosophy, was a member of the Brazilian Academy of Letters, and would eventually be promoted to the ambassador level. His position on Japanese immigration was complex. He believed it would create "an enemy at home" and was "a danger . . . to our national organism [because they] always have to live like a Japanese . . . it is not possible to naturalize a Japanese." Japan's political and military power also scared Guimarães, who believed that within fifty years "millions" of Japanese would enter Brazil and deliver a "fatal" blow to the "whitening" process because they were "spies from birth [and] are our blood enemy." Using the eugenic theories that had formed the intellectual basis of so many Brazilian diplomats, Guimarães suggested that "it seems to me that the physiognomy and the force of a nation depend principally on the unity of race: to inject Asian blood into an organism that is still ethnically stammering will impede the march toward the homogeneity of a national type . . . we will lose the cohesion necessary for a great country, the nation of Brazilians."[31]

Fear of affronting the Japanese government made policy-making difficult. The 1910 Brazilian federal budget, for example, included a clause, slipped in at the last minute by opposition politicians, that prohibited subsidies for Asian immigrants and applied negative stereotypes of Chinese (that they were unassimilable and opium-addicted) to Japanese.[32] Yet prior to the implementation of the budget, diplomats were able to secure a promise from the Brazilian government that Japanese would be excluded "from the category of Asiatics," and before the law was enacted, the offending words were expunged completely.[33]

Reconfiguring Japanese as non-Asians was an important step in creating "ethnic" categories for immigrants, and Japanese diplomats eagerl played on such attitudes with constant reminders that their subjects wei "white."[34] Since many in the Brazilian elite placed Japanese immigrants in a hierarchic position equal to or above Europeans, images of those on the *Kasato-Maru* were positive. São Paulo's inspector of agriculture, J. Amândio Sobral, wrote a front-page story about the landing for the *Correio Paulistano.* He was impressed that almost 70 percent of the colonists were literate and, "in flagrant contrast . . . with our workers," did not seem poor. Class status was accompanied by an ethnic reclassification of immigrants who arrived in "European clothing," all of which "had been purchased in Japan and made in Japanese factories." The attempt to place Japan in a "European" category is clear: unlike the filthy Asians Sobral was expecting, the Japanese had "combed hair that was perfectly in harmony with their ties." The living and eating quarters on the *Kasato-Maru* were in an "absolute state of cleanliness," and everyone had "clean clothes" and "clean bodies" —they even carried kits with toothbrushes, hairbrushes, and razors. The inspector was particularly pleased that the newcomers liked "our food, made in our way and with our spices," an unknowing reflection of the fact that the majority aboard the *Kasato-Maru* were from Okinawa, a tropical region where the eating of pork and highly spiced food was common.[35] The immigrants even seemed eager to learn Portuguese, making them a new "element of production that we will never stop wanting." "The race is very different, but it is not inferior," Sobral gushed, presenting to readers the idea of ethnic difference in the context of hardworking docility.[36] The immigrants themselves were equally pleased: a strange twist of fate put the docking during a *festa junina* celebration, leading the newcomers to believe the fireworks were in their honor.[37]

Elation about the arrival of the *Kasato-Maru* was not diminished by the concerns that Japanese would not adapt, and would "create . . . their own society."[38] New trade relations were established just a week after the immigrants disembarked; a contract was signed to establish fifteen coffee-houses in Japan.[39] Trade, however, was not the only reason for optimism. A "model minority" discourse (to use a contemporary concept) suggested Japanese immigrants would lead Brazil to economic and military power by re-creating the homogeneous society believed to exist in Japan. Nestor Ascoli, a member of Rio de Janeiro's Commission on Justice, Legislation, and Public Instruction, and a deputy in the Legislative Assembly, insisted that "the small and ugly Japanese recently sneered and did what he had to do, beating the tall and formidable Russian. The Japanese is now a better element of progress than the Russian and other European peoples." According to Ascoli, the Japanese grew taller as a result of mandatory public education, and the introduction of Japanese "blood" into the Brazilian racial mix "will have a better result with our national population than [the introduction of] black blood or that of any other nonwhite." By harping on the idea that "intellectually the Japanese is frighteningly superior," Ascoli suggested that Brazil would soon begin to match the production levels of Japanese industry.[40]

Ascoli's mixing of ethnic conceptual categories was far from idiosyncratic and shows how new ideas about ethnicity were erected on the back of old ideas about race. Japan was constructed as a nation whose "nonwhite" race had become superior to most "European peoples," exactly what elites desired for Brazil. Officials and community leaders encouraged such thinking, implying that immigrants were biologically Brazilian and thus would improve local culture. As Sobral noted in a *Correio Paulistano* article later incorporated by Ascoli, "the blood of the Japanese race is not new among us . . . the inhabitants of the north of Brazil are [also] distinguished by their small stature and special shape of their heads."[41] If Japanese were both original and improved Brazilians, their introduction would hasten social unification because Brazilians and Japanese had a special biological relationship that was not shared with Europeans.

Neither the first Japanese immigrants nor Brazil lived up to expectations. Fazendeiros expecting quiet, "diligent and hardworking" colonists found that terrible conditions were no more acceptable to Japanese than to other immigrants.[42] Furthermore, the Paulista planters complained that Japanese cultural traits (mixed-sex bathing, for instance) were "poor" and that "families" were "false" because they were not strictly nuclear.[43] Immigrants who thought they would become rich felt "tricked by the emigration company [although] many say that Brazil is [still] better than Japan."[44] Some of the newcomers fled to Argentina, where salaries were said to be higher, but most ran to urban areas in São Paulo or Santos, or began to form their own small agricultural colonies in underdeveloped areas of São Paulo state. One group of seventy-five Okinawans left the Fazenda Floresta to help build the Northwest Brazilian Railway (Estrada de Ferro Noroeste do Brasil), and eventually settled in Campo Grande, where they were toasted by local residents for helping the city prosper.[45]

In the few cases where the immigrants remained on the fazendas, strikes were common and immigrants rarely extended their contracts. Japanese government officials, interested both in protecting their citizens *and* in ensuring that they remained in Brazil, were less than pleased and began to play an important role in helping to resolve labor problems.[46] In late 1908 Japanese immigrants began a wage strike on the powerful Prado family's Fazenda São Martinho. The legation in São Paulo immediately sent a diplomat and a translator who, upon entering the fazenda, found a contingent of sixteen soldiers. Sensing that the situation would not be resolved easily, the official had the four leaders of the strike, along with twenty-two other people, fired, which forced them to forfeit their wages. He then brought the entire group to Rio de Janeiro at the expense of the Japanese government and arranged other employment in Brazil.[47]

The intervention of the Japanese government did little to keep immigrants at work; an attempt to place one hundred workers at the St. John d'el Rey Mining Company failed when all deserted the mine less than three months after they arrived.[48] The *Correio da Manhã* termed the entry of Japanese "a huge disaster," and a study conducted by the Japanese legation in São Paulo showed that of the approximately 780 immigrants sent to six different fazendas in June 1908, only 359 remained at the end of January 1909. Nine months later, this figure had dropped to 191, with some plantations losing all their Japanese workers.[49] One fazendeiro even received permission from the state secretary of agriculture to withhold payment to Japanese workers until after the harvest.[50] While the governments involved were interested in economic success and stability, the immigrants reacted to the conditions with sadness. A popular song contained the lyrics "It was a lie when they said Brazil was good: the emigration company lied."[51] Shuhei Uetsuka, employed by the Kōkoku Shokumin Kaisha to lead the immigrants on the *Kasato-Maru,* wrote a haiku about his life on a plantation:

Nightfall: in the shade I cry picking coffee
I think about the migrant that fled; starlight on dry meadow.[52]

Nineteen-year-old Riukiti Yamashiro had experiences similar to those of Uetsuka. The oldest son in a family with a medium-sized plot of land in Okinawa, Yamashiro arrived in 1912 after learning about Brazil from neighbors whose family members had already emigrated. After spending a week at the São Paulo immigrant reception center (Hospedaria dos Imigrantes), Yamashiro and his wife, along with fifteen other families, were sent to a fazenda where they worked alongside Spanish immigrants. After only a few months on the plantation, Yamashiro and his friends fled to Santos, hoping to earn more as dockworkers.[53]

The refusal of hardworking and committed immigrants like Yamashiro and Uetsuka to remain on fazendas led to proposals that would create spaces for Japanese rural workers without involving fazendeiros who were as intransigent about selling their land as they were about labor. Japanese officials in Brazil were eager to settle their subjects, believing that the country "could easily accommodate hundreds of millions more inhabitants" and that "Brazil will find in our immigrants an able means of developing her vast national resources and Japan will find in Brazil a convenient vent for her surplus population."[54] Emigration companies began promoting Brazil more aggressively and began to use a new set of kanji characters to spell "Brazil" that could be translated as "dancing and happiness, reasons to stay in Brazil."[55] With the help of the São Paulo government, Japanese firms began to purchase large plots in the Vale de Ribeira area, which, in spite of fertile soil, lots of water, and a good climate, was considered a frontier because a high mountain range cut the region off from the center of the state. The native population of the region, fairly small and involved in subsistence agriculture, was characterized by one U.S. diplomat as "a pleasant, happy carefree people distinguished by the principal traits of hospitality and laziness."[56]

The idea of Japanese-run colonies seemed a perfect solution to the land and labor problems. On the Brazilian side, costly subsidization of individual laborers (who were fleeing the plantations) would be replaced by land grants in regions where little agricultural development had taken place. For the Japanese, state-directed colonies meant an end to headaches with Brazilian landowners and the opportunity to focus on settlement and production in areas where the profits would flow to the immigrants them-

Table 4. Japanese Immigration to Brazil, 1908–1941

Years	Number
1908–1914	15,543
1915–1923	16,723
1924–1935	141,732
1936–1941	14,617

Source: Hiroshi Saito, "Alguns aspectos da mobilidade dos japoneses no Brasil," Kobe Economic and Business Review, 6th Annual Report (1959): 50.

selves, both discouraging them from returning to Japan and encouraging more to leave Japan. In 1913 the Registro colony of one hundred thousand hectares (fifty thousand hectares were ceded by the state of São Paulo and the rest was purchased privately) was established in Iguape, about 185 kilometers southwest of the city of São Paulo. The Japanese syndicate that operated the colony was released from paying taxes for five years and received a small fee for every fifty families it settled. In return the syndicate promised to bring two thousand families and pay a series of settlement fees.[57]

By 1917 there were over five thousand Japanese immigrants residing in numerous colonies in the Registro area. Corn, rice, and beans were sold to the local market via a Brazilian steamer service that plied the Riberão River and its offshoots, meaning immigrant farmers only had to get their produce to the nearest riverbank in order to sell it. Colonial cooperation and the dropping value of the milreis versus the yen led to capital reinvestment in Brazil rather than remittance. This further developed the region economically, providing still more opportunities for newcomers.[58] Soon agricultural production began to shift—in 1908 the rice crop was not sufficient for national consumption, yet fifteen years later it had become an important export. Reinforcing the notion that Japanese immigrants were creating the "país do futuro" (country of the future) that Brazilians could not, a U.S. military observer opined that "one Japanese and his family can and do produce for a given area of land ten times as much per year as does the careless, lazy, shiftless native and his family."[59]

Agricultural success provided the means to create a nascent Japanese-Brazilian culture with constant cultural reinforcement from the homeland. The Taishō School was opened in 1915 in the São Paulo neighborhood of Liberdade and was followed soon after by a number of others, creating a widespread *nihon gakko* (Japanese school) system throughout the state. Officially these schools were targeted toward acculturating children into Brazilian culture, but curricula were modeled on imperial ones and most printed materials came from Japan. A comparison of book imports from Italy and Japan done by Laurence Hallewell shows that by the mid-1930s the gross numbers of Japanese materials far exceeded those from Italy, in spite of the much smaller Japanese immigrant pool.[60] One immigrant remembered taking care of his firstborn child with information provided in Japanese magazines for new parents.

Brazilian-based Japanese-language newspapers, usually printed with fairly sophisticated presses, were critical in establishing a local identity, especially since there were experienced journalists among the immigrants. Indeed, a common saying was "Two Japanese make an association, and three found a newspaper."[61] The *Shūkan Nambei* (South American Weekly), founded in January 1916, was the first of three newspapers published for the 80 to 90 percent of all Japanese and Japanese-Brazilians living in rural areas. The *Nippak Shinbun* (Japanese-Brazilian News), founded six months later, was based in the Liberdade section of São Paulo, and by the late 1920s was published three times a week and claimed a circulation of thirty thousand.

By 1918 three newspapers were published in São Paulo, and in 1929 the *Nippak Shinbun* became the first Japanese paper to publish some pages in Portuguese for the growing number of Brazilian-born *nikkei* (the general term for those of Japanese descent born in Brazil) who were unable to read Japanese.[62] Japanese-Brazilian ethnicity emerged out of these newspapers in two ways. First, they often included information from Brazilian newspapers unavailable in the countryside, providing a window into majority life that was otherwise inaccessible. The papers also provided space for cultural forms that were specific to immigrant life in Brazil. Newspapers like *Shūkan Nambei* and *Brasil Jihō* (The Brazil Review), founded in 1924, usually had as many pages of poetry as they did of news stories. One poem spoke of the betrayal that many Japanese felt upon discovering that life in Brazil would not lead to instant wealth:

Ten years of Brazil
The fatherland left behind
Dreams of gold undone
And I find myself on the zero stake
Vagabond days fly by in tears and laughs
I sleep with booze, tomorrow will be another day [63]

* * *

Just as nikkei ethnicity began to emerge, Brazilian nativists began a new public campaign against the large numbers of "nonwhite" immigrants flowing into the country. Japanese immigrants were a particular target because the Japanese government seemed to rely on emigration for its own economic expansion, combining race and imperialism into a single discussion. Edgard Roquette-Pinto, an anthropologist and professor at the Museu Nacional, noted in 1918 that Japanese were so "ugly" that "aesthetic considerations" led him to oppose mass entry.[64] Dr. Arthur Neiva, the microbiologist who directed São Paulo's Health Services, took a different approach. In a stridently anti-Japanese speech at the opening of the Oswaldo Cruz Nursery, he argued that "if we look for a solution to the problem of the lack of labor with scientific care and an eye to the future of Brazil, we will see that the Oriental races are unassimilable . . . and the Hindu and Japanese immigrants will create fatal ethnic cysts among us."[65]

Unlike many other immigrant groups, Japanese could count on a public defense in the face of nativist attacks. The strategy was twofold. In the public sphere, Japanese and Brazilian diplomats would respond to newspaper columns with articles of their own. Thus, when *A Imprensa* posited that Japanese military strength was a sign of "barbarism" after the carrier *Ikuma* docked in Rio de Janeiro, Ryoji Noda, a diplomat who would write a number of books on Brazil for the Japanese public, immediately declared the newspaper "second rate" and characterized the ideas expressed as "based on the concepts of racial prejudice common in South American Countries."[66] After the *Jornal do Brasil* attacked Japanese immigrants for introducing an "inferior" racial formation, M. O. Gonçalves Pereira, the minister to Japan and China, wrote that a few tens of thousands of Japanese immigrants in "a big state" would never "harm the formation of the Paulista type."[67] Japan, he wrote, "will surely become a great coffee consumer," and its "worldwide reputation" for medicine and public sanitation made it a country whose citizens had much to teach Brazil.[68]

The second line of defense did not seek to discredit highly respected Brazilians like Roquette-Pinto and Neiva, but rather to change their minds by using equally respected members of the Japanese elite. Dr. Mikinosuke Miyajima was a specialist in infectious diseases who had visited Brazil, and his translation of a famous essay on social life was frequently cited as an "authentic" source of information about Japan. Miyajima met Arthur Neiva and his wife a number of times, and was always received with "kindness and friendliness."[69] This connection led him to suggest to the Japanese Foreign Ministry that the director of the Kitasato Institute for Infectious Diseases in Tokyo invite Neiva and his wife to Japan.[70] First-class travel and accommodations and a full-time guide were provided by the Kaigai Kogyo Kabushiki Kaisha (Overseas Development Company, known by Brazilians as the KKKK and by members of the Japanese community as the Kaikō), formed in 1918 by the Japanese government to assist and encourage emigration to Brazil. Neiva accepted with pleasure and, as would numerous other academics and physicians over the next three decades, spent six weeks visiting Japan's most important medical institutions. Yet in spite of his awe of Japanese technical sophistication, he returned to Brazil unimpressed, noting in a letter some years later that "my warnings [against Japanese immigration] were totally justified."[71]

Nativism was a great concern to the Japanese government, which feared that its surplus rural population had few options other than emigration to Brazil.[72] When newspapers like O Paiz claimed that "We have nothing against the Japanese except the fact of their being entirely different from our people and unable to assimilate with them," there were immediate repercussions in Japan.[73] A businessman who had visited the Amazon told the Osaka Mainichi and Tokyo Nichi-Nichi, Japan's most widely circulated English-language newspaper and an affiliate of the huge Mainichi press conglomerate, that "The sentiment of racial discrimination is assuming a more and more concrete form . . . I even noticed editorials . . . strongly urging the Brazilians to shut their doors against the 'yellow races.' "[74] The comments resonated strongly because many in the Japanese government had exactly the opinion of Brazil that the editorial expressed about Japan. One businessman, angry about the lack of help he was getting in conducting business abroad, complained that "The Japanese Ambassador and consuls in Brazil do not at all seem to like their positions and consider themselves . . . exiled in an 'uncivilized' country."[75]

These attitudes, a ban on Okinawan emigration that began in 1920, the difficulty of life in Brazil, and a rise in wages in Japan led emigration to slow from 1920 to 1924, to between five hundred and one thousand people per year.[76] This kept the discussion of Japanese immigration on the fringes of elite society, in spite of Arthur Neiva's attempts to whip up public sentiment. Even Renato Kehl, who would later model his Central Brazilian Commission of Eugenics on the German Society for Race Hygiene, failed to mention Japanese immigrants in a 1923 book proposing a eugenics policy to "improve" Brazil's population.[77] In 1924, however, things began to change. The number of entries jumped to almost 5,000, and in the next decade approximately 130,000 Japanese stepped onto Brazil's shores. Japanese made up 2.3 percent of all immigrants to São Paulo in 1923, 4.0 percent in 1924, 8.7 percent in 1925, and 11.6 percent in 1928. In the decade after 1924, only Portuguese immigrants entered more frequently than Japanese, who in turn outnumbered Italian and German arrivals by about 2:1 and Spanish arrivals by about 2.5:1.[78]

A number of factors explain the dramatic increase in Japanese entry. In the early interwar years Italian farmworkers left plantations for the cities in increasing numbers, and labor agitation led São Paulo planters to seek a more "docile" workforce. Immigration policies in the United States further closed doors to Asian immigrants, culminating with the 1924 National Origins Act. Japanese-Brazilian economic relations were expanding quickly—in early 1925 the Japanese Foreign Office, together with the Tokyo prefecture and Tokyo Chamber of Commerce, eagerly made space for an exhibition of *sixty tons* of Brazilian produce, including coffee, cocoa, cotton, iron, and steel, even as a similarly sized Japanese product shipment was prepared for show in Brazil—and diplomats from both countries tied trade to migration.[79] A stagnating rural economy in Japan increased emigratory pressure as policy makers sought to make leaving a nationalist act. Moriya Sakao, chief of the Japanese Home Ministry's Social Affairs Bureau, asserted that "we must try to spread our civilization, especially our spiritual heritage, in the world and contribute to world peace and the welfare of humanity," while others spoke of the creation of "little Japans" around the globe. Chō Nagata, the author of several books on emigration, was only one of the nationalist intellectuals who argued that Brazil's climate, "mild character," and lack of a "strong national identity" would allow emigrants to create a new civilization under Japanese leadership.[80] With pressure from within and without, in the mid-1920s emigration became a policy priority (called *kokusaku imin*), with most of the emphasis focused on Brazil. The Home Office budget for emigration increased from 350,000 yen in 1923 to 2,000,000 yen seven years later. In that same period the number of government-sponsored public lectures on emigration rose from 27 to 267 per year.[81] The day-to-day project was usually carried out by the Kaigai Kogyo Kabushiki Kaisha, which in 1920 merged with its only remaining competitor and took over most of the land that had been purchased in Brazil by private Japanese companies. This allowed greater investment, and in a 1926 interview the Japanese ambassador noted that the introduction of "capital into Brazil concurrently with the encouragement of emigration . . . is necessary no less for the exploitation of the riches of Brazil than for the progress of our Japanese colonists in that most hospitable and kindly land."[82]

The creation of the kokusaku imin policy was aimed at second and third sons of farmers with tiny plots who had little chance for advancement in Japan. Government guides to Brazil emphasized that the "climate is . . . very much like the summer and autumn in Japan" and that "the majority of the inhabitants [in the colonies] are Japanese."[83] Advertisements placed in large and small popular newspapers promoted government grants that would help pay travel costs in addition to the Kaikō loans for hotel bills and railway fares. Public lectures on emigration were regularly sponsored by municipal and local governments, and emigrants were hailed for their contributions to international harmony.[84] Ken-ichi Nakagawa, who came to Brazil from Hyogo province in 1926 as a twenty-four-year-old, remembered "marvelous" tales of sweet potatoes "so large that they fed children for an entire day" and gun-toting farmers. For Japanese "without hope [in] a country colored gray," Brazil seemed wildly attractive, an idea reinforced when the first boatload of emigrants to leave Kobe was feted with a bon voyage party hosted by the governor of the prefecture and local Brazilian diplomats.[85]

While images of Brazil among the immigrants were often fantastic, there was in fact a great deal of information available. A number of Japanese travelers and diplomats had written books and poetry about the country, and newsreels about settlement were shown regularly. Emigration companies paid for media coverage of their colonies, and encouraging comments by government officials were reprinted over and over in news-papers read by potential emigrants.[86] A typical headline from the *Osaka Mainichi Shinbun*, whose circulation would grow from 670,000 in 1921 to 1,500,000 in 1930, was "SÃO PAULO NEEDS MORE JAPANESE."[87] The daily *The Japan Advertiser* reprinted stories from the Japanese-language press with headlines like "MORE IMMIGRATION FROM JAPAN ASKED FOR BY BRAZILIANS" and "BRAZIL SEEN IDEAL FOR COLONIZATION."[88] "Let's Go! Take Your Family to South America," urged a Japanese government pro-paganda poster first used in 1923, which shows a muscular young man pointing to Brazil; his other hand holds a hoe, and his family sits on his bent arm, one child waving a Japanese flag. Another Kaikō poster featured a large map of South America dotted with photos of colonial life. Super-imposed, a boat of immigrants sailed happily into Rio de Janeiro's Guana-bara Bay with Sugarloaf posed gorgeously overhead.[89] As late as 1932 the bureaucrat-targeted journal *Shimin* (The People) noted that "Brazil was still safer and more congenial for Japanese settlers" than Manchuria.[90]

By the end of the 1920s, passenger ships carrying about eight hundred immigrants each regularly made the forty-five-day journey between Kobe and Santos. The Japanese and nikkei population increased from 49,400 in 1925 to 116,500 in 1930 and almost 193,000 in 1935.[91] L. H. Gourley, a U.S. diplomat in South Africa, traveled to Brazil on the *La Plata Maru*; his report on the voyage gives a sense of the Japanese emigrants and atti-tudes about them. Most impressive to Gourley was that "some were almost as white as if they belonged to the white race and in several instances their features were not noticeably Oriental." Most also "put on European dress and wore shoes instead of the Japanese sandals." Life on the boat was unlike that of most immigrant ships because the colonists were well organized. There was plenty of food and medical care on board, and chil-dren had a regular school schedule while adults participated in gymnastics and morale-boosting. Films were shown about what to expect at the Ilha das Flores immigration center (not unlike the films one sees today on air-planes explaining how to pass through Brazilian Customs) and about life on the colonies.[92] One group forced a Japanese ship captain to make a pub-lic apology, terribly embarrassing given his status in relation to that of the migrants, when his crew did not help a passenger whose luggage was stolen at the port of Santos.[93]

Brazil was an important destination in large part because the Japanese public and private sectors linked immigration and investment in a coher-

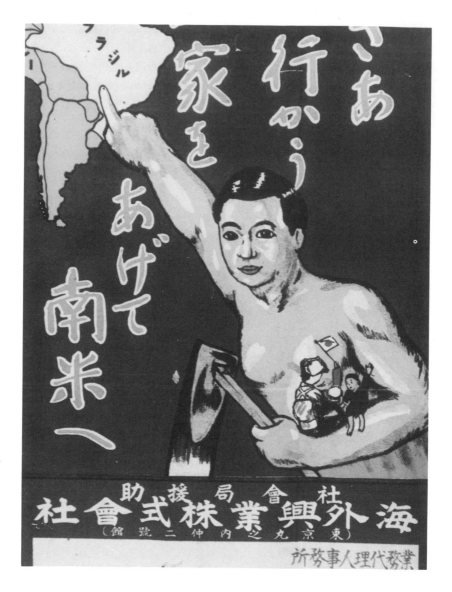

"Let's Go!!! Take Your Family to South America." KKKK propaganda poster, 1920s. Courtesy of Centro de Estudos Nipo-Brasileiros/Museu Histórico da Imigração Japonesa no Brasil, São Paulo.

ent policy. Hachiro Fukuhara's story is illustrative. Fukuhara was a director of the Kanegafuchi Cotton-Spinning Company, a leading textile manufacturer, and "an earnest Christian" of some renown in Japan. He had spent years in South Carolina and Mississippi studying cotton production, and was described by a U.S. diplomat as "a man of superior intelligence." Fukuhara first visited Pará in 1925 to explore cotton production, and upon his return he formed the Nambei Takushoku Kabishiki Kaisha (the Nantaku Company) with heavy backing from the Kanegafuchi Cotton-Spinning Company. The Nantaku Company's half-million-dollar capital base convinced Pará Governor Dionysio Bentes to approve a one million-hectare land grant, and in 1928 Fukuhara returned to Brazil as president of the Companhia Nipônica de Plantação do Brasil (also known as the Fukuhara Company).[94]

Over the next decade some 352 families settled in a colony located about 270 kilometers from Belém, near the town of Tomé-Açu. Fukuhara worked hard at integrating the colonists into local society, often distributing photographs to politicians and businesspeople showing Japanese and Brazilians working together. He even gave free medical services to all residents of the region. He claimed the colonists were "selected . . . from the higher class of farmers" whose impressions might be "communicated to friends at home to advertise the Company and induce new settlers to come out."[95] This, and Brazil's image of wealth in Japan, encouraged emigrants with some capital to establish themselves as independent farmers.[96] Of course having a small stake was no guarantee of success in Brazil's boom-and-bust economy. Many immigrants quickly exhausted their capital and were forced into day labor. Others found themselves conned by sleazy compatriots like the infamous Conde Koma. Koma, whose real name was Mitsuyo Maeda, came to Pará in 1915 or 1920 as a member of an acrobatic troupe but left the company and began giving jujitsu lessons. He sometimes claimed to be an employee of the Japanese government or its "unofficial consul," even convincing a U.S. diplomat and military attaché to let him lead a site visit to Fukuhara's colony. The diplomat, Gerald Drew, believed Koma to be a secret operative preparing a Japanese plot to occupy the Amazon, but other U.S. diplomats were not so sure. The U.S. embassy in Tokyo dismissed Drew's report, saying he "has been prone to cloak the activities of the Japanese with an unnecessary air of mystery," since it was unlikely that Koma "ever had anything whatever to do with the Japanese

Government" and was probably a "China ronin," a Japanese conman who preyed on immigrants by claiming influence with officials.[97]

Between conmen and economic cycles, the numbers returning to Japan as a percentage of entries grew from about 4.5 percent in 1927 to 7.5 percent in 1930 (compared with the almost 50 percent return rate among Middle Easterners). Returnees often "severely denounced" colonization companies in newspaper interviews and gave the impression that "the settlers would have been far better off if they had stayed at home." One immigrant remembered arriving in Santos: "[I saw] Indians with Western clothes: they were Japanese, our old-timers. Would I turn 'savage' within a few years like these Japanese? It was my first disillusionment."[98] Another, who had arrived in 1922, found out that an official refused to send his repatriation request to Japanese diplomats because it would "prejudice the arrival of new immigrants."[99] Soon only those with a high chance of success (those with a trade, engaged in household industry, or in possession of substantial capital) and who would not return with complaints were being sent to Brazil.[100]

*   *   *

The 1920s were a decade of increasing Japanese visibility in Brazil. This helped propel the Campanha Anti-Nipônica into a more public phase. Federal deputy Fidelis Reis, an agronomer and professor at the University of Minas Gerais who led a movement to ban black immigrants, presented motions to the Congressional Commission on Agriculture in 1921 and 1923 that would limit new Asian entries because "the yellow cyst will remain in the national organism, unassimilable by blood, by language, by customs, by religion."[101] This powerful anti-Japanese sentiment was picked up by Miguel Couto, the president of the National Academy of Medicine, who rapidly became the most vocal proponent of the Campanha Anti-Nipônica. In a series of editorials written for O Jornal in 1924 and 1925, Couto claimed that Japanese immigration was part of an expansionist plot to destroy the Brazilian nation.[102] He characterized the newcomers as "cunning, ambitious, warlike and mystical," sentiments echoed by Arthur Neiva and José Felix Alves Pacheco, foreign minister from 1922 to 1926 and owner-editor of the Jornal do Comércio. Couto, Neiva, and Pacheco soon became known as the "Three Heroes of the Anti-Nipponic Campaign," and their presence in debates over immigration and assimilation was constant through the mid-1930s.[103]

Quelling criticism by changing minds continued to be the strategy of those in favor of Japanese immigration. Public responses to newspaper articles were common, and in 1926 Miguel Couto was invited to Japan.[104] The Japanese government circulated translations of rules that emphasized that emigrants must be "strong and healthy in body and soul, love labor, and have perseverance."[105] Such tactics, however, had little effect because most Brazilians had little or no contact with Japanese, thus providing ammunition for those who argued that lack of contact equaled a low index of "assimilation." Rio's *O Jornal* opined that "No one can be in sympathy with these immigrants who do not assimilate, nor even expend their large earnings in the place where they acquire them in so miserly a manner," ideas assimilated with ease by those trained in European pseudo-science.[106] A. Carneiro Leão, director of the Rio de Janeiro school system and an influential modernist educator who was consultant to the Ministry of Labor, Industry, and Commerce, ardently defended the "assimilative power of the Brazilian," arguing that education would guarantee that all immigrants became important cogs in the "future greatness of Brazil."[107] The only group that Leão rejected was the Japanese, whom he judged "unstable, impertinent, excessively proud, aggressively independent [and] disrespectful of contracts." The honorary president of the Brazilian Chamber of Commerce agreed, telling the *Jornal do Comércio* that Japanese were "undesirable inasmuch as these immigrants do not readily assimilate themselves."[108]

Assimilationist concerns were tinged with the nationalist fear that Brazil would be forced to kowtow to an expanding and imperialist "Shin Nihon" (New Japan). This was especially apparent in two areas. First, a 1927 Japanese law created an Overseas Emigration Federation that in turn established the Brasil Takushoku Kumiai (Brazil Colonization Corporation or BRATAC). In 1929 BRATAC bought four huge tracts of land in São Paulo and Paraná. It capitalized the colonies with millions of yen in order to create a system in which migrants would make a down payment in Japan, receive their passage and a twenty-five-hectare lot, and pay back the loan as the land was developed.[109] Landownership in underdeveloped areas of São Paulo led to fear that BRATAC might begin purchasing plots in the Amazon, defined by many Brazilians as the physical embodiment of national identity. When Hachiro Fukuhara was followed to Pará by Japanese diplomatic and military personnel, Vivaldo Coaracy suggested that the Japanese were planning to create a new empire out of Brazilian and Peruvian territory, inhabited by fifty thousand laborers. "We are accustomed to think in years," wrote the equally paranoid and racist Coaracy "[but] the Mongols think in decades or centuries." [110] Diplomats from the United States agreed, classifying Japanese settlement in the Amazon as "a government project." [111] Eugenicists, who less than a decade earlier ignored the Japanese, now began to encourage their students to write anti-Japanese theses.[112] At the First Brazilian Eugenics Conference (1929), A. J. de Azevedo Amaral proposed that non-Europeans (as differentiated from those of African descent) be restricted from entering Brazil; he received support from Xavier de Oliveira and Miguel Couto. The proposal was narrowly defeated because Edgard Roquette-Pinto's position had changed in light of the "marvelous transformation" of Japanese, who now "act like Occidentals." [113]

Public discussions soon spilled into the policy arena. When an immigration inspector in Santos began rejecting immigrant health certificates issued by Japanese physicians in 1929, a battle erupted over whether trachoma was a curable disease. This was widely reported in both the Brazilian and the Japanese press, and led to two resolutions. In the short run Brazilian officials were mollified with a promise by the Kaikō to examine the health of emigrants more carefully and the assertion that colonists were "kept in perfect health so that their work is productive and their adaptation and nationalization is [sic] easy." [114] Yet in the longer term, nativists used biological and nationalist language to assert that Japanese immigrants brought a sickness "that was not domestic," and that health issues were one more front in Japan's invasion of Brazil.[115] In another explosion, Milton Vieira, the consul in Kobe, suggested that the Japanese government used emigration taxes to earn money and that even those who were paralyzed were being certified for emigration. In an interview with the *Osaka Mainichi and Tokyo Nichi-Nichi*, Vieira warned that Brazil would take steps against "bad emigrants," saying, "do not send anyone who cannot work." [116]

Official concern about Japanese immigration led to a widespread public discussion. Guilherme de Almeida's article on a Japanese neighborhood in São Paulo, published as part of his "Cosmópolis" series in *O Estado de S. Paulo,* noted that the area was "small, very small, very very small," but that it had an "absolute concentration" of Japanese, suggesting the idea of a nation within Brazil. This position was also taken by the economist, lawyer, and university professor J. Rodrigues Valle after visiting some Japanese colonies.[117] Ernest Himbloch, commercial secretary of the Department of Overseas Trade at the British embassy in Rio de Janeiro, was "inclined to agree with "the majority [who] are opposed to Japanese immigration . . .

on ethnological grounds [since] they do not assimilate. They live apart. They do not adopt the ways of the country. They do not intermarry."[118]

For every person opposed to Japanese entry there was one in favor of it. Deputy Nestor Ascoli and Professor Bruno Lobo of the Rio de Janeiro Medical School were prominent among them, and their lectures, editorials, and books were widely circulated.[119] Businesspeople were also vocal, seeing Japanese settlement as a small price to pay for increased commercial relations, and the 154 respondents to a questionnaire sent out in 1926 by the Sociedade Nacional de Agricultura (responses regarding Arabs are discussed in the preceding chapter) split almost evenly (seventy-five for entry, seventy-nine against). The SNA journal *A Lavoura* openly supported Japanese immigration as a means of developing the Amazon in spite of Fidelis Reis's directorship of the organization.[120] A letter from Cuiabá (state of Mato Grosso do Sul), published in Rio de Janeiro's *O Paiz*, focused on the economic success of Japanese farmers, who were "reserved and hardworking," as they toiled alongside "caboclos and European colonists" building the Northwestern Brazil Railroad.[121] Rio de Janeiro's Geographical Society condemned "race prejudice" and enthusiastically endorsed "yellow immigration" for its "well-known qualities . . . of industry, discipline, cleanliness, respect for law and order and intelligence."[122]

Pro-Japanese politicians also joined the fray. Francisco Chaves de Oliveira Botelho, a federal deputy from Rio de Janeiro, frequently attacked plans to limit Japanese immigration by discussing his visits to Japanese colonies in São Paulo and Minas Gerais where rice production rose by 400 percent, cotton by 30 percent, and sugarcane by 100 percent. Botelho was also convinced that Japanese integration into Brazilian society would be rapid, insisting to his colleagues that "I can verify that the children born in Brazil are proud to call themselves Brazilians."[123] São Paulo state senators overwhelmingly agreed, eulogizing immigrants during a debate on the Fidelis Reis project.[124] The journalist Waldyr Niemeyer, who began his study of the Japanese in Brazil "under the [negative] influence of North American authors," reached the same conclusion, noting that "the Japanese today occupies an important spot among the people that have brought their affluence to our development."[125]

Since the debate over Japanese immigration was as much about assimilation as about production, the "pro" group had to marshal "scientific" evidence for the position that Japanese would rapidly be transformed into Brazilians. Many hailed Sílvio Romero's "pro-mestiço" positions claiming that Japanese were uniquely assimilable because of high rates of intermarriage. Japanese immigrant newspapers frequently printed statistics in their Portuguese-language sections suggesting that of every one hundred marriages involving a Japanese immigrant, twenty-five were to Brazilians, usually women.[126] Such claims were ludicrous: a massive historical census of the almost four hundred thousand members of Brazil's Japanese community conducted in the late 1950s shows that interethnic marriage among immigrants was rare. Between 1908 and 1942 the rate was less than 2 percent among immigrants and less than 6 percent among nikkei (i.e., all those of Japanese descent). A smaller study, done in the early 1950s, reports that most marriages between Japanese and caboclos "failed abjectly."[127] When Hachiro Fukuhara told U.S. diplomats that "his policy was to discourage his colonists from maintaining their native customs and that he wants them to become Brazilianized as rapidly as possible," his claim was dismissed out of hand.[128]

Whatever the reality of intermarriage and Brazilian identity among immigrants, all those interested in continuing mass Japanese entry realized that the promotion of such ideas was critical. The proposition that Brazilian Indians and Japanese immigrants were of the same biological stock held both political and cultural promise. If true, this assertion made assimilation a given. Asians had become the progenitors of those who resided in the Amazon, Brazil's soul, making them more authentically Brazilian than most residents of Brazil.[129] Roquette-Pinto claimed that modern Japanese had emerged from the mixing of whites (Ainus), yellow (Mongols), and blacks (Indonesians), thus mirroring Brazil's "racial" development.[130] Bruno Lobo, whose ardent public support garnered him the Order of the Rising Sun from the Japanese Empire, asserted that "Mongolian blood . . . incontestably exists in Brazil through the Indians and their descendants of mixed parentage," making Japanese and Brazilians "unique" in their lack of prejudice.[131] He even suggested that since the "Indian was similar to the Japanese" and since Indian-Portuguese mixing had created the "formidable Bandeirante Race," Japanese immigration would strengthen Brazilian society by creating a more original race in areas "abandoned by the European element."[132] An article in Rio's *Gazeta de Notícias* went even farther, claiming that "The Brazilian People already have a strong percentage of Mongol blood," a position repeated by Deputy Oliveira Botelho, who believed that "Our aborigines, of obvious Mongol origin . . . crossed with the Portuguese resulting in the *bandeirantes*. . . . If the crossing of Brazilian with the savage Indian led to such good results . . . why deny the mixing with Japanese blood?"[133] The newspaper *Commércio de Santos,* based in a city with a large Japanese population, agreed, arguing that Japanese children in Brazilian schools and speaking "à paulista" showed the "mixing of the unbreakable Nipponic mettle with our blood."[134]

By suggesting that Japanese were Brazilians and vice versa, those in favor of Japanese immigration were able to wrap eugenics theory around itself. The politician and essayist Alfredo Ellis Júnior, for example, argued that Japanese sexual relations with mestiços would make the resulting progeny more fecund (Ellis was very impressed by the growth of the Japanese population!) and better able to "recross" with the "Italo-Paulista-Syrio" type found in São Paulo.[135] Antonio Baptista Pereira, a widely read essayist and promoter of Brazil's uniqueness (as well as biographer of Rui Barbosa, and collector and annotator of the famous jurist's writings), agreed with Ellis, linking Japan and Brazil by suggesting that "Japan is a mestiço nation where Melanesian migrations took root to form a race whose assimilation to Western progress constitutes the most prodigious in history."[136]

These sentiments reached a wider public with the regular publication of photographs of "Brazilian"-looking children who were, at least ostensibly, of Japanese and Brazilian or European parentage.[137] The pictures were almost always in books and pamphlets published with the financial support (both open and hidden) of Japanese cultural organizations and were of a uniform type: Japanese men married to white Brazilian women (or white European immigrant women) who had produced white children. The symbolism of these photographs was both obvious and hidden. On the surface they gave the message that Japanese immigrants were an elite interested in, and able to attract, only those of high racial status in Brazil. They also suggested that women carried culture in their wombs, thus explaining much of the fear of Asian women so typical in the Brazilian discourse on immigration. Ironically, the photographs had a far different meaning from the Japanese perspective, which viewed culture as patrilineal. Thus children born of Japanese fathers remained genetically Japanese irrespective of their physiognomy.

Japanese-Brazilian miscegenationist imagery can be found throughout Bruno Lobo's aggressively titled *De japonez à brasileiro* (From Japanese to Brazilian), published in 1932 by the National Department of Statistics. Lobo was well-connected to the Japanese government, and his status as a professor at the Rio de Janeiro Medical School provided him with the op-

Family of Eikichi (born in Japan) and Maria Horibe (born in Brazil). From *Cruzamento da ethnia japoneza: Hypóthese de que o japonez não se cruza com outra ethnia* (São Paulo: Centro Nipônico de Cultura, 1934). Courtesy of Centro de Estudos Nipo-Brasileiros, São Paulo.

portunity to publish work for a Brazilian elite audience. Lobo believed that Brazilian racial and climatic conditions, when combined with Japanese "ethnological" characteristics, would cause a cultural and physiological transformation and guarantee a stronger Brazilian race.[138] He thus filled *De japonez à brasileiro* with pages of photographs that "proved" the union of Japanese men and Brazilian women would create Europeanized Brazilian children. In another book, Lobo suggested that "it is not an exaggeration to say that more than 94,000 Nipo-Brazilian children have already been born, children of resident Japanese immigrants, almost 100,000 little future Brazilians."[139] A professionally printed pamphlet paid for by the Centro Nipônico de Cultura, *Cruzamento da ethnia japoneza* (Mixing with the Japanese Ethnicity) used the same approach: it included seven pages of photographs whose captions used the term "ethnicity" (and not race) to suggest that physical transformation was as much cultural as biological.[140]

Theresa Omura (born in Germany) and child. Father was Jorge Jonojo Omura (born in Japan). From *Cruzamento da ethnia japoneza: Hypóthese de que o japonez não se cruza com outra ethnia* (São Paulo: Centro Nipônico de Cultura, 1934). Courtesy of Centro de Estudos Nipo-Brasileiros, São Paulo.

Luiz Hayashy (born in Japan), Maria Martins Hayashy (born in Brazil), and son. From *Cruzamento da ethnia japoneza: Hypóthese de que o japonez não se cruza com outra ethnia* (São Paulo: Centro Nipônico de Cultura, 1934). Courtesy of Centro de Estudos Nipo-Brasileiros, São Paulo.

Brazilians who favored Japanese immigration may have honestly believed that science was on their side when they claimed a special relationship between Japanese and Brazilians. Japanese officials and immigration leaders, however, played with the discourse in ways that appear more strategic than heartfelt. The position had been developed in Peru in the nineteenth century when members of the pro-Japanese movement asserted that the Incas had come from Japan, an idea developed from seventeenth- and eighteenth-century thinkers who linked the Incas and the Chinese.[141] The Japanese linguist Nonami, for example, claimed the indigenous dialects spoken on Brazil's borders with Bolivia were related to Japanese. When Japan's minister in Brazil visited Pará in the early 1920s, he is reported to have frightened a Brazilian caboclo when he confused him with an immigrant and struck up a conversation in Japanese.[142] Hachiro Fukuhara returned from an exploratory trip to the Amazon claiming that Brazil was "founded by Asiatics" because "the natives who live along the River Amazon look exactly like the Japanese. There is also a close resemblance between them in manners and customs . . . [and] a certain Chinese secretary in the German Embassy at Rio [has] made a careful study [of language] and concluded that these Indians descended from Mongols." Fukuhara even stated that he knew of a Buddhist ceremony performed in the Himalayas where a woman holds a tree as she is bearing a child and her husband walks around her. He exclaimed happily, "I saw the same thing in the Amazon."[143] As if to demonstrate the assimilative properties of the Japanese, Fukuhara had "large groups of small children . . . publicly baptized [with] a number of prominent Brazilians serving as godparents." There is no evidence that the colonists maintained the Catholic faith.[144]

Immigrant assertions of a Japanese-Brazilian biological connection were used to create social spaces. (Readers may recall similar stories emerging from the Arab community.) Other strategies included printing parts of Japanese-language newspapers in Portuguese, as much for the nonnikkei population as for the 30 percent of the Brazilian-born nikkei who could not read Japanese. These articles tended to focus on the expansion of Japanese-Brazilian economic ties and on glorifying Japanese life in Brazil, often reprinting positive articles from other papers, and bits and pieces of Bruno Lobo's writings.[145]

Claims of a unique Japanese-Brazilian cultural affinity also emerged from interpretations of religiosity among immigrants. Here again, immigrant elites realized that religious practice was an important component of their public negotiation of national identity in a county where one constitution was promulgated "in the name of the Holy Trinity," nineteenth-century legislation gave the rights of public religious practice only to Catholics, and Jewish and Hindu immigrants faced extra scrutiny as non-Christians.[146] In 1918 Ryoji Noda of the Japanese legation insisted that shrines and temples not be constructed in Brazil, and in the 1930s a member of the Tenrikyō sect, which at the time was actively suppressed in Japan, was given permission to emigrate only after promising he would not proselytize among immigrants. Kumao Takaoka, a scholar whose 1925 book on Brazil was widely read in Japan, suggested that all emigrants convert to Catholicism, and the 1.7 percent of Catholics among Japanese entries between 1908 and 1936 (a percentage significantly higher than the Catholic population in Japan) were featured prominently in articles and books.[147] In the city of São Paulo, a clergyman claimed to have baptized fifteen hundred Japanese, most in public ceremonies. This same padre, and two others who spoke both Portuguese and Japanese, were responsible for baptizing three hundred immigrants and their descendants working on the railroads, and five hundred more in the Iguape colony.[148]

By 1930 there were more "Japanese" Catholics in Brazil than in Japan (this of course included Brazilian-born children of Japanese parents), but the total of some three thousand is far less impressive when it is remembered that some ninety thousand Japanese immigrants had entered Brazil, and that together with their Brazilian children, they numbered about 116,500. Registro's main colony was less than 10 percent Catholic in 1930; most were Brazilian-born children who were nominally Catholic, adopted Afro-Brazilian religions, or created syncretic Japanese-Afro-Brazilian forms of worship.[149] A 1940 study of the Fazenda Tiête by São Paulo's Immigration Department showed that 585 of the 605 residents on the colony were Buddhist and/or adherents of Shinto, and a National Census Service project in the town of Marília suggested that some 85 percent of the Japanese residents were Buddhist.[150] None of this was lost on Oliveira Vianna, who claimed, without providing evidence, that "One time I was in a Catholic country and I met a Japanese Catholic missionary. But a little later I went to a Protestant country and I realized that the same head of the Catholic mission was also the head of the Protestant mission."[151]

The attempt to interpret cultural norms as evidence of a special Japanese ability to become Brazilian can also be seen in sports. A Japanese fascination with gambling, and especially the famed jogo do bicho, a widely played but officially prohibited game of chance based on choosing animals to which numbers correspond, thus became evidence of the transformation of Japanese immigrants. The game, according to legend, began at Rio de Janeiro's Zoological Garden in 1893, and by the time Japanese began arriving some fifteen years later, it was widespread. Whether the immigrants won at the jogo do bicho more than anyone else is doubtful, but stories of Japanese proficiency at the game were legend. One immigrant believed that the Brazilian saying "O bicho leva só vício" (The animal game leads to addiction) had a special meaning for Japanese because the word "vício" was pronounced by Japanese speakers as "bicho." The following story takes a similar approach.

> One day a Japanese immigrant, unsure of which animal he should place his bet [on], was eating a banana to which a grain of rice was stuck. The immigrant realized that the ideogram for "rice" could be decomposed into three parts, one of which represented the number 88. The number 88 in the jogo do bicho represented a tiger, and the immigrant won handsomely with his bet.[152]

The story, of course, is more than one of an immigrant striking it rich. Certainly the role of the banana is superfluous, since it is the ideogram for rice that leads to the winning choice. Yet the placement of the stereotypical Brazilian fruit next to the quintessential Japanese food transforms the story from one about gambling to one about the construction of a Japanese-Brazilian identity.

Such creative attempts to define Japanese-Brazilian ethnicity coexisted with a belief among many migrants that they would remain only temporarily.[153] Typical yearnings and desires to return home wealthy explain a large part of this. Yet there was also a fear that extended residence in Brazil would physically transform them into something other than Japanese. In 1927 Dr. Seizo Toda, a member of Osaka's City Planning Board and a professor at the Tokyo Imperial University Medical School, visited a number of Japanese farming colonies in the state of São Paulo. He complained that his "compatriots' " faces had developed an "ugly color" because of the "uncivilized style of life," suggesting that poverty and relations with Brazilians had "darkened" their skin. The Nippak Shinbun, which published the interview with Toda, drove the point home with its headline "THE CONDITIONS OF OUR COUNTRYMEN ON THE COLONIES ARE THE SAME AS THOSE OF JAPANESE PEASANTS A THOUSAND YEARS AGO."[154]

The idea that Japanese immigrants might somehow become Brazilian indigenes resonated deeply in elite cultural consciousness. An almost neurotic desire for racial improvement made this process frightening. Many Brazilian commentators were convinced that unlike Indians, who were dismissed as members of a weak race, the powerful Japanese "race" would overwhelm the country. Dr. Alvaro de Oliveira Machado, a member of the São Paulo Immigration Department, visited a number of Japanese colonies in 1930 and 1931, and came away confused and deeply fearful. Thus, while the "northeastern population of indigenous origin . . . [was] very similar to the Mongolic race," the per capita production was almost five times that of the "Brazilian," placing national and other immigrant labor at a "disadvantage."[155]

The Japanese government's regular intercession in the lives of emigrants helped confirm beliefs that Brazilians would be swept away in the face of a more powerful race. Oliveira Machado's claims of a "secret plan of expansion and infiltration" were censored by superiors with a simple "Put this in the archives, it shows an ignorance about the topic of colonization," and his report was rewritten by a more sympathetic observer.[156] Even so, the fact that many emigrants were trained in preparation for emigration, received subsidies, and arrived at well-organized colonies caused fear and jealousy among other farmers. An incident involving the Cotia Agricultural Cooperative (CAC), founded outside of São Paulo city in 1928, is illustrative. By the early 1930s the CAC had grown to two thousand members, making it the largest cooperative in Brazil, and was producing about 50 percent of the potatoes in São Paulo. As it began to expand into distribution, Brazilian middlemen of Spanish and Italian descent organized a boycott that failed when the CAC stopped selling to nonmembers. While its director claimed that "this is neither a diplomatic nor an international issue. It is only a conflict between potato producers and merchants," the creation of a permanent distribution system reinforced notions of Japanese power.[157]

These incidents represent different expressions of national identity. The questions were broad: How "Japanese" could or should a "Brazilian" be? How "Brazilian" could a "Japanese" be? Would the economic growth of Brazil be worth a diminished "European" society? Was it more important that immigrants give their labor or their hearts to Brazil? Japanese immigrants found an opportunity to provide one answer in mid-1932 when São Paulo began its "Constitutionalist Revolution" in support of presidential elections that Vargas had been delaying.[158] Two young Japanese-Brazilians joined the unsuccessful revolutionary forces, becoming folk heroes among the nikkei generation and important figures in the battle to define a Japanese-Brazilian ethnic space.

Cassio Kenro Shimomoto, who had arrived as a baby, was a student at São Paulo's São Francisco Law School when he volunteered to fight along with the Brazilian-born José Yamashiro. Both were hailed for their decision after Shimomoto declared to a *Diário de S. Paulo* reporter that he was "before anything . . . a Brazilian."[159] Yamashiro's moment of fame came when a letter from his father published in the *Nippak Shinbun* was translated and sent to the pro-revolutionary *O Estado de S. Paulo*. The elder Yamashiro played on the notion that Japan had a particularly nationalistic culture to suggest that nikkei were uniquely Brazilian, thus leading his son, "as a Brazilian and Paulista, [to] obey the natural impulse to pick up arms to defend his State."[160] Who was a better Brazilian than one whose loyalty was natural? Others in the Japanese-Brazilian community agreed, believing that support of the São Paulo position might help moderate anti-Japanese sentiment. In July 1932 the Liga Japonesa Pro-Cruz Vermelha Brasileira solicited donations to help soldiers. Their advertisement read: "we Japanese who have adopted this blessed land as our second fatherland and the fatherland of our children."[161] The Vargas regime could hardly have been pleased that some nikkei were fighting against it, yet Japan's power was not to be dismissed. At one point a truce between federal and revolutionary forces was called to allow a shipload of Japanese immigrants to pass the tight naval blockade around the port of Santos.[162]

The positive publicity that stemmed from nikkei participation in the 1932 revolt was quickly forgotten the following year when two unrelated issues came together during a period of relatively open political debate. The first was the establishment of a Constitutional Convention, charged with producing what would become the Constitution of 1934, and the second was an increasing Japanese military presence in Manchuria. Debates about Japanese immigration thus became more public as issues of imperialism, assimilation, and nationalism were conflated. Heightening the tension was the dispute over Assyrian entry discussed in the previous chapter. This produced a climate where "exotic" immigrants were lumped together, as Oswald de Andrade did in his semiautobiographical *Marco Zero I—A revolução melancólica* (1937). The novel captured popular images of Japanese and Arab immigrants while asking why a "Japanese" would act "Brazil-

ian." Registro-Gō, Andrade's fictional Japanese colony, was populated with
revolutionaries eager to fight against Vargas as Shimomoto and Yamashiro
had. Warplanes and machine guns were passed by customs inspectors as
agricultural machinery, and a pilot living in the colony desperately wished
to bomb Rio de Janeiro.[163] As telling was the conversation between an
old Italian immigrant and his seatmate on the "Shanghai Express," which
served Registro-Gō:

> An old Italian, with glasses, said:
> — Why would a Japanese need seven Brazilians, two "Turcos," five
> Italians and a half dozen Portuguese . . . .
> — The Japanese want to swallow the world whole. One day they
> will — exclaimed a neighbor.
>   In front of him, on the wooden seat of second class, a Jap smiled
> with satisfaction. It was Muraoka.[164]

* * *

When Japanese immigrants began to enter Brazil in 1908, they were seen
as docile replacements for activist Europeans. Within a decade the honey-
moon had ended: while some in the elite continued to insist that the new
immigrants were perfect, an anti-Japanese movement began to emerge. By
the late 1920s the Campanha Anti-Nipônica was full blown, often focusing on the *nihonjin-kai* (Japanese Associations) that sponsored schools and
helped maintain premigratory culture in the same way that churches often
did for European immigrants.[165] Much of the focus of nativist politicians
was to stop a Japanese "invasion" by keeping settlement out of the Amazon, the "original Brazil." This changed in 1929 when forty-three families
began work on the Fukuhara colony, which within a year had five hundred
"cheerful [and] apparently contented" immigrants "of a fairly high order
of intelligence," each with a twenty-five-hectare plot and a small house.[166]
At first the colonization seemed to please President Vargas, just as had been
the case with the Assyrians. In a visit to Pará in 1933, he exclaimed that
the Japanese "foreshadow a bright future for the almost empty Amazon
Basin." [167] Vargas was half right. There was a shadow in the future, but for
Japanese settlers it was far from bright.

5

Negotiations and New Identities

OUR MENTALITY

We, Brazilian descendants of Japanese, will testify in
the future that we feel our hearts beating strongly,
filled with love for the Brazilian pátria although our
veins flow with Japanese blood.

—*Cassio Kenro Shimonoto's lead editorial in the first issue of*
Gakusei, *a newspaper published by the Nipo-Brazilian Student*
League in 1935[1]

[T]he Japanese colonists . . . are even whiter than the
Portuguese [ones].

—*Federal Deputy Acylino de Leão in a speech before the House,*
18 September 1935[2]

Between 1933 and 1950 the immigrant stream from Japan to Brazil would
slow, but the discussion of the social place of Japanese and their descendants remained a national topic. Immigrants and nikkei alike began to
play an aggressive role in constructing a multifaceted Japanese-Brazilian
identity, one that would be constituted and contested in many ways. Some
insisted on Portuguese as a language of both internal and external commu-
nication, and others fervently supported secret societies linked to emperor

worship. These surface differences, however, masked a shared desire to find a space within the Brazilian nation that would include nikkei identity. The nature of this coveted citizenship was always in dispute, but angry outbursts from nativists and repressive state policies during the World War II era did not prevent a Japanese-Brazilian identity from emerging and flourishing.

*   *   *

In 1933 two things about Japan were well known in Brazil. One was that the Chrysanthemum Throne was effectuating its imperial aspirations in Asia. The other was that half of the entering immigrants came from Japan. These realizations came as politicians and intellectuals who firmly believed in scientific racialism found expression for their ideas during intense public discussion of Brazil's future that flowed from the Constituent Assembly. Delegates with a wide range of political and social outlooks agreed that resolution of "the immigration problem" was fundamental to the creation of a uniform national identity that would include a single Brazilian ethnicity.[3] Speeches about Japanese immigrants in the Assembly were common as delegates wove immigration history and eugenics theory into scenarios about Brazil's future. The debates, however, boiled down to two rather simple positions. For those oriented toward national economic growth, "becoming Brazilian" was a neo-Lamarckian process that would result in increasing production, capital, and foreign trade. Japanese, then, made the "best" possible immigrants.[4] Those who viewed production as secondary saw Brazil's future as a European, Catholic country; divergence from the path would create an increasingly diseased race. Japanese in Brazil, as in other countries in the hemisphere, were constructed simultaneously as a "model minority" and as a "yellow peril."

Antônio Xavier de Oliveira, Miguel Couto, and Arthur Neiva were the delegates most vocal about excluding all immigrant groups judged nonwhite.[5] Their wild rhetoric appealed to the press and the middle classes by combining anti-imperialism with the idea that the "yellow peril" would prevent Brazil from becoming a great power, a position often encouraged by U.S. representatives.[6] Many of the debates conflated the alarming possibility of Assyrian entry with the idea that Japanese lived in secretive rural colonies, making them equally invisible and terrifying. "[L]urid tales . . . of the manner in which the colonies regard themselves as outposts of Japanese imperialism" were told among delegates who reported that visits to the colonies showed that the residents "favored nudism."[7] When Bahia's Partido Social Democrático proposed a constitutional ban on Japanese and other non-Europeans, Arthur Neiva hailed it as "making a splash bigger than anyone expected."[8]

All the deliberations on Japanese immigration were filled with the language of eugenics. São Paulo delegate Morais de Andrade, a former BRATAC lawyer, argued that "science" showed "the free entry of wise and educated Japanese . . . [will aid Brazil's] social, political, religious and esthetic order."[9] When Miguel Couto introduced anti-Japanese evidence from the First Brazilian Eugenics Conference of 1929, Bruno Lobo, his archenemy, called him "violent and intransigent," and his arguments "so weak that no one knows if he is in favor or against" Japanese entry.[10] Xavier de Oliveira cited the work of Herman Lundborg, director of Sweden's Institute of Racial Biology, and Pedro Aurélio de Góis Monteiro, a leader of the Revolution of 1930, argued for a ban on "nonassimilable races."[11]

Such sentiment was widely reported in Japan, forcing Brazilian businesspeople to assuage fears that trade and immigration would be affected. In an interview from his office in Tokyo, the "Coffee King" Antonio de Assumpção, whose chain of coffeehouses had spawned competitors with names like "Café Brasil" and "Café Paulista," hoped that "Saner elements in Brazil, who constitute the majority of the people there, know too well what the Japanese settlers have accomplished and are not blind to the enormous good the industrious Japanese have done Brazil."[12] The powerful owner of the Diários Associados newspaper chain, Assis Chateaubriand, was an ardent defender of "perfect" Japanese immigrants and urged adversaries to be tactful; "otherwise they will injure the pride of a race which for twenty-five years has worked for the grandeur of Brazil."[13] The Vargas government, while eager to dismiss the power of the anti-Japanese movement, found it difficult, given the domestic climate. Foreign Minister Afrânio de Mello Franco's public toast to "Nipponic-Brazilian Solidarity" on the twenty-fifth anniversary of the arrival of the first Japanese colonists led to outrage among socially conservative members of the Constituent Assembly.[14] London's *Evening Standard* perhaps summed up the debates best in an article entitled "Where the Nuts Come From."[15]

Constitutional delegates were eager to appeal to voters in a rare moment of political freedom, which made press coverage important. A survey of Brazilian newspapers shows that articles about Japanese immigration were continuous in 1934 and 1935. Newspapers in Rio de Janeiro and São

Paulo, as well as in João Pessoa, Curitiba, Recife, and Maceió, had regular reports. Of twenty-seven papers in the cities of Rio de Janeiro, São Paulo, Santos, and Campinas, thirteen were in favor of Japanese entry and seven were actively opposed. Six of the papers took no discernible position, usually reprinting reports from other newspapers, while two, *O Globo* (Rio de Janeiro) and *Folha da Manhã* (São Paulo), published articles both for *and* against Japanese entry.[16] This kind of coverage makes sense because newspapers in this period tended to take fixed political party lines and accept prewritten stories for a price. U.S. diplomats were most upset, regularly accusing the Japanese embassy of paying for favorable coverage.[17]

What makes the press reports and the "academic" studies quoted in them worth examining is that they indicate an expansion of the discourse of ethnicity. Prior discussions had focused on whether Japanese immigrants would improve or diminish the "raça," but now the comments included issues of national devotion. As I have shown, Japanese immigrants had proposed since at least the early 1930s that their "natural" devotion to authority had simply shifted to Brazil upon arrival. Those in the anti-Japanese movement twisted the notion by proposing that ethnicity was immutably tied to nationality and that immigrants would always be loyal to Japan.[18] An article in the *Gazeta do Rio,* for example, asserted that the Amazon had become an outpost of Japanese imperialism. The headline, "JAPANESE IMMIGRATION AND THE ALARMING EXAMPLE OF THE INVASION OF MANCHURIA," suggested that the colonists were a "terrible danger" to the "integrity of the Brazilian fatherland." A cordial letter from the Japanese embassy correcting wildly inflated immigration figures was published under the headline "Yellow Peril in Brazil."[19]

Those in favor of Japanese immigration proposed that it would improve the "homen Brasileiro" of the future. Julio de Revorêdo, an immigration specialist in São Paulo's Department of Labor, openly mocked Xavier de Oliveira in his comments on the topic.[20] A study by the University of São Paulo's Institute of Geography hailed the assimilation of Japanese immigrants because "the racial difference between our true caboclos, descendants of Indians, and the Japanese, is very small." Claiming that the immigrants possessed an "indifference to religion" and that more than 25 percent of all immigrant marriages included one Brazilian partner, the study argued that Japanese "possess qualities that you would not find in the elements that might replace them."[21] Such studies, along with the Kaigai Kogyo Kabushiki Kaisha's detailed information booklets, showed that

Japanese colonists were improving sanitation conditions through their cleanliness and health.[22] In a similar vein was a book commemorating the twenty-fifth anniversary of the arrival of the first Japanese immigrants. The title, *Brasil e Japão: Duas civilizações que se completam* (Brazil and Japan: Two Countries That Complete One Another), speaks for itself. Filled with articles by Japanese diplomats and Brazilian scholars, politicians, military leaders, and businessmen (including Roberto Simonsen, Edgard Roquette-Pinto, and Alfredo Ellis Júnior), the book extolled a glorious future for the complementary and spiritually linked Japanese and Brazilian "races." One article romanticizing bushido in the context of Japanese immigration, by the educator and São Paulo State Legislative Assembly Deputy Francisca Pereira Rodrigues, may have surprised constituents used to her nativist positions.[23] São Paulo's *Folha da Manhã* took a similar position, printing long quotes from Bruno Lobo suggesting that Japanese immigrants would spiritually and biologically transform Brazilian society, and republishing photographs of European-looking "Nipo-Brazilian" children.[24]

The KKKK went on the offensive when it began to appear that the new constitution might place limits on Japanese entry. Large advertisements in major newspapers promoted the high levels of production on the colonies and the fact that Japanese immigrants were widely dispersed throughout the country.[25] A family who had settled in the Recife area was extolled for making Brazil modern after setting up the Sorveteria Gemba, the first ice-cream shop in the entire Northeast.[26] The Kaikō also began publishing Portuguese-language books that asserted the "Brazilianness" of Japanese laborers. In the preface to *Aclimação dos emigrantes japonezes* (Acclimation of Japanese Emigrants) Guisuke Shiratori, the Kaikō director in Brazil, wrote, "I have the honor to direct the adaptation and nationalization of the Japanese emigrants . . . who are cultivating the land of this friendly and welcoming country that is Brazil and . . . are integrating themselves into your people, for themselves and for their children." The book included a picture of Shiratori, his wife, and their "four Brazilian children," two of whom, the caption noted, "were awarded distinction after finishing their kindergarten and primary" education in a São Paulo school.[27]

Thousands of pages of debates, articles, advertisements, and books on Japanese immigration circulated in the mid-1930s. Suffice it to say that those who opposed Japanese entry used essentially nationalist (they are stealing our jobs and land) and racist (they will pollute our race) arguments. Those in favor tended to focus on levels of production (in 1936,

Japanese farmers produced 46 percent of the cotton, 57 percent of the silk, and 75 percent of the tea in Brazil even though they comprised less than 3 percent of the population) and the need for a large and docile workforce, often assuming that Japanese were biologically superior to Brazilians of mixed backgrounds.[28] The disparate positions were eventually resolved in the Constitution of 1934, passed in late April, which included an immigration amendment modeled on the U.S. National Origins Act of 1924. Passed by a vote of 146 to 41, it fixed an annual quota of 2 percent of the number of immigrants from each nation who had arrived in the previous fifty years, giving farmers preferential treatment. The national government also gained total authority over immigration.[29]

The amendment was "designed sharply to restrict [Japanese] immigration while causing as little offense as possible to Japan," a buyer of growing quantities of cotton, wool, manganese, and nickel.[30] These commercial ties—one diplomat wrote from his post in Tokyo, "Get me out of here before [they] propose to buy Sugar Loaf [the famous hill overlooking Rio de Janeiro]"—helped to maintain relatively cordial relations in spite of Japanese outrage at what was seen as Brazilian racism.[31] Even so, the new quota officially reduced entry to thirty-five hundred per year, a marked drop from the twenty-three thousand who entered in 1933.

The new constitution was a slap in Japan's face. An "indignant" Juzo Enami, director of the Japan-Brazil Association in Kobe, quit his position by walking out of a public round-table with Brazilian officials at a local restaurant.[32] In the Japanese Diet, members of major parties regularly challenged Foreign Minister Hirota "to keep Brazil open." An editorial in Sapporo's *Hokkai Times* suggested that "Japan must find out the reasons for the movement . . . to exclude the Japanese. If good reasons are shown, something must be done to remedy them at once."[33] For the most part, however, the Japanese press treated the new immigration strictures as yet another example of Western racism. A survey of the English- and Japanese-language press (Portuguese translations are found throughout the Itamaraty files) shows a uniform condemnation of Brazilian legislation as the result of "jealousy due to [immigrant] economic development . . . [that] smack[s] of racial prejudice."[34] Headlines like "Optimism Betrayed" and "Feelings Hurt" were typical, and it was widely reported that Ambassador Kyujiro Hayashi had been "betrayed" by Foreign Minister Afrânio de Mello Franco's claim that the anti-immigration movement was aimed at German and Italian fascists, and that Japan should "maintain a calm attitude and rely on the traditional friendly policy of the Brazilian government."[35]

The new constitution also strained the Japanese government's relations with its colonists. Prohibiting companies with alien shareholders from publishing newspapers led colonists and newspaper owners to demand that officials save Brazil's Japanese-language press.[36] Another amendment mandated that all education be in Portuguese, effectively shutting down the 185 formal primary schools and about 200 backyard schools established by the immigrants.[37] Others angrily pointed out that Ambassador Hayashi "did not notice" the anti-Japanese agitation until months after it had started, and blamed the Tokyo Foreign Office for "having appointed as ambassador a man who is so indifferent to the welfare of his own countrymen."[38] While it appears true that Hayashi never believed the immigration restrictions would be passed, there is evidence that he lobbied aggressively, leading delegates like Arthur Neiva to complain of Japanese influence over "some of our cliquey officials . . . [who] are giving Brazil away to the foreigners."[39] Even so, the Constitution of 1934 left Hayashi "filled with remorse," and he begged, unsuccessfully, to be allowed to quit his post.[40]

The immigration quotas for 1935 were announced in mid-1934, and Japan's low figure of 2,755 (later revised to 2,849) concerned those seeking some way to mollify the Japanese government. Since the quota would not go into effect immediately, officials began to consider innovative ways of circumventing it. Oscar Correia arrived in Kobe in 1934 as the new consul general, just as the Constitution was passed. His comment as he stepped off the boat, "I should think that a way will eventually be found out of this delicate situation," was reported with great emphasis.[41] Foreign Minister Hirota agreed, stating during a visit to New York that "Japan may send almost as many settlers from now on as in the past, since there is reason to believe that the amendment will not be enforced to the letter."[42] Such comments may have been an accurate reflection of the politics of the moment, but the story was reported only in Japan and the United States. In the months after the Constitution was promulgated, Deputy Alfredo Ellis Júnior led the São Paulo Legislative Assembly, and later the São Paulo Constitutional Assembly, in numerous discussions defending the Japanese. In 1935 he proposed circumventing the quotas through the use of *cartas de chamada,* official forms that allowed citizens and permanent residents alike to "call" their relatives by providing them with an affidavit of support.

In spite of the constitutional restrictions, ten thousand Japanese immigrated to Brazil in 1935, a 50 percent reduction from the previous year.[43] For nativists, the drop was less important than the actual number. Complaints that "thousands of immigrants . . . already have their bags packed" were frequently tinged with anti-Vargas over- and undertones, and the president feared he was seen as caving in to foreign pressure. Vargas therefore asked Oliveira Vianna, who had written in 1932 that "The Japanese is like sulfur: insoluble," to expand the purview of his commission on Assyrian entry in order to implement immigration restrictions more effectively.[44] Soothing nativists, however, had to be done with care. Trade between Brazil and Japan was substantial, and many politicians in agricultural states like São Paulo, Minas Gerais, and Rio Grande do Sul claimed that food production would drop precipitously as a result of the "constitutional text that has created the largest labor shortage in the history of Brazilian agriculture."[45] In a speech before the São Paulo Chamber of Deputies, Bento de Abreu Sampaio, president of the Sociedade Rural Brasileira, spoke of defending the Brazilian "race" from undesirable immigrants but attacked those who placed Japanese in this category.

> I know the value of the Japanese as well as anyone. Marília, my dear city, is the largest Japanese center in Brazil. And the people are the most efficient in labor, educated, refined, sober. . . . During those dark nights when the planters could not regularly pay their workers, you never saw a single impatient or complaining Japanese. With regard to race, I do not know if the great physicians [the anti-Japanese Neiva and Couto] are right, because in Marília there are beautiful and robust men and women among the Japanese colonists.[46]

An editorial in Rio de Janeiro's *Gazeta de Notícias* took the same position, mocking Vianna, Couto, and Neiva: "Our eugenicists and patriots should be congratulated. The nation, however, should receive condolences."[47]

The Constitution of 1934 did more than create quotas and formalize xenophobic attitudes into law. The new *carta magna* also had a deep impact on the Brazilian children of Japanese immigrant parents. Many had grown up bilingual in urban areas, interacted with Brazilians of all backgrounds, and believed the rhetoric that Brazil was a country without racism and on the road to world power. Anti-Japanese rhetoric was particularly shocking to the many nikkei who assumed they had neatly integrated into the middle and upper-middle classes.

From the halls of São Paulo's São Francisco Law School, with its progressive and anti-Vargas tradition, came the most sophisticated response to the Constitution of 1934. In 1935, law student and former soldier Cassio Kenro Shimomoto and a number of colleagues founded the Nipo-Brazilian Student League (Liga Estudantina Nippo-Brasiliera) to sponsor cultural, educational, and sporting events. More important, the League sought to promote the place of nikkei within the "Brazilian race." Indeed, the organization's name, with its explicit hyphen, emphasized that ethnicity and nationality were two separate yet connected items. José Yamashiro, another founder of the League, had a simple position on the subject: "since we were here we had to act as Brazilians."[48]

The insistence that those who had lived all or most of their lives in Brazil were or had become Brazilian was explained with regularity and care in the League's two newspapers, the Portuguese-language monthly *Gakusei* (Student), which had a circulation of about five hundred, and the more widely read Japanese-language *Gakuyu*, which appeared only occasionally but may have had a circulation of over two thousand. *Gakusei* remained in existence for about three years and became the first public expression of a hyphenated culture that was simultaneously Brazilian in nationality (including citizenship, language, and culture) and Japanese (albeit a collectively remembered rather than actual Japan in many cases) in terms of ethnicity. It had a transliterated Japanese masthead but was written exclusively in Portuguese, suggesting an attempt to negotiate identity from both within and without. An editorial by Massaki Udihara noted that "We are a strange generation" whose problem was that "from our parents . . . we always received a bit of the East and in our schooling a bit of the West." The editors of *Gakusei* echoed the discourse of the Brazilian elite, insisting that the mixing of Japanese and Brazilian cultures would "create a unique [Brazilian] mentality that condenses in itself the two." This new culture was denominated "dainissei" and was filled with people who were "more Brazilian than Japanese" and who believed "prompt assimilation" would help the country, "whose nationality is still . . . in formation."[49]

The editors of *Gakusei* insisted that hyphenated ethnicity explained the kind of Brazilians that descendants of Japanese had become. The first issue's main editorial was entitled "What We Want" and was explicit in its position: "We Brazilians, children of Japanese . . . have the desire to . . . write in the beautiful language of Camões." Yet to embrace Luso-Brazilian culture did not mean accepting the nativism that had emerged from it, and "accusations that the Japanese form cysts, that they do not assimilate or adapt to Brazilian customs, are without foundation."⁵⁰ All the other issues of *Gakusei* contained articles in the same vein, arguing that "We are Brazilian in every way" while attacking intolerance. Yet the monthly was also an expression of the status quo. Articles on Freud and European music sat comfortably with editorials that tried to energize nikkei out of the sense of "resignation and indifference" with which they had responded to anti-Japanese rhetoric. Other columns expressed nikkei ethnicity through plays on the Japanese and Portuguese languages.⁵¹

José Yamashiro, a fervent advocate of the use of Portuguese, became editor in chief of *Gakusei* in 1937 when new laws demanded that "foreign" publications be transformed into Brazilian ones through directorship modifications. Yamashiro's parents had been among the first emigrants from Okinawa, and as an adult José would become a well-known journalist and publish scholarly work on the history of Japan and Okinawa. Yamashiro sought to explain how hyphenated ethnicity might work to the advantage of Brazilian society in a perhaps hypothetical conversation between an older immigrant and young Japanese-Brazilian student. The younger asked about the concept of "Yamato damashii," which the elder interpreted as a "Japanese soul" that led to an undying loyalty to the emperor. The younger man responded with shock, wondering why he, born in Brazil, had to be loyal to the emperor. The elder's response, however, was pure nikkei: "[You] should defend the Brazilian flag with the same ardor, with the same dedication, as the Japanese soldiers defend their sovereign. What you should not do is interpret 'Yamato damashii' as only linked to the Mikado. . . . If you promise to defend the integrity of the Brazilian fatherland, its institutions and order . . . this is the essence of 'Yamato damashii.'"⁵² Another article asserted that "your fatherland is this land [and you are] the son of this land, Brazil." As had been the case in 1932, the proposition was that something essentially Japanese made the children of immigrants more loyal Brazilians.⁵³

The intention of the Nipo-Brazilian Student League was broadly acculturative, but an examination of *Gakusei* suggests that interpretations of "acculturation" varied. Articles like the one lamenting the nikkei who "prefer Brazilian customs and know almost nothing that is not superficial about the land of their parents" were common.⁵⁴ This collective, albeit limited, knowledge of Japan went hand in hand with a Brazilian education and the speaking of Portuguese as the language of social interaction in urban centers. Thus the advertisements in *Gakusei* show that

Japanese-Brazilian businesses sought to reach nikkei by marketing hyphenated ethnicity. The niche of the Nipo-Brazilian Beauty School, for example, does not appear to have been in hairstyles as much as the context in which "beauty" was taught—"by nikkei and for nikkei." "Casa Mikado" sold Brazilian-made furniture, but its name told potential nikkei patrons that they were especially welcome. Other stores sold explicitly Japanese products that quickly were used in "Japanese" ways unrecognizable in Japan, over time creating an ethnic consumer market for the Brazilian-born with items divorced from their original cultural meanings. By the mid-1930s nikkei households were distinguishable from both Japanese and nonnikkei Brazilian ones by their use of symbols (paper lanterns, photographs of Japan, home temples) that in other contexts would not go together. This was not unique to the nikkei population; it is typical of ethnic culture to place symbols of an unknown collective past together in new ways. "Italian" restaurants in Brazil (as elsewhere) often place the banner of a soccer team from one region of Italy next to a map of another region.[55]

Perhaps the greatest tension in *Gakusei* was between the Brazilian-born editors of the monthly and the Japanese-born students who dominated the leadership of the League. An editorial published in both *Gakusei* and *Gakuyu* by Cassio Kenro Shimomoto that complimented nikkei youth for joining the 1932 Constitutionalist Revolution against the wishes of their elders and referred to Japan as the "pátria dos crisântemos" (chrysanthemum fatherland) was considered so offensive that he was forced to resign from the newspaper and the League.[56] Another article took the Japanese-born members of the movement to task for their "nippophilia" in conducting most business in Japanese and trying to "instill [a] spirit . . . very favorable to Japan." Yet exhortations to Brazilianize were often surrounded by articles with an explicit focus on Japan, and the Nipo-Brazilian Student League accepted funds from the Japanese consulate to pay for its registration with the Brazilian government. Japan's ambassador even treated the League as an imperial project aimed at cementing Japanese-Brazilian relations.[57]

Another struggle, over the language of self-definition, may seem remarkably familiar to those involved in the civil rights and multiculturalist movements in the United States. Throughout the 1920s most nikkei simply called themselves "Japanese," in replication of the majority terminology. Yet after some Japanese-Brazilians had the opportunity to meet Japanese-

The Casa Mikado furniture store, São Paulo. Courtesy of Centro de Estudos Nipo-Brasileiros/Museu Histórico da Imigração Japonesa no Brasil, São Paulo.

A rural *nihon gakko* (Japanese school), São Paulo state. Courtesy of Centro de Estudos Nipo-Brasileiros/ Museu Histórico da Imigração Japonesa no Brasil, São Paulo.

[U.S.] Americans, the term "nissei" (literally "second generation") started to be used to delineate the Brazilian-born from immigrants.[58] As anti-imperialism became increasingly important to Brazilian identity in the 1930s, however, the ostensibly (U.S.) American term "nissei" was dropped in favor of "dainissei." This never took hold, and by the 1940s the term "nikkei" began to distinguish Japanese-Brazilians from both the immigrant generation and Japanese-(U.S.) Americans. During the 1985 Pan-American Nikkei Conference in São Paulo, "nikkei" was formally adopted as the term to describe all those of Japanese descent in the Americas.

The heated debates in the Japanese and Japanese-Brazilian communities about how to situate themselves within Brazilian culture were mirrored in majority society. While immigrant entry dropped markedly between 1935 and 1942 (to a total of fifteen thousand), discussions focused on the Japanese.[59] In a 1935 interview with the *Tokyo Nichi-Nichi Shinbun*, former Minister of War Pedro Aurélio de Góis Monteiro, part of a pro-fascist contingent within the Vargas government who some years earlier had sought a ban on nonwhites, claimed that "[i]n order to form an excellent Brazilian type, I consider it necessary to adopt the excellent Japanese element."[60] Góis Monteiro's comments illustrate a number of key points: an elite affinity for fascism, a political need to assuage the Japanese government in the years after the Constitution of 1934 (the interview was published in Japan, not Brazil), and the growing sense that if Japanese were desirable immigrants, it might mean that they were "white."

One reason social conservatives like Góis Monteiro began to favor Japanese immigration is that by the end of 1935 the domestic political gains of the Constitution were well spent. Indeed, with nativists in line, pressure from the Japanese government and its allies in the Vargas regime to increase the quota numbers was heeded. The Japanese ambassador convinced retired General Moreira Guimarães, who in 1936 was president of the Geographical Society of Rio de Janeiro, to allow a new printing of his *No Extremo Oriente*, a favorable 1907 account of his eighteen-month posting in Tokyo. Representatives of Mitsui and Mitsubishi hinted that their purchases of cotton were contingent on immigration policy.[61] In 1936 the quota rose to 3,480, the result of adding to the Japanese base unfilled portions of quotas from countries that sent few immigrants. In fact, over eight thousand Japanese entered Brazil that year, and relations between Japan and Brazil seemed better than they had in years.[62]

Yet Vargas had miscalculated his ability to control domestic nativism through the Constitution and the public banning of the Assyrians. When news of growing Japanese entry reached the public, the Society of the Friends of Alberto Torres unleashed a violent campaign against the federal government. Fiery broadsheets claimed hundreds of thousands of Japanese were crossing the borders, and Raúl de Paula, a Friend who also sat on the Oliveira Vianna immigration commission, resigned his post with a flourish, telling reporters that Itamaraty "places itself at the service of foreigners against the interests of the nation."[63] Rio de Janeiro's *A Nota* railed that São Paulo had "250 thousand Japanese in cysts and militarily grouped in the northeast, where they publish newspapers in their mysterious language, treating us like foreigners in our own land."[64] The *Jornal do Comércio* and *Folha do Povo* took similarly jingoistic approaches, claiming that a Kaikō demographic map (which had been published in 1932) had been produced by the Japanese military and that the Amazon was slated to become a new Japanese naval base. Copies of the map were published by the *Jornal do Comércio* under the headline "JAPANESE INFILTRATION IN BRAZIL: The Official Map That Is a Precious Document," and by the *Folha do Povo* as "JAPAN INVADES BRAZIL." The specter of a Japanese invasion of the Amazon could be found in press reports throughout 1936 and 1937, and Deputy Antóvila R. M. Vieira of the Legislative Assembly of the state of Amazonas led a movement to strip all state concessions from Japanese-owned colonization companies.[65] Federal Deputy Xavier de Oliveira demanded a ban on "nonwhites," leading to angry protests from the Japanese embassy and congratulations from the *Jornal do Comércio* for his "rigorously Brazilian point of view."[66]

By 1937 a new sense of urgency regarding Japanese entry was felt in the Brazilian Foreign Ministry, the Itamaraty. Oswaldo Aranha, the pro-U.S. foreign minister (and former ambassador to Washington), along with numerous members of the military, believed that Japan was plotting to divide South America into colonies. Diplomats like Jorge Latour, a commercial attaché in Warsaw, wrote lengthy reports on "Japanese Infiltration" that suggested Brazil's population was too racially weak to prevent the plot.[67] In another case, the chief of Itamaraty's Political Division took the same (already published and easily available) Kaikō map mentioned above and slipped it to U.S. Ambassador Hugh Gibson with the cryptic comment that "he was not at liberty to disclose how he came by this map [but] could nevertheless state that it had been prepared at the instance [sic] of the Japanese Embassy in this city."[68]

The imposition of the Estado Novo by Getúlio Vargas in November 1937, just four days after the Japan-Germany Anti-Comintern Pact was extended to include Italy, markedly changed the ways in which immigrant ethnicity would be treated in Brazil. Corporatist in nature, the "New State" was an *auto-golpe* (when an elected president makes himself dictator) encouraged by a group of authoritarian nationalists that included Army Chief of Staff Góis Monteiro, Minister of War Eurico Dutra, pro-Nazi police chief Filinto Müller, and Francisco Campos, the chief ideologue of nondemocratic rule and soon-to-be justice minister. Using a fictitious document that purported to detail a Communist plot to overthrow the government (known as the Cohen Plan) as an excuse, a national emergency was decreed in late September 1937. On November 8 the only moderate left in Vargas's cabinet resigned and a new constitution was approved. Two days later the cavalry surrounded the presidential palace, and the Estado Novo, with Vargas as its head, was declared.[69]

Less than a month after the coup, Vargas banned all political parties, and the nationalist rhetoric that accompanied the decision mobilized nativist groups to attack Japanese immigration viciously.[70] Beginning in April 1938, new decrees sought to diminish foreign influence in Brazil, modifying the ways in which the Japanese and nikkei community operated. *Gakusei* no longer would contain argumentative articles exploring Japanese-Brazilian identity, but instead focused on community news, facts about Japanese and Brazilian history, and the occasional article complimenting Brazil for its hospitality. More important, the editors of *Gakusei* insisted that both immigrants and their children had been "Brazilianized."[71] In September 1938, *Gakusei* printed its last issue.

The Japanese immigrant community maintained a low profile, even in the face of racist attacks, and the Japanese government (unlike that of Germany) rarely criticized Vargas publicly for his antiforeigner positions. Even so, Japanese immigrants and their descendants continued to be seen as the least assimilated, and assimilable, group. A *Jornal do Brasil* editorial in early 1938 demanded that Vargas stop Japanese government control of immigrants and their children, and a secret report from Vargas's Political and Social Police claimed that "the naturalized Japanese is always Japanese."[72] The United States was also involved, labeling a Japanese Catholic goodwill mission as "very astute propaganda indeed," and putting pressure on Brazilian military officials stationed in Japan to minimize contact with locals.[73]

Such pressure led Vargas to initiate his wide-ranging "brasilidade" (Brazilianization) campaign. This state-driven homogenization program sought to preserve Brazilian identity from the encroachment of ethnicity by eliminating distinctive elements of immigrant culture. New legislation controlled entry and prevented foreigners from congregating in residential communities. Now 30 percent of all colonial residents had to be Brazilian, and no more than 25 percent could be of any other one nationality.[74] Decrees required that all schools be directed by native-born Brazilians, and that all instruction be in Portuguese and include "Brazilian" topics. Non-Portuguese-language materials were prohibited, except by permission. This effectively closed some six hundred schools, although many continued clandestinely. Later legislation allowed the state to expel foreign residents and journalists who offended the "dignity of Brazil."[75]

The brasilidade campaign resonated deeply among Japanese immigrants. Many contemplated a return to Japan, and a 1939 study conducted in the Bauru area found that almost 90 percent favored repatriation, in part for nationalist reasons and in part because the anti-Japanese movement left them with a sense that they would never be fully accepted as members of their host society.[76] Action, however, was rare. Few had available cash, and the Japanese government, via BRATAC, pressured immigrants to remain. The widely read magazine *Bunka* (Culture), published in São Paulo but distributed in the countryside, also took a pro-Brazilianization position. Even the Japanese consulate cautioned against repatriation, and in 1939 only two thousand Japanese left Brazil while fifteen hundred entered.[77]

Nikkei had a different attitude than immigrants toward the new laws. Why, they asked, was their Brazilian citizenship not a guarantee of recognition as nonforeigners? In April 1939 the Nipo-Brazilian Student League elected a directorate comprised almost exclusively of nikkei, including, for the first time, a number of women. One of the first decisions was to create *Transição* (Transition), an advertisement-filled magazine edited by the same group of students who had created *Gakusei,* including Massaki Udihara (at the time a medical student at the University of São Paulo) and José Yamashiro. *Transição,* like its predecessor, focused on hyphenated ethnicity. An editorial in the first issue explained:

> We, Brazilian children of Japanese, are a transition. A transition between what was and what will be. A transition between the East and the West. . . . It is the understanding of our parents, the Japanese,

by our brothers, the Brazilians, by a common language, Brazilian. The harmonization of two civilizations, apparently antagonistic. The fusion, in an ideal of mutual comprehension, of the qualities inherent in each. In the end, we are Brazilians conscious and proud of our land and that of our parents.[78]

Transição was targeted to the nikkei community and, perhaps showing how deeply Brazilian the nissei and sansei generations were, often took nationalist positions within the context of Japanese-Brazilian ethnicity. One focus was cultural preservation, and Brazil was painted as a heterogeneous society where eugenics proved that Japanese had become Brazilians.[79] Many articles, including those by nonnikkei, tried to situate Japanese within the larger immigrant stream by suggesting that nikkei had no relation to Japan, and that being born in Brazil and being treated as Brazilian created nationalists. A report asserted that the Taishō-Bandeirante School (Brazil's oldest Japanese school, founded in 1915) was filled with "Brazilians" whose courses in the Japanese language were extraneous.[80] After editor José Yamashiro met with a group from the Los Angeles Japanese-American Citizen League, a series of articles explored differences and similarities, using terms like "melting pot" to characterize Brazil.[81]

In spite of the brasilidade campaign, neither the Brazilian nor the Japanese government desired to break relations at a time when commercial ties were intense. The Japanese Department of Tourism continued publishing Portuguese-language guides to Japan for the Brazilian audience, and through the first half of 1941, Japan (along with Germany) was such a heavy buyer of Brazilian rubber that São Paulo tire manufacturers complained of shortages.[82] The complexity of Brazil's relations with Japan can be seen in a situation that arose in mid-1939 and involved Sack Miura, the publisher of *Nippak Shinbun*. Miura had arrived in Brazil in 1909 aboard a Brazilian naval vessel, and was said to speak German, English, and Portuguese fluently. He took over *Nippak Shinbun* in 1919 and quickly made a reputation for himself as an eccentric (after visiting the Cotia Agricultural Cooperative in 1926, he titled his report "Elegy to the Potato") willing to take on the status quo-oriented editor of the rival *Brasil Jihō* with satiric articles.[83] This delighted the immigrant community, which made *Nippak Shinbun* its most popular newspaper. Miura regularly angered members of the Japanese diplomatic corps, and an article considered insulting to both the emperor and Vargas found its way to the president's office. Vargas, perhaps at the request of the Japanese consulate, decided to deport Miura, an old hand at expulsion; a similar order had gone out in 1931. That time Vargas reversed his order while Miura was en route to Japan, but in 1939 the deportation gave Vargas an opportunity to do what the Japanese government wanted and to demonstrate his government's willingness to force "brasilidade" on the immigrant population. In spite of more than thirty years' residence in Brazil and two Brazilian-born children, Miura was deported to Japan, where he remained until his death.[84]

As the months passed, Brazil took an increasingly bellicose stance toward resident foreigners. In early 1939, Justice Minister Francisco Campos decided that all foreign-language publications had to be accompanied by Portuguese translations. Soon thereafter, Vargas decreed that all public agencies must work for the "complete adaptation" of foreigners in order to create a "common [national] consensus." Indoctrination of youngsters was placed in the hands of the Ministry of Education and Health (an official nod to the influence of eugenics), and the prevention of immigrant residential concentration or land purchases fell under the purview of the Conselho de Imigração e Colonização (CIC, Immigration and Colonization Council). The Ministry of War received the task of drafting children of foreign residents into the army and stationing them outside the regions of their birth. Speaking foreign languages in public and private (including houses of worship) was banned, and the Brazilian children of foreign residents were prohibited to travel abroad.[85] By 1942 the brasilidade campaign was in full swing. Publications like the monthly *Cultura Política*, written by members of Vargas's inner circle, were filled with intellectual-ideological articles on "foreign schools," "immigration and nationalism," and "immigrantism and brasilidade." Justice Minister Campos demanded that Brazil's doors be closed to "undesirable" Japanese.[86]

Vargas would have been happy to present nativists with a drop in Japanese entry and the "brasilidade" policy while leaving the rules unenforced in order to maintain cordial relations with Japan. Yet as the rhetoric intensified, there were growing numbers of complaints demanding investigation of Japanese colonies where only superficial compliance (such as changing street names and shop signs to Portuguese) seemed to be taking place.[87] In late 1939 the Conselho de Imigração e Colonização sent two of its members to Japanese and German, but not Italian, colonies in the states of São Paulo, Santa Catarina, and Paraná. Arthur Hehl Neiva was a member of Rio de Janeiro's Civil Police (a forerunner of the Political and Social

Police, DEOPS), son of one of the most nativist members of the 1934 Constitutional Assembly, and an advocate of allowing unpopular immigrants like Jews to enter Brazil.[88] His coinvestigator was Major Aristóteles de Lima Câmara, a member of the Army General Staff who took an anti-immigrant position. The two visited the Bastos colony (founded 1928) in early 1940 and found the accusations of noncompliance were accurate. The library had only two books in Portuguese, one of which was a Japanese-Portuguese dictionary that no one could find. The only Portuguese-language newspaper in the colony was used to keep dust off a chessboard. Marriage registration was at the Japanese consulate rather than a Brazilian *cartório*. A "clandestine" Japanese school system operated openly.[89]

In an interesting twist, the Neiva-Lima Câmara report was generally favorable to Japanese immigration, concluding only that firmer government input was necessary in order to speed the pace of assimilation. A similar tone was taken by an inspector from the São Paulo Ministry of Agriculture, who urged the creation of "a class of nationalizing teachers," noting that "[t]he Japanese can assimilate all that is ours, but in order for us to achieve this, we need action and perseverance."[90] The moderation of the reports did not stop them from being used as justification for greater suppression. One reason may have been that Lima Câmara took a public posture different from his official one. In lectures he thrilled audiences with reports of Japanese insidiousness and reportedly told the Associação Brasileira de Educação that "smiling and agreeing with everyone, the Japanese has found supporters in all areas of Brazil."[91] In early 1941, Japanese-language newspapers (there were four dailies published in São Paulo with a total circulation of some fifty thousand) were banned, and even the Portuguese-language *Transição* was shut down after the Nipo-Brazilian Student League was declared illegal. When a local official in rural São Paulo decided to enforce the brasilidade measures to the letter, he ended up arresting almost every Japanese resident of the town.[92]

Until the end of 1941, Vargas sought to maintain relations with both the Allied and the Axis powers, but after the attack on Pearl Harbor in December, Brazil moved firmly into the Allied camp. This led to the house arrest of Brazilian diplomats in Japan, intensifying still further wild stories of "fifth column" activity in Japanese (and German) colonies.[93] The police were ordered to round up Japanese citizens and remove them from strategic locations: one family discovered that they had unknowingly lived for decades between a powder dump and munitions factory only after their arrest. The broadcast of weather reports was prohibited for fear they would be crucial to subversives, and articles suggesting that all Japanese were spies were common.[94] The ostensibly left-wing weekly *Diretrizes* waged an open campaign against São Paulo's "yellow cooperatives," and Rio de Janeiro's *O Radical* screamed, "Important Japanese Official Is a Potato Planter in Brazil." *A Notícia* claimed that a family of tomato farmers had a broadcast facility hidden on their farm, and the Vargas insider and journalist Samuel Wainer (who himself was attacked as a "foreign Jew") suggested that the Japanese-Brazilian population's loyalty was "fragile," and that the São Paulo coastline had been "infiltrated" by twenty-two thousand Japanese who had mysteriously disappeared from their colonies.[95] A young immigrant named Tomoo Handa remembered an instance when a group of his friends went fishing outside the city of Santos. A police unit suddenly appeared with a Japanese flag and ordered the fishermen to grab it. They refused, but one officer held a gun on the group while another forced them to stand together in front of the flag. A Japanese photographer whom the police had kidnapped snapped a picture of the "traitors," who were then turned over to authorities. The young men were freed only because news of the "arrest" was given to the police chief prior to its occurrence. The Japanese government regularly complained that Brazilian police were stealing merchandise and cash from Japanese-owned stores on a regular basis.[96]

With the police and population imagining spies behind every building and plant, the DEOPS began producing regular reports on mysterious agents and hidden caches of war propaganda. Immigrants were said to "obey a plan carefully created by the Japanese Army," and when a Chinese diplomat reported that a São Paulo bookstore was filled with propaganda, the well-publicized DEOPS raid attracted large crowds screaming "Get out!" to Japanese and nikkei residents.[97] All those who appeared Asian were branded as Japanese infiltrators; two Chinese businessmen in Belo Horizonte even placed a sign in their shop window saying "Attention: We are Chinese." Such confusion was embarrassing because China was a Brazilian ally, so the DEOPS began circulating a crude sheet titled "How to Tell a Chinese from a Japanese." The information, which may well have been inspired by an earlier, and equally racist, *Time* magazine article entitled "How to Tell Your Friends from the Japs," was complete with pictures and helpful hints: "The Chinese are racially less complex than the Japanese . . . the Japanese is bad, the Chinese is good; the Japanese is false, the Chinese is sincere; the Japanese is mean, the Chinese is nice."[98] Neither internment in concentration camps (as were Japanese-[North] Americans) nor depor-tation to the United States (as took place in Peru and Bolivia) occurred, but this cannot be understood as a respect for human rights. Rather, the decisions were a result of two fears: that the Japanese and nikkei popula-tion was too large and well-armed to intern without creating a rebellion, and that Japan might attack (and defeat) Brazil if Japanese citizens were rounded up.[99]

In March 1942, the Vargas regime ruptured diplomatic relations with Japan. Five months later, German U-boats began sinking ships off Brazil's coast, and war was declared on Italy and Germany. Now the Vargas regime began to attack Japan and the Japanese at every opportunity. The Depart-ment of Press and Propaganda (DIP), charged with spreading the regime's ideological and cultural directives, reported that a nikkei informer had dis-covered a secret Japanese plan to occupy São Paulo with twenty-five thou-sand troops. The soldiers would be met by spies disguised as fishermen who had readied Japanese colonists to blow up strategic military sites near Santos and create a country in the Amazon called "New Japan."[100] Japa-nese officials reacted to the DIP report as "too ridiculous to refute"; private correspondence between the Foreign Ministry and its ambassador makes clear that Japan had no interest in occupying Brazil, and saw colonization only as a population measure.[101] Nevertheless, one prestigious publisher produced a collection of Xavier de Oliveira's speeches against Japanese and Assyrian colonization, and another rereleased a three hundred-page ver-sion of Carlos de Souza Moraes's 1937 A ofensiva japonesa no Brasil, replete with the superimposition of evil-looking Japanese soldiers, warships, and dragons over maps of Brazil.[102]

After breaking off diplomatic relations with the Axis, the Vargas regime compelled Japanese residents (along with Germans and occasionally Ital-ians) to move from areas defined as "strategic."[103] In Belém do Pará the entire Japanese community was sent hundreds of kilometers upriver to Tomé-Açu, a small village near the Fukuhara colony; in Recife the owners of the Sorveteria Gemba fled the city on their own. Three families who re-mained were forcibly moved. In the town of Álvares Machado, some three hundred miles from the city of São Paulo along the Sorocaba rail line, the Japanese cemetery, founded in 1918, was closed.[104] Reports of Japanese spies were carried daily in the press, often with disingenuous claims that they had been disguised as fishermen or farmers.[105] When five cargo boats were torpedoed outside of Santos harbor in July 1943, Vargas ordered all residents with Axis passports, including some four thousand Japanese, to move from the coast to interior regions within twenty-four hours. Japanese cooperatives, previously hailed for their production, now became "centers of economic sabotage" and "fifth columns of food." After Vargas ordered the properties of Axis companies and individuals seized, BRATAC was accused of directing subversives. Its colonies were placed under government supervision, a move that reportedly netted the regime at least one hundred million dollars.[106]

While the secret Japanese plot to invade Brazil never materialized, the social and ethnic tension created by the anti-Japanese attitudes led members of the Japanese and nikkei community to strike back against the public order by becoming increasingly "Japanese." Emperor worship, always strong among those educated in the first quarter of the century, soon began to replace ancestor worship as a form of identity preservation.[107] Those who did not actively show their loyalty to Japan were defined as "enemies," and the underground Japanese-language press was filled with denunciations of those judged to have lost their "right" to be "Japanese."[108] Wild rumors spread by Brazilians about Japanese were replicated by immigrants themselves as each group sought to demonize and dominate the other in the realm of popular language. In Marília, with a population of some fifteen thousand Japanese and nikkei, there was a widely believed report that a monster baby had predicted that Japan would win the war within a year.[109]

The social tension led to the emergence of a series of secret societies whose ultra-Japanese nationalism mixed with a desire to reinforce a space for Japanese-Brazilian identity. Immigrants began to say that "when the war ends, I want to live under the hi-no-maru [Rising Sun]," although whether this was intended to imply a return to Japan or a return to life in a Japanized Brazil is not clear. After the Doko Kai was organized in 1943 to destroy silkworm farms whose produce would ostensibly become parachutes for the U.S. military, numerous secret societies led the tripartite debate on hyphenated ethnicity (between nikkei, Brazilians, and Japanese) to explode into bloodshed and the destruction of property.[110]

Japanese secret societies first came to the attention of the Brazilian public in March 1943 when a National Security judge imprisoned a group from the town of Bastos as subversives. A few months later a Japanese citizen was refused naturalization because police records indicated the petitioner was involved in secret activities.[111] Soon a number of societies began to surface, all taking the position that Japanese and nikkei were obligated to support the emperor and that those who did not were traitors in need of punishment. In Paraná the Akebono (Society of Japanese Youth) began destroying farms that produced mint (believed to be used for cooling oil in U.S. military vehicles), and throughout the state of São Paulo the Seinen Aikoku Undō (Youth Patriotic Movement) and the Tenchugumi (Executors of God's Punishment) wrecked Japanese-owned silkworm farms that the Doko Kai had not attacked.[112]

These movements would be confined to historical footnotes if they did not begin to expand enormously *after* it became clear in 1944 that an Allied victory was assured. In July of that year Brazil sent twenty-five thousand troops (known as the FEB, Brazilian Expeditionary Force), of whom at least one member was a nikkei, to Italy, causing immense nationalist and anti-Axis feeling in Brazil.[113] Bela Lugosi's *Yellow Peril* played to large crowds in São Paulo, and popular music often included anti-Japanese lyrics. In November, the official anti-Japanese propaganda machine began to churn out articles—typical was the one in the regime's large-format and popular *Vamos Ler!* (Let's Read!) that quoted Manuel de Oliveira Lima's 1903 book on his experiences as a diplomat in Japan out of context, with inflammatory headlines like "THE CREATION OF THE MINISTRY OF LIES IN TOKYO," and a text and photos that implied all Japanese women spent some time engaged in prostitution.[114] In December the *Correio Paulistano* warned residents to watch out for Japanese suicide bombers, and after the war in Europe ended in May 1945, Brazil declared war on Japan so that the U.S. military could continue to use bases in the northeast.[115]

For two months, beginning in June and lasting until Japan's surrender after the dropping of atomic bombs by the United States, Japanese immigrants were the last "enemy aliens" in Brazil. It was during this period of intense anti-Japanese propaganda that the secret societies garnered their widest support. The idea of Japan's defeat had little resonance among immigrants and Brazilian-born rural dwellers for a number of reasons. For those educated in Japan or in Japanese-language schools (*nihon gakko*) in Brazil, much of the curriculum was developed with books and ideas from Japan's Education Ministry.[116] This combined with a ban on Japanese-language newspapers and the poor circulation of Brazilian newspapers in rural areas. Widely circulated newsreels of the surrender ceremonies were never seen by Japanese farmers, who had no access to cinemas. Indeed, a 1952 study showed those in rural areas generally got their news about the war from hidden shortwave radios, from clandestine newspapers, or from neighbors.[117] For many Japanese immigrants, the societies represented a counterattack on the way national identity was defined by demanding new spaces for Japanese-Brazilian ethnicity.

The most powerful of the secret societies in Brazil was the Shindo Renmei (Way of the Subjects of the Emperor's League), whose leaders were retired Japanese army officers furious at Brazil for "becoming an enemy country." The group emerged after the Estado Novo was toppled in a 1945 coup and a subsequent period of wide-ranging political debates created openings for maximalist responses. The society's main goal, which became public in August 1945, following Japan's surrender, was to maintain a permanent Japanized space in Brazil through the preservation of language, culture, and religion among nikkei and the reestablishment of Japanese schools.[118] What the Shindo Renmei did *not* promote was a return to Japan. Home was Brazil, and by December the Shindo Renmei claimed a membership of fifty thousand who believed that Japan had won the war.[119]

Critical to the growth of the Shindo Renmei was its monopoly on information, since the ban on the Japanese-language press continued after Vargas's resignation. The group's circulars and secret newspapers were distributed from sixty-four district offices, and found a willing audience among the many immigrants educated to believe in Japan's superiority and invincibility. Personal diaries with notations for 15 August 1945 collected by Susumu Miyao and José Yamashiro are filled with the absolute conviction that news of Japan's defeat was U.S. propaganda, a position repeated over and over in the Shindo Renmei's weekly mimeographed broadsheet.[120] Each Shindo Renmei document mixed fact and fiction, claiming among other things that Charles Lindbergh had been nominated as president of the United States, that General MacArthur had been imprisoned as a war criminal, and that five major newspapers in Rio de Janeiro had been closed by the Vargas regime after reporting Japanese victory in the war.[121] Just a week after Emperor Hirohito broadcast his surrender message over shortwave radio, the Shindo Renmei, playing on rumors already in circulation, released its own statement:

> Emperor Hirohito has been forced to abdicate in favor of a regent because he accepted the conditions imposed by the Potsdam Declaration. The imperial combined fleet has been given the order for immediate action, and in a furious battle in Okinawan waters the

Japanese Navy and Air Force destroyed about four hundred Allied warships, thus deciding the course of the war. The Japanese employed for the first time their secret weapon, the "high-frequency bomb." Only one of the bombs killed more than one hundred thousand American soldiers on Okinawa. [This led to the] "unconditional surrender of the Allies [and] the landing of Japanese expeditionary forces in Siberia and the United States." [122]

The "news" spread quickly via telephone calls, and when a group of prominent Japanese circulated the actual surrender documents, they were accused of being traitors. By 1946 the community had divided into two camps: the *kachigumi* (victorist) and the *makegumi* (defeatist), the latter calling themselves *esclarecidos* in Portuguese (clear-headed or enlightened).[123]

The Shindo Renmei appears to have emerged as an expression of ethnic solidarity, but some members soon began to engage in extortion. Some collected money by claiming that "Prince Asaki" (this may have been a reference to Imperial Prince Asaka Yasuhiko) was en route to Brazil, and that funds were needed to transport his contingent from the port at Santos to various Japanese communities. A man who represented himself as a Japanese secret agent began selling worthless war medals for over a thousand U.S. dollars each, and others sold false pictures of Allied generals accepting defeat aboard the U.S.S. *Missouri*. Most common, however, was the trafficking in worthless 100-yen notes, false tickets for passage to Japan, and plots of land in the Philippines and Java that had been "conquered" by the "victorious" Japanese.[124]

While some Shindo Renmei members were criminal, the rank and file used its claims of a Japanese victory to demand in a convoluted way that Brazilian authorities give them the highest rank in the pantheon of immigrants. The extortion schemes, which were generally small-scale rather than bankrupting, may thus have been seen by immigrants as donations to a cause rather than commercial transactions. In an expression of a desire for a place in Brazil, numerous towns with large Japanese populations left "department stores . . . hard pressed to fill orders for red and white cloth that they used to make Japanese flags" in preparation for the supposed arrival of the imperial delegation in 1945 and 1946.[125] The Japanese-Brazilian public sphere was so important to the secret societies that they placed blacklists of "traitors" in public places, using *ihai* (small tablets, inscribed with ancestors' names, placed in front of shrines) to put evil spells on "defeatists." Such usage was unknown in Japan, and this phenomenon may be an early example of Japanese-Afro-Brazilian religious syncretism.[126]

By mid-1946 Shindo Renmei propaganda included altered photos of President Truman bowing to Emperor Hirohito, "press" reports of Japanese troops landing in San Francisco and marching toward New York, and notices that Getúlio Vargas would be signing surrender documents in Tokyo.[127] Brazilian newspapers, which ran hundreds of stories on the movement, portrayed some rumors as true: the *Correio da Manhã* received a tip from an unidentified "Japanese" that fifteen Imperial Navy ships were anchored near Rio de Janeiro, waiting to disembark an imperial envoy, and *A Noite* reported on the claims of the imminent arrival of "Prince Asaki." [128]

More frightening to Brazilians was the discovery that fanatical youth had been recruited as members of either the Special Attack Team (*tokkōtai*) or the Suicide Platoon (*kesshitai*), whose role was to assassinate those who spoke against the movement, and thus against the place of Japanese in Brazil. The murders began in early March 1946 when five members of the tokkōtai shot the director of the Bastos Cooperative, and continued the following month with the assassination of the former editor of *Nippak Shinbun,* long a tormentor of Japanese officialdom. The same day the home of a former diplomat was attacked, and two of the "terrorists" were captured. Between March and September 1946, sixteen "esclarecidos" were assassinated, including the head of the Japanese Section of Sweden's consulate general and an ex-army colonel who had headed the Cotia Agricultural Cooperative. Thirty other makegumi were seriously injured, and hundreds of others received death threats bearing the Shindo Renmei's trademark skull and crossbones. Numerous silk, cotton, and mint farmers had their homes and fields destroyed.[129]

The killings resonated oddly among Brazilians. Fears of Japanese militarism and ethnic solidarity were confirmed as Brazilians saw the movement as seeking detachment from majority culture. Most incomprehensible was the attitude of tokkōtai members who surrendered to authorities and then insisted that "Japan did not lose the war. As long as there is one Japanese on earth, even if he is the last, Japan will never surrender." [130] Reports that the Shindo Renmei was allied with the criminal Japanese Black Dragon Society were common, and the press screamed "TEAMS OF 'SUICIDE YOUTH' DISEMBARK IN SÃO PAULO TO KILL JAPANESE" and "JAPANESE GESTAPO ORGANIZES IN THE CITY OF SÃO PAULO." [131] When a raid took place on Shindo Renmei headquarters in early 1946, piles of propaganda materials, a mimeograph machine used to produce the organization's weekly newspaper, and a list of 130,000 members were discovered.[132]

For many nikkei trying to assert their identity as a component of the Brazilian nation, such publicity was disastrous. The government, itself in a moment of transition, was equally concerned about its inability to control a civil war within an immigrant community. This created an esclarecido-government alliance that sought to portray secret society members as a small group of criminals. In a letter to São Paulo's *Folha da Manhã* in late 1945, a nikkei demanded police repression of the "criminals." Using a rather different approach, one of the lawyers who helped prosecute Shindo Renmei leaders dedicated his book on the topic to "the Japanese and their children, all Brazilians who contribute to the formation of this great people and respected nation."[133] The coalition became most clear when Mário Botelho de Miranda, a lawyer who had spent several years in Japan, was appointed police interpreter on the Shindo Renmei case and made two nikkei journalists, Hideo Onaga and José Yamashiro, his assistants. Onaga and Yamashiro had worked together on *Gakusei* and *Transição*, and founded the Japanese-Portuguese *Paulista Shinbun* as an openly esclarecido newspaper that attacked the Shindo Renmei and its supporters in issue after issue.[134] This was far from safe. A reporter with the *Paulista Shinbun* remembered that journalists "had a revolver in their drawer and were always prepared."[135] In another instance, an outspoken young man who promoted nikkei ethnicity was kidnapped; he was released only after his father, a merchant in the town of Marília, guaranteed his future silence.[136]

The police arrested four hundred Shindo Renmei members and scheduled eighty leaders for deportation to Japan in early 1946. This heightened tensions, and the new Japanese government was asked to send documents to Brazil that would make clear the Allied victory. The papers, however, were dismissed as false because they were distributed by the Swedish legation, which represented Japan during the war and its immediate aftermath.[137] Finally, in mid-July 1946, São Paulo's federal interventor, former Foreign Minister José Carlos de Macedo Soares, invited police, military officials, diplomats from the Swedish legation, and Shindo Renmei members, including those in jail, to a meeting at the Palácio de Campos Elíseos. This was a stunning acknowledgment of the expansion of Brazilian national identity to include those of non-European descent, even ones who appeared loyal to another nation.

Some six hundred people gathered that night, the majority secret so-

"TEAMS OF 'SUICIDE YOUTH' DISEMBARK IN SÃO PAULO TO KILL JAPANESE." *Correio Paulistano,* 5 April 1946. Courtesy of Centro de Estudos Nipo-Brasileiros/Museu Histórico da Imigração Japonesa no Brasil, São Paulo.

(above)"THE 'HEAD' OF THE 'SHINDO REMMEI.'" *Mundo Policial em Revista* 1:7–8 (May–June 1947). Courtesy of Centro de Estudos Nipo-Brasileiros/ Museu Histórico da Imigração Japonesa no Brasil, São Paulo.

(left) Materials captured after a raid on Shindo Renmei headquarters. *Mundo Policial em Revista* 1:7–8 (May–June 1947). Courtesy of Centro de Estudos Nipo-Brasileiros/Museu Histórico da Imigração Japonesa no Brasil, São Paulo.

ciety members. Macedo Soares begged for the violence to end, calling Japanese residents "a treasure" and "the most important part of the Brazilian population." The Swedish minister spoke in the name of the Japanese government, but as Jorge Americano noted in a mocking essay, he was dismissed because "Hiii eez not Zapanese, ambassadol of Zapan eez Zapanese" (the original reads, "Ere não é zaponês, embaixador do Zapão é zaponês"). The irony of the federal interventor inviting a Japanese secret society to a meeting with "its" Swedish representative was not lost on Americano, at the time rector of the University of São Paulo: "I don't know if the tall, ruddy, and blond 'representative of Japan,' perhaps speaking English, and fixing his blue eyes on the squinty black Japanese eyes, I don't know if he was able to convince them of Japan's loss any more than he, Swedish, tall, ruddy, blond, blue-eyed, speaking English, was able to convince them that he was the defender of the interests of the Japanese in Brazil."[138] Not surprisingly, the meeting ended in failure. The final word came from Sachiko Omasa, who lectured Macedo Soares in front of her Shindo Renmei colleagues that "We Japanese do not believe . . . in Japan's defeat. If Your Excellency wants to end the disputes and terrorist acts, begin by spreading word of Japan's victory and order that all false propaganda about defeat be stopped."[139]

Macedo Soares was impressed by the fervor. He prohibited newspapers from publishing news of Japan's defeat and ordered the term "unconditional surrender" taken out of all official communications. While the press raged that "They lost in Asia but won at Campos Elíseos," the conciliatory approach and a high court decision that those convicted of the murders could not be deported had the opposite effect of that intended: Shindo Renmei members saw the gentle treatment as evidence of Japan's victory and thus took even firmer positions.[140] Local officials felt sabotaged by the federal government. Francisco Luís Ribeiro, a lawyer who interviewed Shindo Renmei prisoners, complained that these "political delinquents . . . consider us the foreigners," and there were regular reports that the police were torturing prisoners and waving pictures of the emperor accepting defeat as interrogation tactics.[141] Shindo Renmei jokes started circulating among the police, all of them using "funny accents" in the punch lines.[142] These attitudes infuriated even the esclarecidos, who began to use the Shindo Renmei movement to gain still more space for Japanese-Brazilian identity.

While the Shindo Renmei began as a movement *within* the Japanese and nikkei community, the violence soon turned outward. In late July 1946 there was a series of incidents between Brazilians and Japanese in the city of Oswaldo Cruz (São Paulo). When a Shindo Renmei member said in a bar that he would "kill three or four Brazilians," a riot took place that ended as three thousand Brazilians hunted down immigrants, screaming, "Lynch the Japanese!"[143] A few months later police and Shindo Renmei members had a shoot-out in Penápolis. A new wave of anti-Japanese sentiment therefore took hold. The *Correio Paulistano* claimed "the error was ours" in allowing Japanese, who had "difficulty in miscegenating" and who "speak a language completely different from ours," to form "racial cysts." The police magazine *Mundo Policial em Revista* published articles and photographs about fanatics who "shamed the uniform of the Japanese Army."[144] José Augusto and Miguel Couto Filho (son of the anti-Japanese politician discussed above), members of a new Constitutional Assembly, used the violence as an excuse for banning all Japanese immigration to Brazil. The vote was tied at 99–99, and only a decision by the president of the assembly stopped the motion from becoming law.[145] In September, a series of presidential decrees allowed the deportation of 177 Japanese immigrants imprisoned near Rio de Janeiro.[146]

While the Brazilian government feared violence, it was also concerned that secret society members might leave Brazil. The government therefore asked U.S. military authorities to send thousands of Japanese newspapers with articles on the defeat because "the leisurely Brazilians want the Japs, who work three times as hard as the natives, to remain in Brazil."[147] Most of the newspapers were destroyed by the Shindo Renmei, and the few that reached the public were denounced as false. Thus, in 1946 and 1947 secret societies experienced continued growth while they collected firearms and circulated hit lists. One hundred and fifty members of São Paulo's Kokumin Zenei-tai (National Vanguard Unit), for example, were arrested with bombs, guns, and surveillance photos of their intended victims' homes. News of the Shindo Renmei soon began to flow to Japanese communities throughout the Americas, and women became increasingly involved in educating children about the "victory" and urging people to report on those who "committed crimes against Japan."[148] In Paraná "defeatist" Japanese began receiving death threats claiming that "soon the Japanese Army will arrive in Rio de Janeiro or Paranaguá, and go directly to Londrina, where they will finish off the Jewish and Communist elements, as well as the yellows who do not believe in the victory of Japan."[149] Shindo Renmei propaganda frequently linked the Brazilian government to "the Jews in Rio" as it sought to discriminate between insiders and outsiders by using both economic and ethnic language. Those who denied Japan's victory were interchangeably "Western capitalists," "Communists," "Jews," "Chinese," or "nissei" (meaning Japanese-[U.S.] American), all terms that dismissed "defeatists" from the category of "Japanese."[150]

A number of factors began to marginalize the kachigumi groups after 1947. Efforts to raise funds for Japanese war victims, without ever declaring winners and losers, created "sympathizer" or "hard-liner" groups (the terms were synonyms) who recognized defeat but, in a typical expression of minority group politics, took the position that a "family matter" should not be discussed with majority society.[151] Then, in early 1950, Japanese Olympic swimming champion Masanori Yusa arrived in Brazil with his team, the "Flying Fish." The group was welcomed emotionally by the Japanese and nikkei communities, and six thousand people greeted the team at Congonhas Airport in São Paulo. An exhibition match at the Pacaembu Stadium (a major *futebol* arena) was sold out, and included music by the State Military Police Band and the presence of the governor of São Paulo, Adhemar de Barros. During an interview, members of the Flying Fish expressed shock when presented with the idea that Japan had *won* the war. As a result, the Shindo Renmei and the Zenpaku Seinen Renmei (All-Brazil Youth League, Liga dos Moços de Todo o Brasil) began poster campaigns claiming the swimmers were Koreans masquerading as Japanese.[152] Nikkei and Japanese alike were offended by the suggestion, and the Brazilian government's indictment of over two thousand Shindo Renmei members was greeted with relief.

A few years later a group of kachigumi brought a troupe of Japanese actors to Brazil to make a commercial film, released under the title *E a paz volta a reinar na época do "Shindo Renmei"* [1956] (Peace Returns in the Time of the Shindo Renmei). The film sought to re-create "the ties of sincere friendship within the community that had existed in the past" while encouraging nikkei to help "the national economy."[153] In a wildly convoluted plot, the hero was a Japanese immigrant engaged to the daughter of a wealthy European fazendeiro; the villain owned a Japanese-language newspaper and plotted to sell millions of worthless yen to unsuspecting immigrants. The message was clear: the kachigumi-makegumi split was not a matter of politics but the result of selfish elements in the community. While *E a paz volta a reinar* did have a commercial run in cities in the interior of São Paulo state, it was never shown in the capital. The owner of the *São Paulo Shinbun* had the film suppressed by city officials, claiming it slandered him by portraying rumors that he had sold worthless yen as true. The secret societies were no more as a newly contested space for nikkei emerged in post-war Brazil.

*　*　*

Between 1933 and 1945, Japanese and Japanese-Brazilians became more sure that their home was in Brazil and less certain on how to place their ethnicity within the context of national identity. As anti-Japanese rhetoric exploded, first in the debates over the Constitution of 1934 and later during the brasilidade campaign, the negotiations between majority and minority were transformed. For members of the Brazilian elite, answers to the question of how Japanese would fit into society were inexorably tied to discussions of economics and assimilation. Even as nikkei integrated into all areas of Brazilian society, both scholars and journalists reported that few Brazilians of European descent were willing to marry those of Japanese descent.[154] Japanese and Japanese-Brazilians, however, began to define their identity in different ways. Young nikkei referred to themselves in a hyphenated fashion while the older generation created secret societies in the shared belief that loyalty to Japan would insure their lives in Brazil. In the end, all parties were left with equal parts satisfaction and anger. Nikkei were now Brazilian even as society at large continued to define them as Japanese.

6

Turning Japanese

No sooner had the European leaped ashore than he
found his feet slipping among the naked Indian
women. . . . The women were the first to offer
themselves to the whites, the more ardent ones
going to rub themselves against the legs of these
beings whom they supposed to be gods.
—*Gilberto Freyre*, The Masters and the Slaves: A Study
in the Development of the Brazilian Nation *(1933)*

[T]he Asiatic woman . . . has something original and
strange that incites sinfulness. . . . [In Japan] men
enjoy a liberty that makes me jealous.
—*Nelson Tabajara de Oliveira*, Japão: Reportagens
do Oriente *(1934)*

There is an oft-repeated Brazilian saying that if you dig a hole deep enough, you will end up in Japan. This popular linkage found its expression in elite circles in an explosion of travel books. Imagining Brazil's future via Japan was a convenient way for intellectuals and policy makers to extract day-to-day pressures from ideological disputes about national identity. If politeness, political survival, and class expectations defined the future at home, once Brazilians arrived in the exotic East, all became clear.

Asia was the root of the postslavery non-European experience in Brazil, and travelers to the region were experts unbound. Many turned their private thoughts public in literature or speeches, and from the late nineteenth century on, travelogues on "the Orient," notably Japan, were produced by Brazil's largest commercial houses. The voyagers may have been clerics or warriors, psychologists or artists, but they all explored the same motif: a Brazil imagined through the lens of otherness. People were objectified and objects were subjectified in an attempt to understand a domestic future by exploring social and economic developments abroad. The power of difference was its ability to function as a representation of self. Travelers created Brazil thousands of kilometers from the physical place. Descriptions of "elsewhere" were always hopes for "here."

It was the Meiji Restoration, with its radical modifications of the political and economic system, that provided a model for domestic growth and international power. Japan appeared to have become wealthy, powerful, and modern overnight, and the growing numbers of trains, streetcars, soldiers, and factories fit perfectly with Brazilian aspirations. Intellectuals were awed by Japanese advances in science and medicine, and politicians were attracted to military expansion and the authoritarian state. All were filled with questions about how Brazil's Japanese and Japanese-descended populations would effect national identity. Brazilian interests were matched by a Japanese desire to impress, and large sums of money were allocated to invite prominent academicians and scientists for official visits. If Brazilian elite culture helped define the kinds of people and objects that travelers saw, so, too, did the Japanese government.

Brazilian travel narratives on Japan stand apart from the books and articles produced by "Western" travelers to the "East." In these, confident European and U.S. North American imperialists portrayed Asia as a place to be occupied, owned, and perhaps redeemed.[1] Brazilian representations, however, tended toward emulation rather than possession. In Japan each traveler hoped to find cultural artifacts and technological innovations that would improve Brazil's social climate and place in the world order. Even so, travelers to Japan were as one convinced that their own European-ness made them superior to Asians. Brazilian voyagers thus felt themselves in *both* the "first" and "third" worlds, and the desire to imitate Japan in the economic and military spheres was matched by repulsion at its non-Christian tradition. If absolute confidence marks most non-Brazilian portrayals of Asia, the Brazilian texts are notable for their lack of certainty. It is simply impossible to imagine Lafcadio Hearn (from the United States) or Sir Rutherford Alcock (from Great Britain) agreeing with Brazilian Ambassador Manuel de Oliveira Lima that the Japanese "are tolerated in practice for material advantage."[2]

The sense of superiority and inferiority, of desire and disgust, led Brazilians to link Japan to Portugal, the European nation to which they had the most ambiguous relationship. Just as Japanese and Arab immigrants sought to explain their places in Brazil through a mythic linkage to Amazon indigenes, Brazilian elites sought to guarantee their national future by proposing that Portuguese culture was critical to Japanese world power. Replicating stories of "discovery" where a European lust for gold was transformed into sexual desire and a new, mixed national race, the writers suggested that the Portuguese "discovery" of both Japan and Brazil would lead the two countries to similar positions of national power.[3] If Brazilian Orientalists sought to possess Japan, it was only so that Brazil could become more like it.

* * *

Brazilian writings about Japan were constructed out of a long history of Luso-Asian relations. The "new world" of the Americas was "discovered" in a search for Cipango (as Columbus called Japan), and diplomats and planters watched with some jealousy in the mid-1800s as Japan promulgated treaties with nations other than Brazil. In the early twentieth century, images came via the work of Wenceslau de Moraes, a Portuguese diplomat who lived in Japan from 1898 until his death in 1929.[4] His eight books contrasting the mythical traditional Japan with a superindustrialized modern state were required reading for those interested in how a nation could rapidly become a world power. After reading Moraes, planters, diplomats, and physicians all posed the same question: If the Meiji Restoration had created "a new civilization from this old people," could Brazil achieve global respect while maintaining charming cultural aspects of African and indigenous civilizations?[5] Japan was a modernizing nation that had retained its exotic soul in an increasingly harmless way—could Brazil do the same?

Brazilian narratives on Japan began to be published following José de Costa Azevedo's 1893 special mission to Asia, a trip that left him as impressed by Japan and the Japanese as he was dismissive of China and the Chinese (see chapter 2).[6] In the decades that followed, some of Brazil's most important politicians, educators, and intellectuals began to add their personal reflections. A kind of international "jet set," many of them spoke numerous languages (although not Asian ones), proudly pointed out that they read European and North American literature, and regularly socialized with foreigners. They lived within and replicated a specific type of travel literature, and in some ways the Brazilian accounts are like those of other visitors. All inexorably focus on the author's experiences as representative of a "true" Japan and begin with obligatory pictures of the Daibutsu (the great image of the Buddha at Kamakura) and Mount Fuji, then continue with discussions of hara-kiri, geishas, and bathhouses.[7]

Brazil's travelers were experts without knowledge. Their visits were relatively short (between two months and two years, tending toward the former), and few spoke the local language. All had read the works of Wenceslau de Moraes, and their frequent trading of introductions and prefaces created a closed form of discourse about Japan. Most of the books were published by the government or by prestigious presses, and were not confined to the bookshelf, coffee table, or salon. Numerous volumes entered into second and third printings as important decision makers looked to the travelers as intermediaries between experience and policy. The literate public took the same approach, and those who visited Japan found that upon return they were in demand as lecturers and as granters of interviews for major newspapers. They titillated the media and the middle and upper classes, helping to form images among many urbanites, who had little contact with Japanese immigrants and their descendants living in Brazil's rural areas.

What is remarkable about the travelogues is how similar the motifs remained over five decades. Early historical chapters portray a wild and precarious premodern Japan suddenly transformed into a powerfully modern state by the Meiji. Statistics on production and photographs of heavy industry and Western-style buildings suggest that the inevitable by-product of economic strength was cultural modernity. Desirable Japan was a Western Japan, filled with electric streetcars and large multistory buildings made of permanent materials. Chapters on modern hotels and their fancy English tearooms, most notably the Frank Lloyd Wright-designed Imperial Hotel, which opened in Tokyo in 1922 as an official residence for foreign dignitaries, were almost obligatory.[8] Japan was glossed as modern, and hence Western, thus mediating Brazil's quest for just this status. In Japan lay the hope for a future Brazil.

The modern Japan that Brazilians hailed, however, had a dark side. The conservation of traditional culture, as different from traditional objects, troubled the travelers. If giant Buddha statues and shogunate-era castles were impressive, "un-Western" people were problematic. This thinking, of course, is typical in European and North American colonialist discourses, where Asian men and women are feminized so that they can be dominated and dismissed. Brazilians, however, did not follow this model. Rather, men were portrayed in a positive light, in order to suggest a "modern" population that was hardworking, smart, and stepping brightly toward the future. Women, on the other hand, represented both the past Brazil wished to flee and the realm of male fantasies.

Dual gendering expressed the contradiction between a Japan despised and a Japan desired. By contrasting modern men in ties with docile, domestic, and thoroughly unmodern Japanese women, Brazilians asserted their first-world (i.e., European) superiority while expressing their third-world (i.e., Brazilian) sense of inferiority. Although Western cultural stereotypes rendered Japan an exotic and mysterious woman, efficiency in the spirit of modernity could not be dismissed. Dual gendering thus allowed elites to portray themselves as thoroughly modern and forward-looking even though their views show them to have been conservative and traditional. While the public expression of such sentiments in early twentieth-century Brazil may have been seen as retrograde, the point could be made via Japan. Contrasting modern men and traditional women also allowed an exploration of Japanese immigration that could be both hopeful and cautious. By suggesting that some Japanese were good and others were not, a role was given to the state (to which all travelers were tied) as a promoter and protector of Brazilian nationhood.

Dual gendering cannot be found in Brazilian writings on the Middle East or other parts of Asia, most notably India and China. In those narratives male travelers bring civilization to "backward culture[s]" populated with weak, intoxicated men and women engaged in lives of sexual license or domestic service.[9] The singular aspects of the dual gendering of Japan, however, should not suggest that travelogues were not heavily oriented toward sex. In fact, their lewd nature at first seems surprising, given that the authors were members of an elite, trained not to offend delicate sensibilities. Leaving home gave license to the imagination, and for Brazilians who sought a future in Japan, sex provided the theater. "The milieu in which Brazilian life began was one of sexual intoxication," wrote Gilberto Freyre in 1933, and in Japan, Brazilians sought reincarnation.[10] The authors, at home both sexually repressed (in elite mixed company) and sexually active (with women of different racial and class backgrounds), were intrigued, excited, and scared by Japan's seemingly open sexuality. Official business (between men) was aimed toward bettering the nation, but what of the private business (and business it was) between Brazilian men and Japanese women? What was the impact of the availability and acceptability of sex in imagining a Brazil with hundreds of thousands of Japanese immigrants and their children? In the end, the cost of portraying a single and unitary Japanese culture was too high for Brazilians who were as sure of the future as they were fearful of the past.

*   *   *

The motifs of emulation, modernity, and sexuality described above can be found even in the earliest travel narratives. Francisco Antonio de Almeida arrived in Japan in 1874 as part of a delegation sent to observe the transit of the planet Venus. While his visit predated the arrival of the *Kasato-Maru* by almost forty years, his desire to remake Brazil along Japanese lines is clear. Almeida did this by tapping into a submerged Christianity that he believed remained from the period of Portuguese contact in the sixteenth century. If Japan was reformulated as a Christian nation, it could become a model for Brazilians who hoped to create the kind of modern state the Meiji had. Reconfiguring Japan as Western, however, flew in the face of assumptions about the "East," and Almeida was both impressed and disappointed that Japanese port officials wore modern military uniforms rather than the hoped-for "long coats [kimonos] and shiny sabers." [11]

Almost a quarter of a century passed between Almeida's visit and the opening of Brazil's first official mission in 1895. During that period important changes took place. China never became a supplier of labor, and Sho Nemoto's visit to São Paulo set the stage for Japanese entry. Brazilian production expanded on the backs of European immigrants whose activism concerned landowners. Diplomats were charged with redesigning Brazilian culture rather than managing simple political affairs.

Aluísio Azevedo was one of the young men posted to run the new consulate in Yokohama. He had gained national and international fame for his social-realist portrayals of Brazil, but much of his life was at the immigration-diplomacy nexus. His father was the Portuguese vice consul in Maranhão, and Aluísio was born out of wedlock to a Portuguese woman living in the state. Portugal was his first diplomatic posting: there he worked almost exclusively on immigration issues related to the expanding Amazon rubber economy. In 1897 Azevedo was elected to the Brazilian Academy of Letters and transferred to Japan, where his efforts helped to set the stage for mass migration a decade later.[12]

Azevedo was a pseudo anthropologist who adopted many local customs, including wearing Japanese clothing and eating Japanese cuisine, both rare practices among his contemporaries. Such eccentricity helped readers (and Azevedo) believe that the author had more than a superficial understanding of Japanese culture. His "discovery of Japan for Brazil" came to the literate public in two articles on women published by the prestigious *Almanaque Brasileiro Garnier* and in numerous speeches. His book-length manuscript *O Japão* (which surfaced in the 1920s and was finally published in 1984) is filled with a sense that Azevedo had turned Japanese: one discarded title was "O Japão como ele é" (Japan as It Is), suggesting not an observer but an insider with absolute knowledge.[13] The reality, however, was that Azevedo spoke no Japanese and knew little of the country's history. *O Japão,* in fact, borders on plagiarism: it reformulated Georges Bosquet's popular *Le Japon de nos jours* (1877) in the comparative style of Wenceslau de Moraes's *Dai-Nippon.*[14] The text is strictly narrative, beginning with the Japanese origin myth of Amaterasu and ending just as Commodore Perry was set to arrive (a final chapter covering 1853–1863 was never written).

The tension between emulation and dismissal is clearly expressed in the *Almanaque Brasileiro Garnier* articles and in *O Japão*'s short introduction. Japan's economic, military, and political successes were hailed without question. Yet Azevedo was confused about the traditional role of women in the kitchen rather than the factory, in the house rather than the street. Women were "sweet prisoners" who upon marriage "transformed themselves into slaves," their "femininity and refinement" so admirable that he wrote of his yearning for them after his return to Brazil.[15] Japan, then, was both a woman and a man; it was a place where "few secrets will remain with its virginity" *and* where the "best-dressed [in a Western sense] and bureaucratic constitutional monarchy" is filled with "ministers in embroidered suits."[16] If the female Japan was to be dominated, the male one was to be modeled by Brazil. Making Japan *like* Brazil was so crucial that Azevedo even considered calling his book "Agonia de uma raça" (Agony of a Race), a title that equates the two countries in a common search for a racial nationality.[17]

Azevedo's views of Japan only skirted the edges of public consciousness until recently; it was the appointment of the famed diplomat and author Manuel de Oliveira Lima as ambassador that brought Brazilian images of Japan to a broad elite audience. *No Japão: Impressões da terra e da gente* (In Japan: Impressions of the Land and of the People) was published in 1903 by Laemmert on high-quality paper and was filled with glossy photographs. The book opens with a photograph of the Daibutsu at Kamakura, and the historical chapters are shaped out of secondary sources. The focus of *No Japão,* however, is on how Brazil might use Japan as a prototype for the rapid overhaul of its national character. Ancient Japanese poetry was "like" modern Brazilian poetry, and this linkage, combined with the odd claim that when they wore Western dress, Japanese "judged themselves morally obliged to imitate the Europeans," showed how Brazil might reshape itself.[18] If Japanese, with their odd religion and un-Western ways, could become European by simply slipping out of a kimono and putting on a suit and tie, perhaps Brazil's marginal populations could do the same.[19]

Oliveira Lima's hopes and fears were most clearly expressed in his fascination with women who were superficially viewed as sexual objects or domestic servants (sometimes both). This is surprising, because the ambassador regularly toured factories where he saw the important role women played in the industrial workforce, mainly in cotton-spinning and silk-reeling factories. He must have known that middle-class women frequently conducted private lives quite separate from their husbands or mother-in-laws, and even created a feminist movement.[20] Yet these modern roles were not ones that he sought for Brazilian womanhood. Rather, the Japanese woman was portrayed as everything the Brazilian was not. From the modern perspective she was "unhappy, because [she was] not emancipated," but in a more traditional construction her "subjection is sweet and voluntary."[21]

The foremost contradiction for Brazilians enthralled by modernization was how to employ industrial Japan as a model if the culture was itself retrograde. Utilizing a tactic as old as the arrival of the first Europeans in the Americas, Oliveira Lima saw Japan's unemancipated women as Christian soldiers who would subvert the social order. Buddhism, which placed women in an "inferior position," thus was constructed as an oppressive national culture that provided a motivation for change.[22] The cultural "inhumanity" of the Asian religion would disappear as Christianity helped women "emancipate themselves" by using the "discreet influence [of their] innate and calculated sweetness." Women would transform an Asian (Buddhist) culture into a Western (Christian) one while staying outside the world of the men who maintained Japanese industry. With the transformation complete, Japan could be admired as Brazil's future. In a series of lectures to Japanese women's groups, Oliveira Lima made clear his expectations:

> Brazilian ladies who eighty years ago were kept in almost Moorish reclusion . . . rank now among the best customers of Parisian dressmakers and milliners, and are as fond of dancing and having an "awful good time" as any American girl of Chicago or San Francisco. Some have taken life more seriously and are doctors, or teachers, or even lawyers. Yet our women have neither despised nor neglected their home duties.[23]

Oliveira Lima's ideas were reinforced by Brazil's military attaché in Japan. Moreira Guimarães' *No Extremo Oriente: O Japão* was as critical of Brazil, where "laws multiply" and "disastrous skepticism" had led to disorder, as it was positive about Japan, where "tradition is respected [and] intelligence was developed at home."[24] Working from a Lamarckian climate-culture model, the attaché linked the traditional and the modern through a mysterious "Japanese soul" that emerged from a convergence of feminine and masculine worlds. Brazil and Japan were both mestiço nations, although the former was racial in nature while the latter took place in the realm of gender. Suggesting that *mestiçagem* was not as much a mixing as a joining, Guimarães proposed that in Japan the "enchanting tenderness of the land [and] gentleness of the plants" created both "the kindness of the Japanese woman" and the bureaucrats and electric trams of the male world.[25] The many photographs that illustrate *No Extremo Oriente* make the same point. While Mount Fuji hovers behind modern Tokyo, deeply bowing Japanese women in kimonos stand next to athletes and soldiers. Ancient temples coexist with dockyards, train stations, and universities.

Modern Japanese and foreign men, dressed in suits and ties, stand behind kimono-clad Japanese women and their hatted, Western-dressed female counterparts.

Government officials like Oliveira Lima and Moreira Guimarães were under pressure to use their positions to help remake Brazil, and their views of Japan reflected this. Yet even those who traveled to Japan by choice replicated many of the same ideas. Monsignor Vicente Lustoza, a member of the Instituto Histórico e Geográfico Brasileiro, made his trip in 1908 after being "seduced" by an image of "greatness in . . . war, in arts and in industry."[26] Much of Lustoza's vision fits neatly with what Mary Louise Pratt has termed the "monarch-of-all-I-survey," where the sights of landscapes are made into momentous events.[27] The landscapes, however, were not all natural ones: he was as impressed by docks as he was by mountains. Admiration of the material did not mask Lustoza's repulsion at the people. Japanese modernity was thus remade into something foreign, and the Grand Hotel where Lustoza stayed was granted first-class status because it was filled with foreigners. Lustoza, in an attempt to link his visit to the glories of earlier European explorers, hailed his own landing in the "*new* old world."[28]

Viagem ao Japão: Circunavegando o globo (1909) was written as a study in striking contrasts. Photos concentrating on the exotic—kimono-clad geishas kneel and touch their heads to the floor in a "typical Japanese greeting" [*sic*]—are juxtaposed to photos of the new Nippon Bank building and the enormous Shinbashi train station. Descriptions of Japanese temples are mixed with discussions of modern hotels. This typical colonialist discourse does not hide the emulatory trope. Lustoza, like Oliveira Lima, sought to transform Japan into a Catholic country as much for nationalistic reasons as for ones of faith. By linking Brazil and Japan, he proposed that a unique Japanese ability "to assimilate with such ease the best of the refined world" would allow Christianity to flourish, and shift Japan from the "old to the new world."[29]

Lustoza had trouble understanding how Japanese industrial development could take place within an "eccentric" culture. Brazil and Japan were linked materially, but the only people mentioned in *Viagem ao Japão* are portrayed as animals. Like the Brazil the Portuguese had found hundreds of years earlier, Japan was available for possession. Lustoza used the term "indigenous" for the local population, and he constructed women as Africans who were "slaves to their husbands [and their] mothers-in-law," and who

spoke only after kneeling down, the act of "a beast of burden." Depravity in
the home led to a lack of public morality, as the following anecdote shows:

> One day in Osaka, we crossed a bridge by jinricksha and in front of us
> we saw two taller-than-average people with their kimonos pulled up,
> showing their legs. At first glance they appeared to be two men, but
> looking at their heads, they had the hairstyles of women. We asked
> the driver: Are they men or women?
> —Women, he said.
> —But why the extravagance?
> —It's the way of women.
> —A terrible way, we replied, that does not respect modesty.[30]

Oliveira Lima, Moreira Guimarães, and Vicente Lustoza all used Japan
to imagine a new, industrially powerful, and socially conservative Brazil.
What they did not picture was a Brazil filled with Japanese immigrants, and
as entry rates increased, questions about culture and labor could no longer
be locked within a geographical space far from Brazil's borders. The proposition that Japan was "like" Brazil would now be tested as Japanese were
asked to become Brazilian and Brazil endeavored to become "Japanese."

Brazilian narratives on Japan after 1908 were uniformly constructed
around the question of immigration, although they show continuity with
the earlier work through the exploration of sexuality. In most cases the
interwar era travelogues are filled with positive comments as human and
commercial ties expanded and diplomatic postings to Japan became increasingly prestigious. Nondiplomatic travelers were often official guests of
the Japanese government, and their stays were turned into festive international events. The upbeat mood helped shift Japan from a model for Brazil
to an actual replication of Brazil. Japanese achievement was Brazilian success as Japanese immigrants improved Brazil by making it more Japanese.

Typical of the enhanced vision was Juliano Moreira's *Impressões de uma
viagem ao Japão* (1935). Moreira was a well-known psychiatrist whose 1928
visit was organized by Dr. Mikinosuke Miyajima, the physician who had
invited Arthur Neiva a decade earlier (see chapter 4). Moreira believed
he was uniquely "qualified" to assess questions of national character, an
attitude the Japanese government encouraged when it awarded him the
Order of the Sacred Treasure, which was reserved for "men of real scientific merit."[31] Since both the Japanese and the Brazilian elite believed that
science, class, and policy were part of the same package, invitations and

awards created a favorable climate for continued Japanese immigration by promoting the "modern" status of both countries. By making state visits into media events—during Moreira's three-and-a-half-month stay, he was interviewed by the million-circulation *Tokyo Nichi-Nichi* newspaper and presented a series of public lectures, including some via radio—Japanese foreign policy coalesced neatly with Brazilian aspirations.

"My life in Japan . . . is to assimilate all that is good from other centers of civilization," noted Moreira in one address. By placing Japan on the same plane as Europe, he suggested that members of the "Brazilian race" had a special ability to understand Japan and its people. Moreira was a mulatto (although the text makes no mention of this) who had a vested interest in promoting the unique "ethnic affinities" of the two countries. Since all Brazilians had "descended from our aborigines," they were especially "sympathetic" to those of the same "racial stock" arriving from Japan. If Brazilians and Japanese were one, then the much-heralded international power of Japan was Brazil's future. In a countrywide radio lecture Moreira took the idea to its logical conclusion, complimenting the Japanese government for sending immigrants who were "good Brazilians of Nipponic origin in the midst of a new fatherland." [32]

While the texts of the psychiatrist's speeches make up most of *Impressões de uma viagem,* the chapter "Is Japanese Immigration Convenient for Brazil?" was written only for Brazilian readers. Here Moreira continued to turn Japanese immigrants into Europeans who were creating a better Brazil: "I am certain that the second-generation Japanese and later, born in Brazil, will be a Brazilian as far from the original type as the child and grandchild of the Portuguese, the Spaniard, the Italian, the German, etc. [They are] born in Brazil [and] are not judged any more tied . . . to the fatherlands of their parents and grandparents." A photograph of Moreira in Hokkaido, receiving an award from a group of men dressed in formal Japanese attire, emphasizes the point. The visual message is decoded via the caption ". . . a representative of the Ainus, the primitive race that peopled Japan." [33] If the uncivilized and un-Westernized Ainu could be transformed into the modern and Western-clothed Japanese who conducted and recognized science, then Brazil could expect the same from its "backward" populations.

A curious addition to *Impressões de uma viagem* were the chapters written by Augusta Peick Moreira. Unlike her husband's presentation of Japan's modern face—university buildings and libraries are described in detail while temples go unmentioned—Augusta describes a charming and unthreatening conservation of the past through the arts. While her approach was different from her husband's, the intent was the same: to provide evidence of a unique biological bond between Brazilians and Japanese. In a clever attempt to appeal to readers who may have been unconvinced by her husband's scientific approach, Augusta used her freedom from methodological constraints to turn personal experience into generalizable truth. Japanese first-class treatment was termed "Brazilian hospitality" while, in what was certain both to titillate and to give hope to the Brazilian audience, "the crossing of Japanese with Europeans [in Japan led to] better-formed people than the pure Japanese," a "fact" that was replicated "not only in Rio de Janeiro but also in São Paulo."[34]

Augusta, unlike her husband, spoke frequently of gender as she lauded Japanese womanhood. In a lecture to the Brazilian Federation for Feminine Progress that had the Mao Zedong-like title "Ten Million Women Gain a Life in Japan," she extolled the virtues of the wives and daughters of diplomats who had spent time outside of Japan, returning to the idea that Japanese immigrants improved Brazil. Expecting to find "Nipponic beauties in gracious costumes," Augusta discovered that the Japanese women were as modern as Brazilian ones, aspiring to high levels of education and wanting to know their future mates.[35] As impressive was the daily life of working women: rural dwellers did "the most uncultivated [rude] work," and urban women were involved in every aspect of industrial life, including "wearing masculine uniforms" as tram conductors. Japanese women brought still another important trait to Brazil: reproduction. "The numbers of children in Japan are fantastic," gushed Augusta, proposing that Japanese women would improve Brazil's national race along with its work ethic.[36]

The Moreiras illustrate how Brazilian conceptions of ethnicity and nationality were constructed in the face of mass non-European immigration. While such notions may not have gained markedly more adherents in the 1930s, they did gain more exposure as growing numbers of Brazilians traveled to Asia. With the expansion of the industrial base came an internationally oriented cadre of business, military, and intellectual leaders and the growth of the urban middle class. This in turn led to an explosion of book reading, and between 1932 and 1938 the prestigious Companhia Editora Nacional's (CEN) output rose from 670,000 to about 3.5 million volumes.[37] As technological changes made transoceanic transportation cheaper and faster, travel books became increasingly popular.

In 1932 the CEN launched its Viagens (Voyages) series, produced to have an identical appearance to the prestigious Brasiliana collection. Volumes included everything from Monteiro Lobato's mocking comments on the United States to Caio Prado Júnior's adoring vision of the Soviet Union.[38] Six of the first fifteen volumes in Colecção Viagens were about Asia; three of them, on Shanghai, Japan, and the "Eastern Route," were written by Nelson Tabajara de Oliveira, a Vargas loyalist whose reward after the Revolution of 1930 was a posting to Shanghai as consul general. Tabajara fancied himself "a reporter," and saw his work in Asia as pure adventure. Within minutes of his arrival in Shanghai, he set out on a nocturnal adventure to a red-light district where prostitutes extended "courtesies only for foreigners."[39] Singapore was a "permanent carnival" filled with women of mixed Asian races who had "something original and strange that incites sinfulness."[40]

While Tabajara's book about Japan was written after "only two weeks of hurried tourism," the lack of wide experience was not an obstacle: "I have studied the history of Japan rigorously and thus arrived at the most just conclusions possible," noted the author. Yet even Tabajara recognized that his expectations of a wildly exotic Japan were not entirely reasonable. Upon leaving his hotel in Tokyo for the first time, he saw a crowd squatting in a circle. "At first sight I thought it must be a 'charmer' stimulating the cobras, or at least a juggler." What the diplomat found was a group of chrysanthemum growers preparing their plants.

Horticulture was far from Tabajara's main interest. A tram ride from Yokohama to Tokyo led to a visit to Yoshiwara, a traditional legal red-light district where the Brazilian was both stimulated and frightened. The experience allowed Tabajara to contrast the virtues of geishas as "life's delight" with "common prostitutes" who were content, if not happy. Women in traditional marriage relationships, however, played a different role. They were miserable sex slaves forced "to submit themselves, without having another God other than the husband."[41] Yet unhappy wives and "vulgar" hookers did not really bother the diplomat, who seemed happy to proclaim that in Japan, women were simply "inferior to men." Indeed, if Tabajara took anything from his short trip, it was "the certainty that men there enjoy a liberty that makes me jealous."[42]

Why this explicit tour of Japanese sexuality? Certainly the allure of the forbidden was at play, and Tabajara pouted that "Brazilian wives would [n]ever agree" to Japan's "wild" sexual mores.[43] Yet Tabajara's comments can also be read as a story of economic expansion without social modernization. Brazilian men, then, could move forward in one realm without fearing the other. What could not be allowed, however, was the entry of Japanese into Brazil. In a nod to eugenics the diplomat worried that the "150,000 Japanese who live in Brazil . . . influenced the cadence of our nationality" by being "natural parasites . . . who only aggravate economic difficulties [as do] the Syrians."[44] Sexuality and intense work habits were a dangerous cocktail, and the consul feared that within fifty years (i.e., by 1985) Brazil would contain one million Japanese and descendants, and that members of the "yellow race" would be sent from São Paulo to the federal House of Deputies.[45] Tabajara, of course, was correct on both counts.

While Tabajara's views of Japan and the Japanese were characteristic of his contemporaries, his conclusions were not. Members of Brazilian "study missions" in the 1930s tended to be very impressed, in part as a result of the Japanese government's decision to use gentle persuasion to keep immigration flowing in the wake of restrictions in the Constitution of 1934. Ernesto de Souza Campos, who visited with a group of his students at the São Paulo College of Medicine (Faculdade de Medicina de São Paulo), was typical. Souza Campos, a specialist in microbiology and immunology, contacted the Japanese consul general in São Paulo after meeting some exchange students. Both the diplomat and the Vargas regime jumped at the chance to "straighten the ties of friendship" bent by the rise of anti-Japanese sentiment.[46] Passages were paid jointly by the Kaigai Kogyo Kabushiki Kaisha (Japan's semiofficial Overseas Development Company) and through a special Brazilian government exchange rate to purchase dollars. Before they left Brazil, there was a going-away party at the Japanese consulate; upon their arrival in Yokohama, another gala was made more festive by the special edition of the *Tokyo Nichi-Nichi* that had been prepared in Campos's honor. The KKKK arranged the official schedule, and Brazil's ambassador was ever present. Within Japan lurked hopes for Brazil, and within the Brazilians was a future for Japanese immigrants.

Souza Campos's trip diary is a boring account filled with notations on who met whom, the numbers of patients examined, and the texts of medical regulations.[47] Yet the narrow arena of unique professional experience did not modify the more general view of Japan. A snow-covered Mount Fuji enticed readers to delve into the exotic land while other photographs focused on meetings with large groups of men or on buildings labeled "modern." A few photographs with titles like "Ancient Japan" or "Picturesque Japan" are of temples or women. What is striking is the comparison with Hong Kong and Ceylon, two other stops on the trip. In these sections the reader sees only the ancient and unchanging poverty that makes up so much of the "Orientalist" vision of Asia. Japan was not situated within the miserable "East"; it was extracted and placed in the West. Contrasting a modern male Japan with a mysterious ancient female one repeats a theme so ingrained that even those uninterested in preparing material for publication did it: a personal album of photographs taken and arranged by Antonio de Assumpção (the "Coffee King"), for example, follows exactly the same pattern.[48]

After the institution of the Estado Novo in late 1937, nativist groups (and all political parties) were banned. This gave President Getúlio Vargas new leeway in promoting Japan for its market potential and its authoritarian similarities to Brazil. Travel books portrayed similar images, and in the space of less than two years the Companhia Editora Nacional published two books on Japan and Editora Record produced another. Each sought to frame Brazilian-Japanese commercial relations (of which immigration was part) in a positive light and, while including the requisite comments on Japanese spirit and antiquity, focused on the modern. All presented fascism as a political system that would work for Brazil, and photographs of mass physical education and massive industrial production were common.[49]

When Brazil joined the Allies and broke relations with Japan, the positive images of the country and its people changed overnight. Rather than a nation to be admired for its industry, Japan became an "enemy," and travel literature reflected the change. The three books on Japan by José de Lima Figueirêdo illustrate the point. Lima Figueirêdo was a career military officer (in 1951, after his promotion to general following Vargas's return to power, he was elected a federal deputy from São Paulo) sent to observe the conflicts that emerged from Japan's establishment of the puppet state of Manchukuo in 1932. He remained military attaché in Japan until 1937, and upon his return to Brazil rose rapidly in the Estado Novo military, achieving the rank of colonel in 1944 and frequently publishing articles in the official monthly *Cultura Política*. In addition to his writings on Asia, Lima Figueirêdo authored ten books about Brazil. *No Japão foi assim* (In Japan It Was Like This, 1941) focused mainly on military and economic matters, and showed an admiration of Japan. It won first prize in a literary competition organized by the Instituto Brasileiro de Cultura Japonese.[50]

When Brazil declared war on Japan, so did Lima Figueirêdo. *O Japão por dentro* (Japan From Within, 1944) was pure propaganda, filled with "modern samurais [who] do not have nerves": they "cry because a beautiful flower loses its petals . . . [and] laugh at seeing a Chinese cut in half." The admirable Japanese culture explored in his earlier books disappeared; now Japan was "an immense barracks [where] the men are born to be soldiers."[51] Images from U.S. propaganda played an important role in Lima Figueirêdo's new vision. The "military spirit is something that the Nip acquires in the cradle," wrote the Brazilian, creating a new derogatory term (*nipão*) out of the English "Nip."[52] One chapter had an English-language title, "Spy Mania" (which was crossed out and translated into Portuguese in the copy that I used from the São Paulo Municipal Library).

What is striking about *O Japão por dentro* is how the shift in interpretations did not greatly modify the search for a Brazilian national identity that had defined travel literature from the early years of the century. Japan was as an "ethnic mélange of Ainus [whites], Malays [blacks] and Chinese, Manchus and Mongols [yellows]" who eventually became "perfectly equal" Japanese. The bracketed "racial" terms were, of course, those in use in Brazil. "Brancos" were European, "negróides" were African, and "amarelos" were indigenous.

While Lima Figueirêdo may have unconsciously seen Japan as a model, his conscious construction of it was as an enemy, and much of the negative portrayal revolved around women. Geishas were transformed from desirable sex objects into holders of secrets whose company was "forever prohibited" to foreigners who might discover the mysteries that lay at the heart of Japan. Women were born to be "mothers of soldiers," he wrote, and brides were sacrificed to the needs of the state in special schools where "all the dreams of a virgin are dedicated to an unknown man" who would use their wombs "to construct the economy of the Country of the Rising Sun."[53] Such notions had a direct impact on Brazil, now filled with "true [Japanese] racial cysts." The only hope was to stop Japanese immigration so that the docile women would be forced to marry Brazilian men.[54]

If Lima Figueirêdo presented a dangerous Japan, his contemporary Mário Botelho de Miranda sought to dig deeply into the local culture by turning Japanese. Botelho studied Japanese (as well as French, English, and Spanish) and helped found the Grêmio Cultural Brasileiro-Nipônico. While his language skills and leadership of the national Jujitsu League tied him to the immigrant and nikkei community, "I knew, in the end, a Japan in Brazil." Young Mário leaped at the opportunity to join a government-sponsored trip from the University of São Paulo in 1940. The other students left after two months, but Botelho remained in hopes of finding the Japan that "always hides itself from the eyes of tourists and official visitors." For three years he was employed by the Brazilian government, becoming fluent in Japanese and winning the 1941 Japanese Oratorical Contest for Foreigners. When Brazil and Japan ruptured diplomatic relations in 1942, he was repatriated. Soon after, he was appointed an official police translator during the Shindo Renmei investigations (see chapter 5).

The jacket of Botelho's *Um brasileiro no Japão em guerra* shows a drawing of a sword emblazoned with the ideograms for "Japan in Wartime" cutting through a serene scene of two geishas walking in front of Mount Fuji. This wildly provocative cover suggested Botelho's unique experience, the expected view of sexuality, and the new aggressive attitude toward Japan. The preface was written by Nelson Tabajara de Oliveira, who had met Botelho in the "famous Imperial Hotel" in Tokyo, and noticed the student's interest in Japan and his difference from his "rapid but noisy" colleagues. While Tabajara was impressed with Botelho the man, he was more cautious about Botelho's vision. Indeed, in the context of World War II, Tabajara repudiated his own "mistakes" about the "Japanese soul," warning that Botelho "rigorously identified" with the Japanese and that readers should "REMEMBER PEARL HARBOR." [55]

Botelho dismissed those (like Tabajara) who saw a Japan of geishas and samurais and who were seduced by notions of Japanese as "hardworking, organized and submissive." [56] His comments on his voyage aboard the *Brasil-Maru*, where Japanese residents of Latin America engaged in broken conversations with Jewish refugees, show Botelho to be an observer unlike many of his Brazilian compatriots. His perceptions of Japan were equally unique. A critique of the culture of alcohol consumption was transformed into a discussion of the nondrinking habits of women. An analysis of Japanese transportation focused on the women who worked in the sector as conductors and cashiers. [57] He condemned those authors who "exaggerated" the different roles women played because they were "indirect observers or hurried." If women appeared to be "slaves," Botelho cautioned, Western observers misunderstood the dynamics at play. The chapter on Yoshiwara questioned whether an absolute morality could be applied across cultures.

Perhaps the most telling vignette in *Um brasileiro no Japão em guerra* comes from a story that Botelho claimed he had overheard in a park. By suggesting the tale was accessible only to Japanese speakers (like himself), it allowed a quick glance into Japan's secret world, the same world that was presumed to exist among the immigrant community. The story, which superficially represents the Japan that Brazilians so despised, was turned into a nationalistic ritual that Brazilians should replicate.

> A candidate for political office, who urgently needed to raise thousands of yen for the expenses and deposits necessary for his campaign, "pawned" his wife in Yoshiwara. His supporters, who knew of this, worked with extra energy for his victory. After the victory, his friends took up a collection and paid for the rescission of the "contract," bringing the "pawn" home. The newspapers and popular sentiment judged them as heroes who had sacrificed for the country.[58]

Brazil was at war with Japan. But the Japanese were still the model for how to be Brazilian.

* * *

Botelho, like others before him, saw Japan through Brazilian eyes. Brazil and Japan could be enemies or friends. Travelers could be sex fiends or clerics. It made no difference to the final analysis. In Brazil was a human piece of Japan, and in Japan, Brazilians found hope. A lack of nationalist spirit could be changed overnight through the wombs of Japanese women whose children would become better Brazilians. The issues raised, however, did not end with the war. Between 1950 and 1990 more than fifty thousand Japanese immigrants settled in Brazil while two hundred thousand nikkei left to work in Japan. Negotiations over national identity were far from over.

7

A Suggestive Epilogue

Taxi driver: Where are you coming from?

Killer: São Paulo

Taxi driver: How's it going down there?

Killer: Same as always. Lots of rain, lots of Japanese

Taxi driver: [Laughs loudly]

—*From the film* Amor bandido, *set in Rio de Janeiro*[1]

. . . white in Brazil is difficult because in Brazil we are
all mestiços [of mixed race]. If you don't agree, then
look behind you. Look at our history. Our ancestors.
Colonial Brazil was not the same as Portugal. The
roots of my country were multiracial. There was
Indian, White, Yellow, Black. We were born a mix,
so why the prejudice?

—*Gabriel o Pensador (Gabriel the Thinker), from his 1993
rap hit "Lavagem cerebral" (Brainwashing)*[2]

Does Brazilian national identity include those of non-European descent? The answer is a qualified yes. Some immigrant groups were able to expand the narrow national paradigm of a "white" or "European" Brazil while others insisted, with some success, that "whiteness" was not a necessary component of Brazilian citizenship. All this took place within a context of often open prejudice and discrimination. How, then, do we interpret the evidence? Certainly it suggests that the apparently static elite discourse on national identity was cracked open. The give-and-take shows that elite discourses on race and ethnicity were surprisingly flexible under specific conditions. The expansion of national identity to include Syrian-Lebanese and nikkei allowed the Brazilian elite to enrich itself at the modest cost of the anger of some openly racist ideologues. Seth Garfield's recent work on the indigenous community in Brazil and Arnd Schneider's new approaches to understanding Argentine identity provide further support for this assertion.[3]

Ideology and policy changed in systematic and logical ways between 1850 and 1950, even as Brazil's political system and demographic composition were altered markedly. The temporal marks that I have imposed should not, however, imply that negotiations over the relationship between national identity and ethnicity ended in the immediate post-World War II era. In the mid-1950s theoreticians like Gilberto Freyre, surely reformulating old notions for the new post-Shoah era, hailed Brazil's "ethnic democracy," which ostensibly provided social spaces for minority cultures not found in the United States or Europe.[4] The rhetoric never led to the disappearance of popular or official prejudice, but it is worth noting that many in the nikkei and Syrian-Lebanese communities found success in the economic, political, military, and artistic arenas after 1945. Today Syrian-Lebanese and nikkei seem more part of the Brazilian nation than do the poor of Polish descent in Paraná.[5]

It was in the 1950s, just as hyphenated Brazilians established themselves in the middle and upper classes, that new immigrants from the Middle East and Asia began to enter in significant numbers. Palestinians, many of them Muslims, have generally been viewed in a negative light, and leaders of the Syrian-Lebanese community work hard to make distinctions between old and new Middle Easterners.[6] The U.S. occupation of Okinawa following World War II led almost fifty-four thousand small landowners and farmers to enter Brazil between 1952 and 1988, some 43 percent following relatives who had migrated prior to the war.[7] Older Japanese residents were shocked

by the new attitudes toward everything from the emperor to sexual relations. The newcomers were equally aghast: they had trouble understanding old dialects filled with Japanized Portuguese words, and wondered if
earlier immigrants had become "Brasil-bokē" (made nuts by Brazil).[8]

Along with Palestinians and Okinawans came tens of thousands of Chinese and Korean immigrants who were stunned to find that in Brazil they
had become "Japanese." There are no reliable statistics on the numbers
of Chinese in Brazil, but the Korean population stands at about one hundred thousand, living mainly in São Paulo. Many in both communities
work in the low-end clothing industry as producers, retailers, or both.[9] As
Korean and Chinese immigrants ascend the economic ladder, propelling
the social integration of their children through university educations, an
ugly joke has started to circulate among the São Paulo elite: "To get a place
at the University of São Paulo, you first have to kill a Japanese." Negotiations about what it means to be Brazilian are already under way for those
of Korean and Chinese descent.

If the new Middle Eastern and Asian immigration has challenged Brazilian national identity from the middle, the migration of millions of
Brazilians from the impoverished northeast of the country to cities in
the south has frightened members of the elite and middle classes from
below. While most *nordestinos* seem to represent Brazil's widely hailed
racial mixture, they are also the antithesis of the desirable "white" immigrant. In São Paulo, Northeasterners have been transformed from Brazilians into foreigners: the name of a bridge on the highway that runs past
the Central Bus Terminal is the "Northeastern Immigrants Bridge." "Brazil" is still a desirable destination, and national identity continues to be
negotiated.

* * *

To judge social place only by economic or political position is a dangerous
business. Public acceptance of hyphenated ethnicity remains contested in
Brazil, and the terms "árabe," "turco," and "japonês" continue to be applied to those of non-European descent whether they are prominent ministers or local bookstore owners. This is more noticeable for nikkei than
for Arab-Brazilians because physiognomy often allows instant categoriza-
tion. Many Arab-Brazilians simply change their names (or give "Brazilian"
names to their children), but a sense among nikkei that they can become Brazilian only by changing their appearance has led many women

to have plastic surgery on their eyes. A high level of interethnic marriage (almost 46 percent overall, and over 60 percent in some regions of the country) is also a fact of life in the nikkei community. Part of the explanation is the entry of the Japanese-Brazilian community into the middle class and above, decreasing the pool of partners for those unwilling to "marry down." Equally important is that many members of the majority have developed a model minority stereotype, making Japanese-Brazilians seem like especially good marriage partners. From the nikkei perspective, however, majority societal pressure to stop "being Japanese" is intense, a point the anthropologist Koichi Mori makes in his discussion of exogamy.[10] Popular language focuses on physiognomy, and a recent issue of the political magazine *Momento Legislativo* headlined a story on Japanese-Brazilian relations "Slanty-Eyed Brazil" and made constant references to "the Brazilian Japan." This language is also used within the nikkei community; a recent article in *Japão Aqui* (Japan Here), a glossy magazine with an initial circulation of about eighty thousand, used "Brazilian Japan" as the title for an article that combined the history of Japanese immigration with a sociological study of the nikkei community.[11]

Strategies like intermarriage and plastic surgery have divided the nikkei population. For the 340,000 "mestiços" in Brazil's population of over 1.2 million of Japanese descent, the use of multiple identities is common. Many nikkei mestiços reject their Japanese background when in social situations, yet in the economic sphere, whether it be in applying for a job or advertising sexual services, there is a belief that being "Japanese" provides an important advantage. For nonmestiço nikkei the situation is somewhat different. They are viewed as "Japanese," which is one important reason that some 135,000 (called *dekassegui*) currently live and work in Japan, along with 55,000 mestiço nikkei and nonnikkei spouses.[12] Since cultural identity is intimately tied to class status, wage differentials play an important role in this migration (almost two billion dollars was remitted officially in 1996, but the actual amount may be twice as high). Even so, oral histories given by dekassegui, most of whom work in factories although almost half have university educations, indicate that questions of identity are critical to the decision to leave Brazil for Japan. A thirty-seven-year-old university professor who migrated in 1991 is typical: "In Brazil I am a stranger even though I like Brazil. I feel like I do not have Brazilian nationality and I feel like a gypsy. I wanted to make myself the perfect Brazilian, but this is impossible. But here in Japan I also feel like a foreigner."[13]

Nikkei and nonnikkei seem to agree on this point, and terms like "remigration" and "return" are often applied to Brazilians moving to Japan for the first time.

In Japan dekassegui are treated as "Brazilians" whose role is to provide temporary labor and nothing more. This leads many nikkei to become Brazilian for the first time. Cultural patterns, such as wearing Brazilian-made Zoomp jeans rather than Levi's, are often used to express identity, and newspapers meant to serve the dekassegui community promote a stereotype of Brazil most often found outside the country. A color photo of a group of bikini-clad young nikkei women, both mestiço and not, was recently splashed across the front page of the Tokyo-based *Jornal Tudo Bem*. "A Guide to Guarantee Your Luck This Summer" reads the headline in a proud nod to the "Brazilianization" of Japan.[14] The phenomenon of becoming Brazilian abroad is, of course, nothing new. In the late nineteenth century, freed slaves returned to Nigeria, where they were known for their Brazilianized identities. Lebanese remigrants often insisted on speaking Portuguese to each other, changing Arabic street names to Brazilian ones, and even playing the Rio de Janeiro "animal game" on a daily basis.[15]

The question of how to maintain a hyphenated identity in a hesitant national culture is as present now as it was in the 1920s and 1930s. Pressure from majority society to become Brazilian is matched by an immigrant generation that complains that the sansei and yonsei generations have become "too Brazilian" (*Japão Aqui*, for example, includes a section on how to cook Japanese food in each issue). In the early 1980s the *Diário Nippak* newspaper began publishing a biweekly Portuguese-language supplement that sought to explore the history of Japanese immigration and "the duality of being Nippo-Brazilian." More recently *Japão Aqui* asked, as *Gakusei* had sixty years ago, "Who are we: Japanese or Brazilian?"[16] The Portuguese-language *Made in Japan* is produced in Tokyo for those "who understand Japan and Brazil," and a São Paulo weekly targeted to teenagers and produced by the primarily Japanese-language *Diário Nippak*, has articles about places for young nikkei to meet. One nineteen-year-old interviewed inside a nikkei dance club stated, "Here [inside the club] we feel at home, we are all from the same nation."[17] These sentiments would undoubtedly be echoed by the many young Afro-Brazilians who have made Afro-dance clubs a rage throughout Brazil.

A search for "home" is not the only nikkei reaction to the general Brazilian rejection of hyphenated identities. Another is the re-creation of

"Japan" as a means for selling oneself as Brazilian. The old notion that nikkei are "Japanese" (read "honest and hardworking"), and thus better "Brazilians" than nonnikkei "Brazilians" (read "corrupt and lazy"), has found its way into popular culture through an advertisement for the state-owned petroleum company in which a grinning and bowing nikkei sells "Brazilian" fuel to a group of hicks. The message is not subtle: Brazilian gas is good because it is "Japanese," and Brazilian country folk are in need of "Japanization" to become modern and stop retarding national growth. São Paulo's sanitation monopoly takes the same approach, proclaiming "Service so good you would think [the company] was founded by Japanese." The suggestion that Japanese ethnicity improves Brazilian national identity is equally noticeable in the political sphere, where nikkei use images of their ancestry as a tool for garnering votes. Luís Gushiken, a three-time federal deputy from the Worker's Party who was the campaign manager for Luís Ignacio Lula da Silva's unsuccessful presidential bid, provides the most striking example. Gushiken gets little support from the generally middle- and upper-class nikkei community because of his left-leaning politics and because he is a member of a well-known Okinawan (i.e., non-Japanese) family. While troubled by the fact that he is referred to as "Japanese" rather than as "Brazilian," Gushiken has deftly deployed "Japanese" symbolism in his recent political campaigns. His political propaganda uses everything from a rising sun, to photographs with Japanese diplomats, to faux Japanese-style lettering. By focusing on the "Japanese" virtues of hard work, honesty, and frugality, Gushiken has sold his ethnicity as making him a better Brazilian. This technique is common among Okinawan nikkei politicians, who believe that their cultural background has made them particularly successful in acculturating. Focusing on climatic and cultural similarities between Okinawa and Brazil, and a legacy of discrimination suffered at the hands of Japanese officials and immigrants, Okinawan nikkei insist that they are more "Brazilian" than any other immigrant group.[18] This, of course, is just the newest formulation of the strategies of inclusion recounted throughout this book.

*   *   *

It has always been deeply ironic that the immigration policies constructed to remake Brazil as "European" in fact created an immensely multicultural society. Thus I have tried to tell the story of a long, strange trip to a country where the rejection and inclusion of immigrant groups are both part of the search for "the spiritual integralization of Brazil." [19] I cannot help but be reminded of Greil Marcus's comment in *Lipstick Traces* that history is the result "of moments that seem to leave nothing behind, nothing but the spectral connections of people long separated by place and time, but somehow speaking the same language." [20] The connections here are indeed spectral: members of the literate national and immigrant elite, be they respected intellectuals or angry pamphlet writers, be they rural planters or urban industrialists, be they federal senators or local politicians, all engaged in great debates: Were Asians and Arabs white? Could Catholics become Muslims with the stroke of a pen? If Japanese and Arab immigrants and their descendants were descended biologically from Amazonian ancestors, were they more Brazilian than most members of the elite? In a land that is multicultural but hyphenless, negotiations over national identity continue.

Notes

Careful readers will note that the sources used for this book are in a multitude of languages. I would like to be fluent in them all, but I am not. In the case of Japanese newspapers, I have used the official Brazilian translations of articles provided by the Itamaraty and have checked them with specialists. Other translations from Japanese have been provided by generous colleagues who are thanked in the endnotes. In the case of Arabic, I have used the translations as published in the works themselves. Translations from French, German, Italian, Portuguese, and Spanish, I have done myself. I have also modernized all Portuguese spellings in the text and notes, except for book titles. Any exceptions to this rule are noted.

Preface

1 Report on Escola General Trompowsky, 1935. Anisio Teixeira Papers, AT pi 35.00.00, Escola General Trompowsky. Centro de Pesquisa e Documentação de História Contemporânea do Brasil, Fundação Getúlio Vargas, Rio de Janeiro [hereafter CPDOC-R]. My thanks to Jerry Davila for sharing this document with me.

1 The Hidden Hypen

1 *Jornal do Imigrante* (São Paulo) 4:422 (September 1981), p. 2. The *Jornal do Imigrante*, a small weekly newspaper aimed at the descendants of European immigrants, generally contained stories about events connected to maintaining premigratory culture or celebrating immigrant culture in Brazil.

2 Ethnically oriented magazines have become quite numerous in Brazil. Other recently introduced titles are *Raça, Made in Japan, Tomodaty Jovem,* and *Shiawase.*

3 Liner notes to *Nissei/Sansei* (São Paulo: Comercial Fonográfica RGE, 1996); Roney Cytrynowicz, ed., *Renascença 75 anos: 1922-1997* (São Paulo: Sociedade Hebraico-

Brasileira Renascença, 1997). Sertanejo music ostensibly emerges out of life on the *sertão* (backlands).

4 Zygmunt Bauman, *Modernity and Ambivalence* (Ithaca, NY: Cornell University Press, 1991), p. 59.

5 Eric Hobsbawm, "Peasants and Politics," *Journal of Peasant Studies* 1:1 (1973), 4; Philip Corrigan and Derek Sayer, *The Great Arch: English State Formation as Cultural Revolution* (Oxford: Oxford University Press, 1985), pp. 4–5. On the creation of new transnational cultures, see Homi K. Bhabha, *The Location of Culture* (London: Routledge, 1994), pp. 86–89. For the "between cultures" position, see Gloria Anzaldúa, *Borderland/La Frontera: The New Mestiza* (San Francisco: Spinsters/aunt lute, 1987); or the essays in Alfred Arteaga, ed., *An Other Tongue: Nation and Ethnicity in the Linguistic Borderlands* (Durham, N.C.: Duke University Press, 1994). For a discussion of how marginalized individuals negotiate their own positions, see Leo Spitzer, *Lives in Between: Assimilation and Marginality in Austria, Brazil, West Africa, 1780–1945* (Cambridge: Cambridge University Press, 1989).

6 Simon Schwartzman, Helena Maria Bousquet Bomeny, and Vanda Maria Ribeiro Costa, *Tempos de Capanema* (Rio de Janeiro: Paz e Terra, 1984), p. 146; Roberto Schwarz, "Brazilian Culture: Nationalism by Elimination," *New Left Review* 167 (January/February 1988), 77–90. The latter essay appears in Portuguese in Schwarz's *Que horas são* (São Paulo: Companhia das Letras, 1987), pp. 29–48.

7 Nancy Leys Stepan, *"The Hour of Eugenics": Race, Gender and Nation in Latin America* (Ithaca, NY: Cornell University Press, 1991); Oswaldo Frota-Pessoa, "Raça e eugenia," in Lilia Moritz Schwarz and Renato da Silva Queiroz, eds., *Raça e diversidade* (São Paulo: EDUSP/Estação Ciência, 1996), pp. 29–46.

8 Sílvio Romero, *O allemanismo no sul do Brasil, seus perigos e meios de os conjurar* (Rio de Janeiro: H. Ribeiro & Co., 1906).

9 Matthew Frye Jacobson, *Special Sorrows: The Diasporic Imagination of Irish, Polish and Jewish Immigrants in the United States* (Cambridge, MA: Harvard University Press, 1995); David Sorkin, *The Transformation of German Jewry, 1780–1840* (New York: Oxford University Press, 1987), pp. 6–7.

10 James C. Scott, *Domination and the Arts of Resistance: Hidden Transcripts* (New Haven: Yale University Press, 1990), and *Weapons of the Weak: Everyday Forms of Peasant Resistance* (New Haven: Yale University Press, 1985); Catriona Kelly and Patrick Joyce, "History and Post-Modernism II," *Past and Present* 133 (November 1991), 209–213.

11 "Campeonato sul-americano—ligeiras considerações," *O Estado de S. Paulo*, 30 May 1919, p. 3; Nelson Rodrigues, "A realeza do Pelé," *Manchete Esportiva*, 8 March 1958, repr. in Nelson Rodrigues, *O melhor do romance, contos e crônicas* (São Paulo: Companhia da Letras, 1993), pp. 117–119. The game, between Santos and América, took place on 25 February 1958, with the victory going to Santos, 5–3. For a broad discussion of the growth of sport, and its relationship to social Darwinist thought, see Nicolau Sevcenko, *Orfeu extático na metrópole: São Paulo sociedade e cultura nos frementes anos 20* (São Paulo: Companhia das Letras, 1992), pp. 42–72.

12 Lyle N. McAlister, *Spain and Portugal in the New World, 1492-1700* (Minneapolis: University of Minnesota Press, 1984), p. 53.

13 Johann Friedrich Blumenbach, *On the Natural Varieties of Mankind: De Generis Humani Varietate Nativa* [1775-1776] (New York: Bergman, 1969), p. 269; Stephen Jay Gould, "The Geometer of Race," *Discover* 15:11 (November 1994), 66.

14 *Novo Michaelis dicionário ilustrado*, vol. 2, *Português-inglês*, 10th ed. (São Paulo: Edições Melhoramentos, 1972), p. 1038.

15 João Cardoso de Menezes e Souza, *Theses sobre colonização do Brazil: Projecto de solução as questões sociaes, que se prendem à este difícil problema* (Rio de Janeiro: Typografia Nacional, 1875), pp. 403, 426. On elite discourse on immigration in Argentina, see Carl Solberg, *Immigration and Nationalism, Argentina and Chile, 1890-1914* (Austin: University of Texas Press, 1970).

16 Sílvio Romero, *História da literatura brasileira* [1888], vol. 1, 2nd ed., 2 vols. (Rio de Janeiro: H Garnier, 1902-1903), p. 67.

17 Edgard Roquette-Pinto, *Ensaios de antropologia brasiliana*, Série Brasiliana 22 (São Paulo: Companhia Editora Nacional, 1936), p. 20; João Baptista Borges Pereira, "Os estudos sobre imigração na antropologia brasileira," *Iberoamericana* (Tokyo) 14:1 (1992), 37-41.

18 Marcos Chor Maio and Ricardo Ventura Santos, eds., *Raça, ciência e sociedade* (Rio de Janeiro: FIOCRUZ/CCBB, 1996), esp. "O Brasil como 'laboratório racial,'" pp. 141-203; Newton Freire-Maia, *Brasil: Laboratório racial* [1973], 7th ed. (Petrópolis: Vozes, 1985); W. D. Borrie, ed., *The Cultural Integration of Immigrants: A Survey Based upon the Papers and Proceeding of the Unesco Conference Held in Havana, April 1956* (New York: UNESCO, 1957).

19 This represents about 15 percent of all immigrants entering in this period. Maria Stella Ferreira Levy, "O papel da migração internacional na evolução da população brasileira (1872 a 1972)," *Revista de Saúde Pública* suppl., 8 (1974), 49-90; "Discriminação por nacionalidade dos imigrantes entrando no Brasil no período 1884-1939," *Revista de Imigração e Colonização* [hereafter RIC] 1:3 (July 1940), 617-638.

20 Jay O'Brien, "Towards a Reconstitution of Ethnicity: Capitalist Expansion and Cultural Dynamics in Sudan," in Jay O'Brien and William Roseberry, eds., *Golden Ages, Dark Ages: Imagining the Past in Anthropology and History* (Berkeley: University of California Press, 1991), p. 126. Anthony Cohen, "Culture as Identity: An Anthropologist's View," *New Literary History* 24:1 (Winter 1993), 195-209; Thomas C. Holt, "Marking: Race, Race-making, and the Writing of History," *American Historical Review* 100:1 (February 1995), 1-20.

21 A number of scholars take a contrary approach, arguing that immigrant ethnicity is structurally defined by premigratory culture: Richard T. Schaefer, *Racial and Ethnic Groups*, 4th ed. (Glenview, IL: Scott, Foresman/Little, Brown Higher Education, 1990), pp. 9-12; Michael Novak, "The New Ethnicity," in John A. Kromkowski, ed., *Race and Ethnic Relations 94/95* (Guilford, CT: Dushkin Publishing Group, 1994), p. 169.

22   José Vasconcellos, *The Cosmic Race: A Bilingual Edition* [1925], trans. and anno-
     tated by Didier T. Jaén (Baltimore: Johns Hopkins University Press, 1997).

23   Evelyn Hu-DeHart, "Racism and Anti-Chinese Persecution in Sonora, Mexico,
     1876–1932," *Amerasia* 9:2 (Fall/Winter 1982), 1–28; Alicia Gojman de Backal, "Mi-
     norías, estado y movimientos nacionalistas de la clase media en México: Liga
     Anti-China y Anti-Judia (siglo XX)," in AMILAT, ed., *Judaica latinoamericana: Es-
     tudios histórico-sociales* (Jerusalem: Editorial Universitaria Magnes, Universidad
     Hebrea, 1988), pp. 174–191.

24   Anita Novinsky, *Cristãos novos na Bahia* (São Paulo: Editora Perspectiva, 1972);
     Arnold Wiznitzer, *Jews in Colonial Brazil* (New York: Columbia University Press,
     1960).

25   E. Constantine Phipps, *Report by Mr. Phipps on Emigration to Brazil. Presented to
     Both Houses of Parliament by Command of Her Majesty, June 1872* (London: Har-
     rison and Sons, 1872), p. 26.

26   Decree Law 528, 28 June 1890, art. 1. See also Jeffrey Lesser, "Are African-Ameri-
     cans African or American? Brazilian Immigration Policy in the 1920's," *Review of
     Latin American Studies* 4:1 (1991), 115–137.

27   Verena Stolcke, "Sexo está para gênero assim como raça para etnicidade?" *Estudos
     Afro-Asiáticos* 20 (June 1991), 118; Antônio Baptista Pereira, *O Brasil e a raça: Con-
     ferência feita na faculdade de direito de São Paulo a 19 de junho de 1928* (São Paulo:
     Empresa Gráfica Rossetti, 1928), p. 129.

28   Pará, *Dados estatísticos e informações para os immigrantes* (Belém do Pará: Typ.
     Diário de Notícias, 1866), pp. 177, 180; *Gazeta de Notícias* (Rio de Janeiro), 29 Sep-
     tember 1935, p. 1; Mario de Sampaio Ferraz, *Cruzar e nacionalizar* [1937], 2nd ed.
     (São Paulo: Typ. Brasil Rothschild Loureiro, 1939), p. 8.

29   I have intentionally used the asymmetrical African (black)/White (European)
     continuum because it represents quite faithfully the traditional ideas and lan-
     guage of race in Brazil. Affonso Arinos de Mello Franco, *Conceito de civilização bra-
     sileira,* Serie Brasiliana 70 (São Paulo: Companhia Editora Nacional, 1936), p. 100;
     Nina Rodrigues, *As raças humanas e a responsibilidade penal no Brasil* [1894], 3rd
     ed., Série Brasiliana 110 (São Paulo: Companhia Editora Nacional, 1938), pp. 117,
     118, 122. Charles Wagley and Marvin Harris's classic *Minorities in the New World*
     (London: Oxford University Press, 1958) is also organized along "Indian/Negro/
     European" lines. A small group of Brazilian scholars have been breaking new
     ground by looking at Afro-Brazilian ethnicity. See Regina Pahim Pinto, "Movi-
     mento negro e etnicidade," *Estudos Afro-Asiáticos* 19 (1990), 109–124; Ilka Boa-
     ventura Leite, "Invisibilidade étnica e identidade: Negros em Santa Catarina,"
     Encontros com a Antropologia (Curitiba) (May 1993), 63–71.

30   George Reid Andrews, *Blacks and Whites in São Paulo, Brazil, 1888–1988* (Madison:
     University of Wisconsin Press, 1991), p. 56. Similar assumptions can be found
     in Robert Stam, *Tropical Multiculturalism: A Comparative History of Race in Brazil-
     ian Cinema and Culture* (Durham, N.C.: Duke University Press, 1998), p. 76; and
     Thomas H. Holloway, *Policing Rio de Janeiro: Repression and Resistance in a 19th-
     Century City* (Stanford: Stanford University Press, 1993), p. 209. In the classic

Raças e classes socias no Brasil, 2nd ed. (Rio de Janeiro: Editora Civilização Brasileira, 1972), Octávio Ianni simply ignores Asians and Arabs.

31 Roger Bastide and Florestan Fernandes, *Brancos e negros em São Paulo: Ensaio sociológico sobre aspectos da formação, manifestações atuais e efeitos do preconceito de cor na sociedade paulistana,* 2nd ed. (São Paulo: Companhia Editora Nacional 1959); Thomas Skidmore, *Black into White: Race and Nationality in Brazilian Thought* (New York: Oxford University Press, 1974); Carl Degler, *Neither Black nor White: Slavery and Race Relations in Brazil and the United States* (New York: Macmillan, 1971); Lilia Moritz Schwarcz, *Retrato em branco e negro: Jornais, escravos e cidadãos em São Paulo no final do século XIX* (São Paulo: Companhia das Letras, 1987); Célia Maria Marinho de Azevedo, *Onda negra, medo branco: O negro no imaginário das elites século XIX* (Rio de Janeiro: Paz e Terra, 1987); Andrews, *Blacks and Whites.* Other well-known studies that take the "triangle" or "black/white" approach are Carlos A. Hasenbalg, *Discriminação e disigualdades racias no Brasil* (Rio de Janeiro: Graal, 1979); Lilia Moritz Schwarcz, *O espetáculo das raças: Cientistas, instituições e questão racial no Brasil, 1870-1930* (São Paulo: Companhia das Letras, 1993); Dain Borges, " 'Puffy, Ugly, Slothful and Inert': Degeneration in Brazilian Social Thought, 1880-1940," *Journal of Latin American Studies* 25 (1993), 235-256.

32 Luiz Peixoto de Lacerda Werneck, for example, argued that the Protestant German "character" was better for Brazil than the Catholic Irish "character." *Idéias sobre colonização precedidas de uma sucinta exposição dos princípios geraes que regem a população* (Rio: Eduardo e Henrique Laemmert, 1855), p. 101. Johann Moritz Rugendas made careful distinctions between different African slave groups in the lithographs in his *Malerische Reise in Brasilien von Moritz Rugendas* (Paris: Engelmann, 1835), published in Portuguese as João Maurício Rugendas, *Viagem pitoresca através do Brasil,* 7th ed., trans. by Sérgio Milliet (São Paulo: Livraria Martins Editora, 1976). A modern examination of African ethnicity in Brazil is in João José Reis, *A morte e uma festa: Ritos fúnebres e revolta popular no Brasil do século XIX* (São Paulo: Companhia das Letras, 1991). See also Reis's *Slave Rebellion in Brazil: The Muslim Uprising of 1835 in Bahia,* trans. by Arthur Brakel (Baltimore: Johns Hopkins University Press, 1993), p. 113; and Barbara J. Fields, "Ideology and Race in American History," in J. Morgan Kousser and James M. McPherson, eds., *Region, Race, and Reconstruction: Essays in Honors of C. Vann Woodward* (New York: Oxford University Press, 1982), p. 144.

2   Chinese Labor and the Debate over Ethnic Integration

1 Eça de Queiroz, *O mandarim* (Pôrto: Lello e Irmão, n.d.), pp. 89-90. English version from *The Mandarin and Other Stories,* trans. Richard Franko Goldman (Athens: Ohio University Press, 1964), p. 51.

2 José de Souza Pereira de Cruz Júnior, "As raças, os sexos e as idades imprimen caracteres reaes na cabeça ossa? Quaes são elles e no que consistem," pages 15-16 of thesis presented to the Faculdade de Medicina do Rio de Janeiro, 15 Septem-

ber 1874, Teses do Rio, 1857, J–V #6, vol. 2, Academia Nacional de Medicina, Rio de Janeiro; Johann Friedrich Blumenbach, *On the Natural Varieties of Mankind: De Generis Humani Varietate Nativa* (New York: Bergman, 1969), p. 273.

3 Recent scientific discussions have dismissed race as a genotypic or phenotypic concept that can be applied widely, and contemporary divisions often propose grouping people by whether they have antimalarial genes or lactase. Albert Weissman, "'Race-Ethnicity': A Dubious Scientific Concept," *Public Health Reports* 105:1 (January–February 1990), 102–103; Jared Diamond, "Race Without Color," *Discover* 15:11 (November 1994), 83–89; L. Luca Cavalli-Sforza, Paolo Menozzi, and Alberto Piazza, *The History and Geography of Human Genes* (Princeton: Princeton University Press, 1994).

4 Brazil, *Annaes do Parlamento brasileiro, Câmara dos srs. deputados—sessão de 1828* (Rio de Janeiro: Typ. Parlamentar, 1876), vol. 2, session of 28 June 1828, p. 62; Brazil, *Annaes do Parlamento brasileiro, Câmara dos srs. deputados—sessão de 1831* (Rio de Janeiro: Typ. H. J. Pinto, 1878), vol. 1, session of 3 June 1831, p. 123; José Honorio Rodrigues, "Brasil e Extremo Oriente," *Política Externa Independente* 2 (August 1965): 61–64.

5 Joaquim Pedro Oliveira Martins, *O Brazil e as colônias portuguezas* [1880], 4th ed. (Lisbon: Parceria Antonio Maria Pereira, 1904), pp. 148, 151.

6 See, for example, letter of Augusto Decosterd, Swiss consul in Bahia, to Sociedade Suiça para o Bem Commun, 23 July 1843, repr. in Visconde de Abrantes, *Memória sobre meios de promover a colonisação* (Berlin: Typ. de Unger Irmãos, 1846), pp. 45–54; and Arthur de Gobineau, "Emigrations actuelles des allemands," *Revue Nouvelle* (Paris) 2 (March 1845), 41. See also Francisco Augusto de Carvalho, *O Brazil, colonização e emigração—Esboço histórico baseado no estudo dos systemas e vantagens que offerecem os Estados Unidos*, 2nd ed. (Pôrto: Imprensa Portugueza, 1876), p. 191.

7 Antonio Galvão, *The Discoveries of the World, from Their First Original unto the Year of Our Lord, 1555* [1555], ed. and trans. Admiral Bethune (London: Hakluyt Society, 1862), p. 19; Pero de Magalhães, *The Histories of Brasil* [1570s?], John B. Stetson, trans. 2 vols. (New York: Cortés Society, 1922), vol. 2, p. 83.

8 Doris Sommer, *Foundational Fictions: The National Romances of Latin America* (Berkeley: University of California Press, 1991), pp. 138–139; Johann Moritz Rugendas, *Viagem pitoresca através do Brasil*, p. 50; James Silk Buckingham, *The Slave States of America*, vol. 1 (London: Fisher, Son, 1842), p. 433; Eugene Ridings, *Business Interest Groups in Nineteenth-Century Brazil* (Cambridge: Cambridge University Press, 1994), p. 174.

9 João Rodrigues de Brito, *Cartas econômico-políticas sobre a agricultura, e commércio da Bahia* (Lisbon: Imprensa Nacional, 1821), p. 35.

10 Luiz Gonçalves dos Santos (Padre Perereca), *Memória para servir a história do reino do Brasil* [1825] (Rio de Janeiro: Zelio Valverde, 1943), vol. 1, p. 331, and vol. 2, pp. 651–652.

11 Wilhelm Ludwig von Eschwege, *Pluto brasiliensis*, trans. Domício de Figueiredo Murta (Belo Horizonte: Ed. Itatiaia; São Paulo: Ed. da Universidade de São Paulo,

1979), vol. 2, p. 267; originally published as *Pluto brasiliensis: Eine Reihe von Abhandlungen über Brasiliens gold-, diamanten- und anderen mineralischen Reichthum, über die Geschichte seiner Entdeckung, uber das Vorkommen seiner Lagerstatten, des Betriebs* (Berlin: G. Reimer, 1833). See also John Luccock, *Notes on Rio de Janeiro and the Southern Parts of Brazil: Taken During a Residence of Ten Years in That Country from 1808 to 1818* (London: Samuel Leigh, in the Strand, 1820), published in Portuguese as *Notas sobre o Rio de Janeiro e partes meridionais do Brasil*, trans. Milton da Silva Rodrigues, foreword by Mário Guimarães Ferri (Belo Horizonte: Ed. Itatiaia; São Paulo: Ed. da Universidade de São Paulo, 1975); Daniel P. Kidder, *Sketches of Residence and Travels in Brazil Embracing Historical and Geographical Notices of the Empire and Its Several Provinces*, 2 vols. (Philadelphia: Sorin and Ball; London: Wiley and Putnam, 1845), vol. 1, p. 251; Harley Farnsworth MacNair, *The Chinese Abroad: Their Position and Protection: A Study in International Law and Relations* (Shanghai: Commercial Press, 1924), p. 96; Maria José Elias, "Introdução ao estudo da imigração chinesa," *Anais do Museu Paulista* 24 (1970), 60; Lynn Pann, *Sons of the Yellow Emperor: A History of the Chinese Diaspora* (Boston: Little, Brown, 1990), p. 67.

12   Brazil, Ministério da Justiça e Negócios Interiores, *Registro de estrangeiros, 1808–1822* (Rio de Janeiro: Arquivo Nacional, 1960), p. 80; José Honório Rodrigues, "Nota liminar," ibid., p. 8; José Paulo de Figueirôa Nabuco Araújo, *Legislação brazileira ou Collecção chronológica das leis, decretos, resoluções de consulta, provisões, etc., etc., no império do Brazil, desde o anno de 1808 até 1831 inclusive, contendo: Além do que se acha publicado nas melhores collecções para mais de duas mil peças inéditas, coligidas pelo conselheiro José Paulo de Figueirôa Nabuco Araújo*, 7 vol. (Rio de Janeiro: Typ. Imp. e Const. de J. Villeneuve 1836–1844), "Aviso de 15 de julho," vol. 2 (1837), p. 149; Francisco Adolfo de Varnhagen, *História geral do Brasil antes da sua separação e independência de Portugal*, ed. Rodolfo Garcia, 3rd ed., 5 vols. (São Paulo: Companhia Melhoramentos, 1936), vol. 5, p. 111, n. 34.

13   Eschwege, *Pluto brasiliensis*, vol. 2, p. 267; Richard Darwin, ed., *Charles Darwin's Beagle Diary* (Cambridge: Cambridge University Press, 1988), pp. 67–68; Luccock, *Notes on Rio de Janeiro*, p. 288. A critique of Chinese tea cultivation can also be found in MacNair, *The Chinese Abroad*, p. 96.

14   Frank Dikötter, *The Discourse of Race in Modern China* (Stanford: Stanford University Press, 1992), pp. 50, 148.

15   Neill Macaulay, *Dom Pedro: The Struggle for Liberty in Brazil and Portugal, 1798–1834* (Durham, N.C.: Duke University Press, 1986), p. 68; Warren Dean, *With Broadaxe and Firebrand: The Destruction of the Brazilian Atlantic Forest* (Berkeley: University of California Press, 1995), p. 172.

16   Rugendas, *Viagem pitoresca*, pp. 122–123; Kidder, *Sketches*, vol. 1, pp. 250–253; José Arouche de Toledo Rondon, "Pequena memória de plantação e cultura do chá," *Auxiliador da indústria nacional* 2 (May 1834), 145–152; 2 (June 1834), 179–184.

17   Letter signed by fifty Chinese laborers on the Fazenda Real to Dom Pedro I, 6 September 1819, Manuscript Collection—General Collection, II 34.27.4, Biblioteca

Nacional, Rio de Janeiro [hereafter BN-R]. All the workers signed both the names they had taken (or had been forced to take) in Brazil (Manuel, Joaquim, Antonio, Luis, José) and their Chinese names in characters.

18 "Parecer sobre a colonização chinesa no Brasil. Sala das sessões do Conselho do estado dos negócios estrangeiros," Rio de Janeiro, 30 May 1846, Manuscript Collection—Colecção Afro-Asiática, I-48, 20, 28, BN-R; *Rio News,* 5 October 1879.

19 Decree 668A, 1 February 1850, in *Collecção das leis do império do Brasil de 1850,* vol. 13, parte 2, sec. 1 (Rio de Janeiro: Typ. Nacional, 1851), pp. 17a, 17b; Brazil, *Annaes do Senado do império do Brasil, 2a sessão da 16a legislatura no mez de setembro de 1877,* vol. 4 (Rio de Janeiro: Typ. do Diário do Rio de Janeiro, 1877), session of 18 September, p. 194; José Pedro Xavier Pinheiro, *Importação de trabalhadores chins: Memória apresentada ao ministério da agricultura, comércio e obras públicas e imprensa por sua ordem* (Rio de Janeiro: Typ. de João Ignacio da Silva, 1869), pp. 35, 49; George P. Browne, "Government Immigration Policy in Imperial Brazil, 1822–1870" (Ph.D. thesis, Catholic University of America, 1972), p. 255.

20 Pinheiro, *Importação de trabalhadores chins,* pp. 45–46; Luis Millones Santagadea, *Minorías étnicas en el Perú* (Lima: Pontificia Universidad Católica del Perú, 1973), pp. 62–87.

21 Sérgio F. de Maceda, "Memória sobre a emigração chinesa e sobre o que se sabe dos resultados em vários paizes" (1855), Código 807, vol. 16, pp. 561–562, Arquivo Nacional, Rio de Janeiro [hereafter AN-R].

22 Cited in Pinheiro, *Importação de trabalhadores chins,* p. 20.

23 Adadus Calpe (pseudonym for Antônio Deodoro de Pascual), "Breves consideraciones sobre colonización por Adadus Calpe" (7 September 1855), código 807, vol. 16, pp. 480 (8)–481 (9), AN-R.

24 Emília Viotti da Costa, *The Brazilian Empire: Myths and Histories* (Belmont, CA: Wadsworth, 1988), p. 97. Luiz Peixoto de Lacerda Werneck was the son of Baron Paty Alferes, Francisco Peixoto de Lacerda Werneck (1795–1861). He should not be confused with Francisco's other son, the ardently pro-Chinese Manoel Peixoto de Lacerda Werneck.

25 The editorials were collected and published in book form as Luiz Peixoto de Lacerda Werneck, *Idéias sobre colonização precedidas de uma succinta exposição dos princípios geraes que regem a população* (Rio de Janeiro: Eduardo e Henrique Laemmert, 1855).

26 Ibid., pp. 14, 28, 98.

27 Ibid., p. 77.

28 Ibid., p. 78.

29 Fábio A. de Carvalho Reis, *Breves considerações sobre a nossa lavoura* (São Luiz: Typ. do Progesso, 1856), p. 22.

30 Brazil, *Annaes da Assembléia legislativa provincial da Bahia, sessões do anno de 1876* (Bahia: Typ. do Correio da Bahia, 1876), 8th ordinary session, 9 May 1876, p. 45. I would like to thank Dr. Dale Graden (University of Idaho) for his generosity and collegeality in sharing his research with me. Cruz Júnior, "As raças, os sexos e as idades imprimen caracteres reaes na cabeça ossa?," p. 20.

31   Joaquim da Silva Rocha, *História da colonização do Brasil, organizado por Joaquim da Silva Rocha, chefe de secção da directoria do serviço de povo-amento*, 3 vols. (Rio de Janeiro: Imprensa Nacional, 1919), vol. 1, p. 86. A discussion of the ideas Rocha presents can be found in Giralda Seyferth, "Construindo a nação: Hierarquias raciais e o papel do racismo na política de imigração e colonização," in Marcos Chor Maio and Ricardo Ventura Santos, eds., *Raça, ciência e sociedade* (Rio de Janeiro: FIOCRUZ/CCBB, 1996), pp. 41–58.

32   Sociedade Auxiliadora da Indústria Nacional, *Discurso pronunciado pelo Dr. I. J. Galvão na sessão de 3 de outubro de 1870 (questão dos chins)* (Rio de Janeiro: Typ. Universal de Laemmert, 1870), p. 23. Pinheiro's *Importação de trabalhadores chins*, pp. 36 and 60, erroneously gives the date as 1866. This error was repeated in José Honório Rodrigues, "Brasil e Extremo Oriente," p. 66, and in Robert Conrad, "The Planter Class and the Debate over Chinese Immigration to Brazil, 1850–1893," *International Migration Review* 9:1 (Spring 1975): 42. See also "Memorandum em que são expostas as vistas do governo imperial à respeito da colonização e imigração para o Brasil," Código 807, vol. 19, p. 275 (16), AN-R; Manoel Felizardo de Sousa e Melo, "Relatório da repartição geral das terras públicas," appendix to Luís Pedreira do Couto Ferraz, *Relatório apresentado à Assembléia geral legislativa na quarta sessão da nona legislatura pelo ministro e secretário d'estado dos negócios do império* (Rio de Janeiro: Typ. Nacional, 1856), pp. 20–21, 91–92; Souza e Melo, quoted in Pinheiro, *Importação de trabalhadores chins*, p. 59.

33   Baron Circal (consul of Brazil in Macao) to Ministro Secretário do Estado dos Negócios Estrangeiros (Rio de Janeiro), 10 January 1856, 02—Repartições Consulares Brasileiras—Macao—Ofícios, 1850–1896, 252/4/6, AHI-R; Brazil, *Annaes do Parlamento brazileiro, Câmara dos srs. deputados, 1868*, vol. 3 (Rio de Janeiro: Typ. do Diário do Rio de Janeiro, 1868), p. 65; Sociedade Auxiliadora da Indústria Nacional, *Discurso pronunciado pelo Dr. I. J. Galvão*, p. 25; Agostinho Marques Perdigão Malheiro, *A escravidão no Brasil: Ensaio histórico-jurídico-social*, Parte 3— *Africanos* (Rio de Janeiro: Typ. Nacional, 1867), pp. 182, 192. Many of Malheiro's comments on the Chinese were simply regurgitations of Werneck's earlier ideas.

34   See, for example, the Nantes newspaper *Phare de la Loire*, 10 August 1866; letter from the London Anti-Slavery Society to Tavares Bastos of 8 May 1865, cited in *Jornal do Comércio* (Rio de Janeiro), 16 August 1865; Richard Graham, *Patronage and Politics in Nineteenth-Century Brazil* (Stanford: Stanford University Press, 1990), p. 190.

35   Aureliano Candido Tavares Bastos, *O valle do Amazonas: A livre navegação do Amazonas, estatística, producções, commércio, questões fiscaes do valle do Amazonas*, 2nd ed., Serie Brasiliana 106 (São Paulo: Comp. Editora Nacional, 1937), p. 364; Carlos Pontes, *Tavares Bastos (Aureliano Candido), 1839–1875*, Serie Brasiliana 136 (São Paulo: Comp. Editora Nacional, 1939), p. 242. Viotti da Costa, *The Brazilian Empire*, p. 7.

36   A. C. (Aureliano Candido) Tavares Bastos, "Memória sobre immigração" in his *Os males do presente e as esperanças do futuro (Estudos Brasileiros)*, Serie Brasiliana 151 (São Paulo: Comp. Editora Nacional, 1939), p. 104. Originally presented on

16 February 1867 as "Memória apresentada à Sociedade international da immigração." The 1867 Annual Report was republished in the *Jornal do Comércio* (Rio de Janeiro), 22 March 1867.

37 Tavares Bastos, *Os males do presente*, pp. 8, 11.

38 Letter XVII of "Solitário" to *Correio Mercantil*, 22 March 1862, Letter XVIII, 23 March 1862, and Letter XXI, 27 March 1862, in Aureliano Candido Tavares Bastos, *Cartas do Solitário ao redactor do Correio Mercantil: Liberdade de cabotagem— Abertura do Amazonas; Communicações com os Estados Unidos* (Rio de Janeiro: Typ. do Correio Mercantil, 1862), pp. 117, 124; *New York Times*, 14 August 1863; Tavares Bastos, *O valle do Amazonas*, pp. 377-379. Aureliano Candido Tavares Bastos, "Notas sobre questões de imigração," unpublished notebook (1867), Manuscript Collection—Colecção Tavares Bastos, 13.1.7, vol. 1, BN-R.

39 Letter of Tavares Bastos published in *Reforma* (Rio de Janeiro), 10 December 1869; letter of Tavares Bastos published in *Correio Paulistano* (São Paulo), 11 June 1871; Tavares Bastos, *A provincia: Estudo sobre a descentralisação no Brasil* [1870], 2nd ed., Serie Brasiliana 105 (São Paulo: Companhia Editora Nacional, 1937), pp. 276-277; Oscar Tenório, "As idéais de Tavares Bastos sobre a imigração," *RIC* 4:3 (September 1943), 395-404.

40 Quintino Bocayuva, *A crise da lavoura: Succinta exposição por Q. Bocayuva* (Rio de Janeiro: Typ. Perseverança, 1868), pp. 39, 43.

41 Ibid., pp. 9, 20, 30, 34.

42 Decree 4547, 9 July 1870, clause 6, in Brazil, *Colleção das leis do império do Brasil de 1870*, vol. 30, part 1 (Rio de Janeiro: Typ. Nacional, 1870), pp. 382-387.

43 Galvão, Menezes de Macedo, and Deschamps de Montmorency, *Parecer da secção de colonização e estatística*, pp. 8, 11, 12.

44 Ibid., p. 3. Also published in *Revista de Sociedade auxiliadora da indústria nacional* 38 (1870), 324.

45 "Dr. Nicolão Moreira, discurso de 16 de agosto de 1870," cited in Sociedade Auxiliadora da Indústria Nacional, *Discurso pronunciado pelo Dr. I. J. Galvão*, p. 7. A similar position was taken by Dr. J. Parigot in *Discurso pronunciado na Sociedade auxiliadora da indústria nacional em sessão de 16 de agosto de 1870* (Rio de Janeiro: Typ. Universal de Laemmert, 1870), pp. 3-4.

46 Sociedade Auxiliadora da Indústria Nacional, *Discurso pronunciado por Joaquim Antonio d'Azevedo em sessão do Conselho administrativo de 3 de outubro de 1870* (Rio de Janeiro: Typ. Universal de Laemmert, 1870), pp. 3, 5, 8.

47 Sociedade Auxiliadora da Indústria Nacional, *Discurso pronunciado por Miguel Calmon Menezes de Macedo na sessão de 30 de dezembro de 1870 (questão dos chins)* (Rio de Janeiro: Typ. Universal de Laemmert, 1871), pp. 12-13.

48 Sociedade Auxiliadora da Indústria Nacional, *Discurso Pronunciado pelo Dr. I. J. Galvão*, pp. 16, 62. Edouard Du Hailly, "Souvenirs d'une campagne l'Extrême Orient," *Revue des Deux Mondes* 36:65 (15 September 1866), 957-983; 36:65 (15 October 1866), 893-924; 36:66 (15 November 1866), 396-420; "De Saigon en France," *Revue des Deux Mondes* 37:67 (15 January 1867), 441-469.

49 Sociedade Auxiliadora da Indústria Nacional, *Discurso pronunciado por José Ricardo*

Moniz na sessão de 30 de dezembro de 1870 (questão dos chins) (Rio de Janeiro: Typ. Universal de Laemmert, 1871), pp. 3, 5.

50 Ibid., pp. 6, 8, 9.

51 João Cardoso de Menezes e Souza, *Theses sobre colonização do Brazil: Projecto de solução as questões sociaes, que se prendem à este difícil problema* (Rio de Janeiro: Typografia Nacional, 1875), pp. 411–423.

52 A. Legoyt, *L'émigration européenne: Son importance, ses causes, ses effets, avec un appendice sur l'émigration africaine, hindoue et chinoise* (Marseilles: Typ. Roux, 1861), pp. 310–319; Malheiro, *A escravidão no Brasil,* pp. 176–200; Sociedade Auxiliadora da Indústria Nacional, *Discurso pronunciado pelo Dr. I. J. Galvão,* pp. 36–39.

53 Sociedade Auxiliadora da Indústria Nacional, *Discurso pronunciado por Joaquim Antonio d'Azevedo,* pp. 6–7; Sociedade Auxiliadora da Indústria Nacional, *Discurso pronunciado por Miguel Calmon Menezes de Macedo,* p. 19. I am unable to confirm that this translation was published.

54 Leonard Wray, *The Practical Sugar Planter. A Complete Account of the Cultivation and Manufacture of the Sugar-Cane, According to the Latest and Most Improved Processes, Describing and Comparing the Different Systems Pursued in the East and West Indies and the Straits of Malacca, and the Relative Expenses and Advantages Attendant upon Each: Being the Result of Sixteen Years' Experience as a Sugar Planter in Those Countries* (London: Smith, Elder, 1848), p. 86. It was published in France as *Manuel pratique du planteur de canne à sucre: Exposé complet de la culture de la canne selon les procédés les plus récentes et les plus perfectionnés* (Dusacq: Librairie Agricole de la Maison Rustique, 1853).

55 Comments of Olavo Góes, 8th ordinary session, 9 May 1876, in Bahia, *Annaes da Assembléia legislativa provincial da Bahia, sessões do anno de 1876* (Bahia: Typ. do Correio da Bahia, 1876), pp. 43–45; Dale Thurston Graden, "From Slavery to Freedom in Bahia, Brazil, 1791–1900" (Ph.D thesis, University of Connecticut, 1991), p. 249.

56 Evelyn Hu-DeHart, "Coolies, Shopkeepers, Pioneers: The Chinese of Mexico and Peru (1849–1930)," *Amerasia* 15:2 (1989), 103–108. See also Jeffrey Lesser, "Asians in South America," in Johannes Wilbert, ed., *Encyclopedia of World Cultures,* vol. 7, *South America* (New York: G. K. Hall/Macmillan, 1995), pp. 58–61.

57 Sociedade Importadora de Trabalhadores Asiáticos de Procedência Chinese, *Demonstração das conveniencias e vantagens à lavoura do Brasil pela introdução dos trabalhadores asiáticos (da China)* (Rio de Janeiro: Typ. de P. Braga, 1877), pp. iii–ix; Francisco Antonio de Almeida, *Da França ao Japão: Narração de viagem e descripção histórica, usos e costumes dos habitantes da China, do Japão e de outros paizes de Asia* (Rio de Janeiro: Typ. do Apóstolo, 1879), p. 170.

58 Decree 5099, 2 October 1872, in Brazil, *Collecção das leis do império do Brasil de 1872,* part 2, vol. 2 (Rio de Janeiro: Typografia Nacional, 1873), p. 855; Decree 5791, 1 November 1874, in Brazil, *Collecção das leis do império do Brasil de 1874,* vol. 37, part 2, vol. 2 (Rio de Janeiro: Typografia Nacional, 1875), p. 1168.

59 Debate of 18 August 1875, read into the record of 64th session, 18 September 1877, in Brazil, *Annaes do Senado do império do Brasil, 2a sessão da 16a legislatura no mez*

de setembro de 1877, vol. 4 (Rio de Janeiro: Typ. do Diário do Rio de Janeiro, 1877), p. 193; Dikötter, *The Discourse of Race.*

60   Nicolão Joaquim Moreira, *Relatório sobre a imigração nos Estados Unidos da América apresentado ao exm. sr. ministro da agricultura, commércio e obras públicas* (Rio de Janeiro: Typografia Nacional, 1877), pp. 91, 94.

61   Carvalho, *O Brazil, colonização e emigração*, p. 192.

62   *Mephistópheles* (Rio de Janeiro), 2:60 (August 1875), 8. My thanks to Peter Beattie for directing me to this cartoon.

63   Brazil, *Annaes do Senado do império do Brasil, 2a sessão da 16a legislatura no mez de setembro de 1877*, vol. 4, 64th session, 18 September 1877, p. 194; "Discurso proferido na sessão de 1 de outubro de 1877—Orçamento do Ministério da agricultura," in Brazil, *Annaes do Senado do império do Brazil, 2a sessão da 16a legislatura no mez de outubro de 1877*, vol 5 (Rio de Janeiro: Typ. do Diário do Rio de Janeiro, 1877), pp. 63-79.

64   Pedro D. G. Paes Leme, "A nossa lavoura," 17 October 1877, repr. in *Diário official* 17:165 (11 July 1878), 6; Sociedade Importadora de Trabalhadores Asiáticos de Procedência Chinese, *Demonstração das conveniencias e vantagens à lavoura do Brasil*, pp. vii, x.

65   The first report can be found in *Diário Official* 17:163 (9 July 1878).

66   Speech of Minister Sinimbú, 8 July 1878, in Brazil, Congresso Agrícola, *Collecção de documentos* (Rio de Janeiro: Typ. Nacional, 1878), pp. 128-129.

67   Paes Leme, "A Nossa Lavoura," p. 6.

68   Brazil, Congresso Agrícola, *Collecção de documentos*, pp. 38-39.

69   Ibid., p. 65.

70   "Proposta de resolução," art. 1, in ibid., p. 83.

71   Nelson Werneck Sodré, *História da imprensa no Brasil* (Rio de Janeiro: Editora Civilização Brasileira, 1966), p. 250. Reprinted in Viotti da Costa, *The Brazilian Empire*, p. 150.

72   Jaguaribe Filho, *Reflexões*, p. v; Warren Dean, *Rio Claro: A Brazilian Plantation System, 1820-1920* (Stanford: Stanford University Press, 1976), p. 148; São Paulo, *Relatório annual apresentado ao cidadão dr. presidente do estado de São Paulo pelo Dr. Jorge Tibiriçá, secretário dos negócios da agricultura, commércio e obras públicas* (São Paulo: Typ. à Vapor de Vanorden, 1894), p. 99.

73   Domingos José Nogueira Jaguaribe Filho, "Do acclimamento das raças sob o ponto de vista de colonisação em relação ao Brasil," pp. 142-143, thesis presented to the Faculdade de Medicina do Rio de Janeiro, 15 September 1874. Teses do Rio, 1874, C–F #8, vol. 2, Academia Nacional de Medicina, Rio de Janeiro.

74   Jaguaribe Filho, *Reflexões*, pp. 203-205.

75   Ibid., pp. 210, 251, 280. Virtually every stereotype about Asians in Brazil, be they Chinese or Japanese, can also be found in bigoted discussions of Jews. See Jeffrey Lesser, *Welcoming the Undesirables: Brazil and the Jewish Question* (Berkeley: University of California Press, 1995).

76   Representative Joaquim da Costa Pinto, in Bahia, *Annaes da Assembléia legislativa provincial da Bahia, 1876*, p. 44. My thanks to Prof. Dale Graden for sharing

this material with me. A twentieth-century example of the same attitude can be found in Mario da Costa Guimarães, Brazilian Legation (Havana), to Octavio Mangabeira, Minister of Foreign Relations, 1 May 1928, Lata 1290, Maço 29616-29622, Arquivo Histórico Itamaraty, Rio de Janeiro [hereafter, AHI-R].

77   Jaguaribe Filho, *Reflexões,* pp. 206, 254.

78   The word *china,* which as a noun can mean either the country or a Chinese woman, was a popular term for an indigenous woman or a woman or girl (*chininha*) of mixed race. *Novo Michaelis, dicionário ilustrado* (São Paulo: Edições Melhoramentos, 1961), p. 285. See also Aurélio Buarque de Holanda Ferreira, *Novo dicionário da língua portuguesa,* 2nd ed. (Rio de Janeiro: Ed. Nova Fronteira, 1986), p. 396; and Adalberto Prado e Silva, ed., *Novo dicionário brasileiro Melhoramentos Illustrado* (São Paulo: Companhia Melhoramentos, 1971), vol. 2, p. 208. These popular usages may have come from Quechua-speaking Peruvian peoples who had contact with Chinese immigrants who settled in the late nineteenth and twentieth centuries. Cid Franco, *Dicionário de expressões populares brasileiras,* 2 vols. (São Paulo: Editoras Unidas, n.d.), vol. 1, p. 229. On issues of sexuality and nation-building, see Homi Bhabha, ed., *Nation and Narration* (New York: Routledge, 1990); Gillian Rose, *Feminism and Geography: The Limits of Geographical Knowledge* (Minneapolis: University of Minnesota Press, 1993).

79   Salvador de Mendonça, *Trabalhadores asiáticos, por Salvador de Mendonça, consul geral do Brazil nos Estados-Unidos. Obra mandada publicar pelo exm. conselheiro João Lins Vieira Cansansão de Sinimbú, presidente do Conselho de ministros e ministro e secretário de estado dos negócios de agricultura, commércio e obras públicas* (New York: Typ. do Novo Mundo, 1879), p. 19; letter of Joaquim Bonifácio do Amaral (Campinas), Viscount Indaiatuba, to Salvador Furtado de Mendonça, 14 May 1881, Manuscript Collection—Coleção Salvador de Mendonça, I-4, 23, 34; letter of José Luís de Campos, Baron Monte Claro (Cidade do Pomba-Minas Gerais), to Salvador Furtado de Mendonça, 30 July 1881, Manuscript Collection—Coleção Salvador de Mendonça, I-4, 23, 48; letter of Manuel Buarque de Macedo (Rio de Janeiro) to Salvador Furtado de Mendonça, 4 May 1881, Manuscript Collection—Coleção Salvador de Mendonça, I-4, 23, 41, BN-R.

80   *Rio News,* 24 September 1879, p. 1.

81   Brazil, *Annaes do Senado do império do Brazil, 1a sessão de 17a legislatura do 10 à 31 de março,* vol. 3. (Rio de Janeiro: Typ. Nacional, 1879), pp. 213, 214.

82   Brazil, *Annaes do Parlamento brazileiro, Câmara dos deputados, prorogação da sessão de 1879,* vol. 5. (Rio de Janeiro: Typ. Nacional, 1879), pp. 21–22; letter of Ambrosio Machado da Cunha Cavalcanti to Luís Felipe de Sousa Leão, 1 May 1879, Coleção Sousa Leão, Lata 457 doc. 40, Instituto Histórico e Geográfico Brasileiro, Rio de Janeiro [hereafter IHGB-R].

83   Letter of Joseph Cooper, Edmund Stinge, and Charles H. Allen to Marquis Tseng, published in *The Anti-Slavery Reporter* (London), August 1879, repr. in *Rio News,* 24 September 1879, p. 1.

84   *Rio News,* 5 October 1879, p. 2; *Rio News,* 15 December 1879, p. 1.

85   Letter from Dr. Halliday Macartney on behalf of Marquis Tseng to Committee of

the British and Foreign Anti-Slavery Society (6 November 1879), published in *Rio News*, 15 December 1879, p. 1; letter of Col. Engenheiro Paulo José Pereira to Lt. Gen. Conselheiro Henrique de Beurepaire Rohan, 1 November 1883, Manuscript Collection-General Collection, II 35, 4, 31, no. 1, BN-R; Miguel Lemos, *Immigração chineza: Mensagem a s. ex. o embaixador do Celeste Imperio junto aos governos de França e Inglaterra* (Rio de Janeiro: Sociedade Positivista, 1881); *La Revue Occidentale* (Paris), 1 May 1880; *La Revue Occidentale* (Paris), 1 September 1881; "THE CHINESE QUESTION," *Rio News*, 24 September 1879, p. 1.

86   *Gazeta de Notícias* (Rio de Janeiro), 15 December 1879; *Rio News*, 24 December 1879.

87   A. Moreira de Barros to Eduardo Callado and Arthur Silveira da Motta, 6 December 1879; Ministry of Agriculture, Commerce, and Public Works, *officio* no. 2 (11 January 1882), in memo of Eduardo Callado and Arthur Silveira da Motta (30 March 1882); Missões Especiais do Brasil no estrangeiro-06; 271/2/2-Barão de Jaceguai (Arthur Silveira da Motta), AHI-R; report from the Ministry of Agriculture, Commerce, and Public Works published in *Diário oficial* 20:206 (27 July 1881), 2; José Pereira Rego Filho, *O Brazil e os Estados Unidos na questão da immigração—Conferência effectuada na augusta presença de sua magestade o imperador em o dia 16 de dezembro de 1880 pelo Dr. José Pereira Rego Filho* (Rio de Janeiro: Typografia Nacional, 1884), p. 19; Conrad, "The Planter Class," p. 45.

88   Discussion of Representative Inglez de Souza, in São Paulo, *Annaes da Assembléia legislativa provincial de São Paulo. Primeiro anno da 23 legislatura (sessão de 1880)* (São Paulo: Typ. da Tribuna Liberal, 1880), 30th session, 18 March 1880, pp. 280–286; 29th session, 17 March 1880, p. 264; 24th session, 11 March 1880, pp. 195–196.

89   Ministry of Agriculture, Commerce and Public Works, *officio* no. 2, 11 January 1882; report from the Ministry of Agriculture, Commerce, and Public Works (27 July 1881); *Rio News*, 4 May 1881, p. 4.

90   *South American Journal* (Rio de Janeiro), 7 June 1883.

91   Marshall C. Eakin, *British Enterprise in Brazil: The St. John d'el Rey Mining Company and the Morro Velho Gold Mine, 1830–1960* (Durham, N.C.: Duke University Press, 1989), p. 48.

92   Letter of Callado to G. C. Butler, 21 January 1881, Missão Especial ao Celeste Imperio China, 1893–1894—Barão do Ladario, Manuscript Collection—Colecção Afro-Asiática, 20, 2, 5, BN-R.

93   Letter of J. H. Gibb Livingston to Ladario, 25 July 1893, Missão Especial ao Celeste Imperio China, 1893–1894—Barão do Ladario," Manuscript Collection-Coleção Afro-Asiática, 20, 2, 5, BN-R. T'ang T'ing-shu was born in 1832 and died in 1892. John King Fairbank, *The Great Chinese Revolution: 1800–1985* (New York: Harper & Row, 1986), p. 110.

94   Chi-kong Lai, "Li Hung-chang and Modern Enterprise: The China Merchants Company, 1872–1885," in Samuel C. Chu and Kwang-Ching Liu, eds., *Li Hung-chang and China's Early Modernization* (Armonk, NY: M. E. Sharpe, 1994), pp.

216–247; Stanley Spector, *Li Hung-chang and the Huai Army: A Study in Nineteenth-Century Chinese Regionalism* (Seattle: University of Washington Press, 1964), pp. ix, 238, 243–244; Albert Feuerwerker, *China's Early Industrialization: Sheng Hsuan-Huai (1844–1916) and Mandarin Enterprise* (Cambridge, MA: Harvard University Press, 1958), pp. 110–111; Fairbank, *The Great Chinese Revolution*, pp. 92, 98, 114.

95   Letter of J. H. Gibb Livingston to Ladario, 25 July 1893; letter from Callado to G. C. Butler, 21 January 1881, Missão Especial ao Celeste Imperio China, 1893–1894-Barão do Ladario, Manuscript Collection-Colecção Afro-Asiática, 20, 2, 5, BN-R.

96   Tong King-sing to Callado, 21 November 1881; Tong King-sing to Callado, 28 December 1881, Missão Especial ao Celeste Imperio China, 1893–1894—Barão do Ladario, Manuscript Collection-Coleção Afro-Asiática, 20, 2, 5, BN-R.

97   Tong King-sing to Callado, 21 November 1881; Tong King-sing to Callado, 28 December 1881, Missão Especial ao Celeste Imperio China, 1893–1894-Barão do Ladario, Manuscript Collection-Coleção Afro-Asiática, 20, 2, 5, BN-R.

98   *Correio Paulistano*, 19 October 1883, p. 2.

99   Henrique C. R. Lisboa, *Os chins do Tetartos* (Rio de Janeiro: Typografia da Empresa Democrática Editora, 1894), p. 11.

100   Carl von Koseritz, *Imagens do Brasil*, trans Afonso Arinos de Melo Franco (Belo Horizonte: Ed. Itatiaia, 1980), pp. 221–223; *Correio Paulistano*, 19 October 1883, p. 2.

101   *Gazeta de Campinas* article "VIAJANTE CHIM," repr. in *Correio Paulistano*, 26 October 1883, p. 1; *Jornal do Agricultor* article "VIAJANTE CHIM," repr. in *Correio Paulistano*, 30 October 1883, p. 1.

102   Tong King-sing, quoted in letter of Charles H. Allen (Secretary of the British Anti-Slavery Society) to Earl Granville, Principal Secretary of State for Foreign Affairs, 6 December 1883, repr. in C. F. van Delden Laërne, *Brazil and Java: Report on Coffee-Culture in America, Asia and Africa* (London: W. H. Allen; The Hague: Martinus Nijhoff, 1885), pp. 149–150; Roberto Simonsen, "Aspectos da história ecônomica do café," in Instituto Histórico e Geográfico Brasileiro, ed., *Anais do Terceiro congresso da história nacional* (Rio de Janeiro: Imprensa Nacional, 1941), pp. 265–266; Maria José Elias, "Introdução ao estudo da imigração chinesa," *Anais do Museu Paulista* 24 (1970), 88.

103   Fidelis Reis and João de Faria, *O problema immigratório e seus aspectos éthnicos: Na câmara e fóra de câmara* (Rio de Janeiro: Typ. Revista dos Tribunaes, 1924), p. 130.

104   Lisboa, *Os chins do Tetartos*, p. 12.

105   Letter of Charles H. Allen (Secretary of the British Anti-Slavery Society) to Earl Granville, Principal Secretary of State for Foreign Affairs, 6 December 1883, repr. in full in Laërne, *Brazil and Java*, pp. 149–150.

106   Tong King-sing (Rio de Janeiro) to Society for the Promotion of Commerce and Immigration from China, 28 October 1883; letter from G. C. Butler to Mr. Chapman (Rio de Janeiro), 8 March 1883, Missão Especial ao Celeste Imperio China, 1893–1894-Barão do Ladario, Manuscript Collection-Coleção Afro-Asiática, 20, 2, 5, BN-R.

107   "GUERRA FRANCO CHINEZA," *Correio Paulistano,* 27 October 1883, p. 2, repr.
       from *L'Epoca* (Genoa); J. O. P. Bland, *Li Hung-Chang* (New York: Henry Holt, 1917),
       pp. 144–146.

108   *Questões agrícolas—Immigração chineza (3 discussão do orçamento). Discurso pronun-
       ciado na Assembléia provincial do Rio de Janeiro na sessão de 23 de novembro de 1888
       pelo bacharel em sciências jurídicas e sociaes Oscar Varady* (Rio de Janeiro: Typo-
       grafia Carioca, 1888).

109   *A immigração* 1: 1 (December 1883), 1; 1: 3 (April 1884), 9; 4:30 (March 1887), 4; 5:
       50 (November 1888), 1; Lisboa, *Os chins do Tetartos,* p. 12. For more on the forma-
       tion of the Sociedade Central da Immigração, see Michael M. Hall, "The Origins
       of Mass Immigration to Brazil, 1817–1914" (Ph.D. dissertation, Columbia Univer-
       sity, 1969), pp. 35–80.

110   *A Immigração* 6: 55 (March 1889), 2–3; Brazil, *Annaes do Senado do império do Bra-
       zil, 3a sessão da 20a legislatura de 1 de outubro a 20 de novembro de 1888,* vol. 6 (Rio
       de Janeiro: Imprensa Nacional, 1888), session of 3 October, p. 51.

111   Brazil, *Annaes do Senado do império do Brazil, 3a sessão da 20a legislatura de 1 de
       outubro a 20 de novembro de 1888,* vol. 6 (Rio de Janeiro: Imprensa Nacional, 1888),
       session of 3 October, p. 51; Decree Law 528, 28 June 1890, art. 1. In 1892 citizens
       of Japan and China were given immigration rights after Brazil signed commer-
       cial and peace treaties with the two countries. This did not, however, lead to any
       spontaneous Chinese or Japanese immigration. Law 97, 5 October 1892, art. 1.

112   Brazil, *Annaes do Senado do império do Brazil, 3a sessão da 20a legislatura de 1 de
       outubro a 20 de novembro de 1888,* vol. 6 (Rio de Janeiro: Imprensa Nacional, 1888),
       session of 4 October, p. 80.

113   *Ceylon Observer,* 6 January 1893; *Jornal do Comércio,* 16 March 1893; *O Estado de
       S. Paulo,* 23 March 1893; *O Estado de S. Paulo,* 25 March 1893; *Correio Paulistano,*
       19 July 1892; Lisboa, *Os chins do Tetartos,* pp. 13–17.

114   Gustavo Penna, *Immigração chineza para o estado de Minas Gerais* (Juiz de Fora:
       Typ. Pereira, 1892), p. 71.

115   Collatino Marques de Souza, *O trabalho dos chins no norte do Brazil, na Amazonia,
       nos estados do Rio de Janeiro e de Minas Gerais* (Rio de Janeiro: Typ. do Jornal do Bra-
       sil, 1892), p. 17; *O Estado de S. Paulo,* 21 June 1892, p. 2; 5 July 1892, p. 2; 18 October
       1892, p. 1; Baron Etienne Hulot, *De l'Atlantique au Pacifique à travers le Canada et le
       nord des Etats-Unis* (Paris: E. Plon Nourrit, 1888), p. 346; letter of Col. Engenheiro
       Paulo José Pereira to Lt. Gen. Conselheiro Henrique de Beurepaire Rohan, 1 Feb-
       ruary 1894, Manuscript Collection—General Collection, II 35, 4, 31, no. 3, BN-R.

116   São Paulo, Câmara dos Deputados do Estado de São Paulo, *Annaes da sessão ordi-
       nária e extraordinária de 1892 (10 anno da 2nda legislatura)* (São Paulo: n.p., 1893),
       p. 427.

117   São Paulo, Câmara dos Deputados do Estado de São Paulo, *Annaes da sessão extra-
       ordinária e ordinária de 1893 (2ndo anno da 2nda legislatura)* (São Paulo: n.p., 1894),
       pp. 140, 166, 246.

118   São Paulo, Câmara dos Deputados do Estado de São Paulo, *Annaes da sessão ordi-
       nária e extraordinária de 1892 (10 anno da 2nda legislatura),* p. 426.

119   General Tcheng-Ki-Tong, *Meu paiz: A China contemporânea* (Rio de Janeiro: Imprensa Nacional, 1892); Lisboa, *Os chins do Tetarto*, p. 21; Law of 5 October 1892, cited in Lisboa, *Os chins do Tetartos*, p. 46.

120   Francisco Fereira de Morais, "Proposta ao governador do estado do Rio sobre a imigração de chineses," Niterói, 25 October 1892, Manuscript Collection-Coleção Afro-Asiática, I-46, 23, 20, BN-R; Lisboa, *Os chins do Tetartos*, p. 22; Dikötter, *The Discourse of Race*, p. 70.

121   "Mensagem enviada à Assembléia legislativa do estado do Rio de Janeiro pelo primeiro vice-presidente Manoel Martins Torres," in Rio de Janeiro, *Annaes da Assembléia legislativa do estado do Rio de Janeiro* (Rio de Janeiro: Typ. Jornal do Comércio, 1894), session of 1 August 1893, p. 7.

122   Minas Gerais, *Relatório apresentado ao dr. presidente do estado de Minas Geraes pelo secretário de estado dos negócios, da agricultura, comércio e obras públicas, Dr. David Moretzsohn Campista, no anno de 1893* (Ouro Preto: Imprensa Official de Minas Gerais, 1893), p. 7. Moretzsohn received sixty-four responses to his questionnaire. One question regarded the type of worker preferred, based on nationality, and those who responded frequently put more than one answer. The totals were as follows: Chinese, 17; Portuguese, 14; Brazilians, 13; Italian, 9; German, 8; Asians, 6 (no one put both Asian and Chinese); No preference, 3; Spanish, 2; English, 2; Other, 1; French, 1; Japanese, 1; African, 1.

123   Minas Gerais, Congresso Mineiro, *Annaes do Senado mineiro, terceira sessão da primeira legislatura no anno de 1893* (Ouro Prêto: Imprensa Official de Minas Gerais, 1893); Decree 612 of 6 March 1893, in Minas Gerais, *Collecção das leis e decretos do estado de Minas Geraes em 1893* (Ouro Prêto: Imprensa Official de Minas Geraes, 1893), pp. 277–284; Law 102 of 24 July 1894, in Minas Gerais, *Collecção das leis e decretos do estado de Minas Geraes em 1894* (Ouro Preto: Imprensa Official de Minas Gerais, 1895), p. 27. For more on Minas Gerais, see Norma de Góes Monteiro, "Esbôço da política imigratória e colonizadora do governo de Minas Gerais, 1889–1930," *Revista Brasileira de Estudos Políticos* 29 (July 1970), 195–216.

124   *O Estado de S. Paulo*, 24 November 1892, p. 2; *Correio Paulistano*, 19 August 1892, p. 2; Arlinda Rocha Nogueira, *Companhias interessadas na introdução de asiáticos em São Paulo nos primeiros anos de República* (São Paulo: Centro de Estudos Nipo-Brasileiros, 1979), pp. 11–16.

125   "LO QUE SON LOS CHINOS," *Correio Paulistano*, 19 July 1892, 21 July 1892, 22 July 1892, 24 July 1892, 26 July 1892, 28 July 1892, 31 July 1892, 4 August 1892. See also *Correio Paulistano*, 19 August 1892, p. 2.

126   *Correio Paulistano*, 15 December 1892, p. 3; *O Paiz* (Rio de Janeiro), 23 December 1892, p. 1; *Correio Paulistano*, 29 December 1892, p. 2; *O Estado de S. Paulo*, 8 January 1893, p. 2; *Correio Paulistano*, 1 February 1893, p. 2; letter of Dr. Manoel Peixoto de Lacerda Werneck, in *Jornal do Comércio*, 18 December 1893, repr. in *Hong Kong Daily Press*, 4 April 1894. Macao's *O Independente* (7 April 1894) criticized the *Jornal do Comércio* article, pointing out numerous errors of fact and suggesting that Brazilians had little sense of the reality of Asia. See also *China Mail* (Hong Kong), 1 June 1893, article repr. from *San Francisco Chronicle*. C. Fabri, *Memórial sobre a*

questão de immigração apresentado aos illustres membros do Congresso nacional (Rio de Janeiro: Typografia do Jornal do Commércio, 1893), p. 8.

127   Letter of José de Costa Azevedo to Felisbello Firmma de Oliva Freire (Brazilian Minister of Foreign Affairs), 1 July 1893; letter of José de Costa Azevedo to Cassiano de Nascimento, 2 April 1894, 06-Missões Especiais do Brasil no Estrangeiro, 271/2/3, Barão de Ladario-Missões Especias, China, 1893–1894, AHI-R; *China Mail* (Hong Kong), 1 June 1893; *Hong Kong Daily Telegraph,* 28 November 1893.

128   *China Mail* (Hong Kong), 10 June 1893.

129   Baron Asumpção (Consul of Brazil in Macao) to Felisbello Firmma de Oliva Freire (Brazilian Minister of Foreign Affairs), 28 August 1893, 02-Repartições Consulares Brasileiras, Macao-Ofícios-1850–1896—252/4/6, AHI-R.

130   *Hong Kong Daily Press,* 9 March and 15 March 1894. Regulations on transport of Chinese from Macao (chapter I, arts. 2, 3, and 5) were published in *Boletim da província de Macau e Timor* 29:31 (4 August 1893), 1. The full contract can be found in Lisboa, *Os chins do Tetartos,* pp. 74–76. See also *Echo Macaense* (Macao), 7 March 1894; *China Mail,* 8 March 1894.

131   The figure of 375 comes from Barão de Asumpção (Consul of Brazil in Macao) to Felisbello Firmma de Oliva Freire (Brazilian minister of foreign affairs), 19 October 1893, 02-Repartições Consulares Brasileiras, Macao-Ofícios-1850–1896—252/4/6, AHI-R. The figure of 474 was reported in Custodio de Borja (Governor of Macao) to William Robinson, (Governor of Hong Kong), 8 January 1894, 02-Repartições Consulares Brasileiras, Hong Kong (5)-Ofícios-1880–1899—250/2/5, AHI-R. The figure of 475 can be found in both "Mensagem enviada à Assembléia legislativa do estado do Rio De Janeiro pelo presidente Dr. José Thomaz da Porciuncula," in Rio de Janeiro, *Annaes da Assembléia legislativa do estado do Rio De Janeiro* (Rio de Janeiro: Typ. Jornal do Comércio, 1894), p. 8; and Lisboa, *Os chins do Tetartos,* p. 23.

132   Baron de Asumpção (Consul of Brazil in Macao) to Felisbello Firmma de Oliva Freire (Brazilian Minister of Foreign Affairs), 19 October 1893, 02-Repartições Consulares Brasileiras, Macao-Ofícios-1850–1896—252/4/6; J. do Amaral (Itamaraty) to Agostinho Guilherme Romano (Brazilian Consul in Hong Kong), 8 November 1893, 02-Repartições Consulares Brasileiras, Hong Kong (5)-Despachos-1887–1899—250/2/7, AHI-R.

133   Custodio de Borja to William Robinson, 12 December 1893, *Boletim official do governo da província de Macau e Timor* (27 December 1893), 3; open letter from William Robinson to Custodio de Borja, 27 December 1893, *Boletim official do governo da província de Macau e Timor* (27 December 1893), 3; Custodio de Borja to William Robinson, 8 January 1893, *Boletim official do governo da província de Macau e Timor* (13 January 1894), 13; *Hong Kong Daily Press,* 18 May 1893; speech of William Robinson, *Boletim official do governo da província de Macau e Timor* (13 January 1894), 13. See also Customs Notification no. 55 of H. Elgar Hobson, Commissioner for Kowloon and District Office of Customs, 26 February 1894; *Hong Kong Daily Press,* 28 February 1894; *Hong Kong Daily Press,* 21 July 1894.

134   Letter of Cassiano de Nascimento (Itamaraty) to Costa Azevedo, 28 May 1894, Missão especial ao Celeste Imperio China, 1893–1894—Barão do Ladario, Manuscript Collection—Colecção Afro-Asiática, 20, 2, 5, BN-R; José Honório Rodrigues, "Brasil e Extremo Oriente," p. 72.

135   Proclamation of the Tsungli Yamēu to superintendent of trade for the southern ports and governor-general of the Liangkiang Provinces, trans. in *New China Daily News*, 4 March 1894, and printed verbatim in *Hong Kong Daily Press*, 15 March 1894.

136   "Mensagem enviada à Assembléia legislativa do estado do Rio De Janeiro pelo presidente Dr. José Thomaz da Porciuncula," in Rio de Janeiro, *Annaes da Assembléia legislativa do estado do Rio De Janeiro* (Rio de Janeiro: Typ. Jornal do Comércio, 1894), p. 8.

137   *Jornal do Comércio*, 18 December 1893, repr. in *Hong Kong Weekly Press*, 4 April 1894.

138   *Jornal do Comércio*, 25 December 1893, reprinted in *China Mail* (Hong Kong), 13 February 1894. Henrique Lisboa agreed with this distinction, pointing out that Hakkas and Puntis resident in Macao were the only Chinese worth recruiting for agricultural labor. Lisboa, *Os chins do Tetartos*, p. 51, n. 1.

139   Lisboa, *Os chins do Tetartos*, p. 81.

140   "Os chins," *Gazeta de Notícias*, 9 March 1894.

141   The Chinese government estimated in 1916 that twenty thousand of its subjects lived in Brazil. H. T. Montague Bell and H. G. W. Woodhead, *The China Year Book—1916* and *The China Year Book—1919/1920* (repr. Nedeln/Liechtenstein: Kraus-Thomson Organization, 1969), p. 37. In what must be considered a great understatement, the authors noted, "The figures are probably too high." For a brief analysis of more recent Chinese immigration to Brazil, see Lesser, "Asians in South America," pp. 58–61.

142   Jeffrey Lesser, "Always Outsiders: Asians, Naturalization and the Supreme Court," *Amerasia Journal* 12:1 (1985–1986), 83–100; Stuart Miller, *The Unwelcome Immigrant: The American Image of the Chinese, 1785–1882* (Berkeley: University of California Press, 1969).

143   João do Rio (Paulo Barreto), "Visões d'ópio. Os chins no Rio," in *A alma encantadora das ruas* [1908] (Rio de Janeiro: Edição da Organização Simões, 1951) pp. 84–92. The article was first published in *Gazeta de Notícias* (Rio de Janeiro) on 1 July 1905. For a different kind of analysis of João do Rio's comments on Chinese, see Dain Borges, "Intangible Influences in Metropolitan Rio de Janeiro, ca. 1900–1910," lecture given at the Getty Center for the History of Art and the Humanities, Santa Monica, CA, 12 December 1994.

3   Constructing Ethnic Space

1   Luiz Gonçalves dos Santos (Padre Perereca), *Memória para servir à história do reino do Brasil* [1825], 2 vols. (Rio de Janeiro: Zelio Valverde, 1943), vol. 1, p. 333; Jorge Amado, *Gabriela, Clove and Cinnamon*, trans. James L. Taylor and William L. Grossman (New York: Knopf, 1962), p. 3.

2   The term "Syrian-Lebanese" is used throughout much of the Southern Cone.

3   Eça de Queiroz, *O Egipto: Notas de viagem* [1926], 5th ed. (Pôrto: Lello e Irmão, 1946), pp. 123–140; José de Souza Larcher, *Viagens no Oriente: O que eu vi e ouvi atravez do Egypto e da velha Europa* (Rio de Janeiro: Livraria Schettino, n.d.), part II, pp. 23, 167. *Viagens no Oriente* was essentially a Portuguese version of Gerard de Nerval's *Voyage en Orient* [1851] (Paris: Garnier-Flammarion, 1980). An economic perspective on the Middle East can be found in José Bonifácio Andrada e Silva's twenty-four-page handwritten notebook, Coleção José Bonifácio-O Patriarca, Lata 191 Doc. 34 M. 4880, Instituto Histórico e Geográfico Brasileiro-Rio de Janeiro [hereafter IHGB-R].

4   Eduardo Prado, *Viagens: A Sicilia, Malta e o Egypto*, 2nd ed. (São Paulo: Escola Typográfica Salesiana, 1902), p. 143; Francisco Antonio de Almeida, *Da França ao Japão: Narração de viagem e descripção histórica, usos e costumes dos habitantes da China, do Japão e de outros paizes de Asia* (Rio de Janeiro: Typ. do Apóstolo, 1879), pp. 44–45.

5   Afrânio Peixoto, *Viagem sentimental* (Rio de Janeiro: Editora Americana, 1931), pp. 55–65; T. Duoun, *Confissões e indiscrições: Meio século de experiências em quatro continentes (com um album intercalado de 60 gravuras)* (São Paulo: n.p., 1943), pp. 108, 121, 175. See also Ali Behdad, *Belated Travellers: Orientalism in the Age of Colonial Dissolution* (Durham, NC: Duke University Press, 1994), pp. 18–19.

6   From an unsigned, reserved, and confidential letter of 5 September 1857 under the heading "Imigração," Coleção Instituto Histórico, Lata 477 Doc. 21, IHGB-R; Cezar Magalhaens, *Pela brazilidade (discursos e conferências)* (Rio de Janeiro: Typ. A. Pernambucana Hermes Poffes, 1925), p. 6.

7   Teófilo Braga, *A pátria portugueza: O território e a raça* (Pôrto: Lello e Irmão, 1894), pp. 283–293. Braga may have been influenced by theories that Brazil's indigenous population had descended from the Israelites. See Ambrósio Fernandes Brandão, *Dialogues of the Great Things of Brazil* [*Diálogos das grandezas do Brasil*] (Albuquerque: University of New Mexico Press, 1987), p. 103. Gilberto Freyre took much the same position as Braga in *The Masters and the Slaves: A Study in the Development of the Brazilian Nation* [1933], trans. Samuel Putnam, 2nd English ed. (Berkeley: University of California Press, 1986), p. 85. For a complete discussion of theories of the origins of American indigenous peoples, see Lee Eldridge Huddleston, *Origins of the American Indians: European Concepts, 1492–1729* (Austin: University of Texas Press, 1967); Angus MacKay, *Spain in the Middle Ages: From Frontier to Empire, 1000–1500* (London: Macmillan Press, 1977), 20; Joseph F. O'Callaghan, *A History of Medieval Spain* (Ithaca, NY: Cornell University Press, 1975), p. 96.

8   Braga, *A pátria portugueza*, pp. 283–293; Friedrich Max Müller, *Introduction to the*

Science of Religion [1873] (New York: Arno Press, 1978), pp. 159–165. For a discussion of the Turanian connection and the scholars who supported it, see Elisabeth Tooker, "Lewis H. Morgan and His Contemporaries," *American Anthropologist* 94:2 (June 1992), 357–375, esp. 364–365.

9   One of Brazil's most important social thinkers, Silvio Romero, mocked Braga's ideas as "absurd." Silvio Romero, *A pátria portugueza. O território e a raça. Apreciação do livro de igual título de Theóphilo Braga* (Lisbon: Livraria Clássica Editora de A. M. Teixeira e Companhia, 1905), p. 443. For a complete discussion of Romero's various attacks on Braga and those supporting the Turanian/Tupí notion, see Roberto Ventura, *Estilo tropical: História cultural e polêmicas literárias no Brasil, 1870–1914* (São Paulo: Companhia das Letras, 1991), pp. 85–86.

10 Freyre, *The Masters and the Slaves*, pp. 208–220, included in Salomão Jorge's *Album da colônia sírio-libanesa no Brasil* as "A influência do mouro na civilização do Brasil" (São Paulo: Sociedade Impressora Brasileira, 1948), pp. 39–66; Luís da Câmara Cascudo, *Mouros, franceses e judeus (três presenças no Brasil)* (Rio de Janeiro: Editora Letras e Artes, 1967), pp. 17–52.

11 Vicomte Enrique Onffroy de Thoron, *Voyages des flottes de Salomon et d'Hiram en Amérique: Position géographique de Parvaim, Ophir & Tarschisch* (Paris: Imp. G. Towne, 1868); "O rei Salomão no Rio Amazonas," in Júnior Amarilio, *As vantagens da immigração Syria no Brasil: Em torno de uma polêmica entre os snrs. Herbert V. Levy e Salomão Jorge, no "Diario de São Paulo"* (Rio de Janeiro: Off. Gr. da S. A. A. Noite, 1925), pp. 87–103; Viriato Correia, "O rei Salomão no Rio Amazonas," in Jorge, *Album da colonia sírio-libanesa*, pp. 471–479.

12 Plínio Salgado, *O estrangeiro (crônica da vida paulista)* [1926], 4th. ed. (São Paulo: Edições Panorama, 1948). Plínio Salgado, "Oriente (impressões de viagens) 1930," in his *Obras completas*, vol. 18 (São Paulo: Editora das Americas, 1956), p. 307.

13 Plínio Salgado, *O Oriente*, cited in Jorge, *Album da colônia sírio-libanesa*, p. 447.

14 Salomão Jorge, *Tudo pelo Brasil* (São Paulo: n.p., 1943), p. 147, new ed. published as *Tudo pelo Brasil: Discursos, ensaios e artigos literários* (São Paulo: Nova Época Editorial, 1975 [1976?]); Jorge, *Album da colonia sírio-libanesa*; Taufik Duoun, *A emigração sirio-libanesa as terras de promissão* (São Paulo: Tipografia Árabe, 1944); Jamil Safady, *O café e o mascate* (São Paulo: Editora Safady, 1973); Wadih Safady, *Cenas e cenários dos caminhos de minha vida* (Belo Horizonte: Estabelecimentos Gráficos Santa Maria, 1966); Sadalla Amin Chanem, *Impressões de viagem (Líbano-Brasil)* (Niterói: Gráfica Brasil, 1936).

15 A similar assertion was made by the Brazilian author Manoelito de Ornellas in his *Gaúchos e beduinos: A origem étnica e a formação social do Rio Grande do Sul* (Rio de Janeiro: José Olympio, 1948). See also Tanus Jorge Bastani, *O Líbano e os libaneses no Brasil* (Rio de Janeiro: n.p., 1945), pp. 133, 137.

16 Bastani, *O Líbano e os libaneses no Brasil*, pp. 133, 137.

17 There is an extensive non-Arabic bibliography on Arab immigration to countries other than Brazil. See Ignacio Klich, "Introduction to the Sources for the History of the Middle Easterners in Latin America," *Temas de Africa y Asia—Africanos y Mediorientales en América (siglos XVIII-XX)* (Buenos Aires) 2 (1993), 205–233;

Michael W. Suleiman, "Los árabes en América Latina: Bibliografía preliminar," *Estudios migratorios latinoamericanos* (Buenos Aires) 9:26 (April 1994), 165–188; Ignacio Klich, "Sources on the Lebanese and Other Middle Easterners in Latin America," Centre for Lebanese Studies (Oxford), *Papers on Lebanon* 16 (March 1995). While I use the term "mahjar" as synonomous with "diaspora," I am aware that Arab authors who refer to a Palestinian diaspora do not use the word.

18   José Daniel Colaco (Consul) to João da M. Machado (Minister of Foreign Relations), 20 August 1884, 02-Repartições Consulares Brasileiras, Tangier-Ofícios-1876–1890—265/1/10, AHI-R.

19   Interview by author with Sr. J., Belém do Pará, 13 April 1994.

20   Michael M. Laskier, *The Alliance Israélite Universelle and the Jewish Communities of Morocco: 1862–1962* (Albany: State University of New York Press, 1983), pp. 133–137; Robert Ricard, "Notes sur l'émigration de Israélites marocains en Amérique espagnole et au Brésil," *Revue africaine* 88 (1944), 1–6.

21   Edmund Burke III, *Prelude to Protectorate in Morocco: Precolonial Protest and Resistance, 1860–1912* (Chicago: University of Chicago Press, 1976), pp. 36–37; Salamão Serebrenick and Elias Lipiner, *Breve história dos judeus no Brasil* (Rio de Janeiro: Edições Biblos, 1962), p. 95.

22   Maïr Lévy, "Rapport sur l'émigration à Tétouan" (1891–1892), Archives of the Alliance Israélite Universelle (Tétouan), VI B 25, repr. in Sarah Leibovici, *Chronique des juifs de Tétouan (1860–1896)* (Paris: Editions Maisonneuve & Larose, 1984), pp. 287–296; Laskier, *The Alliance Israélite Universelle,* p. 137; Norman A. Stillman, *The Jews of Arab Lands in Modern Times* (Philadelphia: Jewish Publication Society, 1991), p. 38.

23   Barbara Weinstein, *The Amazon Rubber Boom, 1850–1920* (Stanford: Stanford University Press, 1983), pp. 50–51, 259–260; Abraham Ramiro Bentes, *Primeira comunidade israelita brasileira: Tradições, genealogia, pré-história* (Rio de Janeiro: Gráfica Borsoi, 1989).

24   *Yehudim al g'dot ha Amazonas/Jews on the Banks of the Amazon* (Tel Aviv: Beth Hatefutsoth—The Nahum Goldmann Museum of the Jewish Diaspora, 1987).

25   Robert Ricard, "L'émigration des juifs marocains en Amérique du sud," *Revue de géographie marocaine* 7:8 (2nd and 3rd trimesters, 1928), 3; Isaac Benchimol, "La langue espagnole au Maroc," *Revue des écoles de l'AIU* 2 (July–September 1901), 128. On the protégé system see Laskier, *The Alliance Israélite Universelle,* pp. 38–54.

26   See naturalization case of Mimom Elbás in Egon Wolff and Frieda Wolff, *Dicionário biográfico,* vol. 4, *Processos de naturalização de israelitas, século XIX* (Rio de Janeiro: n.p., 1987), p. 211.

27   José Daniel Colaco (consul) to Carlos de Carvalho (minister of foreign affairs), 18 September 1895, 02-Repartições Consulares Brasileiras, Tangier-Ofícios-1891–1895—265/1/11, AHI-R.

28   Ministry of Justice annex to José Daniel Colaco (Consul) to Carlos de Carvalho (Minister of Foreign Affairs), 18 September 1895, 02-Repartições Consulares Brasileiras, Tangier-Ofícios-1891–1895—265/1/11, AHI-R.

29   Letter of Simão Nahmias in Wolff and Wolff, *Dicionário biográfico,* vol. 4, p. 349.

30   *Al-Shogreb Al-Aksa* (Tangier), 27 August 1902, 02-Repartições Consulares Brasileiras, Tangier-Ofícios-1900–1925—265/1/13, AHI-R.

31   Confidential letter of A. Mauritz de Calinerio (Consul in Tangier) to Olyntho Máximo de Magalhaes (Minister of Foreign Affairs), 15 September 1902, 02-Repartições Consulares Brasileiras, Tangier-Ofícios-1900–1925—265/1/13, AHI-R.

32   *El Imparcial* (Madrid), 20 August 1902.

33   Confidential letter of A. Mauritz de Calinerio (Consul in Tangier) to Olyntho Máximo de Magalhaes (Minister of Foreign Relations), 6 October 1902, 02-Repartições Consulares Brasileiras, Tangier-Ofícios-1900–1925—265/1/13, AHI-R.

34   Letter of William R. Gordon (Brazilian Vice Consul in Tangier) to Itamaraty, 4 March 1903, 02-Repartições Consulares Brasileiras, Tangier-Ofícios-1900–1925 —265/1/13, AHI-R.

35   F. de B. Accioli de Vasconcellos, *Guia do emigrante para o império do Brazil pelo inspector geral das terras e colonização* (Rio de Janeiro: Typ. Nacional, 1884), pp. 36, 39; São Paulo, Secretaria dos Negócios da Agricultura, Comércio, e Obras Públicas, *Relatório apresentado ao dr. Francisco de Paula Rodrigues Alves, presidente do estado, pelo dr. Antonio Candido Rodriques, secretário da agricultura—Anno de 1900* (São Paulo: Typografia do Diário Oficial, 1901), p. 138; Weinstein, *The Amazon Rubber Boom*, pp. 50-51. On Christian emigration, see Albert H. Hourani, *Syria and Lebanon: A Political Essay* (London: Oxford University Press, 1946); A. L. Tibawi, *A Modern History of Syria Including Lebanon and Palestine* (London: Macmillan, 1969).

36   Since immigrants were categorized in different ways by the Brazilian government, statistics rarely coincide. "Discriminação por nacionalidade dos imigrantes entrando no Brasil no período 1884–1939," *RIC* 1:3 (July 1940), 617–642, and 1:4 (October 1940), 617–638; "Movimento imigratório no Brasil de 1819 à 1947," in J. Fernando Carneiro, *Imigração e colonização no Brasil* (Rio de Janeiro: Faculdade Nacional de Filosofia, 1950), p. 64; Meir Zamir, *The Formation of Modern Lebanon* (London: Croom Helm, 1985), p. 15. See also Duoun, *A emigração sírio libanesa*, p. 89; Rollie E. Poppino, *Brazil: The Land and People* (New York: Oxford University Press, 1973), p. 194; Clark S. Knowlton, "Spatial and Social Mobility of the Syrians and Lebanese in the City of São Paulo, Brazil" (Ph.D. thesis, Vanderbilt University, 1955), p. 50 and table 1, pp. 58–59. Published in Portuguese as *Sírios e libaneses* (São Paulo: Editora Anhembi, 1960).

37   Kohei Hashimoto, "Lebanese Population Movement, 1920-1939: Towards a Study," in Albert Hourani and Nadim Shehadi, eds., *The Lebanese in the World: A Century of Emigration* (London: I. B. Tauris; New York: St. Martin's Press, 1992), table A.1, pp. 89, 91.

38   There are no exact statistics on Syro-Lebanese emigration. According to Kohei Hashimoto, there were 688, 917 migrants between 1921 and 1926: 29.0 percent (199,785) resided in the United States, 25.7 percent (177,051) in Brazil, and 16.0 percent (110,226) in Argentina. Other significant populations in the Americas were in Mexico, Cuba, Canada, and Venezuela. "Lebanese Population Movement, 1920-1939," figure C.1, p. 107.

39   Albert Hourani, "Introduction," in Hourani and Shehadi, eds., *The Lebanese in the World*, pp. 4–7; David C. Gordon, *Lebanon: The Fragmented Nation* (London: Croom Helm, 1980), p. 112.

40   Charles Issawi, "The Historical Background of Lebanese Emigration, 1800–1914," in Hourani and Shehadi, eds., *The Lebanese in the World*, pp. 13–31; A. Ruppin, "Migration from and to Syria, 1860–1914," in Charles Issawi, ed., *The Economic History of the Middle East, 1800–1914* (Chicago: University of Chicago Press, 1966), pp. 269–273.

41   Among those identified as Syrians, Greek Orthodoxy was the most commonly listed religion. "Entradas de imigrantes pelo Pôrto de Santos, segundo a religião, 1908–1936," Secretaria da Agricultura, Indústria e Comércio, *Boletim da Directória de terras, colonização e imigração* 1:1 (October 1937), 64; *Boletim do Serviço de imigração e colonização* 2 (October 1940), 155, and 4 (December 1940), 11, 53. In 1939, for example, 63 percent of the Lebanese entering with "temporary visas" were listed as Catholic and 22 percent were listed as Muslim. For Syrians, 52 percent were listed as Orthodox, 24 percent as Catholic, and 17 percent as Muslim. These numbers, it must be emphasized, are far from conclusive. RIC 1:4 (October 1940), 127–128.

42   "Treaty of Friendship Between Turkey and Brazil," repr. in *L'Akcham* (Constantinople), 16 April 1928; and *Le Milliett* (Constantinople), 13 April 1928. Brazil had no diplomatic relations with Turkey between 1912 and 1927. This treaty shows the legal justification of Syrian-Lebanese entering Brazil as "turcos."

43   Oswaldo M. S. Truzzi, "Etnicidade e diferenciação entre imigrantes síriolibaneses em São Paulo," *Estudios Migratorios Latinoamericanos* (Buenos Aires) 9:26 (April 1994), 18. In contemporary Brazil the terms "Arab" and "Syrian-Lebanese" are used interchangeably. In cases where I can distinguish between Syrian and Lebanese immigrants, I will do so. Otherwise I will also use "Arab" and "Syrian-Lebanese" as synonyms.

44   Safady, *O café*, pp. 115–116.

45   Hildebrando Rodrigues, ed., *Album do Pará: Organizado sob os auspícios do governo do estado e com o apoio da Associação commercial do Pará, sendo interventor federal senhor excellencia o sr. dr. José Carneiro da Gama Malcher* (Belém: Typ. Novidades, 1939), p. 15; Bastani, *O Líbano e os libaneses;* Jacy Siqueira, "A presença síriolibanesa em Goiás" (Goiânia, Goias, 1993), pp. 22, 26 (mimeo). See the oral histories in Wilson de Lima Bastos, *Os sírios em Juiz de Fora* (Juiz de Fora, Minas Gerais: Edições Paraibuna, 1988), pp. 47–186. A novel that treats this theme is Emil Farhat, *Dinheiro na estrada: Uma saga de imigrantes* (São Paulo: T. A. Queiroz, 1986).

46   Assis Feres, "O mascate," cited in Safady, *Cenas e cenários*, pp. 184–185.

47   A slightly different version can be found in Claude Fahd Hajjar, *Imigração árabe: 100 anos de reflexão* (São Paulo: Icone Editora, 1985), p. 145.

48   Safady, *Cenas e cenários*, p. 139. On the earliest peddlers in Brazil, see José Alipio Goulart, *O mascate no Brasil* (Rio de Janeiro: Editora Conquista, 1967), esp. pp. 165–189; Safady, *O café*.

49   Pierre Deffontaines, "Mascates ou pequenos negociantes ambulantes do Brasil," *Geografia* 2:1 (1936), 28. For an analysis of the economic ascension of Arab immigrants in Brazil, see Jeffrey Lesser, "From Pedlars to Proprietors: Lebanese, Syrian and Jewish Immigrants in Brazil," in Hourani and Shehadi, eds., *The Lebanese in the World*, pp. 393-410.

50   Oswaldo Truzzi, *De mascates a doutores: Sírios e libaneses em São Paulo* (São Paulo: Editora Sumaré, 1991), pp. 8-9. See also *Boletim do Serviço de imigração e colonização* (December 1941), 132-166; Knowlton, "Spatial and Social Mobility," p. 113.

51   Arab immigrants to Brazil in the 1980s and 1990s repeated this process, and the press has continued to question their aims. "Enclave suspeito," *Veja* 28:7 (15 February 1995), 50-52.

52   Clark S. Knowlton, "The Social and Spatial Mobility of the Syrian and Lebanese Community in São Paulo, Brazil," in Hourani and Shehadi, eds., *The Lebanese in the World*, pp. 285-312; José Carlos G. Durand, "Formação do pequeno empresariado têxtil em São Paulo (1880-1950)," in Henrique Rattner, ed., *Pequena empresa: O comportamento empresarial na acumulação e na luta pela sobrevivência*, vol. 1 (São Paulo: Brasiliense, 1985), p. 112; Richard B. Morse, *From Community to Metropolis* (Gainesville: University of Florida Press, 1958), p. 254; Elie Safa, *L'Émigration libanaise* (Beirut: Université Saint-Joseph, 1960), pp. 55-57.

53   *A Imigração—Orgão da Sociedade central da imigração* (Rio de Janeiro) 5:43 (March 1888), 3. The *Mariannense* (Mariana, Minas Gerais) article, "A emigração turca," was reprinted in full.

54   A. Tavares de Almeida, *Oeste paulista: A experiência etnográfica e cultural* (Rio de Janeiro: Alba Editora, 1943), pp. 171-173. The larger fine was 500$000 (U.S. $158, roughly equivalent to U.S. $2,310 in 1994); the smaller was 10$000 (U.S. $3.17, roughly equivalent to U.S. $46 in 1994). Exchange rates can be found in Linda Lewin, *Politics and Parentela in Paraíba: A Case Study of Family-Based Oligarchy in Brazil* (Princeton: Princeton University Press, 1987), p. 430; Eugene Ridings, *Business Interest Groups in Nineteenth-Century Brazil* (Cambridge: Cambridge University Press, 1994), p. xiii.

55   São Paulo, *Relatório apresentado ao vice-presidente do estado pelo secretário dos negócios da justiça de S. Paulo José Getúlio Monteiro relativo ao Anno de 1897* (São Paulo: Typ. Espindola, Siqueira, 1898), p. 151; São Paulo, *Relatório apresentado ao secretário dos negócios da justiça do estado de S. Paulo pelo chefe de polícia Theodoro Dias de Carvalho Júnior em 31 de janeiro de 1895* (São Paulo: Typ. Espindola, Siqueira, 1898), p. 59; Thomas H. Holloway, *Policing Rio de Janeiro* (Stanford: Stanford University Press, 1993), p. 255.

56   "TURCOS," *A Imigração* 6: 60 (August 1889), 7; John Higham, *Strangers in the Land: Patterns of American Nativism, 1860-1925* [1955] (New York: Atheneum, 1973), p. 56.

57   Safady, *Cenas e cenários*, p. 201; Tanus Jorge Bastani, "A emigração libanesa para o Brasil," in Jorge, *Album da colonia sírio-libanesa*, p. 87. For a discussion of "naming" among Lebanese immigrants to the United States, see John G. Moses, *The*

Lebanese in America (Utica, NY: J. G. Moses, 1987), pp. 16-19. I would like to thank Dr. E. Nassar for directing me to this material.

58   Alfredo Ellis Júnior, *Populações paulistas*, Serie Brasiliana 27 (São Paulo: Companhia Editora Nacional, 1934), p. 203; Edgard Roquette-Pinto, *Rondonia* [1917], 3rd ed., Serie Brasiliana 22 (São Paulo: Companhia Editora Nacional, 1935), p. 81. *Rondonia* was awarded the Pedro II Prize by the Instituto Histórico e Geográfico Brasileiro. In 1930 El Salvador prohibited Syrian and Lebanese immigrants from translating or Hispanicizing their names. Ignacio Klich, "Sources on the Lebanese and Other Middle Easterners in Latin America," p. 7.

59   Hajjar, *Imigração árabe*, p. 70; Safady, *Cenas e cenários*, p. 146; Joseph L. Love, *São Paulo in the Brazilian Federation, 1889-1937* (Stanford: Stanford University Press, 1980), p. 91; Safa, *L'Émigration libanaise*, pp. 64-66. Viscount Philippe de Tarrazi's study of the Arab press noted the existence of ninety-five Arabic newspapers and magazines in Brazil prior to 1933. Phillipe de Tarrazi, *Ta'rikh al-Sihafah al-'Arabiyah* (History of the Arab Press) (Beirut[?]: Al-Matba'ah al-'Adabiyyah, 1913-1933). A study of Arabic use among Lebanese immigrants in São Paulo is Neuza Neif Nabhan, *O imigrante libanês em São Paulo: Estudo de fala* (São Paulo: FFLCH/Universidade de São Paulo, 1989).

60   C. Nijland, "The Fatherland in Arab Emigrant Poetry," *Journal of Arabic Literature* 20: 1 (March 1989), 61-62; M. M. Badawi, *A Critical Introduction to Modern Arabic Poetry* (Cambridge: Cambridge University Press, 1975), pp. 196-203; Salma Khadra Jayyusi, ed., *Modern Arabic Poetry: An Anthology* (New York: Columbia Press, 1987), pp. 68-71; Robin Ostle, ed., *Modern Literature in the Near and Middle East, 1850-1970* (London: Routledge, 1991); Safa, *L'Émigration libanaise*, p. 67; Jorge Safady, *Antologia árabe do Brasil* (São Paulo: Editora Comercial Safady, n.d.); Farid Aoun, *Do cedro ao mandacaru* (Recife: FIDA-Editorial Comunicação Especilizada S/C, 1979).

61   C. Nijland, "A 'New Andalusian' Poem," *Journal of Arabic Literature* 17 (1987), 102-103.

62   Ruppin, "Migration from and to Syria," p. 271.

63   Safady, *Cenas e cenários*, p. 168; Philip K. Hitti, *Lebanon in History: From the Earliest Times to the Present* (London: Macmillan, 1957), pp. 474-475. See also Afif I. Tannous, "Emigration, a Force of Social Change in an Arab Village," *Rural Sociology* 7:1 (March 1942), 62-74; Ruppin, "Migration from and to Syria," p. 271.

64   "Movimento migratório pelo pôrto do Santos, 1908-1936," *Boletim da Directória de terras, colonização e imigração* 1:1 (October 1937), table A-4, p. 54. After 1923 Turkish Jews made up a significant part of the emigration of "Turcos."

65   "Como os brasileiros foram recebidos no Líbano—Uma admiravel impressão do Padre José de Castro," in Amarilio, *As vantagens*, pp. 135-156; Duoun, *A emigração sírio-libanesa*, p. 288. Also see Chanem, *Impressões de viagem*, pp. 85-86.

66   *Brazilian-American*, 21 August 1926. Many thanks to Joel Wolfe for sharing this article with me.

67   Chanem, *Impressões de viagem*, pp. 24-25, 83; Duoun, *Confissões e indiscrições*, p. 19.

68   Julio de Revorêdo, *Immigração* (São Paulo: Empresa Gráfica Revista dos Tribunaes, 1934), pp. 92–93.

69   By 1930 there were at least thirty such groups in São Paulo alone. Duoun, *A emigração sírio-libanesa*, pp. 165–203.

70   *Correio Paulistano*, 12 April 1917; *O Estado de S. Paulo*, 8 September 1918.

71   Ugo Fleres, *Ettore Ximenes: Sua vita e sue opere* (Bergamo: Instituto Italiano d'Arti Grafiche, 1928), pp. 175–180; São Paulo, Prefeitura Municipal, *Catálogo das obras de arte em logradouros públicos de São Paulo: Regional sé* (São Paulo: Dept. do Patrimônio Histórico, 1987), p. 39.

72   Ettore Ximenes, quoted in *O Estado de S. Paulo*, 3 May 1928, p. 9. For a short discussion of a similar monument constructed by the Lebanese community in Tucumán, Argentina, see Michael Humphries, "Ethnic History, Nationalism and Transnationalism in Argentine Arab and Jewish Cultures," *Immigrants and Minorities* 16:1–2 (March/July 1997), 167–188.

73   *O Estado de S. Paulo*, 4 May 1928.

74   "O discurso do Sr. Nagib Jafet," in Duoun, *A emigração sírio-libanesa*, pp. 153–156.

75   Ilyās Farhāt, September 1928, trans. by Afonso Nagib Sabbag in Farhat, *Dinheiro na estrada*, p. 3.

76   Duoun, *A emigração sírio-libanesa*, p. 22.

77   Sadallah Amin Ghanem, "O Líbano, Conferência realizada no Club Libanez de Curityba, 1 set. 1934," Misc. 191.2.2 no. 18, p. 16, IHGB. Though the spelling is slightly different, the author appears to be the same as Sadalla Amin Chanem, author of *Impressões de viagem*.

78   Roberto Grün, *Negócios e famílias: Armênios em São Paulo* (São Paulo: Editora Sumaré, 1992), p. 32; Maria Isaura Pereira de Queiroz, "Assimilação de três famílias em São Paulo," *Sociologia* 12:1 (March 1950), 22–32.

79   The *New York Herald Tribune* article, written by Francis McCullagh, was republished in the *Japanese Advertiser* and attached to the diplomatic note of Silvio Rangel de Castro (Commercial Attaché, Tokyo legation) to Felix Pacheco (Minister of Foreign Relations), 7 October 1926, 01-Missões Diplomáticas Brasileiras, Tóquio-Ofícios-1923-1926—26/232/3/2, AHI-R.

80   Guilherme de Almeida, "Cosmópolis: O Oriente mais próximo," *O Estado de S. Paulo*, 19 May 1929, p. 6. The eight articles were published in book form as *Cosmópolis: São Paulo/29* (São Paulo: Companhia Editora Nacional, 1962).

81   Salgado, "Oriente," p. 308.

82   Unsigned confidential note from the Brazilian Consular Section, Alexandria, to Octavio Mangabeira, Minister of Foreign Relations, 14 April 1930, Lata 1290, Maço 29616-29622; Dulphe Pinheiro Machado, Director, Ministry of Agriculture, Industry, and Commerce, to Joaquim Eulalio, Director of Economic and Commercial Services, Diretoria Geral do Serviço de Povoamento, 9 June 1930, Lata 1290, Maço 29616-29622, AHI-R.

83   J. Rodrigues Valle, *Pátria vindoura (em defesa do Brasil)* (São Paulo: Gráfico Editora Monteiro-Lobato, 1926), pp. 61, 55.

84   Sociedade Nacional de Agricultura, *Immigração: Inquerito promovido pela Sociedade*

nacional de agricultura (Rio de Janeiro: Villani e Barbero, 1926), pp. 281–282, 51, 61.

85   Boris Fausto, *A revolução de 1930: Historiografia e História* (São Paulo: Brasiliense, 1986), p. 29; Wilson Suzigan, *Indústria brasileira: Origem e desenvolvimento* (São Paulo: Brasiliense, 1986), pp. 74–115.

86   Decree 19.482, 12 December 1930, in Brazil, *Collecção da leis da República dos Estados Unidos do Brasil de 1930*, vol. 2, *Actos da junta governativa provisória e do governo provisório (outubro a dezembro)* (Rio de Janeiro: Imprensa Nacional, 1931), p. 82; Commercial Attaché (Alexandria) to Octavio Mangabeira (Foreign Minister, Rio), 17 April 1930, Maço 29625/29 (1291), AHI-R. This was representative of comments made in justifying restrictive immigration policies throughout the Americas. See, for example, Evelyn Hu-DeHart, "Racism and Anti-Chinese Persecution in Sonora, Mexico, 1876–1932," *Amerasia* 9:2 (1982), 1–28.

87   "Entradas de imigrantes pelo pôrto de Santos, segundo a profissão, 1908–1936," table A-17; "Entradas de imigrantes pelo pôrto de Santos, segundo o sexo, 1908–1936," table A-10; "Entradas de imigrantes pelo pôrto de Santos, segundo a educação, 1908–1936," table A-11; "Entradas de imigrantes pelo pôrto de Santos, segundo o estado civil, 1908–1936," table A-12; *Boletim da Diretória de terras, colonização e imigração* 1:1 (October 1937), pp. 67, 69, 74. Knowlton cites statistics to the same effect through 1941. See also Getúlio Vargas, quoted in Revorêdo, *Immigração*, p. 146.

88   Albert Hourani has pointed out that persecution may have been less important at the time of emigration than it seems now. "Introduction," in Hourani and Shehadi, eds., *The Lebanese in the World*, pp. 4–7. For similar examples from the United States, see Matthew Frye Jacobson, *Special Sorrows: The Diasporic Imagination of Irish, Polish, and Jewish Immigrants in the United States* (Cambridge: Harvard University Press, 1995), pp. 15–53.

89   Hajjar, *Imigração árabe*, pp. 62–64. Compare the work in Arabic with that in Portuguese, filled with "Persian carpets" and "hot kisses." Salomão Jorge, "Canção do beduino," in *Arabescos—poesias 1918–1928* (São Paulo: Irmãos Pongetti Editores, 1941), p. 16.

90   Labib Zuwiyya Yamak, *The Syrian Social Nationalist Party: An Ideological Analysis* (Cambridge, MA: Center for Middle Eastern Studies/Harvard University Press, 1966), pp. 53–59; Hitti, *Lebanon in History*, p. 498.

91   Ilyās Farhāt, *Dīwān* (São Paulo, n.p. 1932), trans. by C. Nijland in "The Fatherland," pp. 64–65. Years later Rashīd Salīm Khūrī (al-Shafir al-Qarawi) was decorated by President Nasser of Egypt for his adherence to the nationalist Arab line.

92   Vivaldo Coaracy, *Problemas nacionaes* (São Paulo: Sociedade Impressora Paulista, 1930), p. 121. See also Lúcia Lippi Oliveira, Eduardo Rodrígues Gomes, and Maria Celina Whately, *Elite intelectual e debate político nos anos 30: Uma bibliografia comentada da revolução de 1930* (Rio de Janeiro: Fundação Getúlio Vargas/Instituto Nacional do Livro, 1980), pp. 148–150.

93   Deffontaines, "Mascates," p. 27. In a similar vein Richard Morse has argued that although Italians monopolized peddling until the 1880s, "they were soon to be

displaced by the even cannier Syrians." Morse, *From Community to Metropolis*, p. 175.

94 Salgado, "Síria," in Jorge, *Album da colonia sírio-libanesa*, p. 448.

95 Alfredo Ellis Júnior, *Raça de gigantes: Civilização no planalto paulista* (São Paulo: Novíssima Editora, 1926), and *Pedras lascadas* [1928], 2nd ed. (São Paulo: Editora Piratininga, 1933), p. 140.

96 Ellis Júnior, *Pedras lascadas*, pp. 80–82.

97 Companhia Editora Nacional, *Catálogo brasiliana: Comemorativo do 200 volumes. Síntese dos volumes da coleção "Brasiliana"* (São Paulo: Companhia Editora Nacional, 1941 [?]), p. 5; Laurence Hallewell, *Books in Brazil: A History of the Publishing Trade* (Metuchen, NJ: Scarecrow Press, 1982), pp. 216–217.

98 Ellis Júnior, *Populações paulistas*, pp. 197–211.

99 The Assyrians are mentioned numerous times in the Hebrew Bible as a group continually pressuring the biblical Israelites in approximately the eighth century before the common era. Early in the Christian era a number of groups in Asia Minor converted to Christianity and also became known as Assyrians.

100 Phebe Marr, *The Modern History of Iraq* (Boulder, CO: Westview Press, 1985), pp. 57–59; Khaldun S. Husry, "The Assyrian Affair of 1933 (I)," *International Journal of Middle East Affairs* 5:2 (1974), 161–176, and "The Assyrian Affair of 1933 (II)," *International Journal of Middle East Affairs* 5:3 (1974): 348–352.

101 "Protection of Minorities," *Monthly Summary of the League of Nations* 14:1 (January 1934), 17; "Report by the Committee for the Settlement of the Assyrians of Iraq, Submitted to the Council on May 17th, 1934," *League of Nations—Official Journal* 6:1 (June 1934), 545.

102 Letter of Afrânio de Melo Franco (Minister of Foreign Relations) to Tancredo Soares de Souza, 20 June 1931, 6(04).0034, Lata 401, Maço 6048, AHI-R. As in Brazil and its position on the Assyrians, there was a general reluctance throughout Latin America to accept refugees. See, for example, Haim Avni, "Latin America and the Jewish Refugees: Two Encounters, 1935 and 1938," in Judith Laikin Elkin and Gilbert W. Merkx, eds., *The Jewish Presence in Latin America* (Boston: Allen and Unwin, 1987), pp. 45–70.

103 Memo of Raúl P. do Rio Branco (Geneva) to Afrânio de Melo Franco, 20 November 1933, 6(04).0034, Lata 401, Maço 6048, AHI-R. Vargas's first minister of education and public health, Francisco Campos, issued a decree less than a year after the revolution of 1930 reinstating religious training in public schools. Charles F. O'Neil, "The Search for Order and Progress: Brazilian Mass Education, 1915–1933" (Ph.D. thesis, University of Texas at Austin, 1975), p. 293.

104 Memo of Raúl P. do Rio Branco (Geneva) to Afrânio de Melo Franco, 20 November 1933, 6(04).0034, Lata 401, Maço 6048, AHI-R; Sterndalle Bennett to López Olivan (president of Assyrian Committee of the League of Nations), 6 April 1934, FO371/17836, E2209/1/93, Public Records Office, London [hereafter PRO-L].

105 Petition of Arthur Thomas to Ministry of Labor, 6 December 1933, 6(04).0034, Lata 401, Maço 6048, AHI-R.

106   Major Johnson (Nansen Office) to Mr. Bennett, 3 January 1934, FO371/17832, E182/1/93, PRO-L.

107   Unsigned telegram of 4 January 1934, EM 4/1/34; telegram of Salgado Filho, 22 February 1934, EM 21/22/2/34, 6(04).0034, Lata 401, Maço 6048, AHI-R.

108   Unsigned telegram of 4 January 1934, 601.34(04). Lata 401, Maço 6048, AHI-R.

109   "Protection of Minorities," p. 17; Foreign Office memo from Mr. Rendel, 17 March 1934, FO371/17835, E1813/L/93, PRO-L; *The Times* (London), 20 January 1934; *Daily Mail* (London), 20 January 1934; *Morning Post* (London), 20 January 1934; *Daily Telegraph* (London), 20 January 1934.

110   *League of Nations—Official Journal* 2:1 (February 1934), 152; "Report of the Committee of the Council, Approved by the Council on January 19th, 1934," *League of Nations—Official Journal* 2:1 (February 1934), 226.

111   Major Johnson (Rio de Janeiro) to President of League of Nations, 3 March 1934, FO371/17835, E1653/1/93, PRO-L.

112   Military Attaché Sackville to U.S. Ambassador in Brazil, 28 December 1933, 832.5593/1, National Archives and Record Center, Washington, DC. [hereafter NARC-W].

113   Frederico A. Rondón, *Pelo Brasil central,* Serie Brasiliana 27 (São Paulo: Companhia Editora Nacional, 1934), p. 25.

114   *Correio da Manhã,* 28 March 1934; *Diário de Notícias,* 2 April 1934.

115   *Jornal do Brasil,* 25 January 1934; Lesser, "From Pedlars to Proprietors."

116   *A nação,* 4 February 1934 and 7 March 1934.

117   *A Nação,* 3 February 1934; *Correio da Manhã,* 28 March 1934. See comments of Dr. Hostilio de Araújo in Instituto da Ordem de Advogados do Paraná, *Anuário contendo os fatos de maior relevância da sua atividade no ano social do 1934 principalmente a campanha contra a imigração dos assírios* (Curitiba: Instituto da Ordem des Advogados do Paraná, 1936), pp. 40–41.

118   *Platéa* (São Paulo), 21 May 1934; *Diário Carioca,* 12 April 1934.

119   *Diário de Notícias,* 1 February 1934.

120   William Seeds to Brigadier Browne, 9 February 1934, FO371/17835, E1312/1/93, PRO-L.

121   *A Nação,* 7 March 1934.

122   Memo of Sterndalle Bennett, 1 June 1934, FO371/17832, E199/1/93, PRO-L; memo of conversation between Mr. Rendal and Mr. J. C. Sterndalle Bennett (Foreign Office) and Canon Douglas (Honorary Secretary of the Church of England on behalf of the Archbishop of Canterbury), 2 March 1934, FO371/17835, E1411/1/93, PRO-L; *L'Asie française* (Paris) 319 (April 1934), 126.

123   "Report by the Committee for the Settlement of the Assyrians of Iraq, Submitted to the Council on May 17th, 1934," *League of Nations—Official Journal* 6:1 (June 1934), 547.

124   Last Paper of 23 February 1934, FO371/17835, E 1245/1/93, PRO-L.

125   Ibid.

126   Seeds (Rio) to Foreign Office, 20 March 1934, FO371/17835, E1813/1/93; Stern-

dalle Bennett to López Olivan (President of Assyrian Committee of the League of Nations), 6 April 1934, FO371/17836, E2209/1/93, PRO-L.

127 Letter of the President of the Associação dos Agrônomos e Médico Veterinários do Paraná to Minister of Foreign Affairs, 1 March 1934, 15/5 6(04).0034, Lata 401, Maço 6048, AHI-R.

128 *San Francisco Chronicle*, 4 March 1934.

129 *The Times* (London), 22 May 1934.

130 See, for example, the handwritten label on the letter of President of the Associação dos Agronômos e Médico Veterinários do Paraná to Minister of Foreign Affairs, 1 March 1934, or the typewritten label on the letter of Cavalcanti de Lacerda to Nabuco de Gouvêa (Special Envoy of Brazil in Bern), 24 July 1934, NP/27/601.34(04), Lata 401, Maço 6048, AHI-R.

131 Alberto Torres (1865–1917) rejected concepts of racial superiority. Alberto Torres, *A organização nacional. Primeira parte, a constituição* (Rio de Janeiro: Imprensa Nacional, 1914), p. 136; Douglas McLain, Jr., "Alberto Torres, Ad Hoc Nationalist," *Luso-Brazilian Review* 4 (December 1967), 17–34; Adalberto Marson, *A ideologia nacionalista em Alberto Torres* (São Paulo: Duas Cidades, 1979).

132 Letter of Samuel Guy Inman to Committee on Cooperation in Latin America (New York), 15 April 1935, James G. McDonald Papers, "Inman, S. G. — Interviews, 1935," D356-H16, in Herbert H. Lehman Papers, Columbia University.

133 *Jornal do Comércio*, 2 May 1934; Society of the Friends of Alberto Torres Report in letter of Seeds to Simon, 15 March 1934, FO371/17835, E1686/1/93; Seeds to Simon, 8 March 1934, FO371/17836, E1986, PRO-L.

134 Undated press release, 000232, Lata 401, Maço 6048, AHI-R; *Diário de Notícias*, 11 March 1934.

135 Seeds to Simon, 8 March 1934, FO371/17836, E1986. Sir W. Seeds (Rio de Janeiro) to Sir John Simon (Foreign Office), 25 February 1934, FO 371/17835, E 1341/1/93, PRO-L.

136 E.g., *Correio da Manha*, 20 and 24 February 1934; *Diário Carioca*, 11, 15, and 20 February 1934.

137 *Anglo-Brazilian Chronicle* (Rio), 28 April 1934; handwritten memo of K. R. Johnstone on Foreign Office Last Paper of 17 June 1934, FO371/17840, E3871/1/93, PRO-L.

138 Emphasis added. *Folha da Noite* (São Paulo), 3 April 1934. Similar articles were published in *A Nação*, 7 March 1934; *Correio da Manhã*, 8 March 1934.

139 *Jornal do Comércio*, 5 February 1934.

140 Sir W. Seeds (Rio de Janeiro) to Sir John Simon (Foreign Office), 25 February 1934, FO371/17835, E1341/1/93, PRO-L.

141 Undated telegram from William Seeds (Rio de Janeiro) to Foreign Office, FO371/17839, E34308/1/93, PRO-L.

142 Constituição de 16 de julho de 1934, art. 5, para. 19 (g), and art. 121, para. 6. Hélio Silva, *1934—A constituinte* (Rio de Janeiro: Editora Civilização Brasileira, 1969), pp. 209–217.

143   Valdemar Carneiro Leão, *A crise da imigração japonesa no Brasil (1930–1934): Contornos diplomáticos* (Brasília: Fundação Alexandre de Gusmão/IPRI, 1990); Patrick M. Fukunaga, "The Brazilian Experience: The Japanese Immigrants During the Period of the Vargas Regime and the Immediate Aftermath, 1930–1946" (Ph.D. thesis, University of California, Santa Barbara, 1983), pp. 74–83.

144   Arthur Neiva, in Brazil, *Annaes da Assembléia nacional constituente organizados pela redação das annaes e documentos parlamentares,* vol. 7 (Rio de Janeiro: Imprensa Nacional, 1935), 66th session, 3 February 1934, pp. 328–329; exchange between Xavier de Oliveira and Morais Andrade, in Brazil, *Annaes da Assembléia nacional constituente organizados pela redação das annaes e documentos parlamentares,* vol. 8 (Rio de Janeiro: Imprensa Nacional, 1935), 76th session, 21 February 1934, p. 266. See menu attached to papers in AN 16.11.27, Centro de Pesquisa e Documentação de História Contemporânea do Brasil [hereafter CPDOC-RJ]. For more on Neiva's trip to Japan, see chapter 4.

145   Brazil, *Annaes da Assembléia nacional constituinte organizados pela redação das annaes e documentos parlamentares,* vol. 4 (Rio de Janeiro: Imprensa Nacional, 1935), pp. 211–216 (Neiva) and 546–549 (Xavier de Oliveira).

146   Xavier de Oliveira, in Brazil, *Annaes da Assembléia nacional constituente organizados pela redação das annaes e documentos parlamentares,* vol. 6 (Rio de Janeiro: Imprensa Nacional, 1935), 58th session, 25 January 1934, p. 451.

147   Pedro Aurélio de Góes Monteiro, "Discurso ao Assembléia constituente de 1934," Secção de Arquivos Particulares-Pedro Aurélio de Góes Monteiro, AP 51 (12)– "Communismo, 1930–1936," AN-R.

148   Morais de Andrade, in Brazil, *Annaes da Assembléia nacional constituente organizados pela redação das annaes e documentos parlamentares,* vol. 6 (Rio de Janeiro: Imprensa Nacional, 1935), 55th session, 22 January 1934, p. 348; Brazil, *Annaes da Assembléia nacional constituente organizados pela redação das annaes e documentos parlamentares,* vol. 8 (Rio de Janeiro: Imprensa Nacional, 1935), 76th session, 21 February 1934, p. 266. This constitution was the most liberal in Brazil up to that time, in terms of guaranteeing personal freedoms. At the same time, it was the first to impose general restrictions on immigration.

149   *Jornal do Comércio,* 1 November 1934. For more on the McDonald mission, see Jeffrey Lesser, *Welcoming the Undesirables* (Berkeley: University of California Press, 1995), pp. 68–77.

150   Telegrams from Itamaraty to London embassy, 4 January 1934, 601.34(04) and EM/4/1/34, Lata 401, Maço 6048, AHI-R; Tacúrcio Tôrres, in Brazil, *Annaes da Assembléia nacional constituente organizados pela redação das annaes e documentos parlamentares,* vol. 8 (Rio de Janeiro: Imprensa Nacional, 1935), 76th session, 21 February 1934, p. 258.

151   Telegram of Alberto Cruz (Federação Operária) and Oscar Martins Gomes (Instituto da Ordem de Advogados do Paraná), in Brazil, *Annaes da Assembléia nacional constituente organizados pela redação das annaes e documentos parlamentares,* vol. 12 (Rio de Janeiro: Imprensa Nacional, 1936), p. 399; 105th session, 27 March 1934, in Instituto da Ordem de Advogados do Paraná, *Anuário,* p. 33.

152   Dr. Hostilio de Araújo, "Basta de achincalhes!," in Instituto da Ordem de Advogados do Paraná, *Anuário*, p. 39.

153   Dr. Ulisses Vieira, "Contra a imigração assíria," ibid.

154   Foreign Office minute, 2 March 1934, FO371/17835, E1376/1/93, PRO-L; *A Batalha*, 10 April 1934; *The Times* (London), 1 March 1934 and 20 March 1934; *Morning Post* (London), 24 March 1934; *Sunday Times* (London), 25 March 1934; letter of Nissan Yavou (President of the Community of Assyrians of Athens) to Getúlio Vargas, 7 April 1934, Lata 401, Maço 6048, AHI-R.

155   Jeffrey D. Needell, "History, Race and the State in the Thought of Oliveira Vianna," *Hispanic American Historical Review* 75:1 (February 1995), 2, 11-20; Élide Rugai Bastos, "Oliveira Vianna e a sociologia no Brasil (um debate sobre a formação do povo)," in Élide Rugai Bastos and João Quartim de Moraes, eds., *O pensamento de Oliveira Vianna* (Campinas: Editora da UNICAMP, 1993), pp. 405-428.

156   Oliveira Vianna, *Populações meridonais do Brasil,* 5th ed., vol. 1 (Rio de Janeiro: José Olympio, 1952), p. 13, and *Raça e assimilação* (São Paulo: Companhia Editora Nacional, 1932), pp. 93-126; Nancy Leys Stepan, *"The Hour of Eugenics"* (Ithaca, NY: Cornell University Press, 1991), p. 156; Thomas E. Skidmore, *Black into White* (New York: Oxford University Press, 1974), p. 64.

157   Dulphe Pinheiro Machado, general comments on immigration, 9 January 1937, Presidência da República-Relações-Fundo Conselho Nacional de Economia-Serie Intercambio Comercial, Lata 174-no. 468-1936, AN-R.

158   Copy of the committee charge drawn up by Oliveira Vianna and sent to Salgado Filho, "Comissão de inquérito sobre imigração assíria," 16 April 1934, 601.34(04), Lata 401, Maço 6048, AHI-R; reserved memo of Cavalcanti de Lacerda (Acting Minister of Foreign Affairs) to Salgado Filho, 4 May 1934, NP/95/601.34(04), Lata 401, Maço 6048, AHI-R; *L'Asie française* (Paris) 319 (April 1934), 126; summary of the report on Brazil by General Browne, in "Protection of Minorities," p. 122.

159   The full text was reprinted in *Jornal do Comércio,* 2 May 1934. See also *Jornal do Comércio,* 14 March 1934 and 17 April 1934; memo of Acting Foreign Minister Cavalcanti de Lacerda to Nabuco de Gouvêa (Special Envoy of Brazil in Bern), 24 July 1934, NP/27/601.34(04), Lata 401, Maço 6048, AHI-R; memo of Nabuco de Gouvêa to Foreign Minister José Carlos de Macedo Soares, 6 September 1934, #107, 601.34(04), Lata 401, Maço 6048, AHI-R.

160   Decree 24,215, art. 2, no. 8, 9 May 1934, *Diário Oficial,* 18 May 1934; Decree 24,258, 16 May 1934, *Diário Oficial,* 11 June 1934. For a discussion of similar earlier bans on those of African descent, see Jeffrey Lesser, "Are African-Americans African or American? Brazilian Immigration Policy in the 1920's," *Review of Latin American Studies* 4:1 (1991), 115-137, published in Portuguese as "Legislação imigratória e dissimulação racista no Brasil (1920-1934)," *Arché* 3:8 (1994), 79-98.

161   Memo of Seeds to Simon, 21 May 1934, FO371/17491, A4554/2862/6, PRO-L.

162   *Correio da Manhã,* 28 March 1934.

163   Muniz to Cavalcanti de Lacerda, 18 May 1934, #40, Lata 401, Maço 6048, AHI-R.

164   *O Jornal* (Rio), 31 May 1934.

165 *Jornal do Comércio*, 14 March 1934.

166 W. Seeds to Foreign Office, 4 February 1935, FO371/19405, N 479/41/97, PRO-L; "Summary of the Month," *Monthly Summary of the League of Nations* 14:6 (June 1934), 132, 147; *The Times* (London), 8 June 1934.

167 *Diário Carioca* (Rio de Janeiro), 11 April 1934; *Correio da Manhã* (Rio de Janeiro), 29 June 1934; Lindolpho Pessôa, "A missão dos brasileiros," in Instituto da Ordem de Advogados do Paraná, *Anuário*, pp. 93-94.

168 Paulo Cursino de Moura, *São Paulo de outrora: Evocações da metrópole* [1932] (Belo Horizonte: Editora Itatiaia; [Sao Paulo]: Editora da Universidade de Sao Paulo, 1980), p. 174; Manuel Diégues Júnior, *Etnias e cultura no Brasil* [1952] (São Paulo: Círculo do Livro, 1976), p. 147.

169 R. Paulo Souza, "Contribuição à etnologia paulista," *Revista do Arquivo municipal de São Paulo* 3:35 (January 1937), 96; Oscar Egídio de Araújo, "Enquistamentos étnicos," *Revista do Arquivo Municipal de São Paulo* 6:65 (March 1940), 230-231, 233; Knowlton, "Spatial and Social Mobility," 112.

170 Deffontaines, "Mascates," p. 29; Oscar Egídio de Araújo, "Latinos e não latinos no município de São Paulo," *Revista do Arquivo Municipal de São Paulo* 7:75 (April 1941), 93; Tavares de Almeida, *Oeste paulista*, pp. 171-173; Moura, *São Paulo de outrora*, p. 174.

171 Herbert Levy, *Problemas actuaes na economia brasileira* (São Paulo: Empresa Gráfica da Revista dos Tribunaes, 1934), pp. 96, 104.

172 Jeffrey Lesser, " 'O judeu é o turco de prestação': Etnicidade, assimilação e imagens das elites sobre árabes e judeus no Brasil," *Estudos Afro-Asiáticos* 27 (April 1995), 65-85.

173 Salomão Jorge, "Carta aberta ao Dr. José Maria Whitaker," in Amarilio, *As vantagens*, p. 25. Using this same flawed logic, Jorge could also have easily argued that Bank of Brazil head Ricardo Jafet was also Jewish because Yefet is a common biblical name.

174 Ibid., pp. 27, 33, 35.

175 Herbert Levy, "A propósito de uma carta aberta ao dr. José Maria Whitaker," in Amarilio, *As vantagens*, pp. 39, 47.

176 Amarilio, *As vantagens*, pp. 43, 157-161. The Ação Integralista Brasileira, formed in 1932, was the first Brazilian fascist movement to gain national prominence. It was modeled after the Italian and Portuguese fascist movements but used Nazi-influenced trappings such as the brown shirt and the swastika-like Greek sigma. Its nationalistic goal was an "integral" state with a single authoritarian leader. See Hélgio Trindade, *Integralismo: O fascismo brasileiro na década de 30*, 2nd ed. (São Paulo: DIFEL, 1979).

177 Eduardo B. Jafet, *Impressões de viagem* (São Paulo: n.p., 1936), p. 176.

178 Amarilio, preface to *As vantagens*.

179 Alfredo Romario Martins, *Quanto somos e quem somos: Dados para a história e a estatística do povoamento de Paraná* (Curitiba: Empresa Gráfica Paranaense, 1941), p. 177.

180   George Lian, "Aspectos e particularidades da imigração árabe," *Digesto econômico* 2:13 (December 1945), 74-77.

181   Ornellas, *Gaúchos e beduínos.*

182   Roger Bastide, *Brasil: Terra de contrastes,* 2nd ed. (São Paulo: Difusão Européia do Livro, 1964), p. 183. Originally published as *Brésil, terre des contrastes* (Paris: Hachette, 1957).

183   Duoun, *A emigração sírio-libanesa,* p. 268; Knowlton, "Spatial and Social Mobility," pp. 297, 188. Richard Morse played on similar stereotypes of Arabs in his *From Community to Metropolis,* p. 254.

184   Bastos, *Os sírios em Juiz de Fora,* p. 27.

4   Searching for a Hyphen

1   Thomas H. Holloway, *Immigrants on the Land* (Chapel Hill: University of North Carolina Press, 1980), pp. 36, 48.

2   *Correio Paulistano,* 20 October 1894, p. 1. See also *Estado de S. Paulo,* 30 September 1894; *Correio Paulistano,* 24 October 1894.

3   Sandra Wilson, "The 'New Paradise': Japanese Emigration to Manchuria in the 1930's and 1940's," *International History Review* 17:2 (May 1995), 249.

4   Hiroshi Saito, *O japonês no Brasil: Estudo de mobilidade e fixação* (São Paulo: Editora Sociologia e Política, 1961), pp. 26-27.

5   Arthur Jaceguay *O dever do momento: Carta a Joaquim Nabuco* (Rio de Janeiro: Typ. Levzinger, 1887), pp. 11-12. Memo of Eduardo Callado and Arthur Silveira da Motta, 30 March 1882, Missões Especiais do Brasil no Estrangeiro-06; 271/2/2-Barão de Jaceguay (Arthur Silveira da Motta), AHI-R.

6   Unfortunately, it is impossible to tell which newspaper this clipping came from. Secretaria da Agricultura, série 6, Imigração e Colonização, subsérie 1, Imigração, SA 6-1, #880-Recortes, December 1885, Arquivo Público de Minas Gerais, Belo Horizonte.

7   *Correio Paulistano* (São Paulo), 5 August 1892, p. 3. The perfume was actually a French product.

8   Law 97, 5 October 1892, arts. II and III.

9   Brazil, *Relatório apresentado ao presidente da república dos Estados Unidos do Brazil pelo ministro do estado das relações exteriores Carlos Augusto de Carvalho em maio de 1895* (Rio de Janeiro: Imprensa Nacional, 1895), pp. 44-45; Barão de Ladario to Cassiano do Nascimento (minister of foreign affairs), 7 February 1894; Barão de Ladario to Cassiano do Nascimento (minister of foreign affairs), 2 April 1894, Missões Especiais do Brasil no Estrangeiro-06; 271/2/3, Barão de Ladario-Missões Especiais, China, 1893-1894, AHI-R.

10   Henrique C. R. Lisboa, *Os chins do Tetartos* (Rio de Janeiro: Typografia da Empreza Democrática Editora, 1894), pp. 149, 152.

11   Barão de Ladario to Cassiano do Nascimento (Minister of Foreign Affairs), 7 Feb-

ruary 1894, 06-Missões Especiais do Brasil no Estrangeiro, 271/2/3, Barão de Ladario-Missões Especiais, China, 1893–1894, AHI-R; Eugene Ridings, *Business-Interest Groups in Nineteenth-Century Brazil* (Cambridge: Cambridge University Press, 1994), p. 174.

12   Mário Botelho de Miranda, *Um brasileiro no Japão em guerra* (São Paulo: Companhia Editora Nacional, 1944), pp. 106–109; Nelson Tabajara de Oliveira, *Japão: Reportagens do Oriente*, Coleção Viagens, vol. 4 (São Paulo: Companhia Editora Nacional, 1934), p. 122. A fascinating discussion of both the language and the location of homosexuality can be found in Peter Beattie, "Conflicting Penal Codes: Modern Masculinity and Sodomy in the Brazilian Military, 1860–1916," in Daniel Balderston and Donna J. Guy, eds., *Sex and Sexuality in Latin America* (New York: New York University Press, 1997), pp. 65–85.

13   Raymundo Cyriaco Alves da Cunha, *Obras públicas, terras e colonização* (Belém do Pará: n.p., 1895), pp. 26–28.

14   Lisboa, *Os chins do Tetartos*, pp. 155, 158.

15   Henrique Lisboa (legation in Tokyo) to Dionísio E. de Castro Cerqueira (Itamaraty), 1 November 1897, 01-Missões Diplomáticas Brasileiras, Tóquio-Ofícios-1897–1899—26/232/2/1, AHI-R.

16   Director, Department of Foreign Business, Japanese Ministry of Foreign Affairs, to governors of the provinces of Kanagawa, Hyōgo, and Osaka, 11 May 1897; "Miscellaneous Documents Relating to Japanese Immigration to Brazil" (*Burajirukoku imin kankei zakken*), Japanese Ministry of Foreign Affairs, Tokyo, Japan, 1868–1945, Meiji-Taisho 38280 14/15/16 [hereafter JMFA-MT]; Shyōchi Omori (Governor of Hyōgo) to Baron Shigenobu Okuma (Foreign Minister), 26 May 1897, JMFA-MT 38280 20/21. (JMFA-MT was microfilmed for the Library of Congress, 1949–1951.) All materials cited have been read by the author in Portuguese translations by Prof. Katsunori Wakisaka in the Archives of the Centro de Estudos Nipo-Brasileiros (São Paulo) [hereafter ACENB-SP]. See also Arlinda Rocha Nogueira, *Imigração japonesa na história contemporânea do Brasil* (São Paulo: Centro de Estudos Nipo-Brasileiros, 1983), p. 87.

17   Saito, *O japonês no Brasil*, pp. 27–28. Oliveira Lima's comments are cited in Valdemar Carneiro Leão, *A crise da imigração japonesa no Brasil (1930–1934): Contornos diplomáticos* (Brasília: IPRI/Fundação Alexandre de Gusmão, 1989), p. 22.

18   Henrique Lisboa (legation in Tokyo) to Dionísio E. de Castro Cerqueira (Minister of Foreign Affairs), 18 February 1898. The clipping from *The Japan Times* (no date) was attached to Lisboa's memo; 01-Missões Diplomáticas Brasileiras, Tóquio-Ofícios-1897–1899—26/232/2/1, AHI-R; Brazil, Secretaria dos Negócios da Agricultura, Comércio e Obras Públicas, *Relatório apresentado ao dr. Francisco de Paula Rodrigues Alves, presidente do estado, pelo dr. Antonio Candido Rodriques, secretário da agricultura—Anno de 1900* (São Paulo: Typografia do Diário Official, 1901), p. 122; Alan Takeo Moriyama, *Imingaisha: Japanese Emigration Companies and Hawaii, 1894–1908* (Honolulu: University of Hawaii Press, 1985), p. 151. The *Japan Times* was one of a large group of English-language newspapers founded in the latter half of the nineteenth century and widely read by members of Japan's business

and political elite as well as foreign residents. See James L. Huffman, *Politics of the Meiji Press: The Life of Fujuchi Gen'ichirō* (Honolulu: University Press of Hawaii, 1980), pp. 49–50.

19   Fukashi Suguimura to Tarō Katsura (Substitute Minister of Foreign Affairs), 2 October 1905, JMFA-MT 38280 104/105/106/107/108/109/110/111/112/113, ACENB-SP; Marshall C. Eakin, *British Enterprise in Brazil* (Durham, NC: Duke University Press, 1989), p. 48. Translations of Suguimura's impressions of São Paulo can be found in Tereza Hatue de Rezende, *Ryu Mizuno: Saga japonesa em terras brasileiras* (Curitiba: Secretaria de Estado da Cultura, 1991), pp. 13–20.

20   Tokujiro Araki (headman of the village of Shirosatoi, Gumma province) to Viscount Toh Hayashi (Department of Foreign Business, Japanese Ministry of Foreign Affairs), 5 December 1906, JMFA-MT 38280 97/98/99, ACENB-SP.

21   Arlinda Rocha Nogueira, "Antecedentes da imigração japonesa no Brasil," in Comissão de Elaboração da História dos 80 Anos da Imigração Japonesa no Brasil, ed., *Uma epopéia moderna: 80 anos da imigração japonesa no Brasil* (São Paulo: Editora Hucitec, 1992), p. 49; *Diário oficial do estado de São Paulo*, 12 December 1897; "Memorial à respeito da imigração japonesa dirigido à Sociedade paulista de agricultura," Secretaria da Agricultura-1906, Maço s/no, Arquivo do Estado de São Paulo [hereafter AESP].

22   Hideki Arimatsu (governor of Mie) to Kikujiro Ishii, director, Department of Foreign Business, Japanese Ministry of Foreign Affairs, 4 June 1908, JMFA-MT 38280 136/137, ACENB-SP; *Yorodzu Choho* (Yokohama), 6 December 1907.

23   *Afarodzu Choho* (Tokyo), 20 January 1908.

24   *Japan Times* (Tokyo), 4 March 1908; *Japan Gazette* (Tokyo), 5 March 1908 and 16 March 1908.

25   Cited in Saito, *O japonês no Brasil*, p. 29.

26   São Paulo, *Relatório apresentado ao dr. Jorge Tibiriçá, presidente do estado, pelo dr. Carlos Botelho, secretário da agricultura, relativo ao ano de 1907* (São Paulo: Secretaria da Agricultura, 1908), pp. 23–24, 138–142; "Parecer apresentado à Assembléia legislativa do estado do Rio de Janeiro pelo relator da Commissão de justiça, legislação e instrução pública, e por esta unanimente assinado, em 30 de outubro de 1909, sobre o contrato de novembro de 1907 firmado entre o governo desse estado e os srs. Rio Midzuno e Raphael Monteiro para a Fundação de núcleos coloniaes de japonezes na Baixada Fluminense," in Nestor Ascoli, *A immigração japoneza para a baixada do estado do Rio de Janeiro*, 2nd ed. (Rio de Janeiro: Ediçao da Revista de Língua Portuguesa, 1924), p. 17.

27   Secretaria da Agricultura-Diretória de Terras, Colonização e Immigração, 30 June 1908, file Wilson, Sons and Co., Ltd., no. 121, pp. 3–7, Setor Manuscritos-Secretaria da Agricultura-Requerimentos Diversos, Ano 1908, Maço 38, Caixa 39, Ordem 7255, AESP.

28   Shūhei Hosokawa, "A história da música entre os nikkei no Brasil enfocando as melodias japonesas," *Anais do IV encontro nacional de professores universitários de língua, literatura e cultura japonesa* (São Paulo: Centro de Estudos Japoneses da Universidade de São Paulo, 1993), p. 127.

29   Nakano Makiko, *Makiko's Diary: A Merchant Wife in 1910 Kyoto*, trans. Kazuko Smith (Stanford: Stanford University Press, 1995), pp. 22, 51, 232.

30   Antonio Coutinho Gomes Pereira, *Viagem de circunavegação do navio-escola "Benjamin Constant" (de 22 de janeiro à 16 de Dezembro de 1908)* (Rio de Janeiro: Imprensa Nacional, 1909), p. 40; Alcino Santos Silva (Consul in Yokohama) to Barão do Rio Branco (Itamaraty), 3 May 1908; Alcino Santos Silva (Consul in Yokohama) to Barão do Rio Branco (Itamaraty), 22 September 1908, 02-Repartições Consulares Brasileiras, Yokohama-Ofícios-1900–1910—267/1/2, AHI-R.

31   Luiz Guimarães (Second Secretary of the legation in Tokyo) to Barão do Rio Branco (Itamaraty), 2 January 1907; Luiz Guimarães (Second Secretary of the legation in Tokyo) to Barão do Rio Branco (Itamaraty), 23 September 1907; Luiz Guimarães (Second Secretary of the legation in Tokyo) to Barão do Rio Branco (Itamaraty), 22 June 1908, 01-Missões Diplomáticas Brasileiras, Tóquio-Ofícios-1907–1910—26/232/2/6, AHI-R.

32   *Japan Times* (Tokyo), 9 October 1907. This lumping together of the Chinese and Japanese was common throughout the first half of the twentieth century. See, for example, Joaquim da Silva Rocha, *História da colonização do Brasil*, vol. 1, *Chinezes e japonezes* (Rio de Janeiro: Imprensa Nacional, 1919), pp. 83–90.

33   Unsigned (Rio de Janeiro) to Ministers Komura and Uchida (Tokyo), 16 November 1909, JMFA-MT 38280 284/285/285a; Ryoji Noda (Provisional Minister Substitute in Brazil) to Jutaro Komura (Minister of Foreign Affairs, Tokyo), 6 January 1910. JMFA-MT 38280 326/327/327a, ACENB-SP.

34   *Correio da Manhã* (Rio de Janeiro), 30 November 1908.

35   Okinawans (Ryukyuans) were considered a lower-status minority group. They spoke a dialect related to ancient Japanese that was incomprehensible to most mainland Japanese (*naichi-jin*). Between 1908 and 1912 almost 17 percent of all Japanese entries in Brazil were from Okinawa (746/4,540), making Okinawans the second largest group after those from Kumamoto (24 percent; 1,083/4,540) and more numerous than those from Hiroshima (14 percent; 629/4,540). This information was generated from the disembarkation lists held at the Hospedaria dos Imigrantes in São Paulo as published by Nogueira, *A Imigração japonesa*, p. 153, and confirmed in the original by the author.

36   J. Amândio Sobral, "Os japonezes em S. Paulo," *Correio Paulistano*, 25 June 1908, p. 1.

37   Teijiro Suzuki, secretary of the Hospedaria dos Imigrantes, quoted in Tomoo Handa, *Memória de um imigrante japonês no Brasil* (São Paulo: T.A. Queiroz/Centro de Estudos Nipo-Brasileiros, 1980), 1986.

38   *Correio paulistano*, 23 June 1908, p. 1; *A Tribuna* (Santos), 19 June 1908, p. 1; Masuji Kiyotani and José Yamashiro, "Os imigrantes do *Kasato-Maru*," in Comissão de Elaboração da História dos 80 Anos da Imigração Japonesa no Brasil, ed., *Uma epopéia moderna*, p. 69.

39   *Correio Paulistano*, 27 June 1908, p. 1.

40   Republished as "Parecer apresentado à Assembléia legislativa do estado do Rio de

Janeiro pelo relator da Commissão de justiça, legislação e instrucção pública," in Ascoli, *A immigração japoneza*, p. 22.

41 Ibid.

42 Letter of Virgilio Ruiz Alves (fazenda owner) to Luiz Ferras, director of Agencia Official de Colonização e Trabalho no Estado, 8 January 1908, Secretaria da Agricultura-Diretoria de Terras, Colonização e Immigração, 30 June 1908, file Wilson, Sons and Co. Ltd., no. 121, pp. 30–32, Setor Manuscritos-Secretaria da Agricultura-Requerimentos Diversos, Ano 1908, Maço 38, Caixa 39, Ordem 7255, AESP.

43 *Relatório apresentado ao dr. M. J. Albuquerque Lins, presidente do estado, pelo dr. Antônio Cândido Rodrigues, secretário da agricultura, referente ao ano de 1908* (São Paulo: Secretaria da Agricultura, 1909), p. 125; *Correio Paulistano*, 2 December 1908; notes of an interview by Hiroshi Saito with K. Nakagawa, 10 October 1953, Donald Pierson Papers (Box 8), Department of Special Collections, George A. Smathers Libraries, University of Florida [hereafter SL-UF]; Nogueira, *Imigração japonesa*, p. 108; Katsuo Uchiyama, Tetsuya Taijiri, and José Yamashiro, "Cresce o número de emigrantes," in Comissão de Elaboração da História dos 80 Anos da Imigração Japonesa no Brasil, ed., *Uma epopéia moderna*, p. 140.

44 Report to Toyo Imin Goshi Kaisha Emigration Company, 11 January 1909, JMFA-MT 38280 371/371a/372/372a/373/373a/374/374a/375/375a/376/376a/377/377a/378/378a, ACENB-SP.

45 Handa, *Memória de um imigrante japonês*, p. 59; Tomoo Handa, *O imigrante japonês: História de sua vida no Brasil* (São Paulo: T. A. Queiroz/Centro de Estudos Nipo-Brasileiros, 1987), p. 388; Associação Okinawa do Brasil, *Guia de endereços—1995* (São Paulo: Associação Okinawa do Brasil, 1995), p. 5; *Jornal do Comércio* (Campo Grande) (3 April 1924), 3.

46 Sadatsuchi Uchida (Japanese Minister Plenipotentiary in Brazil) to Count Jutaro Komura (Minister of Foreign Affairs), 20 March 1909, JMFA-MT 38280 315/316/317/318/319/320; report to Toyo Imin Goshi Kaisha Emigration Co., 11 January 1909, JMFA-MT 38280 371/371a/372/372a/373/373a/374/374a/375/375a/376/376a/377/377a/378/378a, ACENB-SP. See also the comments of the Japanese government translator Noda quoted in Handa, *O imigrante japonês*, p. 47.

47 Sadatsuchi Uchida (Japanese Minister Plenipotentiary in Brazil) to Count Jutaro Komura (Minister of Foreign Affairs), 15 September 1908, JMFA-MT 38280 245/246/246a/247/248/248a/249, ACENB-SP; Zempati Ando and Katsunori Wakisaka, "Sinopse histórica da imigração japonesa no Brasil," in Eurípides Simões de Paula, ed., *O japonês em São Paulo e no Brasil* (São Paulo: Centro de Estudos Nipo-Brasileiros, 1971), p. 26; Zempati Ando, *Estudos sócio-históricos da imigração japonesa* (São Paulo: Centro de Estudos Nipo-Brasileiros, 1976), p. 138.

48 Sadatsuchi Uchida (Japanese Minister Plenipotentiary in Brazil) to Count Jutaro Komura (Minister of Foreign Affairs), 8 November 1909, JMFA-MT 38280 286/287/248/288/289/290, ACENB-SP; *Annual Report of the St. John d'el Rey Mining Company, 1913*, p. 8; letter of A. G. N. Chalmers to directors, 7 August 1925, St.

John d'el Rey Archive, Nova Lima. My thanks to Marshall Eakin for generously sharing his research on the St. John d'el Rey Mining Company with me.

49   *Correio da manhã* (Rio de Janeiro), 30 November 1908; Kiyotani and Yamashiro, "Os imigrantes do *Kasato-Maru*," pp. 75-76; Nogueira, *Imigração japonesa*, pp. 108-109.

50   Letter of Godofredo da Fonseca to Antonio Candido Rodrigues, Secretary of Agriculture, 19 September 1908, and attached correspondence and internal memos, Secretaria da Agricultura-Diretoria de Terras, Colonização e Immigração, 19 September 1908, file Godofredo da Fonseca, no. 1685, Setor Manuscritos-Secretaria da Agricultura-Requerimentos Diversos, Ano 1908, Maço 40, Caixa 41, Ordem 7257, AESP.

51   Handa, *O imigrante japonês*, p. 164.

52   Kiyotani and Yamashiro, "Os Imigrantes do *Kasato-Maru*," p. 73. Portuguese trans. from the Japanese in the original. The translation to English is from a free translation to Portuguese and does not attempt to follow the poetic style.

53   Part of Riukiti Yamashiro's handwritten diary was translated into Portuguese by his son. José Yamashiro, *Trajetória de duas vidas: Uma história de imigração e integração* (São Paulo: Aliança Cultural Brasil-Japão/Centro de Estudos Nipo-Brasileiros, 1996), pp. 20-31.

54   "The Brazilian Government—Japanese Impressions of Brazil," *Japan Magazine* 4:6 (October 1913), 305-309.

55   The official spelling of Brazil used characters that phonetically produced the word "Bu-ra-zhi-ru." The new spelling produced the same sound but had an obvious second meaning.

56   Report of Naval Attaché Glenn Howell, "Status of Japanese Colonists in Brazil," 1 May 1924, 832.5594/29, NARC-W.

57   São Paulo Law 1,299 (29 December 1911); Handa, *O imigrante japonês*, p. 185.

58   Howell, "Status of Japanese Colonists in Brazil."

59   Ibid.; majority report of the Geographical Society of Rio de Janeiro, cited in Mr. Ramsey (Rio de Janeiro) to Austen Chamberlain, 14 August 1925, FO371/10960, F4467/15/23, PRO-L.

60   Hiromi Shibata, "As escolas japonesas paulistas (1915-1945): A afirmação de uma identidade étnica" (Ph.D. dissertation, University of São Paulo, 1997), pp. 23-31; Laurence Hallewell, *Books in Brazil* (Metuchen, NJ: Scarecrow Press, 1982), table 40, p. 432.

61   Notes of an interview by Hiroshi Saito with K. Nakagawa, 10 October 1953, Donald Pierson Papers (Box 8), SL-UF. I would like to thank Marcos Chor Maio for pointing out these documents, and to thank Carl Van Ness for his help in organizing and copying them for me. See also Masuji Kiyotani and José Yamashiro, "Em busca de independência econômica," in Comissão de Elaboração da História dos 80 Anos da Imigração Japonesa no Brasil, ed., *Uma epopéia moderna*, pp. 93-94; Takashi Maeyama, "Ethnicity, Secret Societies, and Associations: The Japanese in Brazil," *Comparative Studies in Society and History* 21:4 (1979), 589.

62   Interview by author with Tetsuya Tajiri (a former journalist), 24 June 1994, Cen-

tro de Estudos Nipo-Brasileiros, São Paulo. A complete discussion of Japanese newspapers in Brazil can be found in Handa, *O imigrante japonês*, pp. 602–616.

63   Translated from Japanese to Portuguese by Hosokawa, "A história da música entre os nikkei no Brasil," p. 130. Translation to English by the author.

64   Interview with Roquette-Pinto, *Correio da Manhã* (Rio de Janeiro), 2 May 1918.

65   Arthur Neiva, "Discurso na inauguração do Horto Oswaldo Cruz," São Paulo, 1918. Cited in Vivaldo Coaracy, *O perigo japonês* (Rio de Janeiro: Jornal do Comércio, 1942), pp. 140–141.

66   *A imprensa* (Rio de Janeiro) 13 June 1910; Ryoji Noda (Japanese Minister in Brazil) to Jutaro Komura (Minister of Foreign Affairs), 22 October 1910. JMFA-MT 38280 390/391/392/393/394/395/396/397/398/399, ACENB-SP; Akira Iriye, *Pacific Estrangement: Japanese and American Expansion, 1897–1911* (Cambridge, MA: Harvard University Press, 1972), pp. 57, 213.

67   Luiz Gomes in *Jornal do Brasil* (Rio de Janeiro), 30 April 1912; M. O. Gonçalves Pereira in *Jornal do Comércio* (Rio de Janeiro), 5 May 1912.

68   M. O. Gonçalves Pereira in *Jornal do comércio* (Rio de Janeiro), 5 May 1912.

69   M. Miyajima (Tokyo) to Arthur Neiva, 11 November 1919, Papers of Artur Neiva [hereafter AN] 16.11.27, Centro de Pesquisa e Documentação de História Contemporânea do Brasil, Fundação Getúlio Vargas, Rio de Janeiro [hereafter CPDOC-RJ]; Kakichi Mitsukuri, *La vie sociale au Japon publié par Mikinosuke Miyajima* (Paris: Société Franco-Japonaise de Paris, 1922); Mikinosuke Miyajima, "L'abus de l'opium et sa répression au Japon," in Mitsukuri, *La vie sociale au Japon*, pp. 127–140; Bruno Lobo, *Japonezes no Japão—No Brasil* (Rio de Janeiro: Imprensa Nacional, 1926), p. 5.

70   S. Kitasato to Arthur Neiva, 20 November 1919, AN 16.11.27, CPDOC-RJ. In this letter, Dr. Kitasato mentions that Miyajima spoke to the foreign minister, who then spoke to him.

71   Arthur Neiva to the directors of the Liga Agrícola Brasileira, 12 November 1923, AN 18.03.09, CPDOC-RJ. See, for example, Olympio O. R. da Fonseca, *Posse do dr. Olympio Oliveira Ribeiro da Fonseca na Academia nacional de medicina em 21 de junho de 1928, seguida de conferência impressões de Ordem médica sobre o Japão* (Rio de Janeiro: Typografia América, 1928); Antônio Xavier de Oliveira, "Três heróis da campanha anti-nipônica," *RIC* 6:2–3 (May–September 1945), 243.

72   See, for example, letter of Sadatsuchi Uchida (Japanese Minister Plenipotentiary in Brazil) to Count Jutaro Komura (Minister of Foreign Affairs), 22 December 1908, JMFA-MT 38280 220/220a/221, ACENB-SP.

73   *O Paiz* (Rio de Janeiro), 25 September 1920.

74   *Osaka Mainichi and Tokyo Nichi-Nichi*, 16 March 1927. On the press in Japan, see John Lee, "English-Language Press of Asia," in John A. Lent, ed., *The Asian Newspapers' Reluctant Revolution* (Ames: Iowa State University Press, 1971), pp. 12–26; Hisao Komatsubara, "Japan," in Lent, *The Asian Newspapers' Reluctant Revolution*, pp. 65–87; and John W. Dower and Timothy S. George, *Japanese History and Culture from Ancient to Modern Times: Seven Basic Bibliographies*, 2nd ed. (Princeton: Markus Weiner, 1995), pp. 351–352.

75   Hachiro Fukuhara, director of the Kanegafuchi Spinning Co., quoted in *The Osaka Mainichi and Tokyo Nichi-Nichi,* 16 March 1927.

76   According to the Japanese emigration companies, the 1920–1924 total was 2,949, and according to the Departamento de Imigração, Ministério do Trabalho, Comércio e Indústria do Brasil, the number was 3,973. Total immigration in that period was 373,000. "Discriminação por nacionalidade dos imigrantes entrando no Brasil no período 1924–1933," *RIC* 1:3 (July 1940), 633–638.

77   Renato Kehl, *A cura da fealdade (eugenía e medicina social)* (São Paulo: Monteiro Lobato, 1923), pp. 171–179. For another eugenics work that discusses immigration but fails to mention Japanese, see Paulo de Godoy, *Eugenía e seleção* (São Paulo: Editorial Helios, 1927).

78   Antonio Gavião Gonzaga, "Contribuição para o estudo das imigrações no Brasil," *RIC* 3:1 (April 1942), 90. The exact numbers were Portuguese, 242,381; Japanese, 131,354; Italians, 72,684; Germans, 65,357; and Spanish, 53,384. "Discriminação por nacionalidade dos imigrantes entrando no Brasil no período 1924–1933 e 1934–1939," *RIC* 1:3 (July 1940), 633–638.

79   Edgar Bancroft, U.S. embassy, Tokyo, to Secretary of State, 19 February 1925, 732.94, NARC-W.

80   Wilson, "The 'New Paradise,'" pp. 258, 260; Akira Iriye, "The Failure of Economic Expansion, 1918–1931," in Bernard S. Silberman and H. D. Harootunian, eds., *Japan in Crisis: Essays on Taishō Democracy* (Princeton: Princeton University Press, 1974), pp. 237–269, esp. 254–256.

81   Edwin L. Neville, Chargé d'Affaires, U.S. embassy, Tokyo, to Secretary of State, 26 February 1931, 832.52 J 27/69, NARC-W; Iriye, "The Failure of Economic Expansion," pp. 237–269, esp. 253.

82   "Booming Brazil in Japan," *Literary Digest,* 8 January 1927, p. 20.

83   See translation of "Folder for Prospective Emigrants to Brazil" in Joseph C. Grew to Secretary of State, 2 November 1934, 832.52 J 27/777, NARC-W.

84   See translated advertisement in Document File from Mr. Woods (U.S. embassy, Tokyo) to Secretary of State, 22 May 1924, 832.5594/29, NARC-W. Iriye, "The Failure of Economic Expansion," pp. 237–269, esp. 255–256.

85   Notes of an interview by Hiroshi Saito with K. Nakagawa, 10 October 1953, Donald Pierson Papers (Box 8), SL-UF.

86   Alexandre Konder, "Os grandes amigos do Brasil," in *Brasil e Japão: Duas civilizações que se completam* (São Paulo: Empresa Gráfica da Revista dos Tribunaes, 1934), pp. 166–172; memorandum of Gerald A. Drew, U.S. Vice Consul in Brazil, to Dr. Munroe, 27 June 1930, 832.52 J27/68, NARC-W.

87   Headline taken from *Osaka Mainichi and Tokyo Nichi-Nichi,* 17 June 1927, pertaining to an article translated into English from the *Osaka Mainichi Shinbun;* circulation figures from Gregory J. Kasza, *The State and the Mass Media in Japan, 1918–1945* (Berkeley: University of California Press, 1988), p. 28.

88   *Japanese Advertiser,* 13 June 1927 and 20 June 1927. See, for example, *Japan Advertiser*'s reprint of stories on Brazil from the *Nagoya Shiaichi,* 17 May 1993.

89   Gastão Moreira, *Colonização japoneza por Gastão Moreira, engenheiro fiscal do go-*

verno do estado de São Paulo junto a Kaigai Kogyo Kabushiki Kaisha (Rio de Janeiro: Pimenta de Mello, 1923), pp. 1, 32.

90   Report of Vice Consul Robert Mills McClintock (Kobe), "Japanese Emigration to Brazil," 1 November 1933, 894.56/69, NARC-W; Wilson, "The 'New Paradise,'" p. 258.

91   Statistics from *Waga Kokumin no Kaigai Hatten* (Tokyo: Foreign Ministry, Consular Emigration Section, 1971), cited in Comissão de Elaboração da História dos 80 Anos da Imigração Japonesa no Brasil, ed., *Uma epopéia moderna*, p. 205; "Memorandum on Japan's Population and Food Supply," attached to John Tilley to Austen Chamberlain, 17 December 1926, F 5581/647.23, PRO-L. According to the Japanese emigration companies, the total was 126,434, and according to the Departamento de Imigração, Ministério do Trabalho, Comércio e Indústria do Brasil, the number was 131,354.

92   L. H. Gourley to Secretary of State, 3 March 1927, 894.5632/2, NARC-W.

93   Notes of an interview by Hiroshi Saito with K. Nakagawa, 10 October 1953, Donald Pierson Papers (Box 8), SL-UF.

94   Bentes granted a similar concession to Henry Ford and a twenty-five thousand-hectare plot to another Japanese company. The Nantaku Company's initial objectives and financial statements can be found in Edwin L. Neville, Chargé d'Affaires, U.S. embassy, Tokyo, to Secretary of State, 26 February 1931, 832.52 J 27/69, NARC-W. For more on Japanese settlement in the area, see Masao Gamou, "Japoneses no Pará," trans. Teiti Suzuki, *Estudos de antropologia teórica e prática* 3:B (August 1956; a special issue entitled, *Memórias do I Painel Nipo-Brasileiro*, ed. Antonio Rubbo Müller and Hiroshi Saito), 56–59; Ernesto Cruz, *Colonização do Pará* (Belém: Conselho Nacional de Pesquisas, Instituto Nacional de Pesquisas da Amazônia, 1958), pp. 145–149; Fernando Moreira de Castro, *50 anos da imigração japoneza na Amazonia* (Belém do Pará: n.p., 1979).

95   Memorandum of Gerald A. Drew, U.S. Vice Consul in Brazil, to Dr. Munroe, 27 June 1930, 832.52 J27/68, NARC-W. Philip Staniford conducted a fascinating anthropological study of Tomé-Açu in the mid-1960s that was published as *Pioneers in the Tropics: The Political Organization of Japanese in an Immigrant Community in Brazil* (New York: Humanities Press, 1973).

96   Edgar Bancroft, U.S. embassy, Tokyo, to Secretary of State, 19 February 1925, 732.94, NARC-W.

97   Memorandum of Gerald A. Drew, U.S. Vice Consul in Brazil, to Dr. Munroe, 27 June 1930, 832.52 J27/68; Edwin L. Neville, Chargé d'Affaires, U.S. embassy, Tokyo, to Secretary of State, 26 February 1931, 832.52 J27/69, NARC-W.

98   Notes of an interview by Hiroshi Saito with K. Nakagawa, 10 October 1953, Donald Pierson Papers (Box 8), SL-UF.

99   Notes of an interview by Hiroshi Saito with Haruo Kasahara, 31 August 1953, Donald Pierson Papers (Box 8), SL-UF.

100   Edwin L. Neville, Chargé d'Affaires, U.S. embassy, Tokyo, to Secretary of State, 26 February 1931, 832.52 J 27/69, NARC-W.

101   Fidelis Reis, *Paiz a organizar* (Rio de Janeiro: A. Coelho Branco, 1931), pp. 233–

238; Projecto 391, art. 5, 22 October 1923; "Parecer apresentado à Comissão de finanças da Câmara dos deputados em 4 de julho de 1924 por s. exca. o sr. dr. Francisco Chaves de Oliveira Botelho, deputado pelo estado do Rio de Janeiro," *Diário do Congresso nacional,* 8 July 1924; letter of Clovis Bevilaqua to Fidelis Reis, 17 October 1921, in Calvino Filho, ed., *Factos e opinões sobre a immigração japoneza* (Rio de Janeiro: n.p., 1934), p. 44; Thomas E. Skidmore, *Black into White* (New York: Oxford University Press, 1974), p. 195; R. Teixeira Mendes to Fidelis Reis, 15 August 1921, in Lobo, *Japonezes no Japão—No Brasil,* pp. 129-139. For more on the prohibition on black immigrants, see Jeffrey Lesser, "Are African-Americans African or American?" *Review of Latin American Studies* 4:1 (1991), 115-137; and Jair de Souza Ramos, "Dos males que vêm com o sangue: As representações raciais e a categoria do imigrante indesejável nas concepções sobre imigração da década de 20," in Marcos Chor Maio and Ricardo Ventura Santos, eds., *Raça, ciência e sociedade* (Rio de Janeiro: FIOCRUZ/CCBB, 1996), pp. 59-84.

102   *O Jornal* (Rio de Janeiro), 30 May 1924, 26 October 1924, 4 January 1925, 24 January 1925. These editorials, along with other statements against Japanese immigration made by Couto, were collected by his son and published as Miguel Couto, *Seleção social: Campanha antinipônica* (Rio de Janeiro: Irmãos Pongetti Editores, 1942).

103   "Uma carta ao embaixador Raul Fernandes, January, 1926," in Couto, *Seleção social,* p. 40; Antônio Xavier de Oliveira, "Três heróis da campanha antinipônica."

104   Guenka Kokichi, *Um japonês em Mato-Grosso (subsídio para história da colonização japonesa no Brasil)* (np: n.p., 1958), pp. 21-22; diplomatic note of Rangel de Castro (Tokyo) to Felix Pacheco (Minister of Foreign Relations), 7 October 1926, 01-Missões Diplomáticas Brasileiras, Tóquio-Ofícios-1923-1926—26/232/3/2, AHI-R; *Tokyo Nichi-Nichi Shinbun,* 29 September 1926.

105   See translation of "Folder for Prospective Emigrants to Brazil" in Joseph C. Grew to Secretary of State, 2 November 1934, 832.52 J 27/777, NARC-W.

106   *O Jornal* (Rio de Janeiro), 26 November 1924.

107   A. Carneiro Leão, *S. Paulo em 1920* (Rio de Janeiro: Annuário Americano, 1920), p. 52.

108   *Jornal do Comércio,* 18 July 1926.

109   James L. Tigner, *The Okinawans in Latin America,* Scientific Investigations in the Ryukyu Islands (SIRI) Report #7 (Washington, DC: Pacific Science Board, National Research Council/Department of the Army, 1954), p. 35. Few Japanese actually took up the offer, and BRATAC filled its colonies only when it shifted its sights toward families already in Brazil. In 1940 BRATAC transformed itself into the Banco América do Sul. For a discussion of the history of Japanese colonization in Paraná, see Rezende, *Ryu Mizuno,* pp. 73-94.

110   Vivaldo Coaracy, *Problemas nacionaes* (São Paulo: Sociedade Impressora Paulista, 1930), p. 123; A. Gaulin, U.S. Consul General, Rio, to Secretary of State, 16 August 1926, 832.55/56, NARC-W.

111   Memorandum of Gerald A. Drew, U.S. Vice Consul in Brazil, to Dr. Munroe,

27 June 1930, 832.52 J27/68, NARC-W; Leão, *S. Paulo em 1920*, pp. 73–74. Such positions could also be found among the Peruvian elite, led by former President Francisco García Calderón. J. F. Normano and Antonello Gerbi, *The Japanese in South America: An Introductory Survey with Special Reference to Peru* (New York: John Day, 1943), p. 72.

112 Pedro Monteleone, *Os 5 problemas da eugenia brasileira* (São Paulo: Faculdade de Medicina de São Paulo, 1929), pp. 119–121. See also Azevedo Antunes' Faculdade de Medicina de São Paulo thesis "Eugenia e imigração," cited in ibid., p. 121.

113 Interview with Roquette-Pinto, *Correio da Manhã* (Rio de Janeiro), 2 May 1924; Primeiro Congresso Brasileiro de Eugenia, *Actas e trabalhos*, vol. 1 (Rio de Janeiro: n.p., 1929), pp. 16–42, 79, 330. Another pro-Japanese eugenicist was Antonio de Queiroz, whose speech to the Rotary Club of São Paulo was published as "O problema immigratório e o futuro do Brasil," *Boletim de Eugenia* 11 (November 1929), 3. See also Nancy L. Stepan, *"The Hour of Eugenics"* (Ithaca, NY: Cornell University Press, 1991), pp. 161–162.

114 Kaigai Kogyo Kabushiki Kaisha, *Aclimação dos emigrantes japonezes: Actividades da Kaigai Kogyo Kabushiki Kaisha do Brasil* (São Paulo: Kaigai Kogyo Kabushiki Kaisha, 1934), p. 31; editorial in *Tokyo Nichi-Nichi Shinbun*, 20 May 1929; Carlos Elias Latorre Lisboa (Second Secretary in Tokyo) to Octavio Mangabeira (Minister of Foreign Affairs), 10 June 1929, 01-Missões Diplomáticas Brasileiras, Tóquio-Ofícios-1929—26/232/3/4, AHI-R. See translation of "Folder for Prospective Emigrants to Brazil" in Joseph C. Grew to Secretary of State, 2 November 1934, 832.52 J 27/777, NARC-W.

115 *Jornal do Brasil*, 14 April 1935.

116 *Osaka Mainichi and Tokyo Nichi-Nichi*, 27 June 1929; Milton Vieira (Consul in Kobe) to Mangabeira (Itamarty), 27 June 1929, 02-Repartições Consulares Brasileiras, Kobe-Ofícios-1927–1929—250/4/14, AHI-R.

117 Guilherme de Almeida, "O bazar das bonecas," *O Estado de S. Paulo*, 17 March 1929; J. Rodrigues Valle, *Pátria vindoura (em defesa do Brasil)* (São Paulo: Gráfico Editora Monteiro-Lobato, 1926), p. 55.

118 Ernest Himbloch, Commercial Secretary of the Department of Overseas Trade, British embassy (Rio de Janeiro), to Department of Overseas Trade (London), 10 May 1923, FO371/8454, A 2783/10151, PRO-L.

119 *Tokyo Nichi-Nichi Shinbun*, 29 September 1926; "Conferência realizada no salão de honra da Escola normal de Nichteroy, em 26 de setembro de 1924," in Ascoli, *A immigração japoneza*, pp. 29–55; interview with Dr. Bruno Lobo, *Correio da Manhã* (Rio de Janeiro), 26 April 1924; Bruno Lobo, *De japonez a brasileiro (adaptação e nacionalisação do imigrante* (Rio de Janeiro: Typ. do Dep. Nacional de Estatística, 1932). For other examples, see the articles by Antonio Prado in *O Estado de S. Paulo* 10 January 1918; and Custódio de Viveiros, *Gazeta de Notícias* (Rio de Janeiro), 1 January 1924.

120 Ramos, "Dos males que vêm com o sangue," p. 73.

121 Unsigned letter of 8 December 1919, republished as "Cartas Matto-Grossenses," *O Paiz* (Rio de Janeiro) 11 January 1920.

122   "Paracer do conselho diretor da Sociedade de geografia do Rio de Janeiro, assinado em 20 de dezembro de 1923," in Ascoli, *A immigração japoneza*, pp.
175–177; Sociedade Nacional de Agricultura, *Immigração: Inquérito promovido pela Sociedade nacional de agricultura* (Rio de Janeiro: Villani e Barbero, 1926), pp. 22–23;
Mr. Ramsey (Rio de Janeiro) to Austen Chamberlain, 14 August 1925, FO371/
10960 F 4467/15/23, PRO-L.

123   Francisco Chaves de Oliveira Botelho, *A immigraçao japoneza: O parecer do ilustre
deputado Oliveira Botelho, apresentado em 8 de julho de 1925, a Comissão de finanças
da Câmara dos deputados* (Rio de Janeiro: n.p., 1925), pp. 13, 26; *A notícia*, 9 September 1924.

124   See comments of senators Padua Salles, João Sampaio, Eduardo Canto, and Fontes
Júnior in the following debates: "Discurso pronunciado pelo sr. dr. Antonio de
Padua Salles, em sessão de 26 de outubro de 1923, no Senado do estado de São
Paulo"; "Discurso pronunciado pelo sr. dr. Fontes Júnior, em sessão de 26 de
outubro de 1923, no Senado do estado de São Paulo"; "Discurso pronunciado
pelo sr. dr. João Martins, em sessão de 26 de outubro de 1923, no Senado do estado de São Paulo," in Ascoli, *A immigração japoneza*, pp. 151–171.

125   Waldyr Niemeyer, *O japonez no Brasil (um face de nosso problema imigratório)* (Rio
de Janeiro: Editora Brasileira Lux, 1925), p. 18.

126   *Nippak Shinbun* (São Paulo), 19 December 1934.

127   Comissão de Recenseamento da Colônia Japonesa, *The Japanese Immigrant in Brazil*, 2 vols. (Tokyo: University of Tokyo Press, 1964), vol. 1, *Statistical Tables*, p. 356.
The study shows the majority of interethnic marriages between Japanese men
and non-Japanese women. Tigner, *The Okinawans in Latin America*, p. 51. For a
more recent comment on "ethnic" Japanese marriage, see P. Pereira dos Reis, "A
miscigenação e a etnia brasileira," *Revista de História* 12:48 (October–December
1961), 334–336. For a fascinating discussion of the consequences of interethnic
relationships, see Hiroshi Saito, "O suicídio entre os imigrantes japoneses e seus
descendentes," *Sociologia* 15:2 (May 1953), 120–121.

128   Memorandum of Gerald A. Drew, U.S. Vice Consul in Brazil, to Dr. Munroe,
27 June 1930. 832.52 J27/68, NARC-W.

129   See, for example, the editorial in *O Brasil* (Rio de Janeiro), 26 April 1924.

130   Edgard Roquette-Pinto, *Ensaios de antropologia brasiliana* [1933], 2nd ed. (São
Paulo: Editora Nacional, 1978), p. 103.

131   Lobo, *Japonezes no Japão—No Brasil*, pp. 151–152, 157; Lobo, *De japonez à brasileiro*,
back cover. See similar comments in Alfredo Ellis Júnior, *Pedras lascadas* [1928],
2nd ed. (São Paulo: Editora Piratininga, 1933), p. 79.

132   Interview with Dr. Bruno Lobo, *Correio da Manhã* (Rio de Janeiro), 26 April 1924.
A more recent notion of Japanese immigrants as "bandeirantes" can be found in
Agostinho Rodrigues Filho, *Bandeirantes do Oriente: Drama íntimo dos japoneses no
Brasil* (São Paulo: Empresa Editora Bandeirantes, 1949).

133   *Gazeta de Notícias* (Rio de Janeiro), 8 May 1924; Botelho, *A immigraçao japoneza*,
p. 35. A similar position is taken in Niemeyer, *O japonez no Brasil*, p. 26.

134   *Comércio de Santos*, 27 April 1924. A decade later a group of Japanese-Brazilian

students traveled to the interior and found that only a few students being educated at Japanese schools were unable to speak Portuguese. *Gakusei: Orgão da Liga Estudantina Nippo-brasileira* (São Paulo) 1:5 (29 April 1936), p. 1.

135 Ellis Júnior, *Pedras lascadas,* 152.

136 Antônio Baptista Pereira, *O Brasil e a raça: Conferência feita na Faculdade de direito de São Paulo a 19 de junho de 1928* (São Paulo: Emp. Gráfica Rossetti, 1928), pp. 20–22, 94.

137 *Folha da manhã* (São Paulo), 5 July 1934; Lobo, *Japonezes no Japão—No Brasil,* p. 159; Filho, ed., *Factos e opinões sobre a immigração japoneza,* pp. 17, 33, 97, 112; *Cruzamento da ethnia japoneza: Hypóthese de que o japonez não se cruza com outra ethnia* (São Paulo: Centro Nippônico de Cultura, 1934).

138 Lobo, *De japonez à brasileiro,* pp. 129–135.

139 Bruno Lobo, *Esquecendo os antepassados: Combatendo os estrangeiros* (São Paulo: Editorial Alba, 1935), p. 144.

140 *Cruzamento da ethnia japoneza.*

141 Normano and Gerbi, *The Japanese in South America,* p. 63; Lee Eldrige Huddleston, *Origins of the American Indians: European Concepts, 1492–1729* (Austin: University of Texas Press, 1967), pp. 73–74, 120–121.

142 *Gazeta de Notícias* (Rio de Janeiro), 8 May 1924; interview with Dr. Bruno Lobo, *Correio da Manhã* (Rio de Janeiro), 26 April 1924.

143 Hachiro Fukuhara, "BRAZIL FOUNDED BY ASIATICS?" *Japan Times and Mail,* 26 June 1927. The Kanegafuchi Cotton-Spinning Company was known for its innovative use of dormitories and health services as a means of maintaining female labor. See E. Patricia Tsurumi, *Factory Girls: Women in the Thread Mills of Meiji Japan* (Princeton: Princeton University Press, 1990), p. 154. See also "NIPPONESE GETS 2,500,000 ACRES AS A BASIS FOR A VAST COLONY," *Japan Times and Mail,* 11 May 1930.

144 Memorandum of Gerald A. Drew, U.S. Vice Consul in Brazil, to Dr. Munroe, 27 June 1930, 832.52 J27/68, NARC-W.

145 Kokichi, *Um japonês em Mato-Grosso,* p. 27. The entire collection of the *Nippak Shinbun* can be found in the Archives of the Centro de Estudos Nipo-Brasileiros, São Paulo.

146 *Constituição de 25 de março de 1824,* sec. I, art. 5; Geraldo Fernandes, "A religião nas constituicões republicanas do Brasil," *Revista eclesiástica brasileira* 8:4 (December 1948), 830–857; George P. Browne, "Government Immigration Policy in Imperial Brazil" (Ph.D. thesis, Catholic University of America, 1972), p. 301; Jeffrey Lesser, *Welcoming the Undesirables: Brazil and the Jewish Question* (Berkeley: University of California Press, 1995), pp. 56–57.

147 Takashi Maeyama, "O imigrante e a religião: Estudo de uma seita religiosa japonesa em São Paulo" (M.A. thesis, Fundação Escola de Sociologia e Política de São Paulo, 1967), pp. 85–87; *DTCI: Boletim da Diretoria de terras, colonização e imigração* 1 (October 1937), 38.

148 Kaigai Kogyo Kabushiki Kaisha, *Aclimação dos emigrantes japonezes,* p. 43.

149 Lobo, *De japonez à brasileiro,* pp. 142–144, 183; Kaigai Kogyo Kabushiki Kaisha,

Aclimação dos emigrantes japonezes, pp. 41–45; notes of an interview by Hiroshi Saito with K. Nakagawa, 10 October 1953, Donald Pierson Papers (Box 8), SL-UF.

150   Report of Octaviano Constant de Oliveira, "Processo—nacionalização de núcleo japonês—Fazenda Tietê," 4 July 1941, fundo Hospedaria dos Imigrantes, seção Documentação Administrativa, série 2: Processos, datas 1 July 1941–17 July 1941, 4161B: 17 July 1941, Archives of the Secretaria do Estado da Promoção Social— Centro Histórico do Imigrante, São Paulo [hereafter SEPS/CHI-SP]; "O maior núcleo japonês no Brasil: Os amarelos em Marília," *Revista do Arquivo Municipal* 9:91 (May–June 1944), 207–208. Ten years later the percentage of Buddhists and Shintoists in Marília had dropped only slightly, to about 77 percent. Roger Bastide, *Brasil: Terra de contrastes,* 2nd ed. (São Paulo: Difusão Européia do Livro, 1964), p. 181. A study of changes in Japanese religious practice in Brazil is Takashi Maeyama, "Japanese Religions in Southern Brazil: Change and Syncretism," *Latin America Studies* (Tsukuba, Japan) 6 (1983), 181–238.

151   Report of Amilcar Alencastre, head of S/5 DEOPS, "A infiltração japoneza no Brasil e suas trágicas conseqüências" (1940?), Arquivos das Polícias Politícas, setor Japonês [hereafter APP, SJ], pasta II, Arquivo Público do Estado do Rio de Janeiro [hereafter APE-RJ].

152   Handa, *O imigrante japonês,* p. 185. On the jogo do bicho, see Renato José Costa Pacheco, ed., *Antologia do jogo do bicho* (São Paulo: Simões Editora, 1957).

153   A 1939 survey of immigrants showed that 90 percent desired to return to Japan. Cited in Y. Kumusaka and H. Saito, "Kachigumi: A Collective Delusion Among the Japanese and Their Descendants in Brazil," *Canadian Psychiatric Association Journal* 15:2 (April 1970), 168.

154   *Nippak Shinbun* (São Paulo), 26 August 1927, trans. in Masuji Kiyotani and José Yamashiro, "Do *Kasato-Maru* até a década de 1920," in Comissão de Elaboração da História dos 80 Anos da Imigração Japonesa no Brasil, ed. *Uma epopéia moderna,* p. 107; Nogueira, *Imigração japonesa,* pp. 120–127.

155   Dr. Alvaro de Oliveira Machado, "Estudos e observações sobre KKKK," fundo Hospedaria dos Imigrantes, seção Documentação Administrativa, série 2: Processos, datas: 19 February 1931 à 27 February 1931, no. 67: 24 February 1931, SEPS/CHI-SP.

156   Dr. Salvio Azevedo, chefe da Seção de Agricultura, "Uma visita à colônia japonesa do Registro," fundo Hospedaria dos Imigrantes, seção Documentação Administrativa, série 2: Processos, datas: 19 September 1931 to 22 October 1931, no. 374: 21 September 1931, SEPS/CHI-SP.

157   Zempati Ando, *Pioneirismo e cooperativismo: História da cooperativa agrícola de Cotia,* trans. José Yamashiro (São Paulo: Editora Sociologia e Política, 1961), p. 65; Hiroshi Saito, *O cooperativismo e a comunidade: Case da cooperativa agrícola de Cotia* (São Paulo: Editora Sociologia e Política, 1964); Dráuzio Leme Padilha, *CAC: Cooperativismo que deu certo* (São Paulo: Cooperativa Agrícola de Cotia, Cooperativa Central, 1989).

158   Hélio Silva, *1932: A guerra paulista* (Rio de Janeiro: Editora Civilização Brasileira,

1967); Thomas E. Skidmore, *Politics in Brazil, 1930–1964: An Experiment in Democracy* (New York: Oxford University Press, 1967), pp. 17–19.

159 *Diário de S. Paulo* article quoted in *Brasil e Japão: Duas civilizações que se completam,* pp. 238–240.

160 *O Estado de S. Paulo,* 19 September 1932; José Yamashiro, *Trajetória de duas vidas,* pp. 111–117.

161 *Nippak Shinbun,* 21 July 1932.

162 Normano and Gerbi, *The Japanese in South America,* pp. 49–50.

163 Oswald de Andrade, *Marco Zero I—A revolução melancólica* [1937], 2nd ed. (Rio de Janeiro: Editora Civilização Brasileira, 1978), p. 16. For more on *Marco zero,* see Alcir Lenharo, *Sacralização da política* (Campinas: Papirus/Editora da UNICAMP, 1986), pp. 129–134; and Renato José Costa Pacheco, "O imigrante na literatura brasileira de ficção," *Sociologia* 18:3 (August 1956), 201–232.

164 Andrade, *Marco zero I,* p. 24.

165 Saito, *O japonês no Brasil,* pp. 215–219.

166 "Booming Brazil in Japan," *The Literary Digest,* 8 January 1927, p. 20; memorandum of Gerald A. Drew, U.S. Vice Consul in Brazil to Dr. Munroe, 27 June 1930, 832.52 J27/68, NARC-W; Moreira de Castro, *50 anos da imigração japoneza na Amazônia,* pp. 41–42; Tsuguo Koyama, "Japoneses na Amazônia: Alguns aspectos do processo de sua integração sócio-cultural," in Hiroshi Saito, ed., *A presença japonesa no Brasil* (São Paulo: T. A. Queiroz/EDUSP, 1980), pp. 11–28; Philip Staniford, "Competição e conflito em Tomé-Açu, Pará," in Hiroshi Saito and Takashi Maeyama, eds. *Assimilação e integração dos japoneses no Brasil* (São Paulo: Vozes/EDUSP, 1973), pp. 346–360.

167 *Japan Times,* 4 February 1934.

5 *Negotiations and New Identities*

1 *Gakusei: Orgão da Liga estudantina nippo-brasileira* (São Paulo) 1, no. 1 (October 1935).

2 Speech of Acylino de Leão, 18 September 1935, in Brazil, República dos Estados Unidos do Brasil, *Annaes da Câmara dos deputados: Sessões de 16 à 24 de setembro de 1935,* vol. 17 (Rio de Janeiro: Off. Gráfica d' A Noite, 1935), p. 432.

3 See speeches of Teotônio Monteiro de Barros (São Paulo) and Xavier de Oliveira (Ceará) in Brazil, República dos Estados Unidos do Brasil, *Annaes da Assembléia nacional constituinte organizados pela redação das annaes e documentos parlamentares* [hereafter AANC], vol. 6 (Rio de Janeiro: Imprensa Nacional, 1935), pp. 232, 449. For a detailed discussion of the constitutional debates, see Valdemar Carneiro Leão, *A crise da imigração japonesa no Brasil (1930–1934): Contornos diplomáticos* (Brasília: IPRI/Fundação Alexandre de Gusmão, 1989); Flávio V. Luizetto, "Os constituintes em face da imigração (Estudo sobre o preconceito e a discriminação racial e étnica na Constituinte de 1934)" (M.A. thesis, Universidade de São

Paulo, 1975); Nancy L. Stepan, *"The Hour of Eugenics"* (Ithaca, NY: Cornell University Press, 1991), pp. 165–167; Hélio Silva, *1934—A constituinte* (Rio de Janeiro: Editora Civilização Brasileira, 1969), pp. 209–217; Angela Maria de Castro Gomes, "A representação de classes na Constituinte de 1934," in Gomes, ed., *Regionalismo e centralização política* (Rio de Janeiro: Editora Nova Frontera, 1980), pp. 427–491; Thomas E. Skidmore, *Politics in Brazil* (New York: Oxford University Press, 1967), p. 30.

4   Brazilian exports to Japan grew from 2,931 pounds sterling in 1913 to 158,000 in 1935 (peaking at 2.1 million in 1937). Comissão de Elaboração da História dos 80 Anos da Imigração Japonesa no Brasil, ed., *Uma Epopéia moderna* (São Paulo: Editora Hucitec, 1992), p. 198.

5   The three were linked to anti-Japanese movements throughout the Americas. Letter of V. S. McClatchy, Executive Secretary, California Joint Immigration Committee, to Arthur Neiva, 8 April 1934, AN 33.06.22, CPDOC-R.

6   One report from a U.S. military attaché lauded the fact that "some Brazilians are thoroughly awake to the unassimilable quality of the Japanese, their pitiless competition with the native, their deceit, adoption of Christianity for political purposes and imperialistic ideas." Military Attaché Sackville to U.S. Ambassador in Brazil, 28 December 1933, 832.5593/1, NARC-W.

7   Williams Seeds to John Simon, 8 March 1934, FO 371/17836, E1376/1/93, PRO-L; AANC, vol. 8, p. 346.

8   *Anteprojeto da constituição emendada pela representação do partido Social demócratico da Bahia* (Bahia: Imprensa Oficial do Estado, 1934), pp. 59–64; Arthur Neiva to Juracy Magalhães, 27 March 1934, AN31.06.03, CPDOC-R.

9   AANC, vol. 6, pp. 336–362.

10   Ibid., vol. 4, p. 294, and vol. 8, p. 78; Bruno Lobo, *Esquecendo os antepassados* (São Paulo: Editora Alba, 1935), p. 36.

11   AANC, vol. 6, pp. 458–459.

12   *Osaka Mainichi and Tokyo Nichi-Nichi Shinbun,* 20 March 1934; Mário Botelho de Miranda, *Um brasileiro no Japão em guerra* (São Paulo: Companhia Editora Nacional, 1944), p. 80.

13   Assis Chateaubriand's comments were reported in *Japan Advertiser,* 25 March 1934.

14   *Diário de São Paulo,* June 1933, cited in AANC, vol. 6, p. 351.

15   *Evening Standard* (London), 20 March 1934.

16   See, for example, *Folha da Manhã* (São Paulo), 5 July 1934 and 28 March 1935.

17   Arthur Neiva to Juracy Magalhães, 27 March 1934, AN31.06.03, CPDOC-R; *Osaka Mainichi and Tokyo Nichi-Nichi Shinbun,* 9 May 1934; report of U.S. Military Attaché Sackville, 28 December 1933, 832.55/93/1; John M. Cabot, Third Secretary, U.S. embassy, Rio de Janeiro, to Secretary of State, 31 May 1934, 832.55/94, NARC-W.

18   Nicolau Debané, "Algumas considerações sobre o problema da imigração no Brasil," *Jornal do comércio,* 3 June 1934; Wilson Martins, *História da inteligência brasileira,* (1915–1933), 6 (São Paulo: Cultrix, 1978), pp. 78, 191.

19   *Gazeta do Rio*, 30 December 1933. The article and the letter mentioned in the text were published side by side in the *Gazeta* that day.

20   Julio de Revorêdo, *Immigração* (São Paulo: Empresa Gráfica Revista dos Tribunaes, 1934), pp. 168–175.

21   *Nippak Shinbun*, 19 December 1934.

22   Statistics on illnesses by type/month from the Registro Colony, kept by Kaigai Kogyo Kabushiki Kaisha, cited in Bruno Lobo, *De japonez à brasileiro* (Rio de Janeiro: Typ. do Dep. Nacional de Estatística, 1932), p. 185.

23   *Brasil e Japão: Duas civilizações que se completam* (São Paulo: Empreza Gráphica da Revista dos Tribunaes, 1934); Francisca Pereira Rodrigues, *O braço estrangeiro* (São Paulo: Imprensa Oficial do Estado, 1938).

24   *Folha da Manhã*, 5 July 1934, 28 March 1935. See discussion in chapter 4. Bruno Lobo, *Japonezes no Japão-No Brasil* (Rio de Janeiro: Imprensa Nacional, 1926), p. 159; Calvino Filho, ed., *Factos e opinões sobre a immigração japoneza* (Rio de Janeiro: n.p., 1934), pp. 17, 33, 97, 112; *Cruzamento da ethnia japoneza: Hypóthese de que o japonez não se cruza com outra ethnia* (São Paulo: Centro Nipônico de Cultura, 1934).

25   *Folha da Manhã*, 5 July 1934, 28 March 1935.

26   Rodriques Caldas, "O estado de Minas Geraes e a immigração japonesa," *Jornal do Comércio*, December 1920, repr. in Nestor Ascoli, *A immigração japoneza para a baixada do estado do Rio de Janeiro*, 2nd ed. (Rio de Janeiro: Ediçao da Revista de Língua Portuguesa, 1924), pp. 115–127; Maria de Fátima Y. Asfora, "Colonos japoneses no brejo Pernambuco: Análise de uma trajetória (1956–1994)," paper presented at the IV Encontro Regional de Antropólogos do Norte e Nordeste, João Pessoa, 28–31 May 1995, p. 9; Moacyr Flores, "Japoneses no Rio Grande do Sul," *Veritas* (Porto Alegre) 77 (1975), 73.

27   Kaigai Kogyo Kabushiki Kaisha, *Aclimação dos emigrantes japonezes: Actividades da Kaigai Kogyo Kabushiki Kaisha do Brasil* (São Paulo: Kaigai Kogyo Kabushiki Kaisha, 1934), pp. 3, 39. A similar book is Kaigai Kogyo Kabushiki Kaisha, *Introdução dos imigrantes japonezes no Brasil e seu orgão instrutivo: Actividades da Kaigai Kogyo Kabushiki Kaisha em São Paulo* (São Paulo: Kaigai Kogyo Kabushiki Kaisha, 1932).

28   J. F. Normano and Antonello Gerbi, *The Japanese in South America* (New York: John Day, 1943), p. 39. See the pro-Japanese positions of Evaristo de Moraes and Bruno Lobo, *O Jornal*, 27 March 1934, 28 March 1934.

29   Constituição de 16 de julho de 1934, art. 5, para. 19 (g), and art. 121, para. 6.

30   Report of Joseph C. Grew (U.S. embassy, Tokyo), 4 August 1934, 739.94/2, NARC-W; John M. Cabot, Third Secretary, U.S. embassy, Rio de Janeiro, to Secretary of State, 31 May 1934, 832.55/94, NARC-W.

31   Carlos Martins Pereira e Sousa (Brazilian diplomat in Tokyo and later wartime Ambassador to the United States), quoted in Stanley E. Hilton, *Brazil and the Great Powers, 1930–1939: The Politics of Trade Rivalry* (Austin: University of Texas Press, 1975), p. 11.

32   *Osaka Mainichi and Tokyo Nichi-Nichi Shinbun*, 5 June 1934.

33   Comments of Kaju Nakamura, Seiyukai party, to Foreign Minister Hirota, as reported in *Japan Times and Mail*, 25 March 1934. *Hokkai Times* article repr. in *Japan Advertiser*, 22 April 1934.

34   *Japan Times and Mail*, 21 March 1934; *Tokyo Asahi Shinbun*, 26 May 1934 and 7 June 1934; *Osaka Mainichi and Tokyo Nichi-Nichi Shinbun*, 26 May 1934 and 11 November 1934. Translations in L323 M4552 and L612 M9599, AHI-R. See letter of (illegible) of Brazilian embassy in Tokyo to Felix de Barros Cavalcanti de Lacerda (Itamaraty), 15 January 1934, L323 M4552, AHI-R.

35   See articles in *Osaka Mainichi and Tokyo Nichi-Nichi Shinbun*, 25 March 1934 and 17 April 1934; *Japan Advertiser*, 22 April 1934 and 26 May 1934; *Tokyo Nichi-Nichi Shinbun*, 17 April 1934. Translation in L323 M4552, AHI-R.

36   Constituição de 16 de julho de 1934, art. 131; report of Joseph C. Grew (U.S. embassy, Tokyo), 4 August 1934, 739.94/2, NARC-W.

37   See comments of Consul-General Uchiyama in *Osaka Mainichi and Tokyo Nichi-Nichi Shinbun*, 6 June 1934, and the editorial in *Jiji Shinbun* (Tokyo), 5 June 1934. Translation in L323 M4552, AHI-R. Statistics from the Kaigai Kogyo Kabushiki Kaisha cited in Lobo, *De japonez à brasileiro*, p. 149. In 1932 the school had 211 Japanese-speaking and 141 Portuguese-speaking teachers.

38   *Osaka Mainichi and Tokyo Nichi-Nichi Shinbun*, 26 May 1934.

39   Arthur Neiva to Juracy Magalhães, 27 March 1934, AN31.06.03, CPDOC-R.

40   *Tokyo Asahi Shinbun*, 31 May 1934; *Tokyo Nichi-Nichi Shinbun*, 31 May 1934. Translation in L323 M4552, AHI-R.

41   *Osaka Mainichi and Tokyo Nichi-Nichi Shinbun*, 29 May 1934.

42   Ibid., 29 September 1934.

43   São Paulo, *Annaes da sessão ordinária de 1935, Assembléia legislativa do estado de São Paulo* (São Paulo: n.p., 1935), vol. 1, pp. 658–704, 790–807, 994–1025; vol. 2, pp. 84–97; vol. 3, pp. 542–553; Projeto de lei 49, 1 October 1935, São Paulo State Legislative Assembly, quoted in Oscar Tenório, *Immigração* (Rio de Janeiro: Pimenta de Mello, 1936), p. 271; *Annaes da Assembléia constituinte de 1935* (São Paulo: Sociedade Impressora Paulista, 1935), vol. 1, pp. 246–253; vol. 2, pp. 360–361, Table 1; "Entrada de imigrantes japoneses no Brasil (de 1908 à 1941)," *RIC* 1:3 (October 1940): 123–124 (misprinted). More than one hundred thousand Japanese entered Brazil in the eight years before 1934; about half that number arrived in the eight years after. Comissão de Elaboração da História dos 80 Anos da Imigração Japonesa no Brasil, ed., *Uma epopéia moderna*, p. 138.

44   Editorial, "Uma explicação que não explica nada," *Correio da Manhã*, 7 May 1935, repr. in *Jornal do Comércio*, 8 May 1935; Oliveira Vianna, *Raça e assimilação* (São Paulo: Companhia Editora Nacional, 1932), p. 209.

45   Eighty percent of the vegetable production around the city of São Paulo came from Japanese farmers. *Gazeta de Notícias*, 5 November 1935. A compilation of similar speeches and editorials in the press can be found in Tenório, *Immigração*.

46   Speech of Bento de Abreu Sampiao before the São Paulo Chamber of Deputies, 22 September 1935, repr. in *Gazeta de Notícias*, 24 September 1935. For a study

of ethnicity in Marília in the mid-1960s, see Francisca Isabel Schurig Vieira, *O japonês na frente de expansão paulista: O processo de absorção do japonês em Marília* (São Paulo: Pioneira/Ed. da Universidade de São Paulo, 1973), pp. 83–89; Tetsuo Nakasumi and José Yamashiro, "O fim da era de imigração e a consolidação da nova colônia nikkei," in Comissão de Elaboração da História dos 80 Anos da Imigração Japonesa no Brasil, ed., *Uma epopéia moderna,* pp. 417–458.

47 *Gazeta de Notícias,* 5 November 1935.

48 Interview with José Yamashiro by author, Michael Molasky, and Koichi Mori, São Paulo, 12 December 1995; John W. F. Dulles, *The São Paulo Law School and the Anti-Vargas Resistance (1938–1945)* (Austin: University of Texas Press, 1986), pp. 26–30.

49 Interview with José Yamashiro by author, Michael Molasky, and Koichi Mori, São Paulo, 12 December 1995; Risseli, "Os dainiseis e a instrução primária," *Gakusei* 2:11 (October 1936) and 2:12 (November 1936). See also *Gakusei* 1:4 (March 1936).

50 *Gakusei* 1:1 (October 1935).

51 Ibid. 1:3 (February 1936); Rose Fukugawa, "Sob teu olhar," *Gakusei* 1:3 (February 1936).

52 José Yamashiro, "Um diálogo," *Gakusei* 1:5 (April 1936).

53 *Gakusei* 1:9 (August 1936).

54 Ibid. 2:17 (September 1937).

55 Koichi Mori, "Por que os brasileiros começaram a apreciar a culinária japonesa? As condições de aceitação da culinária japonesa na cidade de São Paulo," unpublished paper (1997) used by permission of the author.

56 Tomoo Handa, *O imigrante japonês* (São Paulo: T. A. Queiroz/Centro de Estudos Nipo-Brasileiros, 1987), pp. 623–624; José Yamashiro, "Os niseis entre dois penhascos," in Comissão de Elaboração da História dos 80 Anos da Imigração Japonesa no Brasil, ed., *Uma epopéia moderna,* p. 173; interview with José Yamashiro by author, Michael Molasky, and Koichi Mori, São Paulo, 12 December 1995.

57 *Gakusei* 1:4 (March 1936) and 1:5 (April 1936).

58 The term "nikkei" that is used throughout this text is the modern usage, which includes all the generations born in Brazil.

59 Eddy de F. Crissiuma, "Concentração japonesa em São Paulo," *Geografia* 1:1 (1935), 110–114; Astrogildo Rodrigues de Mello, "Immigração e colonização," *Geografia* 1:4 (1935), 25–49.

60 Translation of *Tokyo Nichi-Nichi Shinbun,* 30 May 1935, in L622 M9653, AHI-R. For similar comments see Areobaldo E. de Oliveira Lima, *A imigração japonesa para o estado de Paraíba do Norte* (São Paulo: Empresa Gráfica Revista dos Tribunais, 1936).

61 Moreira Guimarães, *No Extremo Oriente: O Japão* (Rio de Janeiro: Editora Alba, 1936); U.S. Ambassador Hugh Gibson to Secretary of State, 8(?) May 1936, 832.55/115, NARC-W.

62 São Paulo, Secretaria da Agricultura, Indústria e Comércio, *DTCI: Boletim da Directória de terras, colonização e imigração* 1:1 (October 1936), 96; Comissão de Elaboração da História dos 80 Anos da Imigração Japonesa no Brasil, ed., *Uma epopéia moderna,* p. 138.

63 *Japan Review,* May 1935.

64 *A Nota,* 24 January 1937. For another attack on those who maintained aspects of premigratory culture, see Leão Padilha, *O Brasil na posse de si mesmo* (Rio de Janeiro: Gráfica Olímpica, 1941), esp. pp. 63–76.

65 "A colonização japonesa no Amazonas," *Jornal do Brasil,* 24 June 1936; "Ainda os japoneses na Amazônia," *Jornal do Brasil,* 26 June 1936; "A concessão nipônica no Amazonas," *Jornal do Brasil,* 22 July 1936; Antóvila Rodrigues Mourao Vieira, *O perigo amarelo na Amazônia brasileira: Discursos pronunciados, em 1936, na extinta Assembléia legislativa do Amazonas, pelo então deputado Antóvila R. M. Vieira, contra a concessão de terras amazonenses* (Manaus: Secção de Publicidade da Interventoria do Estado do Amazonas, 1942).

66 Letter of Hugh Gurney to Anthony Eden, 12 March 1937, E1702/1/92, PRO-L; *Jornal do Comércio,* 15 August 1937; *Folha do Povo,* 10 September 1937; Baily W. Diffie, "Some Foreign Influences in Contemporary Brazilian Politics," *Hispanic American Historical Review* 20 (August 1940), 410. The original map is in Kaigai Kogyo Kabushiki Kaisha, *Introdução dos imigrantes japonezes no Brasil,* p. 10.

67 Frank D. McCann, Jr., *The Brazilian-American Alliance, 1937–1945* (Princeton: Princeton University Press, 1973), p. 116; Hilton, *Brazil and the Great Powers,* p. 13; Jorge Latour (Warsaw), "A infiltração japoneza no Brasil: Estudo offerido à Secretaria de estado das relações exteriores por Jorge Latour" (May 1936), L622 M9653, AHI-R. Latour was also a vociferous opponent of Jewish entry to Brazil. See Jeffrey Lesser, *Welcoming the Undesirables* (Berkeley: University of California Press, 1995), pp. 84, 89.

68 Kaigai Kogyo Kabushiki Kaisha, *Aclimação dos emigrantes japonezes,* p. 12; Gibson to Secretary of State, 17 April 1936, 832.52 J127/80, NARC-W.

69 Robert Levine, *The Vargas Regime* (New York: Columbia University Press, 1970), p. 138; Edgard Carone, *A Terceira República* (São Paulo: Difel/Difusão Editorial, 1976), pp. 26–28.

70 R.C.P., "Um perigo para a nacionalidade: A immigração japoneza," *Mensário do Jornal do Comércio* 1:1 (January 1938), 119–124.

71 *Gakusei* 3:22 (April 1938).

72 *Jornal do Brasil,* 19 January 1938; secret report on Japanese colonies, 18 June 1939, APP, SJ, pasta II, APE-RJ.

73 Jefferson Caffery (U.S. embassy, Rio de Janeiro) to Secretary of State, 11 July 1938, 732.94/4 LH; confidential memorandum of Lt. Col. Harry Creswell (U.S. Military Attaché, Tokyo), 1 June 1939, 732.94/7 LH, NARC-W.

74 Decree Law 406 (4 May 1938).

75 Decree Law 479 (8 June 1938), art 2, no. 1a; Decree Law 1,377 (27 June 1938).

76 Susumu Miyao and José Yamashiro, "A comunidade nipônica no período da guerra," in Comissão de Elaboração da História dos 80 Anos da Imigração Japonesa no Brasil, ed., *Uma epopéia moderna,* pp. 248–249, 255.

77 This notice from Junzo Sakane, Consul General of Japan in São Paulo, was published in Japanese newspapers throughout Brazil. Translation from Miyao and Yamashiro, "A comunidade nipônica no período da guerra," pp. 252–253.

78   *Transição* 1:1 (June 1939), 5.

79   João Hirata, "A quem cabe engrandecer o Brasil," and Massaki Udihara, "Assimilação," *Transição* 1:1 (June 1939), 7-10.

80   "Uma visita à Escola Taishô-Bandeirante," *Transição* 1:2 (September 1939), 42-43.

81   Yamashiro, "Os niseis entre dois penhascos," p. 178.

82   Japan, Department of Tourism, *Guia de algibeira do Japão: Com uma descrição especial dos costumes, história, educação, arte, divertimentos, etc.* (Tokyo: Direção Geral de Turismo, Ministério de Estradas de Ferro do Japão, 1941); *New York Times,* 13 July 1939; McCann, *The Brazilian-American Alliance,* pp. 253, 388; "Rio Rubber Crisis," *Business Week* (12 July 1941): 78-79.

83   Zempati Ando, *Pioneirismo e cooperativismo,* trans. José Yamashiro (São Paulo: Editora Sociologia e Política, 1961), p. 34.

84   Handa, *O imigrante japonês,* p. 606; *New York Times,* 9 July 1939.

85   Decree Law, 1,545 (25 August 1939), arts. 1, 4, 7, 8, 13, 15, 16.

86   Pedro Calheiros Bonfim, "As escolas estrangeiras no Brasil," *Cultura política* 2:13 (March 1942), 30-34; R. P. Castello Branco, "Imigração e nacionalismo," *Cultura política* 2:15 (May 1942), 26-31; Xavier Marques, "Imigrantismo e brasilidade," *Revista da Academia brasileira de letras* 41:63 (January-June 1942), 11-17; Francisco Campos, "Imigração japonesa," *Boletim do Ministério do trabalho, indústria e comércio* 10:114 (February 1944), 263-270. The report was presented to Vargas in May 1941. For a careful study of the journal see Haruf Salmen Espindola, "O centauro maquiavélico: Ideologia da revista *Cultura política* (1941-1945)" (M.A. thesis, Universidade de Brasília, 1988), pp. 126-128.

87   São Paulo, Secretaria de Agricultura, Indústria e Comércio, *DTCI: Boletim da Directória de terras, colonização e imigração* 1 (October 1937), 54; Emílio Willems and Hiroshi Saito, "Shindo Renmei: Um problema de aculturação," *Sociologia* 9 (1947), 137; Comissão de Recenseamento da Colônia Japonesa, *The Japanese Immigrant in Brazil,* 2 vols. (Tokyo: University of Tokyo Press, 1964), vol. 1, *Statistical Tables,* pp. 644-645.

88   Neiva's long treatise on the benefits of Jewish entry was suppressed by the CIC until 1944. Arthur Hehl Neiva, "Estudos sobre a imigração semita no Brasil," *RIC* 5:2 (June 1944), 215-422.

89   Aristóteles de Lima Câmara and Arthur Hehl Neiva, "Colonizações nipônica e germânica no sul do Brasil," *RIC* 2:1 (January 1941), 39-121.

90   Report of Octaviano Constant de Oliveira, "Processo-Nacionalização de núcleo japonês—Fazenda Tietê," 4 July 1941, Fundo Hospedaria dos Imigrantes, Seção Documentação Administrativa, série 2: Processos, Datas: 1 July 1941-17 July 1941, 4161B: 17 July 1941, SEPS/CHI-SP. A similar pro-Japanese position, based on observations in the Rio Preto region, can be found in A. Tavares do Almeida, *Oeste paulista* (Rio de Janeiro: Editora Alba, 1943), pp. 155-163.

91   Lima Câmara and Neiva, "Colonizações nipônica e germânica"; São Paulo, *Relatório apresentado ao exmo. snr. dr. Getúlio Vargas, presidente da República, pelo dr. Adhemar Pereira de Barros, interventor federal em S. Paulo, 1938-1939* (São Paulo:

Empresa Gráfica da Revista dos Tribunais, 1940), pp. 82–83. Lima Câmara speech cited in report of head of S/5 DEOPS, Amilcar Alencastre, "A infiltração japoneza no Brasil e suas trágicas consequências" (1940?), APP, SJ, pasta II, APE-RJ.

92 Takashi Maeyama, "Ethnicity, Secret Societies and Associations," *Comparative Studies in Society and History* 21:4 (April 1979) 598; Y. Kumusaka and H. Saito, "Kachigumi: A Collective Delusion Among the Japanese and Their Descendants in Brazil," *Canadian Psychiatric Association Journal* 15:2 (April 1970), 167–175.

93 *Diário Carioca,* 8 March 1942; Mário Botelho de Miranda, *Um brasileiro no Japão em guerra* (São Paulo: Companhia Editora Nacional, 1944), pp. 265–266.

94 *O Globo,* 3 March 1942; *New York Times,* 4 March 1942.

95 *Diretrizes,* 21 May 1942; *O Radical,* 6 March 1942; *A Notícia,* 11 March 1942; *O Carioca,* 26 February 1942; Samuel Wainer, *Minha razão de viver: Memórias de um repórter* (Rio de Janeiro: Record, 1988).

96 Handa, *O imigrante japonês,* p. 635; "Brazil Warned for Treatment of Immigrants," *Japan Chronicle and Japan Mail,* 27 September 1947, p. 1.

97 Unsigned DEOPS report, "Niponismo na zona de Registro," 27 September 1941, APP, SJ, Pasta I; DEOPS report of Amilcar Alencastre, 20 May 1943, APP, SJ, Pasta I; DEOPS report of Amilcar Alencastre, "As cooperativas japonesas, centros de sabotagem econômicas," 13 April 1943, APP, SJ, Pasta II, APE-RJ; Handa, *O imigrante japonês,* p. 636.

98 Undated DEOPS translation of report from agent "Nagai" to agent "Hayão"; "Como distinguir um chinez de um japonez," 22 February 1943, APP, SJ, Pasta I, APE-RJ; *Time,* 22 December 1941, p. 33. I would like to thank two of my students, Aimee Blanchette and Jonathan Le, for directing me to the *Time* article, and my colleague and friend Kerry Smith for identifying the exact issue with incredible speed. For a superb treatment of some of the racial issues that characterized Japanese-U.S. relations, see John W. Dower, *War Without Mercy: Race and Power in the Pacific War* (New York: Pantheon Books, 1986).

99 C. Harvey Gardiner, *Pawns in a Triangle of Hate: The Peruvian Japanese and the United States* (Seattle: University of Washington Press, 1981). For an update on this story, see Tim Golden, "Held in War, Latins Seek Reparations," *New York Times,* 29 August 1996.

100 *O Globo,* 21 March 1942; *Correio da Manhã,* 22 March 1942; *New York Times,* 22 March 1942.

101 *Osaka Mainichi and Tokyo Nichi-Nichi,* 24 March 1942; Patrick Fukunaga, "The Brazilian Experience: The Japanese Immigrants During the Period of the Vargas Regime and the Immediate Aftermath" (Ph.D. dissertation, University of California, Santa Barbara, 1983), p. 126.

102 Antônio Xavier de Oliveira, *O problema imigratório na América Latina: O sentido político-militar da colonisação japonesa nos países do novo mundo* (Rio de Janeiro: A. Coelho Branco, 1942); Carlos de Zouza Moraes, *A ofensiva japonesa no Brasil: Aspecto social, econômico e político da colonização nipônica,* 2nd ed. (Pôrto Alegre: Edição da Livraria do Globo), 1942.

103   *Diário da Noite,* 30 September, 1942.

104   Asfora, "Colonos japoneses no brejo Pernambuco," p. 9; *Diário Nippak* (São Paulo), 11 July 1980, p. 1.

105   E.g., *O Estado de S. Paulo,* 8 April 1942.

106   *New York Times,* 12 April 1942, 4 and 29 October 1943; DEOPS report of Amilcar Alencastre, 13 April 1943, APP, SJ, Pasta II, APE-RJ.

107   Christopher A. Reichl, "Stages in the Historical Process of Ethnicity: The Japanese in Brazil, 1908–1988," *Ethnohistory* 42:1 (Winter 1995), 42.

108   Maeyama, "Ethnicity, Secret Societies, and Associations," p. 594.

109   Handa, *O imigrante japonês,* p. 640. A broader analysis of the social meanings of rumor can be found in Patricia A. Turner, *I Heard It Through the Grapevine: Rumor in African-American Culture* (Berkeley: University of California Press, 1993).

110   *New York Times,* 15 November 1942; *O Estado de S. Paulo,* 16 December 1942; Yukio Fujii and T. Lynn Smith, *The Acculturation of the Japanese in Brazil* (Gainesville: University of Florida Press, 1959), p. 49.

111   *O Estado de S. Paulo,* 5 March 1943 and 24 July 1943.

112   Circular no. 889/44, 12 July 1944, Delegacia de Ordem Política e Social, Estado de Paraná, Secretaria de Estado de Segurança Pública, Departamento da Polícia Civil, Divisão de Segurança e Informações, no. 1956—Sociedade dos Jovens Japoneses, Arquivo Público Paraná, Curitiba; *Diário de São Paulo,* 4 April 1946; Francisca Vieira, *O japonês na frente de expansão Paulista,* pp. 236–237.

113   *O Estado de S. Paulo,* 25 April 1945.

114   *Correio Paulistano,* 2 December 1944; *Vamos Ler!,* 2 November 1944, 14–16; Christovão de Alencar and Paulo Barbosa, *Ping-pong* (São Paulo: Editoras Litero-Musical Tupy, 1943), recorded by Lauro Borges (Manduca) on the RCA label; João de Barro and Alberto Ribeiro, *A guerra do amor* (São Paulo: A Melodia, n.d.). I would like to thank Roney Cytrynowicz for sharing this information with me. Oliveira Lima's discussion was about the social meanings of "lying" and how they differed in Brazil and Japan. Manuel de Oliveira Lima, *No Japão: Impressões da terra e da gente,* 2nd ed. (Rio de Janeiro: Laemmert, 1905), pp. 125–126.

115   *New York Times,* 7 June 1945. The Brazilian-U.S. military treaty stated that all bases would revert to Brazil six months after the end of the war.

116   Hiromi Shibata suggests that São Paulo's Japanese schools were as much an affirmation of Nipo-Brazilian identity as they were of Japanese nationalism. Shibata, "As escolas japonesas paulistas (1915–1945)" (Ph.D. dissertation, University of São Paulo, 1997), p. 9.

117   Kumusaka and Saito, "Kachigumi: A Collective Delusion."

118   Hekisui Yoshii, "Gokuchū Kaiko-roku" (Memories from Prison), manuscript, 1948. Cited in translation by Miyao and Yamashiro, "A comunidade nipônica no período da guerra," p. 262. Translation of Shindo Renmei documents can be found in "Perigosa atividade nipônica em São Paulo," *Arquivos da polícia civil de São Paulo* 8:2 (1944), 567–571; and Willems and Saito, "Shindo Renmei: Um problema de aculturação," p. 143. Analysis of the Shindo Renmei and similar

movements can be found in Maeyama, "Ethnicity, Secret Societies and Associations"; Susumu Miyao and José Yamashiro, "A comunidade enfrenta um caos sem precedentes," in Comissão de Elaboração da História dos 80 Anos da Imigração Japonesa no Brasil, ed., *Uma epopéia moderna*, pp. 265-360; and James L. Tigner, "Shindo Remmei: Japanese Nationalism in Brazil," *Hispanic American Historical Review* 41:4 (November 1961), 515-532.

119 See translation of Shindo Renmei objectives and statutes in report of João André Dias Paredes to Major Antonio Pereira Lira (State Police Chief, Paraná), 30 April 1949, Secretaria de Estado de Segurança Pública, Departamento da Polícia Civil, Divisão de Segurança e Informações, no. 1971—Sociedade Terrorista Japonesa, Arquivo Público Paraná, Curitiba; Mário Botelho de Miranda, *Shindo Renmei: Terrorismo e extorsão* (São Paulo: Edição Saraiva, 1948), p. 11; James L. Tigner, *The Okinawans in Latin America,* Scientific Investigations in the Ryuku Islands Report #7 (Washington, DC: Pacific Science Board, National Research Council/Department of the Army, 1954), p. 42.

120 The only Japanese-language competition to the Shindo Renmei weekly was the Cotia Cooperative *Information Bulletin,* which rarely tackled political issues. Miyao and Yamashiro," A comunidade enfrenta um caos sem precedentes," pp. 266-280; Dráuzio Leme Padilha, *CAC: Cooperativismo que deu certo* (São Paulo: Cooperativa Agrícola de Cotia, Cooperativa Central, 1989), p. 90.

121 The documents were found in a raid on Shindo Renmei headquarters in Santo André and published in translation in Herculano Neves, *O processo da "Shindo-Renmei" e demais associações secretas japonesas* (São Paulo: n.p., 1960), pp. 288-290.

122 Reprinted in *Paulista Shinbun,* 29 April 1947.

123 Handa, *O imigrante japonês,* pp. 651-655.

124 José Yamashiro, "Algumas considerações sobre o 'fanatismo japonês,'" *Jornal Paulista (Paulista Shinbun),* 29 April 1947; *A Noite* (Rio de Janeiro), 25 May 1946; Handa, *O imigrante japonês,* p. 678. There were some kachigumi groups among Hawaii's large Japanese population, but support appears to have been minimal. See John J. Stephan, *Hawaii Under the Rising Sun: Japan's Plans for Conquest After Pearl Harbor* (Honolulu: University of Hawaii Press, 1984), pp. 172-173. A brief discussion of "victorist" movements in Hawaii is in Gwenfread Allen, *Hawaii's War Years: 1941-1945* (Honolulu: University of Hawaii Press, 1950), p. 364.

125 Tigner, *The Okinawans in Latin America,* p. 44.

126 I would like to thank John Nelson, Robert J. Smith, and Erica D. Swarts for their kindness in responding to a query on ihai via the H-Japan listserv. Japanese-Afro-Brazilian syncretism is especially noticeable in religious movements whose membership is predominantly of Okinawan descent.

127 *O Estado de S. Paulo,* 26 March 1946; *Correio da Manhã,* 6 April 1946; *A Noite* (Rio de Janeiro), 13 April 1946. Other newspapers that regularly ran stories, often on a daily basis for weeks in a row, were *Correio Paulistano, Diário de São Paulo,* and *Folha da Noite.* See also Neves, *O processo da "Shindo-Renmei,"* pp. 97, 124.

128 *Correio da Manhã,* 13 April 1946; *A Noite,* 25 May 1946.

129   *O Dia,* 6 April 1946 and 4 May 1946; Miranda, *Shindo Renmei,* pp. 160–161; Handa, *O imigrante japonês,* p. 660; Tigner, *The Okinawans in Latin America,* p. 45.

130   Handa, *O imigrante japonês,* p. 673.

131   *Correio Paulistano,* 5 April 1946; *Folha da Manhã,* 1 April 1946. See also *O Estado de S. Paulo,* 26, 28, 31 March 1946; *A Noite,* 4 and 5 April 1946. U.S. military attempts to confirm a Shindo Renmei-Black Dragon Society connection were inconclusive. Memo of Rolf Larson, "Secret Japanese Societies in Brazil," 10 May 1946, APP, SJ, Pasta II, APE-RJ. For an example of Brazilian propaganda on the Black Dragon Society, see José de Lima Figueiredo, *O Japão por dentro,* Coleção Guerra e Paz, vol. 7 (São Paulo: Companhia Editora Nacional, 1944), p. 35.

132   *Folha da Manhã,* 3 April 1946.

133   *Folha da Manhã,* 14 March 1946; Neves, *O processo da "Shindo-Renmei,"* n.p.; *Diário de São Paulo,* 6 April 1946.

134   José Yamashiro, "Apoio à minoria," *Jornal Paulista (Paulista Shinbun),* 19 April 1947.

135   Interview by Jeffrey Lesser with Masuji Kiyotani, 27 July 1995, at the Centro de Estudos Nipo-Brasileiros (São Paulo).

136   Neves, *O processo da "Shindo-Renmei,"* pp. 26–27.

137   "As atividades das sociedades secretas japonesas e a ação repressiva da polícia de São Paulo, publicadas pela impressa," *Arquivos da Polícia Civil de São Paulo* 12:2 (1946), 523–530.

138   Jorge Americano, "Shindo Remei (1946)," in Americano, *São Paulo atual, 1935–1962* (São Paulo: Edições Melhoramentos, 1963), pp. 186–187.

139   Information on the meeting from *Correio Paulistano,* 20 July 1946; *Diário de São Paulo,* 20 July 1946; *A Gazeta,* 20 July 1946; *Jornal de São Paulo,* 20 July 1946; Miyao and Yamashiro, "A comunidade enfrenta um caos sem precedentes," pp. 300–305.

140   *Correio Paulistano,* 21 July 1946; Tigner, *The Okinawans in Latin America,* p. 45.

141   Jouji Nakadate, "O Japão venceu os aliados na Segunda guerra mundial? O movimento Shindo Renmei em São Paulo, (1945/1949)" (M.A. thesis, Pontifícia Universidade Católica, 1988), p. 278. José Sant'Anna do Carmo (a DEOPS translator), "Breve relatório sobre a "SHINDO-RENMEI" e a atuação da polícia de São Paulo, particularmente elaborado segundo o meu modo de ver os trabalhos dessas duas entidades," 12 October 1946, Secretaria da Segurança Pública do Estado de São Paulo-Departmento de Ordem Política e Social (DEOPS) #108981-Ordem Política/Shindo Remmey-Vol. 2, AESP. Francisco Luís Ribeiro, "O japonês como deliqüente político," *Investigações: Revista do Departamento de Investigações* (São Paulo) 1:8 (August 1949), 61.

142   Orlando Criscuolo, "Piadas nipo-crisuolinas: Ouvindo japoneses," *Mundo Policial em Revista* 1:7-8 (May–June 1947), 35.

143   *Revista Cruzeiro* (Rio de Janeiro), 31 August 1946.

144   *Correio Paulistano,* 11 April 1946; *Mundo Policial em Revista* 1:7-8 (May–June 1947), 27–33. Similar articles can be found in *Diário de São Paulo,* 18 April 1946, 13 October 1946, and 2 October 1946.

145   Emenda 3.165, 109th session of 22 August 1946 and 111th session of 24 August 1946, *Anais da Assembléia constituinte de 1946* (Rio de Janeiro: Imprensa Nacional, 1949), vol. 19.

146   *Jornal do Comércio*, 28 September 1946; Handa, *O imigrante japonês*, p. 663; Miyao and Yamashiro, "A comunidade enfrenta um caos sem precedentes," p. 291; Kumusaka and Saito, "Kachigumi: A Collective Delusion."

147   U.S. Secretary of State Acheson, agreeing with a reporter's comment in *New York Mirror*, 2 December 1945.

148   *Correio da Manhã*, 7 April 1946; *Jornal do Comércio*, 30 August 1946. One character in John Okada's novel *No-No Boy* receives regular letters from Brazil referring to news of Japan's victory. John Okada, *No-No Boy* (Seattle and San Francisco: Combined Asian American Resources Project, 1976), pp. 13, 24. I would like to thank Andrew Shin for pointing this out to me.

149   See translation of Shindo Renmei death threat to Akuguro Omura by official DEOPS translator, 18 January 1950, Secretaria de Estado de Segurança Pública, Departamento da Polícia Civil, Divisão de Segurança e Informações, no. 1971-Sociedade Terrorista Japonesa, Arquivo Público Paraná, Curitiba.

150   DEOPS attempts to link the Shindo Renmei to communism were not successful. Unsigned confidential São Paulo DEOPS report, "Atividades atuais no seio da colônia japoneza sobre rearticulação do movimento fanático-terrorista-chatagista," March 1950, Secretaria de Segurança Pública do Estado de São Paulo-Departmento de Ordem Política e Social (DEOPS) #108981-Ordem Política/ Shindo Remmey-vol. 1, AESP; Guido Fonseca, "DEOPS—Um pouco de sua história," *Revista da Associação dos Delegados de Polícia do Estado de São Paulo* 10:18 (December 1989), 41–86, esp. 67–70.

151   "PERIGOS DA IMPRENSA JAPONESA NO BRASIL," *Folha de Pinheiros*, 9 July 1949; *Burajiru Jiho* (*Notícias do Brasil*), 5 April 1949, trans. in Secretaria da Segurança Pública do Estado de São Paulo-Departamento de Ordem Política e Social (DEOPS) #108981-Ordem Política/Shindo Remmey-vol. 2, AESP; Pasquale Petrone, organizer, *Pinheiros: Estudo geográfico de um bairro paulistano* (São Paulo: Editora da Universidade de São Paulo, 1963), p. 67; Handa, *O imigrante japonês*, p. 687.

152   *Folha da Noite*, 21 March 1950; Handa, *O imigrante japonês*, pp. 746–752.

153   *E a paz volta a reinar na época do "Shindo Renmei,"* directed by Den Ohinata (São Paulo: Produção Cinematográfica Liberdade, 1956); Produção Cinematográfica Liberdade, *E a Paz Volta a Reinar na época do "Shindo Renmei"* (São Paulo: Produção Cinematográfica Liberdade, 1956), 1.

154   Emílio Willems, "Aspectos da aculturação dos japoneses no estado de São Paulo," *Boletim da Faculdade de filosofia, ciências e letras da USP* 3:82 (1948); Rubem Braga, "Conversa com japonês em Araçatuba: Notas de viagem," *Revista do Arquivo Municipal* 6:71 (October 1940), 216.

6   Turning Japanese

1   Most academic analysis of travel literature focuses on "first world" views of colonial regions. Edward Said, *Orientalism* (New York: Random House, 1978); Mary Louis Pratt, *Imperial Eyes: Travel Writing and Transculturation* (London and New York: Routledge, 1992); Ram Chandra Prassad, *Early English Travellers in India: A Study in the Travel Literature of the Elizabethan and Jacobean Periods with Particular Reference to India*, 2nd ed. (Delhi: Motilal Banarsidass, 1980); David Spurr, *The Rhetoric of Empire: Colonial Discourse in Journalism, Travel Writing, and Imperial Administration* (Durham, NC: Duke University Press, 1993); Flora Süssekind, *O Brasil não é longe daqui: O narrador, a viagem* (São Paulo: Companhia das Letras, 1990); Stephen Greenblatt, *Marvelous Possessions: The Wonder of the New World* (Chicago: University of Chicago Press, 1991); Toshio Yokoyama, *Japan in the Victorian Mind: A Study of Stereotyped Images of a Nation, 1850–80* (London: Macmillan, 1987); Ali Behdad, *Belated Travelers: Orientalism in the Age of Colonial Dissolution* (Durham, NC: Duke University Press, 1994); Christopher Mulvey, *Anglo-American Landscapes: A Study of Nineteenth-Century Anglo-American Travel Literature* (Cambridge: Cambridge University Press, 1983); Patrick Anderson, *Over the Alps: Reflections of Travel and Travel Writing, with Special Reference to the Grand Tours of Boswell, Beckford and Byron* (London: Rupert Hart-David, 1969); Nicholas Thomas, *Colonialism's Culture: Anthropology, Travel and Government* (Princeton: Princeton University Press, 1994); Anthony Pagden, "The Effacement of Difference: Colonialism and the Origins of Nationalism in Diderot and Herder," in Gyan Prakash, ed. *After Colonialism: Imperial Histories and Postcolonial Displacements* (Princeton: Princeton University Press, 1995), pp. 129–152.

2   Latcadio Hearn, *Glimpses of Unfamiliar Japan*, 2 vols. (Boston: Houghton, Mifflin, 1894); Rutherford Alcock, *The Capital of the Tycoon: A Narrative of a Three Years' Residence in Japan*, 3 vols. (New York: Harper & Brothers, 1863); Manuel de Oliveira Lima, *No Japão: Impressões da terra e da gente*, 2nd ed. (Rio de Janeiro: Laemmert, 1905), p. 326; Yokoyama, *Japan in the Victorian Mind*, pp. 67–72.

3   Richard G. Parker, *Bodies, Pleasures and Passions: Sexual Culture in Contemporary Brazil* (Boston: Beacon Press, 1991), p. 20.

4   Armando Martins Janeiro, *Um intérprete português do Japão: Wenceslau de Moraes* (Macao: Instituto Luís de Camões/Imprensa Nacional, 1966).

5   Letter of Azevedo to H. Garnier (a publisher), 11 September 1897. Cited in Luiz Dantas's introduction to Azevedo's *O Japão* (São Paulo: Roswitha Kempf Editores, 1984), p. 13.

6   Letter of José de Costa Azevedo to Felisbello Firmma de Oliva Freire (Brazilian Minister of Foreign Affairs), 1 July 1893; letter of José de Costa Azevedo to Cassiano de Nascimento, 2 April 1894, 06-Missões Especiais do Brasil no Estrangeiro, 271/2/3, Barão de Ladario-Missões Especias, China, 1893–1894, AHI-R; *China Mail* (Hong Kong), 1 June 1893; *Hong Kong Daily Telegraph*, 28 November 1893.

7   A wide-ranging discussion of stereotypes of Japan among foreign travelers can be found in Yokoyama, *Japan in the Victorian Mind*.

8   Cary James, *The Imperial Hotel: Frank Lloyd Wright and the Architecture of Unity* (Rutland, VT, and Tokyo: Charles E. Tuttle, 1968); Neil Levine, *The Architecture of Frank Lloyd Wright* (Princeton: Princeton University Press, 1996), pp. 114–124.

9   A similar construction can be found in Henrique C. R. Lisboa's comments on Japan, as discussed in chapter 3. Lisboa, *Os chins do Tetartos* (Rio de Janeiro: Tyfographia de Empreza Democrática Editora, 1894), p. 149. For a provocative article on gender and travel literature, see Louis Montrose, "The World of Gender in the Discourse of Discovery," in Stephen Greenblatt, ed., *New World Encounters* (Berkeley: University of California, 1993), pp. 177–217.

10 Gilberto Freyre, *The Masters and the Slaves*, 2nd ed., trans. Samuel Putnam (Berkeley: University of California Press, 1986), p. 85.

11 Francisco Antonio de Almeida, *Da França ao Japão* (Rio de Janeiro: Typ. do Apóstolo, 1879), p. 152.

12 Azevedo had come to prominence in 1881 with the publication of *O mulato*, and his *O cortiço* was published in the late 1920s in the United States. Herberto Sales, *Para conhecer melhor Aluísio Azevedo* (Rio de Janeiro: Bloch Editores, 1973); Wilson Martins, *História da inteligência brasileira*, vol. 4 *(1877–1896)* (São Paulo: Cultrix, 1978), pp. 18, 28, 543–548; Aluísio Azevedo, *Mulatto*, trans. Murray Graeme Mac-Nicoll, ed. Daphne Patai (Cranbury, NJ: Associated University Presses, 1990), pp. 8–9; Aluísio Azevedo, *A Brazilian Tenement*, trans. Harry W. Brown (New York: R. M. McBride, 1926); Samuel Putnam, *Marvelous Journey: A Survey of Four Centuries of Brazilian Writing* (New York: Alfred A. Knopf, 1948), p. 188.

13 Jean-Yves Mérian, *Aluísio Azevedo: Vida e obra (1857–1913). O verdadeiro Brasil do século XIX* (Rio de Janeiro: Editora Espaço e Tempo, 1988), p. 625.

14 Luiz Dantas, introduction to Azevedo, *O Japão*, p. 36; Georges Bosquet, *Le Japon de nos jours et les échelles de l'Extrême-Orient*. (Paris: Hachette, 1877).

15 Aluísio Azevedo, "Japonesas e norte-americanas: O comportamento das mulheres japonesas e norte-americanas," *Almanaque Brasileiro Garnier* (1904), 217–220; and "A mulher no Japão," *Almanaque Brasileiro Garnier* (1906), 410–412; Mérian, *Aluísio Azevedo*, pp. 607–610.

16 Azevedo, introduction to *O Japão*.

17 Mérian, *Aluísio Azevedo*, p. 625.

18 Oliveira Lima, *No Japão*, pp. 255, 213, 261, 267.

19 At the turn of the century everything from yellow fever vaccinations to public school norms to the destruction of *cortiços* (residential areas for the poor) was viewed as a way to change popular culture overnight. Teresa A. Meade, *"Civilizing Rio": Reform and Resistance in a Brazilian City, 1889–1930* (University Park: Pennsylvania State University Press, 1997); Sidney Chalhoub, "The Politics of Disease Control: Yellow Fever and Race in Nineteenth Century Rio de Janeiro," *Journal of Latin American Studies* 25:3 (October 1993), 455–459; Jeffrey D. Needell, *A Tropical Belle Epoque: Elite Culture and Society in Turn-of-the-Century Rio de Janeiro* (Cambridge: Cambridge University Press, 1987), pp. 137–141; Lúcio Kowarick and Clara Ant, "Cem anos de promiscuidade: O cortiço na cidade de São Paulo," in Lúcio Kowarick, org., *As lutas sociais e a cidade: São Paulo, passado e presente* (Rio

de Janeiro: Paz e Terra, 1988), pp. 49–71; Sidney Chalhoub, *Cidade febril: Cortiços e epidemias na corte imperial* (São Paulo: Companhia das Letras, 1996).

20   E. Patricia Tsurumi, *Factory Girls: Women in the Thread Mills of Meiji Japan* (Princeton: Princeton University Press, 1990); Nakano Makiko, *Makiko's Diary: A Merchant Wife in 1910 Kyoto*, trans., with an introduction and notes, by Kazuko Smith (Stanford: Stanford University Press, 1995); Sharon H. Nolte and Sally Ann Hastings, "The Meiji State's Policy Toward Women, 1890–1910," in Gail Lee Bernstein, ed., *Recreating Japanese Women, 1600–1945* (Berkeley: University of California Press, 1991), pp. 151–174; and Laurel Rasplica Rodd, "Yosano Akiko and the Taishō Debate over the New Woman," in Gail Lee Bernstein, ed., *Recreating Japanese Women, 1600–1945* (Berkeley: University of California Press, 1991), pp. 175–198.

21   Oliveira Lima, *No Japão*, p. 200.

22   Ibid., pp. 205, 207, 212.

23   Lecture at the Getsu Yo Kai (Monday Club), Tokyo, 10 March 1902. In Oliveira Lima, *No Japão*, pp. 338–345.

24   Moreira Guimarães, preface to Henrique Paulo Bahiana, *O Japão que eu vi*, Coleção Viagens, vol. 14 (São Paulo: Companhia Editora Nacional, 1937), p. 15.

25   Moreira Guimarães, *No Extremo Oriente: O Japão* (Rio de Janeiro: Editora Alba, 1936), p. 37.

26   Vicente Lustoza, *Viagem ao Japão: Circunavegando o globo* (Rio de Janeiro and Paris: H. Garnier, 1909), pp. 2–3.

27   Pratt, *Imperial Eyes*, pp. 201–202.

28   Lustoza, *Viagem ao Japão*, pp. 49–50.

29   Ibid., pp. 70–71, 76–77.

30   Ibid., pp. 84–85, 141–146.

31   Juliano Moreira, *Impressões de uma viagem ao Japão em 1928* (n.p.: Biblioteca Juliano Moreira, 1935), pp. 127–129.

32   Ibid., pp. 39, 40, 92, 113.

33   Ibid., pp. 111–114.

34   Augusta Peick Moreira, "No Oriente (impressões de viagem)," in Juliano Moreira, *Impressões de uma viagem*, p. 133.

35   Augusta Peick Moreira, "Dez milhões de mulheres ganham a sua vida no Japão," lecture presented to the Federação Brasileira pelo Progresso Feminino, 17 November 1929. In Juliano Moreira, *Impressões de uma viagem*, pp. 139–144.

36   Peick Moreira, "No Oriente," pp. 130, 131.

37   Laurence Hallewell, *Books in Brazil* (Metuchen, NJ: Scarecrow Press, 1982), table 9, p. 216.

38   Monteiro Lobato, *América*, Coleção Viagens, vol. 1 [1932], 2nd ed. (São Paulo: Companhia Editora Nacional, 1934); Caio Prado Júnior, *U.R.S.S. Um novo mundo*, Coleção Viagens, vol. 3 (São Paulo: Companhia Editora Nacional, 1934).

39   Nelson Tabajara de Oliveira, *Shanghai: Reportagens do Oriente*, Coleção Viagens, vol. 2 (São Paulo: Companhia Editora Nacional, 1934), pp. 17–19.

40   Nelson Tabajara de Oliveira, *O roteiro do Oriente*, Coleção Viagens, vol. 8, 2nd ed. (São Paulo: Companhia Editora Nacional, 1935), pp. 164–165.

41   The estimate came from a Japanese official in 1929. Modern scholarship has shown that prostitutes were often quite desperate to leave life in Yoshiwara. A 1900 law allowed prostitutes to leave the brothels if they or their families had no debts to the brothel owners, a rare situation indeed. See Sheldon Garon, "The World's Oldest Debate? Prostitution and the State in Imperial Japan, 1900-1945," *American Historical Review* 98:3 (June 1993), 713-715.

42   Nelson Tabajara de Oliveira, *Japão: Reportagens do Oriente,* Coleção Viagens, vol. 4 (São Paulo: Companhia Editora Nacional, 1934), pp. 157-160.

43   Ibid., pp. 151-156.

44   Ibid., pp. 7-12, 139.

45   Ibid., pp. 141-143, 130.

46   Cantido de Moura Campos, "Prefácio" to Ernesto de Souza Campos, *Japão visto através de uma viagem ao Oriente realizada por universitários da Faculdade de medicina de São Paulo* (São Paulo: Imprensa Oficial do Estado, 1935).

47   Campos, *Japão visto atraves de uma viagem.*

48   I would like to thank Assumpção's grandson for showing me the photographs.

49   Bahiana, *O Japão que eu vi;* Armando Mendes, *O Japão que avança: Aspectos econômicos, estudos e impressões de viagem ao Japão* (São Paulo: Editora Record, 1937); Garibaldi Dantas, *Extremo Oriente,* Coleção Viagens, vol. 15 (São Paulo: Companhia Editora Nacional, 1938); Claudio de Souza, *Impressões do Japão* (Rio de Janeiro: Instituto Brasileiro de Cultura Japonesa, 1940). In 1928 Souza published a two-volume set on his trip to the Middle East, *De Paris ao Oriente* (Rio de Janeiro: Gráphica Sauer, 1928).

50   José de Lima Figueiredo, *No Japão foi assim* (Rio de Janeiro: Editora Século XX, 1941). Lima Figueiredo's view of Brazil can be found in his *A conquista do Brasil pelos brasileiros* (Rio de Janeiro: Conselho Nacional de Geografia, 1943).

51   José de Lima Figueiredo, *O Japão por dentro,* Coleção Guerra e Paz, vol. 7 (São Paulo: Companhia Editora Nacional, 1944), p. 7.

52   Ibid.

53   Ibid., pp. 7-8, 29, 33.

54   Ibid., pp. 75-77.

55   Nelson Tabajara de Oliveira, "Considerações de Nelson Tabajara de Oliveira," in Mário Botelho de Miranda, *Um brasileiro no Japão em guerra* (São Paulo: Companhia Editora Nacional, 1944), pp. 11-13.

56   Botelho de Miranda, *Um brasileiro no Japão,* p. 15.

57   Ibid., pp. 74, 112. The only other author to mention this was Augusta Peick Moreira.

58   Botelho de Miranda, *Um brasileiro no Japão,* p. 135.

7   A Suggestive Epilogue

1   *Amor Bandido,* directed by Bruno Barretto (Rio de Janeiro: Produções Cinematográficas, 1979).

2   Gabriel o Pensador, "Lavagem cerebral," on *Gabriel o Pensador* (Rio de Janeiro: Sony/Chaos, 1993).

3   Seth Garfield, " 'Civilized' but Discontent: The Xavante Indians and Government Policy in Brazil, 1937-88" (Ph.D. thesis, Yale University, 1996); Arnd Schneider, "The Transcontinental Construction of European Identities: A View from Argentina," *Anthropological Journal on European Cultures* 5:1 (1996), 95-105.

4   Gilberto Freyre, "O Brasil, democracia étnica," *Cruzeiro,* 6 and 19 June 1953; Arthur Hehl Neiva, *Deslocados de guerra: A verdade sobre sua seleção* (Rio de Janeiro: n.p., 1949).

5   There are no reliable statistics on Syrian-Lebanese economic ascension. A 1995 Datafolha survey found that 8 percent of nikkei families in São Paulo had incomes of at least ten minimum salaries; in the total population, only 30 percent had salaries that high. The same study showed that 53 percent of nikkei adults had university educations, compared with only 9 percent of the total adult population. *Folha de São Paulo,* 19 October 1995. See also Boris Fausto, Oswaldo Truzzi, Roberto Grün, and Célia Sakurai, *Imigração e política em São Paulo* (São Paulo: Editora Sumaré/FAPESP, 1995); *Vida e sangue de polacko,* documentary film directed by Silvio Back (Curitiba, Paraná), in Coleção Silvio Back, Museu de Imagen e Som, São Paulo, C 309/93; Octávio Ianni, *Raças e classes socias no Brasil,* 2nd ed. (Rio de Janeiro: Editora Civilização Brasileira, 1972), pp. 169-198.

6   "Enclave suspeito," *Veja* 28:7 (15 February 1995), 50-52.

7   Between 1953 and 1959 over thirty thousand new Japanese immigrants settled in Brazil, followed by another sixteen thousand in the next decade. Over 81 percent of all Japanese emigrants between 1952 and 1965 settled in Brazil. Moacyr Flores, "Japoneses no Rio Grande do Sul," *Veritas* (Pôrto Alegre) 77 (1975), 65-98; Tetsuo Nakasumi and José Yamashiro, "O fim da era de imigração e a consolidação da nova colônia nikkei," in Comissão de Elaboração da História dos 80 Anos da Imigração Japonesa no Brasil, ed., *Uma epopéia moderna* (São Paulo: Editora Hucitec, 1992), table 2, p. 424; Harold D. Sims, "Japanese Postwar Migration to Brazil: An Analysis of the Data Presently Available," *International Migration Review* 6:3 (Fall 1972), 246-266. On post-1950 emigration to the Dominican Republic, see Sumire Kunieda, "JAPANESE EMIGRANTS TO DOMINICAN REPUBLIC DEMAND GOVERNMENT COMPENSATION," *Mainichi Daily News,* 10 October 1997.

8   Francisca Isabel Schurig Vieira, *O japonês na frente de expansão paulista: O processo de absorção do japonês em Marília* (São Paulo: Pioneira Ed. da Universidade de São Paulo, 1973), pp. 83-89. Nakasumi and Yamashiro, "O fim da era de imigração," pp. 422-23; Tomoo Handa, *O imigrante japonês* (São Paulo: T. A. Queiroz/Centro de Estudos Nipo-Brasileiros, 1987), p. 715.

9   Jeffrey Lesser, "Asians in South America," in *Encyclopedia of World Cultures,* vol. 7, *South America,* ed. Johannes Wilbert (New York: G. K. Hall/Macmillan, 1995),

pp. 58–61; Keum Joa Choi, "Além do arco-íris: A imigração coreana no Brasil" (M.A. thesis, University of São Paulo, 1991); "Novos imigrantes: Quinhentos mil cidadãos do terceiro mundo sobrevivem hoje clandestinamente no país," *Istoé*, 10 April 1985, 30–35; Ivan Light and Edna Bonacich, *Immigrant Entrepreneurs: Koreans in Los Angeles, 1965–1982* (Berkeley: University of California Press, 1988).

10 Centro de Estudos Nipo-Brasileiros, *Pesquisa da população de descendentes de japoneses residentes no Brasil, 1987–1988* (São Paulo: Centro de Estudos Nipo-Brasileiros, 1990); Gleice Carvalho, "Sutis diferenças," *Japão aqui* 1:2 (May 1997), 26–29. Koichi Mori, "Mundo dos brasileiros mestiços descendentes de japoneses," unpublished paper (1994) used by permission of the author.

11 *Momento Legislativo* 3:27 (August 1993); *Japão Aqui* 1:1 (April 1997), 11–15.

12 Centro de Estudos Nipo-Brasileiros, *Pesquisa da população*, table 2-1, p. 19, and table 3-4, p. 43. Thirty-five thousand Peruvian nikkei also live in Japan.

13 Masako Watanabe, ed., *Kyōdōkenkyū dekassegui-nikkei-baurajiru-jin: Shiryō-hen* (Group Study—Brazilian Dekaseguis), vol. 2 (Tokyo: Akashi Shoten, 1995), pp. 350–351. I would like to thank Prof. Koichi Mori for translating the interviews in this volume for me.

14 *Jornal Tudo Bem*, 19 July 1997; Daniel Linger, "Brazil Displaced: Restaurante 51 in Nagoya, Japan," *Horizontes Antropológicos* (Porto Alegre) 5 (1997), 181–203, and "The Identity Path of Eduardo Mori," in Jean Lave and Dorothy Holland, eds., *History in Person: Enduring Struggles and Identities in Practice* (Santa Fe, NM: School of American Research Press, forthcoming); Koichi Mori, "Evolução e situação vigente dos dekasseguis brasileiros no Japão" and "O significado do fenômeno dekassegui na comunidade nipo-brasileira," in Masako Watanabe, ed., *Os dekasseguis brasileiros de origem japonesa—Coletânea de Teses* (Tokyo: Editora Fukutake, 1995); Masato Ninomia, ed., *Dekassegui: Palestras e exposições do simpósio sobre o fenômeno chamado dekassegui* (São Paulo: Estação Liberdade/Sociedade Brasileira de Cultura Japonesa, 1992); Charles Tetsuo Chigusa, ed., *A quebra dos mitos: O fenômeno dekassegui através de relatos pessoais* (Tokyo: IPC, 1994); Keiko Yamanaka, "Return Migration of Japanese Brazilians to Japan: The *Nikkeijin* as Ethnic Minority and Political Construct," *Diaspora* 5, no. 1 (Spring 1996): 65–97, and "Factory Workers and Convalescent Attendants: Japanese-Brazilian Migrant Women and Their Families in Japan," in *International Female Migration and Japan: Networking, Settlement and Human Rights* (Tokyo: International Peace Research Institute, Meiji Gakuin University, 1996), pp. 87–116; Yoko Sellek, "Nikkeijin: The Phenomenon of Return Migration," in Michael Weiner, ed., *Japan's Minorities: The Illusion of Homogeneity* (London: Routledge, 1997), pp. 178–210.

15 Manuela Carneiro da Cunha, *Negros, Estrangeiros: Os escravos libertos e sua volta à África* (São Paulo: Brasiliense, 1985).

16 "Imigrantes japoneses: Na união, a sobrevivência," *Diário Nippak página um*, 19 September 1980; "Criação x Identidade x Formação: Os descendentes e a literatura," *Diário Nippak página um*, 12 July 1980; *Japão Aqui* 1:3 (July 1997), 38–44; *Japão Aqui* 1:1 (April 1997), 63.

17   Advertisement for *Made in Japan* in *Jornal Tudo Bem,* 19 July 1997; "Bailes agitam a noite da moçada nikkei," *Revista Nippak Jovem* 1:2 (13 April 1997), 28–34.

18   Interview of Luís Gushiken by Jeffrey Lesser, Michael Molasky, and Koichi Mori, 8 December 1995. Getúlio Hanashiro (Brazilian Social Democratic Party), a sociologist who was exiled during the military dictatorship and has served as São Paulo's minister of transportation and minister of health, uses a marketing strategy similar to Gushiken's. Interview of Getúlio Hanashiro by Jeffrey Lesser, Michael Molasky, and Koichi Mori, 12 December 1995.

19   Antônio Baptista Pereira, *O Brasil e a Raça: Conferência feita na Faculdade de direito de São Paulo a 19 de junho de 1928* (São Paulo: Empresa Gráfica Rossetti, 1928), p. 17.

20   Greil Marcus, *Lipstick Traces: A Secret History of the Twentieth Century* (Cambridge, MA: Harvard University Press, 1989), p. 4.

Bibliography

Official Publications

Bahia. *Annaes da Assembléia legislativa provincial da Bahia, sessões do anno de 1876* (Bahia: Typ. do Correio da Bahia, 1876).

Brazil. *Collecção das leis do império do Brasil de 1850*. Rio de Janeiro: Typografia Nacional, 1851.

———. *Annaes do Parlamento brazileiro, Câmara dos srs. deputados, 1868*. Vol. 3. Rio de Janeiro: Typ. do Diário do Rio de Janeiro, 1868.

———. *Colleção das leis do império do Brasil de 1870*. Rio de Janeiro: Typografia Nacional, 1870.

———. *Colleção das leis do império do Brasil de 1872*. Rio de Janeiro: Typografia Nacional, 1873.

———. *Colleção das leis do império do Brasil de 1874*. Tomo 37, parte II, vol. 2. Rio de Janeiro: Typografia Nacional, 1875.

———. *Annaes do Parlamento brazileiro, Câmara dos srs. deputados — sessão de 1828*. Rio de Janeiro: Typ. Parlamentar, 1876.

———. *Annaes do Senado do império do Brasil, 2a sessão da 16a legislatura no mez de setembro de 1877*. Rio de Janeiro: Typ. do Diário do Rio de Janeiro, 1877.

———. *Annaes do Senado do império do Brazil: 2a sessão da 16a legislatura no mez de outubro de 1877*. Vol. 5. Rio de Janeiro: Typ. do Diário do Rio de Janeiro, 1877.

———. *Annaes do Parlamento brazileiro, Câmara dos srs. deputados — sessão de 1831*. Rio de Janeiro: Typ. H. J. Pinto, 1878.

———. *Annaes do Parlamento brazileiro, Câmara dos deputados, prorogação das sessão de 1879*. Vol. 5. Rio de Janeiro: Typ. Nacional, 1879.

———. *Annaes do Senado do império do Brazil, la sessão de 17a legislatura do 10 à 31 de março*. Vol. 3. Rio de Janeiro: Typ. Nacional, 1879.

———. *Annaes do Senado do império do Brazil*. Rio de Janeiro: Imprensa Nacional, 1888.

———. *Relatório apresentado ao presidente da república dos Estados Unidos do Brazil pelo ministro do estado das relações exteriores Carlos Augusto de Carvalho em maio de 1895.* Rio de Janeiro: Imprensa Nacional, 1895.

——. *Collecção das leis da república dos Estados Unidos do Brasil de 1930.* Vol. 2, *Actos da junta governativa provisória e do governo provisório (outubro à dezembro).* Rio de Janeiro: Imprensa Nacional, 1931.

——. *Annaes da Assembléia constituinte de 1935.* São Paulo: Sociedade Impressora Paulista, 1935.

——. *Annaes da Assembléia nacional constituente organizados pela redação das annaes e documentos parlamentares.* Vol. 8. 12 vol. Rio de Janeiro: Imprensa Nacional, 1935–1936.

——. *Annaes da Assembléia nacional constituente organizados pela redação das annaes e documentos parlamentares.* Rio de Janeiro: Imprensa Nacional, 1935.

——. *Annaes da Câmara dos deputados: Sessões de 16 à 24 de setembro de 1935.* Vol. 17. Rio de Janeiro: Off. Gráfica d'A Noite, 1935.

——, Congresso Agrícola. *Collecção de documentos.* Rio de Janeiro: Typ. Nacional, 1878.

——, Ministério da Justiça e Negócios Interiores. *Registro de estrangeiros, 1808–1822.* Rio de Janeiro: Arquivo Nacional, 1960.

——, Secretaria da Agricultura, Indústria e Comércio. *Boletim do Serviço de imigração e colonização.*

——, Secretaria dos Negócios da Agricultura, Comércio e Obras Públicas. *Relatório apresentado ao dr. Francisco de Paula Rodrigues Alves, presidente do estado, pelo dr. Antonio Candido Rodriques, secretário da agricultura—ano de 1900.* São Paulo: Typografia do Diário Official, 1901.

——, Serviço de Estatística Econômica e Financeira do Tesouro Nacional, Ministério da Fazenda. *Quadros estatísticos, resumo anual de estatísticas econômicas, 1932–1939.* Rio de Janeiro: Imprensa Nacional, 1941.

Japan, Comissão de Recenseamento da Colônia Japonesa. *The Japanese Immigrant in Brazil.* Tokyo: University of Tokyo Press, 1964–1969.

——, Consulado Geral do Japão. *Emigração japonesa no Brasil.* São Paulo: Consulado Geral do Japão, 1973.

——, Department of Tourism. *Guia de algibeira do Japão: Com uma descrição especial dos costumes, história, educação, arte, divertimentos, etc.* Tokyo: Direção Geral de Turismo, Ministério de Estradas de Ferro do Japão, 1941.

League of Nations. *League of Nations—Official Journal.*

——. *Monthly Summary of the League of Nations.*

Minas Gerais. *Collecção das leis e decretos do estado de Minas Geraes em 1893.* Ouro Prêto: Imprensa Oficial de Minas Gerais, 1893.

——. *Relatório apresentado ao dr. presidente do estado de Minas Geraes pelo secretário de estado dos negócios da agricultura, comércio e obras públicas, dr. David Moretzsohn Campista, no anno de 1893.* Ouro Prêto: Imprensa Oficial de Minas Gerais, 1893.

——, *Collecção das leis e decretos do estado de Minas Geraes em 1894.* Ouro Prêto: Imprensa Oficial de Minas Gerais, 1895.

——, Congresso Mineiro. *Annaes do Senado mineiro, terceira sessão da primeira legislatura no Anno de 1893.* Ouro Prêto: Imprensa Oficial de Minas Gerais, 1893.

Pará. *Dados estatísticos e informações para os immigrantes*. Belém do Pará: Typ. Diário de Notícias, 1866.

Rio de Janeiro. *Questões agrícolas—immigração chineza (3 discussão do orçamento)*. Discurso *pronunciado na Assembléia provincial do Rio de Janeiro na sessão de 23 de novembro de 1888 pelo bacharel em sciências jurídicas e sociaes Oscar Varady*. Rio de Janeiro: Typografia Carioca, 1888.

———. *Annaes da Assembléia legislativa do estado do Rio de Janeiro*. Rio de Janeiro: Typ. Jornal do Comércio, 1894.

São Paulo. *Annaes da Assembléia legislativa provincial de São Paulo. Primeiro anno da 23 legislatura (sessão de 1880)*. São Paulo: Typ. da Tribuna Liberal, 1880.

———. *Relatório annual apresentado ao cidadão dr. presidente do estado de São Paulo pelo dr. Jorge Tibiriçá, secretário dos negócios da agricultura, Commércio e obras públicas*. São Paulo: Typ. à Vapor de Vanorden, 1894.

———. *Relatório apresentado ao vice-presidente do estado pelo secretário dos negócios da justiça de S. Paulo, José Getúlio Monteiro relativo ao anno de 1897*. São Paulo: Typ. Espindola, Siqueira, 1898.

———. *Relatório apresentado ao secretário dos negócios da justiça do estado de S. Paulo pelo chefe de polícia Theodoro Dias de Carvalho Júnior em 31 de janeiro de 1895*. São Paulo: Typ. Espindola, Siqueira, 1898.

———. *Relatório apresentado ao dr. Jorge Tibiriçá, presidente do estado, pelo dr. Carlos Botelho, secretário da agricultura, relativo ao ano de 1907*. São Paulo: Secretaria da Agricultura, 1908.

———. *Relatório apresentado ao exmo. snr. dr. Getúlio Vargas, presidente da república, pelo dr. Adhemar Pereira de Barros, interventor federal em S. Paulo, 1938–1939*. São Paulo: Empresa Gráfica da Revista dos Tribunais, 1940.

———, Câmara dos Deputados do Estado de São Paulo. *Annaes da sessão ordinária e extraordinária de 1892 (10 anno da 2nda legislatura)*. São Paulo: n.p., 1893.

———. *Annaes da sessão extraordinária e ordinária de 1893 (2ndo anno da 2nda legislatura)*. São Paulo: n.p., 1894.

———, Prefeitura Municipal. *Catálogo das obras de arte em logradouros públicos de São Paulo: Regional sé*. São Paulo: Dept. do Patrimônio Histórico, 1987.

———, Secretaria da Agricultura, Indústria e Comércio. *DTCI: Boletim da Directória de terras, colonização e immigração*.

———. Secretaria dos Negócios da Agricultura, Comércio e Obras Públicas. *Relatório apresentado ao dr. Francisco de Paula Rodrigues Alves, presidente do estado, pelo dr. Antonio Candido Rodriques, secretário da agricultura—Anno de 1900*. São Paulo: Typografia do Diário Oficial, 1901.

Newspapers, Journals, and Bulletins

Afarodzu Choho (Tokyo)
L'Akcham (Constantinople)
Al-Shogreb al-Aksa (Tangier)

Anglo-Brazilian Chronicle (Rio de Janeiro)
The Anti-Slavery Reporter (London)
L'Asie Française (Paris)
A Batalha (São Paulo)
Boletim da Província de Macau e Timor (Macao)
Boletim do Serviço de Imigração e Colonização (Rio de Janeiro)
Boletim Oficial do Governo da Província de Macau e Timor (Macao)
O Brasil (Rio de Janeiro)
Brazilian-American (Rio de Janeiro)
Burajiru Jiho (*Notícias do Brasil*) (São Paulo)
Business Week (New York)
O Carioca (Rio de Janeiro)
Ceylon Observer
China Mail (Hong Kong)
Comércio de Santos
Correio da Manhã (Rio de Janeiro)
Correio Mercantil (São Paulo)
Correio Paulistano (São Paulo)
Daily Mail (London)
Daily Telegraph (London)
Diário Carioca (Rio de Janeiro)
Diário de Notícias (Rio de Janeiro)
Diário Nippak (São Paulo)
Diretrizes (Rio de Janeiro)
Echo macaense (Macao)
L'Epoca (Genoa)
O Estado de S. Paulo
Evening Standard (London)
Folha da Manhã (São Paulo)
Folha da Noite (São Paulo)
Folha de Pinheiros (São Paulo)
Folha do Povo (Rio de Janeiro)
Gakusei: Orgão da Liga Estudantina Nippo-Brasileira (São Paulo)
Gazeta de Campinas
Gazeta de Notícias (Rio de Janeiro)
Gazeta do Rio
O Globo (Rio de Janeiro)
Hong Kong Daily Press
Hong Kong Daily Telegraph
Hong Kong Weekly Press
A Immigração—Orgão da Sociedade Central da Immigração (Rio de Janeiro)
El Imparcial (Madrid)
A Imprensa (Rio de Janeiro)
O Independente (Macao)

Investigações: Revista do Departamento de Investigações (São Paulo)
Istoé (São Paulo)
Japan Advertiser (Tokyo)
Japan Gazette (Tokyo)
Japan Magazine (Tokyo)
Japan Times (Tokyo)
Japan Times and Mail (Tokyo)
Japanese Advertiser (Tokyo)
Jiji Shinbun (Tokyo)
O Jornal (Rio de Janeiro)
Jornal do Agricultor (São Paulo)
Jornal do Brasil (Rio de Janeiro)
Jornal do Comércio (Campo Grande)
Jornal do Comércio (Rio de Janeiro)
Jornal do Imigrante (São Paulo)
Literary Digest (Tokyo)
Manchete Esportiva (Rio de Janeiro)
Mariannense (Mariana, Minas Gerais)
Mephistópheles (Rio de Janeiro)
Le Milliett (Constantinople)
Morning Post (London)
Mundo Policial em Revista (São Paulo)
A Nação (Rio de Janeiro)
New China Daily News (Hong Kong)
New York Herald Tribune
New York Times
Nippak Shinbun (São Paulo)
A Notícia (São Paulo)
Osaka Mainichi and Tokyo Nichi-Nichi Shinbun (Tokyo)
O Paiz (Rio de Janeiro)
Phare de la Loire (Nantes)
Platéa (São Paulo)
O Radical (São Paulo)
Reforma (Rio de Janeiro)
Revista Cruzeiro (Rio de Janeiro)
Revista de Imigração e Colonização (Rio de Janeiro)
Revue des Deux Mondes (Paris)
Revue Occidentale (Paris)
Rio News
San Francisco Chronicle
South American Journal (Rio de Janeiro)
Sunday Times (London)
Time (New York)
The Times (London)

Tokyo Asahi Shinbun
Tokyo Nichi-Nichi Shinbun
Transição (São Paulo)
A Tribuna (Santos)
Vamos Ler! (Rio de Janeiro)
Veja (São Paulo)
Yorodzu Choho (Yokohama)

Books, Articles, Theses

Abrantes, Visconde de. *Memória sobre meios de promover a colonisação.* Berlin: Typ. de Unger Irmãos, 1846.

Alcock, Rutherford. *The Capital of the Tycoon: A Narrative of a Three Years' Residence in Japan.* 3 vols. New York: Harper & Brothers, 1863.

Alencar, Christovão de, and Paulo Barbosa. *Ping-pong.* São Paulo: Editoras Litero-Musical Tupy, 1943. Recorded by Lauro Borges (Manduca) on the RCA label.

Allen, Gwenfread. *Hawaii's War Years: 1941-1945.* Honolulu: University of Hawaii Press, 1950.

Almeida, A. Tavares de. *Oeste paulista: A experiência etnográfica e cultural.* Rio de Janeiro: Editora, Alba, 1943.

Almeida, Francisco Antonio de. *Da França ao Japão: Narração de viagem e descripção histórica, usos e costumes dos habitantes da China, do Japão e de outros paizes de Asia.* Rio de Janeiro: Typ. do Apóstolo, 1879.

Almeida, Guilherme de. *Cosmópolis: São Paulo/29.* São Paulo: Companhia Editora Nacional, 1962.

Alves da Cunha, Raymundo Cyriaco. *Obras públicas, terras e colonização.* Belém do Pará: n.p., 1895.

Amado, Jorge. *Gabriela, Clove and Cinnamon.* Translated from the Portuguese by James L. Taylor and William L. Grossman. New York: Knopf, 1962.

Amarilio, Júnior. *As vantagens da immigração siria no Brasil: Em torno de uma polêmica entre os snrs. Herbert V. Levy e Salomão Jorge, no "Diário de São Paulo."* Rio de Janeiro: Off. Gr. da S. A. A Noite, 1925.

Amemiya, Kozy K. *The Bolivian Connection: U.S. Bases and Okinawan Emigration.* JPRI Working Paper 25. Washington, D.C.: Japan Policy Research Institute, 1996.

Americano, Jorge. *São Paulo atual, 1935-1962.* São Paulo: Edições Melhoramentos, 1963.

AMILAT, ed. *Judaica latinoamericana: Estudios histórico-sociales.* Jerusalem: Editorial Universitaria Magnes, Universidad Hebrea, 1988.

Anderson, Benedict. *Imagined Communities: Reflections on the Origin and Spread of Nationalism.* London: Verso, 1983.

Anderson, Patrick. *Over the Alps: Reflections of Travel and Travel Writing, with Special Reference to the Grand Tours of Boswell, Beckford and Byron.* London: Rupert Hart-David, 1969.

Ando, Zempati. *Pioneirismo e cooperativismo: História da cooperativa agrícola de Cotia.* Translated by José Yamashiro. São Paulo: Editora Sociologia e Política, 1961.

————. *Estudos sócio-históricos da imigração japonesa.* São Paulo: Centro de Estudos Nipo-Brasileiros, 1976.

Andrade, Oswald de. *Marco Zero I—A revolução melancólica* [1937]. 2nd ed. Rio de Janeiro: Editora Civilização Brasileira, 1978.

Andrews, George Reid. *Blacks and Whites in São Paulo Brazil, 1888–1988.* Madison: University of Wisconsin Press, 1991.

Anzaldúa, Gloria. *Borderland/La Frontera: The New Mestiza.* San Francisco: Spinsters/aunt lute, 1987.

Aoun, Farid. *Do cedro ao mandacaru.* Recife: FIDA-Editorial Comunicação Especializada S/C, 1979.

Araújo, José Paulo de Figueirôa Nabuco. *Legislação brazileira ou collecção chronológica das leis, decretos, resoluções de consulta, provisões, etc., etc., no império do Brazil, desde o anno de 1808 até 1831 inclusive, contendo: Além do que se acha publicado nas melhores collecções para mais de duas mil peças inéditas, colligidas pelo conselheiro José Paulo de Figueirôa Nabuco Araújo.* 7 vols. Rio de Janeiro: Typ. Imp. E. Const. de J. Villeneuve, 1836–1844.

Araújo, Oscar Egídio de. "Enquistamentos étnicos." *Revista do Arquivo Municipal de São Paulo* 6:65 (March 1940), 227–246.

————. "Latinos e não latinos no município de São Paulo." *Revista do Arquivo Municipal de São Paulo* 7:75 (April 1941), 65–98.

Arteaga, Alfred, ed. *An Other Tongue: Nation and Ethnicity in the Linguistic Borderlands.* Durham, NC: Duke University Press, 1994.

Ascoli, Nestor. *A immigração japoneza para a baixada do estado do Rio de Janeiro.* Rio de Janeiro: Typ. Jornal do Comércio de Rodrigues e Co., 1910. 2nd ed., Rio de Janeiro: Edição da Revista de Lingua Portuguesa, 1924.

Associação Okinawa do Brasil. *Guia de endereços—1995.* São Paulo: Associação Okinawa do Brasil, 1995.

"As atividades das sociedades secretas japonesas e a ação repressiva da polícia de São Paulo, publicadas pela imprensa." *Arquivos da Polícia Civil de São Paulo* 12:2 (1946), 523–530.

Avila, Fernando Bastos de. *L'immigration au Brésil: Contribution à une théorie générale de l'immigration.* Rio de Janeiro: AGIR, 1956.

Azevedo, Aluísio. "Japonesas e norte-americanas: O comportamento das mulheres japonesas e norte-americanas." *Almanaque Brasileiro Garnier* (1904), 217–220.

————. "A mulher no Japão." *Almanaque Brasileiro Garnier* (1906), 410–412.

————. *A Brazilian Tenement.* Translated by Harry W. Brown. New York: R. M. McBride, 1926.

————. *O Japão.* São Paulo: Roswitha Kempf Editores, 1984.

————. *Mulatto.* Translated by Murray Graeme MacNicoll and edited by Daphne Patai. Cranbury, NJ: Associated University Presses, 1990.

Azevedo, Célia Maria Marinho de. *Onda negra, medo branco: O negro no imaginário das elites século XIX.* Rio de Janeiro: Paz e Terra, 1987.

Babha, Homi K. *The Location of Culture*. London: Routledge, 1994.

Backal, Alicia Gojman de. "Minorías, estado y movimientos nacionalistas de la clase media en México: Liga anti-china y anti-judía (siglo XX)." In *Judaica latinoamericana: Estudios histórico-sociales*, edited by AMILAT, pp. 174-191. Jerusalem: Editorial Universitaria Magnes, Universidad Hebrea, 1988.

Badawi, M. M. *A Critical Introduction to Modern Arabic Poetry*. Cambridge: Cambridge University Press, 1975.

Bahiana, Henrique Paulo. *O Japão que eu vi*. São Paulo: Companhia Editora Nacional, 1937.

Baily, Samuel L. "The Adjustment of Italian Immigrants in Buenos Aires and New York, 1870-1914." *American Historical Review* 88:2 (April 1983), 281-305.

Balderston, Daniel, and Donna J. Guy, eds. *Sex and Sexuality in Latin America*. New York: New York University Press, 1997.

Barretto, Bruno, director. *Amor bandido*. Rio de Janeiro: Produções Cinematográficas, 1979.

Barretto, Castro. "Seleção e assimilação de imigrantes." *Revista Brasileira de Medicina Pública* 12 (March-April 1947), 3-28.

Barro, João de, and Alberto Ribeiro. *A guerra do amor*. São Paulo: A Melodia, n.d.

Bastani, Tanus Jorge. *O Líbano e os libaneses no Brasil*. Rio de Janeiro: n.p., 1945.

Bastide, Roger. *Brasil: Terra de contrastes*. 2nd ed. São Paulo: Difusão Européia do Livro, 1964. Originally published as *Brésil, terre des contrastes*. Paris: Hachette, 1957.

Bastide, Roger, and Florestan Fernandes. *Brancos e negros em São Paulo: Ensaio sociológico sobre aspectos da formação, manifestações atuais e efeitos do preconceito de cor na sociedade paulistana*. 2nd ed. São Paulo: Companhia Editora Nacional, 1959.

Bastos, Élide Rugai, and João Quartim de Moraes, eds. *O pensamento de Oliveira Vianna*. Campinas: Editora da UNICAMP, 1993.

Bastos, Wilson de Lima. *Os sírios em Juiz de Fora*. Juiz de Fora: Edições Paraibuna, 1988.

Bauman, Zygmunt. *Modernity and Ambivalence*. Ithaca, NY: Cornell University Press, 1991.

Beattie, Peter. "Conflicting Penal Codes: Modern Masculinity and Sodomy in the Brazilian Military, 1860-1916." In *Sex and Sexuality in Latin America*, edited by Daniel Balderston and Donna J. Guy, pp. 65-85. New York: New York University Press, 1997.

———. "Penal Servitude Versus Conscription: Honor, Race, Nation and Army Enlisted Service in Brazil, 1864-1945." Unpublished manuscript used with permission of author.

Behdad, Ali. *Belated Travelers: Orientalism in the Age of Colonial Dissolution*. Durham, NC: Duke University Press, 1994.

Bell, H. T. Montague, and H. G. W. Woodhead. *The China Year Book—1916* and *The China Year Book—1919/1920*. Nedeln/Liechtenstein: Kraus-Thomson Organization, 1969.

Beloch, Israel, and Alzira Alves de Abreu, eds. *Dicionário histórico-biográfico brasileiro, 1930-1983*. 4 vols. Rio de Janeiro: Editora Forense-Universitária, 1984.

Benchimol, Isaac. "La langue espagnole au Maroc." *Revue des écoles de l'AIU* 2 (July-September 1901), 127-133.

Bentes, Abraham Ramiro. *Primeira comunidade israelita brasileira: Tradições, genealogia, pré-história.* Rio de Janeiro: Gráfica Borsoi, 1989.

Beth Hatefutsoth. *Yehudim al g'dot ha Amazonas/Jews on the Banks of the Amazon.* Tel Aviv: Beth Hatefutsoth—The Nahum Goldmann Museum of the Jewish Diaspora, 1987.

Bhabha, Homi, ed. *Nation and Narration.* New York: Routledge, 1990.

Bland, J. O. P. *Li Hung-Chang.* New York: Henry Holt, 1917.

Blumenbach, Johann Friedrich. *On the Natural Varieties of Mankind: De Generis Humani Varietate Nativa.* New York: Bergman, 1969.

Bocayuva, Quintino. *A crise da lavoura: Succinta exposição por Q. Bocayuva.* Rio de Janeiro: Typ. Perseverança, 1868.

Bonfim, Pedro Calheiros. "As escolas estrangeiras no Brasil." *Cultura Política* 2:13 (March 1942), 30–34.

Borges, Dain. "'Puffy, Ugly, Slothful and Inert': Degeneration in Brazilian Social Thought, 1880–1940." *Journal of Latin American Studies* 25 (1993), 235–256.

———. "Intangible Influences in Metropolitan Rio de Janeiro, ca. 1900–1910." Lecture given at the Getty Center for the History of Art and the Humanities, Santa Monica, CA, 12 December 1994. Used with permission of the author.

Borrie, W. D., ed. *The Cultural Integration of Immigrants: A Survey Based upon the Papers and Proceeding of the UNESCO Conference Held in Havana, April 1956.* New York: UNESCO, 1957.

Bosquet, Georges. *Le Japon de nos jours et les échelles de l'Extrême Orient.* Paris: Hachette, 1877.

Botelho, Francisco Chaves de Oliveira. *A immigração japoneza: O parecer do illustre deputado Oliveira Botelho, apresentado em 8 de julho de 1925, à Comissão de finanças da Câmara dos deputados.* Rio de Janeiro: n.p., 1925.

Braga, Rubem. "Conversa com japonês em Araçatuba: Notas de viagem." *Revista do Arquivo Municipal de São Paulo* 6:71 (October 1940), 209–217.

Braga, Teófilo. *A pátria portugueza. O território e a raça.* Pôrto: Lello e Irmão, 1894.

Brasil e Japão: Duas civilizações que se completam. São Paulo: Empreza Gráfica da Revista dos Tribunaes, 1934.

Brito, João Rodrigues de. *Cartas econômico-políticas sobre a agricultura, e commércio da Bahia.* Lisbon: Imprensa Nacional, 1821.

Browne, George P. "Government Immigration Policy in Imperial Brazil, 1822–1870." Ph.D. thesis. Catholic University of America, 1972.

Buckingham, James Silk. *The Slave States of America.* Vol. 1. London: Fisher, Son, 1842.

Burke, Edmund III. *Prelude to Protectorate in Morocco: Precolonial Protest and Resistance, 1860–1912.* Chicago: University of Chicago Press, 1976.

Calhoun, Craig. "Nationalism and Ethnicity." *Annual Review of Sociology* 19 (1993), 211–239.

Câmara, Aristóteles de Lima, and Arthur Hehl Neiva. "Colonizações nipônica e germânica no sul do Brasil." *Revista de Imigração e Colonização* 2:1 (January 1941), 39–121.

Campos, Ernersto de Souza. *Japão visto através de uma viagem ao Oriente realizada por universitarios da Faculdade de medicina de São Paulo*. São Paulo: Imprensa Oficial do Estado, 1935.

Campos, Francisco. "Imigração japonesa." *Boletim do Ministério do trabalho, indústria e comércio* 10:114 (February 1944), 263–270.

Cardoso, Ruth Corrêa Leite. "Estrutura familiar e mobilidade social: Estudo dos japoneses no estado de São Paulo." Ph.D. thesis. University of São Paulo, 1972.

Carneiro, J. Fernando. *Imigração e colonização no Brasil*. Rio de Janeiro: Faculdade Nacional de Filosofia, 1950.

Carone, Edgard. *A Terceira República (1937–1945)* São Paulo: Difel/Difusão Editorial, 1976.

Carvalho, Francisco Augusto de. *O Brazil, colonização e emigração—Esboço histórico baseado no estudo dos systemas e vantagens que offerecem os Estados Unidos*. 2nd ed. Porto: Imprensa Portuguesa, 1876.

Carvalho, Gleice. "Sutis diferenças." *Japão Aqui* 1:2 (May 1997), 26–29.

Carvalho Reis, Fabio A. de. *Breves considerações sobre a nossa lavoura*. São Luiz: Typ. do Progesso, 1856.

Cascudo, Luís de Câmara. *Mouros, franceses e judeus (três presenças no Brasil)*. Rio de Janeiro: Editora Letras e Arte, 1967.

Castello Branco, R. P. "Imigração e nacionalismo." *Cultura Política* 2:15 (May 1942), 26–31.

Castro, Fernando Moreira de. *50 anos da imigração japoneza na Amazônia*. Belém do Pará: n.p., 1979.

Cavalli-Sforza, L., Luca Paolo Menozzi, and Alberto Piazza. *The History and Geography of Human Genes*. Princeton: Princeton University Press, 1994.

Centro de Estudos Nipo-Brasileiros. *Pesquisa da população de descendentes de japoneses residentes no Brasil, 1987–1988*. São Paulo: Centro de Estudos Nipo-Brasileiros, 1990.

Chalhoub, Sidney. "The Politics of Disease Control: Yellow Fever and Race in Nineteenth Century Rio de Janeiro." *Journal of Latin American Studies* 25:3 (October 1993), 441–463.

———. *Cidade febril: Cortiços e epidemias na corte imperial*. São Paulo: Companhia das Letras, 1996.

Chanem, Sadalla Amin. *Impressões de viagem (Líbano-Brasil)*. Niterói: Gráfica Brasil, 1936.

Chigusa, Charles Tetsuo, ed. *A quebra dos mitos: O fenômeno dekassegui através de relatos pessoias*. Tokyo: IPC, 1994.

Choi, Keum Joa. "Além do arco-íris: A imigração coreana no Brasil." M.A. thesis. University of São Paulo, 1991.

Chu, Samuel C., and Kwang-Ching Liu, eds. *Li Hung-chang and China's Early Modernization*. Armonk, NY: M. E. Sharpe, 1994.

Cintra, José Thiago. *La migración japonesa en Brasil (1908–1958)*. Mexico City: Colegio de México, Centro de Estudios Orientales, 1971.

Coaracy, Vivaldo. *Problemas nacionaes*. São Paulo: Sociedade Impressora Paulista, 1930.

Cohen, Anthony. "Culture as Identity: An Anthropologist's View." *New Literary History* 24:1 (Winter 1993), 195–209.

Comissão de Elaboração da História dos 80 Anos da Imigração Japonesa no Brasil, ed.

Uma epopéia moderna: 80 anos da imigração japonesa no Brasil. São Paulo: Editora Hucitec, 1992.

Comissão de Recenseamento da Colônia Japonesa. *The Japanese Immigrant in Brazil.* 2 vols. Tokyo: University of Tokyo Press, 1964.

Companhia Editora Nacional. *Catálogo brasiliana: Comemorativo do 200 volumes. Síntese dos volumes da coleção "Brasiliana."* São Paulo: Companhia Editora Nacional, 1941.

Conrad, Robert. "The Planter Class and the Debate over Chinese Immigration to Brazil, 1850–1893." *International Migration Review* 9:1 (Spring 1975), 41–55.

Corrigan, Philip, and Derek Sayer. *The Great Arch: English State Formation as Cultural Revolution.* Oxford: Oxford University Press, 1985.

Costa, Emília Viotti da. *The Brazilian Empire: Myths and Histories.* Belmont, CA: Wadsworth, 1988.

Couto, Miguel. *Seleção social: Campanha antinipônica.* Rio de Janeiro: Irmãos Pongetti Editores, 1942.

Criscuolo, Orlando. "Piadas nipo-crisuolinas: Ouvindo japoneses." *Mundo Policial em Revista* 1:7-8 (May-June 1947), 35.

Crissiuma, Eddy de F. "Concentração japonesa em São Paulo." *Geografia* 1:1 (1935), 110–114.

Cruz, Ernesto. *Colonização do Pará.* Belém: Conselho Nacional de Pesquisas, Instituto Nacional de Pesquisas da Amazônia, 1958.

Cruz Júnior, José de Souza Pereira de. "As raças, os sexos e as idades imprimen caracteres reacs na cabeça ossa? Quaes são elles e no que consistem." Thesis presented to the Faculdade de Medicina do Rio de Janeiro, 15 September 1874. Teses do Rio, 1857, J-V #6, vol. 2, Academia Nacional de Medicina, Rio de Janeiro.

Cruzamento da ethnia japoneza: Hypóthese de que o japonez não se cruza com outra ethnia. São Paulo: Centro Nippônico de Cultura, 1934.

Cunha, Manuela Carneiro da. *Negros, Estrangeiros: Os escravos libertos e sua volta à África.* São Paulo: Brasiliense, 1985.

Cytrynowicz, Roney, ed. *Renascença 75 anos: 1922-1997.* São Paulo: Sociedade Hebraico-Brasileira Renascença, 1997.

Daniels, Roger. *The Politics of Prejudice: The Anti-Japanese Movement in California and the Struggle for Japanese Exclusion.* Berkeley: University of California Press, 1962.

Dantas, Garibaldi. *Extremo Oriente.* São Paulo: Companhia Editora Nacional, 1938.

Darwin, Richard, ed. *Charles Darwin's Beagle Diary.* Cambridge: Cambridge University Press, 1988.

Dean, Warren. *The Industrialization of São Paulo, 1880-1945.* Austin: University of Texas Press, 1969.

———. *Rio Claro: A Brazilian Plantation System, 1820-1920.* Stanford: Stanford University Press, 1976.

———. *With Broadaxe and Firebrand: The Destruction of the Brazilian Atlantic Forest.* Berkeley: University of California Press, 1995.

Deffontaines, Pierre. "Mascates ou pequenos negociantes ambulantes do Brasil." *Geografia* 2:1 (1936), 26–29.

Degler, Carl. *Neither Black nor White: Slavery and Race Relations in Brazil and the United States.* New York: Macmillan, 1971.

Diamond, Jared. "Race Without Color." *Discover* 15:11 (November 1994), 83–89.

Diégues Júnior, Manuel. "Estudos de assimilação cultural no brasil." *Estudos de antropologia teórica e prática* 3:B (August 1956; a special issue entitled *Memórias do I painel nipo-brasileiro,* edited by Antonio Rubbo Müller and Hiroshi Saito.), 15–27.

———. *Imigração, urbanização e industrialização: Estudo sobre alguns aspectos da contribuição cultural do imigrante no Brasil.* Rio de Janeiro: Ministério da Educação, 1964.

———. *Etnias e cultura no Brasil.* São Paulo: Círculo do Livro, 1976.

Diffie, Baily W. "Some Foreign Influences in Contemporary Brazilian Politics." *Hispanic American Historical Review* 20 (August 1940), 410.

Dikötter, Frank. *The Discourse of Race in Modern China.* Stanford: Stanford University Press, 1992.

Dower, John W. *War Without Mercy: Race and Power in the Pacific War.* New York: Pantheon Books, 1986.

Dower, John W., and Timothy S. George. *Japanese History and Culture from Ancient to Modern Times: Seven Basic Bibliographies.* 2nd ed. Princeton: Markus Weiner, 1995.

Dulles, John W. F. *The São Paulo Law School and the Anti-Vargas Resistance (1938–1945).* Austin: University of Texas Press, 1986.

Duoun, T. *Confissões e indiscrições: Meio século de experiências em quatro continentes (com um album intercalado de 60 gravuras).* São Paulo: n.p., 1943.

Duoun, Taufik. *A emigração sírio-libanesa às terras de promissão.* São Paulo: Tipografia Árabe, 1944.

Durand, José Carlos G. "Formação do pequeno empresariado têxtil em São Paulo (1880–1950)." In *Pequena empresa: O comportamento empresarial na acumulação e na luta pela sobrevivência,* edited by Henrique Rattner, vol. 1, pp. 110–126. São Paulo: Brasiliense, 1985.

Eakin, Marshall C. *British Enterprise in Brazil: The St. John d'el Rey Mining Company and the Morro Velho Gold Mine, 1830–1960.* Durham, NC: Duke University Press, 1989.

Elias, Maria José. "Introdução ao estudo da imigração chinesa." *Anais do Museu Paulista* 24 (1970), 57–100.

Ellis Júnior, Alfredo. *Raça de gigantes: Civilização no planalto paulista.* São Paulo: Novissima Editora, 1926.

———. *Pedras lascadas.* [1928]. 2nd ed. São Paulo: Editora Piratininga, 1933.

———. *Populações paulistas.* Serie Brasiliana 27. São Paulo: Companhia Editora Nacional, 1934.

Espindola, Haruf Salmen. "O centauro maquiavélico: Ideologia da *Revista Cultura Política* (1941–1945)." M.A. thesis. Universidade de Brasília, 1988.

Eschwege, Wilhelm Ludwig von. *Pluto brasiliensis.* 2 vols. Translated by Domício de Figueiredo Murta. Belo Horizonte: Ed. Itatiaia; São Paulo: Ed. da Universidade de São Paulo, 1979. Originally published as *Pluto Brasiliensis: Eine Reihe von Abhandlungen über Brasiliens Gold-, Diamanten- und anderen mineralischen Reichthum, über die Geschichte seiner Entdeckung, über das Vorkommen seiner Lagerstatten, des Betriebs.* Berlin: G. Reimer, 1833.

Fabri, C. *Memorial sobre a questão de immigração apresentado aos illustres membros do Congresso nacional.* Rio de Janeiro: Typografia do *Jornal do Commércio*, 1893.

Fairbank, John King. *The Great Chinese Revolution: 1800–1985.* New York: Harper & Row, 1986.

Farhat, Emil. *Dinheiro na estrada: Uma saga de imigrantes.* São Paulo: T. A. Queiroz, 1986.

Fausto, Boris. *A revolução de 1930: Historiografia e história.* São Paulo: Brasiliense, 1986.

Fausto, Boris, Oswaldo Truzzi, Roberto Grün, and Célia Sakurai. *Imigração e política em São Paulo.* São Paulo: Editora Sumaré/FAPESP, 1995.

Fernandes, Florestan. "Immigration and Race Relations in São Paulo." In *Race and Class in Latin America,* edited by Magnus Mörner, pp. 122–142. New York: Columbia University Press, 1970.

Fernandes, Geraldo. "A religião nas constituicões republicanas do Brasil." *Revista eclesiástica brasileira* 8:4 (December 1948), 830–857.

Ferreira, Aurélio Buarque de Holanda. *Novo dicionário da língua portuguesa.* 2nd ed. Rio de Janeiro: Editora Nova Fronteira, 1986.

Feuerwerker, Albert. *China's Early Industrialization: Sheng Hsuan-Huai (1844–1916) and Mandarin Enterprise.* Cambridge, MA: Harvard University Press, 1958.

Filho, Calvino, ed. *Factos e opinões sobre a immigração japoneza.* Rio de Janeiro: n.p., 1934.

Fiola, Jan. *Race Relations in Brazil: A Reassessment of the "Racial Democracy" Thesis.* Program in Latin American Studies Occasional Paper no. 24. Amherst: University of Massachusetts, 1990.

Fleres, Ugo. *Ettore Ximenes: Sua vita e sue opere.* Bergamo: Instituto Italiano d'Arti Grafiche, 1928.

Flores, Moacyr. "Japoneses no Rio Grande do Sul." *Veritas* (Pôrto Alegre) 77 (1975), 65–98.

Fonseca, Guido. "DOPS—Um pouco de sua história." *Revista da Associação dos Delegados de Polícia do Estado de São Paulo* 10:18 (December 1989), 41–86.

Fonseca, Olympio Oliveira Ribeiro da. *Posse do dr. Olympio Oliveira Ribeiro da Fonseca na Academia nacional de medicina em 21 de junho de 1928 seguida de conferencia impressões de ordem médica sobre o Japão.* Rio de Janeiro: Typografia América, 1928.

Fontaine, Pierre-Michel, ed. *Race, Class and Power in Brazil.* Los Angeles: Center for Afro-American Studies, UCLA, 1985.

Fontes, Martins. *Schaharazade.* São Paulo: Estabelecimento Gráfico Irmãos Ferraz, 1929.

Fox, R., ed. *Recapturing Anthropology: Working in the Present.* Santa Fe, NM: School of American Research Press, 1991.

Franco, Cid. *Dicionário de expressões populares brasileiras.* 2 vols. São Paulo: Editoras Unidas, n.d.

Freire-Maia, Newton. *Brasil: Laboratório racial* [1973]. 7th ed. Petrópolis: Vozes, 1985.

French, John D. *The Brazilian Workers' ABC: Class Conflict and Alliances in Modern São Paulo.* Chapel Hill: University of North Carolina Press, 1992.

Freyre, Gilberto. "O Brasil, democracia étnica." *Cruzeiro,* 6 and 19 June 1953.

———. *The Masters and the Slaves: A Study in the Development of Brazilian Civilization.* 2nd English ed. Translated by Samuel Putnam. Berkeley: University of California Press, 1986.

Frota-Pessoa, Oswaldo. "Raça e eugenia." In *Raça e diversidade,* edited by Lilia Moritz Schwarz and Renato da Silva Queiroz, pp. 29–46. São Paulo: EDUSP/Estação Ciência, 1996.

Fujii, Yukio, and T. Lynn Smith. *The Acculturation of the Japanese in Brazil.* Gainesville: University of Florida Press, 1959.

Fukunaga, Patrick N. "The Brazilian Experience: The Japanese Immigrants during the Period of the Vargas Regime and the Immediate Aftermath, 1930–1946." Ph.D. dissertation. University of California, Santa Barbara, 1983.

Gabriel o Pensador. "Lavagem cerebral." On *Gabriel o Pensador.* Rio de Janeiro: Sony/Chaos, 1993.

Galvão, Antonio. *The Discoveries of the World, from Their First Original unto the Year of Our Lord, 1555.* [1555]. Edited and translated by Admiral Bethune. London: Hakluyt Society, 1862.

Galvão, I. C. *Sociedade auxiliadora da indústria nacional, discurso pronunciado pelo dr. I. J. Galvão na sessão de 3 de outubro de 1870 (questão dos chins).* Rio de Janeiro: Typ. Universal de Laemmert, 1870.

Galvão, I. C., M. C. Menezes de Macedo, and Thomaz Deschamps de Montmorency. *Parecer da Secção de colonização e estatística sobre a questão "Se convirá ao Brasil a importação de colonos chins."* Rio de Janeiro: Typ. Universal de Laemmert, 1870.

Gamou, Masão. "Japoneses no Pará." Translated by Teiti Suzuki. *Estudos de antropologia teórica e prática* 3:B (August 1956; a special issue entitled, *Memórias do I Painel Nipo-Brasileiro.* Edited by Antonio Rubbo Müller and Hiroshi Saito), 56–59.

Gardiner, C. Harvey. *Pawns in a Triangle of Hate: The Peruvian Japanese and the United States.* Seattle: University of Washington Press, 1981.

Garfield, Seth. " 'Civilized' but Discontent: The Xavante Indians and Government Policy in Brazil, 1937–88." Ph.D. thesis. Yale University, 1996.

Garon, Sheldon. "The World's Oldest Debate? Prostitution and the State in Imperial Japan, 1900–1945." *American Historical Review* 98:3 (June 1993), 710–732.

Gellner, Ernest. *Encounters with Nationalism.* Oxford: Oxford University Press, 1994.

Glick-Schiller, Nina, et al., eds. *Towards a Transnational Perspective on Migration: Race, Class, Ethnicity and Nationalism Reconsidered.* Vol. 645 of *Annals of the New York Academy of Sciences.* New York: New York Academy of Sciences, 1992.

Gobineau, Arthur de. "Emigrations actuelles des allemands." *Revue Nouvelle* (Paris) 2 (March 1845), 41.

Godoy, Paulo de. *Eugenia e seleção.* São Paulo: Editorial Helios, 1927.

Góes Monteiro, Norma de. "Esbôço da política imigratória e colonizadora do governo de Minas Gerais, 1889–1930." *Revista Brasileira de Estudos Políticos* 29 (July 1970), 195–216.

Gomes, Angela Maria de Castro. "A representação de classes na Constituinte de 1934." In *Regionalismo e centralização política: Partidos e constituinte nos anos 30,* Angela Maria de Castro Gomes, ed., pp. 427–491. Rio de Janeiro: Editora Nova Fronteira, 1980.

———, ed. *Regionalismo e centralização política: Partidos e constituinte nos anos 30.* Rio de Janeiro: Editora Nova Fronteira, 1980.

Gonçalves dos Santos, Luiz (Padre Perereca). *Memória para servir à história do reino do Brasil.* [1825]. 2 vols. Rio de Janeiro: Zelio Valverde, 1943.

Gonzaga, Antonio Gavião. "Contribuição para o estudo das imigrações no Brasil." *Revista de Imigração e Colonização* 3:1 (April 1942), 89–98.

Gordon, David C. *Lebanon: The Fragmented Nation.* London: Croom Helm, 1980.

Goulart, José Alipio. *O mascate no Brasil.* Rio de Janeiro: Editora Conquista, 1967.

Gould, Stephen Jay. "The Geometer of Race." *Discover* 15:11 (November 1994), 64–69.

Graden, Dale Thurston. "From Slavery to Freedom in Bahia, Brazil, 1791–1900." Ph.D. thesis. University of Connecticut, 1991.

Graham, Richard. *Patronage and Politics in Nineteenth-Century Brazil.* Stanford: Stanford University Press, 1990.

———, ed. *The Idea of Race in Latin America, 1870–1940.* Austin: University of Texas Press, 1990.

Greenblatt, Stephen. *Marvelous Possessions: The Wonder of the New World.* Chicago: University of Chicago Press, 1991.

Grün, Roberto. *Negócios e famílias: Armênios em São Paulo.* São Paulo: Editora Sumaré, 1992.

Guimarães, Moreira. *No Extremo Oriente: O Japão.* Rio de Janeiro: Editora Alba, 1936.

Hailly, Edouard du. "Souvenirs d'une campagne en l'Estrême Orient," *Revue des Deux Mondes* 36:64 (15 September 1866), 957–983; 36:65 (15 October 1866), 893–924; 36:66 (15 November 1866), 396–420.

———. "De Saigon en France." *Revue des Deux Mondes* 37:67 (15 January 1867), 441–469.

Hajjar, Claude Fahd. *Imigração árabe: 100 anos de reflexão.* São Paulo: Icone Editora, 1985.

Hall, Michael M. "The Origins of Mass Immigration to Brazil, 1871–1914." Ph.D. dissertation. Columbia University, 1969.

———. "New Approaches to Immigration History." In *New Approaches to Latin American History,* edited by Richard Graham and Peter H. Smith, pp. 175–193. Austin: University of Texas Press, 1974.

Hallewell, Laurence. *Books in Brazil: A History of the Publishing Trade.* Metuchen, NJ: Scarecrow Press, 1982.

Handa, Tomoo. *Memória de um imigrante japonês no Brasil.* São Paulo: T. A. Queiroz/Centro de Estudos Nipo-Brasileiros, 1980.

———. *O imigrante japonês: História de sua vida no Brasil.* São Paulo: T. A. Queiroz/Centro de Estudos Nipo-Brasileiros, 1987.

Hasenbalg, Carlos A. *Discriminação e desigualdades raciais no Brasil.* Rio de Janeiro: Graal, 1979.

Hashimoto, Kohei. "Lebanese Population Movement, 1920–1939: Towards a Study." In *The Lebanese in the World: A Century of Emigration,* edited by Albert Hourani and Nadim Shehadi, pp. 65–108. London: I. B. Tauris; New York: St. Martin's Press, 1992.

Hearn, Lafcadio. *Glimpses of Unfamiliar Japan.* 2 vols. Boston: Houghton, Mifflin, 1894.

Higham, John. *Strangers in the Land: Patterns of American Nativism, 1860–1925.* [1955]. New York: Atheneum, 1973.

Hilton, Stanley E. *Brazil and the Great Powers, 1930-1939: The Politics of Trade Rivalry.* Austin: University of Texas Press, 1975.

Hitti, Philip K. *Lebanon in History: From the Earliest Times to the Present.* London: Macmillan, 1957.

Hobsbawm, Eric. "Peasants and Politics." *Journal of Peasant Studies* 1:1 (1973), 3-22.

Holloway, Thomas H. *Immigrants on the Land.* Chapel Hill: University of North Carolina Press, 1980.

———. *Policing Rio de Janeiro: Repression and Resistance in a 19th-Century City.* Stanford: Stanford University Press, 1993.

Holt, Thomas C. "Marking: Race, Race-making, and the Writing of History." *American Historical Review* 100:1 (February 1995), 1-20.

Hosokawa, Shūhei. "A história da música entre os nikkei no Brasil enfocando as melodias Japonesas." In *Anais do IV encontro nacional de professores universitários de língua, literatura e cultura japonesa,* pp. 125-147. São Paulo: Centro de Estudos Japoneses da Universidade de São Paulo, 1993.

Hourani, Albert H. *Syria and Lebanon: A Political Essay.* London: Oxford University Press, 1946.

Hu-DeHart, Evelyn. "Racism and Anti-Chinese Persecution in Sonora, Mexico, 1876-1932." *Amerasia* 9:2 (Fall/Winter 1982), 1-28.

———. "Coolies, Shopkeepers, Pioneers: The Chinese of Mexico and Peru (1849-1930)." *Amerasia* 15:2 (1989), 91-116.

Huddleston, Lee Eldrige. *Origins of the American Indians: European Concepts, 1492-1729.* Austin: University of Texas Press, 1967.

Huffman, James L. *Politics of the Meiji Press: The Life of Fujuchi Gen'ichirō.* Honolulu: University Press of Hawaii, 1980.

Hulot, Baron Etienne. *De L'Atlantique au Pacifique à travers le Canada et le nord des Etats-Unis.* Paris: E. Plon/Nourrit, 1888.

Humphries, Michael. "Ethnic History, Nationalism and Transnationalism in Argentine Arab and Jewish Cultures." *Immigrants and Minorities* 16:1 and 2 (March/July 1997), 167-188.

Husry, Khaldun S. "The Assyrian Affair of 1933 (I)." *International Journal of Middle East Affairs* 5:2 (1974), 161-176.

———. "The Assyrian Affair of 1933 (II)." *International Journal of Middle East Affairs* 5:3 (1974), 348-352.

Ianni, Octávio. *Raças e classes sociais no Brasil.* 2nd ed. Rio de Janeiro: Editora Civilização Brasileira, 1972.

Instituto da Ordem de Advogados do Paraná. *Anuário contendo os fatos de maior relevância da sua atividade no ano social do 1934 principalmente a campanha contra a imigração dos assírios.* Curitiba: Instituto da Ordem de Advogados do Paraná, 1936.

Iriye, Akira. *Pacific Estrangement: Japanese and American Expansion, 1897-1911.* Cambridge, MA: Harvard University Press, 1972.

———. "The Failure of Economic Expansion, 1918-1931." In *Japan in Crisis: Essays on Taishō Democracy,* edited by Bernard S. Silberman and H. D. Harootunian, pp. 237-269. Princeton: Princeton University Press, 1974.

Issawi, Charles. "The Historical Background of Lebanese Emigration, 1800–1914." In *The Lebanese in the World: A Century of Emigration,* edited by Albert Hourani and Nadim Shehadi, pp. 13–31. London: I. B. Tauris; New York: St. Martin's Press, 1992.

Jaceguay, Arthur. *O dever do momento: Carta a Joaquim Nabuco.* Rio de Janeiro: Typ. Levzinger, 1887.

Jafet, Eduardo B. *Impressões de viagem.* São Paulo: n.p., 1936.

Jaguaribe Filho, Domingos José Nogueira. *Reflexões sobre a colonização no Brazil.* São Paulo and Paris: A. L. Garraux, 1878.

Janeiro, Armando Martins. *Um intérprete português do Japão: Wenceslau de Moraes.* Macao: Instituto Luís de Camões/Imprensa Nacional, 1966.

Jayyusi, Salma Khadra, ed. *Modern Arabic Poetry: An Anthology.* New York: Columbia University Press, 1987.

Jorge, Salomão. *Arabescos—Poesias 1918–1928.* São Paulo: Irmãos Pongetti Editores, 1941.

———. *Tudo pelo Brasil.* São Paulo: n.p., 1943. New edition published as *Tudo pelo Brasil: Discursos, ensaios e artigos literários.* São Paulo: Nova Época Editorial, 1975 or 1976.

———. *Album da colônia sírio libanesa no Brasil.* São Paulo: Sociedade Impressora Brasileira, 1948.

Kaigai Kogyo Kabushiki Kaisha. *Introdução dos imigrantes japonezes no Brasil e seu orgão instrutivo: Actividades da Kaigai Kogyo Kabushiki Kaisha em São Paulo.* São Paulo: Kaigai Kogyo Kabushiki Kaisha, 1932.

———. *Aclimação dos emigrantes japonezes: Actividades da Kaigai Kogyo Kabushiki Kaisha do Brasil.* São Paulo: Kaigai Kogyo Kabushiki Kaisha, 1934.

Kakichi Mitsukuri. *La vie sociale au Japon publié par Mikinosuke Miyajima.* Paris: Société Franco-Japonaise de Paris, 1922.

Kasza, Gregory J. *The State and the Mass Media in Japan, 1918–1945.* Berkeley: University of California Press, 1988.

Kehl, Renato. *A cura da fealdade (eugenia e medicina social).* São Paulo: Monteiro Lobato, 1923.

Kelly, Catriona, and Patrick Joyce. "History and Post-Modernism II." *Past and Present* 133 (November 1991), 204–213.

Kidder, Daniel P. *Sketches of Residence and Travels in Brazil Embracing Historical and Geographical Notices of the Empire and Its Several Provinces.* 2 vols. Philadelphia: Sorin and Ball; London: Wiley and Putnam, 1845.

Klich, Ignacio. "Introduction to the Sources for the History of the Middle Easterners in Latin America." *Temas de Africa y Asia* (Buenos Aires) 2 (1993), 205–233. The theme for this issue was *Africanos y mediorientales en América (siglos XVIII–XX).*

———. "Sources on the Lebanese and Other Middle Easterners in Latin America." In Centre for Lebanese Studies (Oxford), *Papers on Lebanon* 16 (March 1995).

Klich, Ignacio, and Jeffrey Lesser, eds. *Arab and Jewish Immigrants in Latin America: Images and Realities.* London: Frank Cass, 1998.

———. *Turco Immigrants in Latin America.* Special issue of *The Americas* 53:1 (July 1996).

———. *Cárdenas, Vargas, Perón and the Jews.* Special issue of *Canadian Journal of Latin American and Caribbean Studies* 20:39–40 (1995).

Knowlton, Clark S. "Spatial and Social Mobility of the Syrians and Lebanese in the City of São Paulo, Brazil." Ph.D. thesis. Vanderbilt University, 1955.

———. *Sírios e libaneses.* São Paulo: Editora Anhenmbi, 1960.

———. "The Social and Spatial Mobility of the Syrian and Lebanese Community in São Paulo, Brazil." In *The Lebanese in the World: A Century of Emigration,* edited by Albert Hourani and Nadim Shehadi, pp. 285–312. London: I. B. Tauris; New York: St. Martin's Press, 1992.

Kokichi, Guenka. *Um japonês em Mato-Grosso (subsídio para história da colonização japonesa no Brasil).* N.p.: n.p., 1958.

Komatsubara, Hisão. "Japan." In *The Asian Newspapers' Reluctant Revolution,* edited by John A. Lent, pp. 65–87. Ames: Iowa State University Press, 1971.

Konder, Alexandre. "Os grandes amigos do Brasil." In *Brasil e Japão: Duas civilizações que se completam,* pp. 166–172. São Paulo: Empreza Gráfica da Revista dos Tribunaes, 1934.

Koseritz, Carl von. *Imagens do Brasil.* Translated by Afonso Arinos de Melo Franco. Belo Horizonte: Ed. Itatiaia, 1980.

Kousser, J. Morgan, and James M. McPherson, eds. *Region, Race, and Reconstruction: Essays in Honor of C. Vann Woodward.* New York: Oxford University Press, 1982.

Kowarick, Lúcio, org. *As lutas sociais e a cidade: São Paulo, passado e presente.* Rio de Janeiro: Paz e Terra, 1988.

Kowarick, Lúcio, and Clara Ant. "Cem anos de promiscuidade: O cortiço na cidade de São Paulo." In *As lutas sociais e a cidade: São Paulo, passado e presente,* organized by Lúcio Kowarick, pp. 49–71. Rio de Janeiro: Paz e Terra, 1988.

Koyama, Tsuguo. "Japoneses na Amazônia: Alguns aspectos do processo de sua integração sócio-cultural." In *A presença japonesa no Brasil,* edited by Hiroshi Saito, pp. 11–28. São Paulo: T. A. Queiroz/EDUSP, 1980.

Kromkowski, John A., ed. *Race and Ethnic Relations 94/95.* Guilford, CT: Dushkin Publishing Group, 1994.

Kumusaka, Y., and H. Saito. "Kachigumi: A Collective Delusion Among the Japanese and Their Descendants in Brazil." *Canadian Psychiatric Association Journal* 15:2 (April 1970), 167–175.

Kunieda, Sumire. "JAPANESE EMIGRANTS TO DOMINICAN REPUBLIC DEMAND GOVERNMENT COMPENSATION." *Mainichi Daily News,* 10 October 1997.

Kushigian, Julia. *Orientalism in the Hispanic Literary Tradition: In Dialogue with Borges, Paz, and Sarduy.* Albuquerque: University of New Mexico Press, 1991.

Laërne, C. F. Van Delden. *Brazil and Java: Report on Coffee-Culture in America, Asia and Africa.* London: W. H. Allen; The Hague: Martinus Nijhoff, 1885.

Lai, Chi-kong. "Li Hung-chang and Modern Enterprise: The China Merchants Company, 1872–1885." In *Li Hung-chang and China's Early Modernization,* edited by Samuel C. Chu and Kwang-Ching Liu, pp. 216–247. Armonk, NY: M. E. Sharpe, 1994.

Larcher, José de Souza. *Viagens no Oriente: O que eu vi e ouvi atravez do Egypto e da velha Europa.* Rio de Janeiro: Livraria Schettino, n.d.

Laskier, Michael M. *The Alliance Israélite Universelle and the Jewish Communities of Morocco: 1862-1962.* Albany: State University of New York Press, 1983.

Leão, A. Carneiro. *S. Paulo em 1920.* Rio de Janeiro: Anuário Americano, 1920.

Leão, Valdemar Carneiro. *A crise da imigração japonesa no Brasil (1930-1934): Contornos diplomáticos.* Brasília: IPRI/Fundação Alexandre de Gusmão, 1990.

Legoyt, Alfred. *L'émigration européenne: Son importance, ses causes, ses effets avec un appendice sur l'émigration africaine, hindoue et chinoise.* Marseilles: Typ. Roux, 1861.

Leibovici, Sarah. *Chronique des juifs de Tétouan (1860-1896).* Paris: Editions Maisonneuve & Larose, 1984.

Leite, Ilka Boaventura. "Invisibilidade étnica e identidade: Negros em Santa Catarina." *Encontros com a antropologia* (Curitiba) (May 1993), 63-71.

Lemos, Miguel. *Immigração chineza: Mensagem a s. ex. o embaixador do Celeste Império junto aos governos de França e Inglaterra.* Rio de Janeiro: Sociedade Positivista, 1881.

Lenharo, Alcir. *Sacralização da política.* Campinas: Papirus/Editora da UNICAMP, 1986.

Lent, John A., ed. *The Asian Newspapers' Reluctant Revolution.* Ames: Iowa State University Press, 1971.

Lesser, Jeffrey. "Always Outsiders: Asians, Naturalization and the Supreme Court." *Amerasia Journal* 12:1 (1985-1986), 83-100.

———. "From Pedlars to Proprietors: Lebanese, Syrian and Jewish Immigrants in Brazil." In *The Lebanese in the World: A Century of Emigration,* edited by Albert Hourani and Nadim Shehadi, pp. 393-410. London: I. B. Tauris; New York: St. Martin's Press, 1992.

———. "Are African Americans African or American? Brazilian Immigration Policy in the 1920's." *Review of Latin American Studies* 4:1 (1991), 115-137. Published in Portuguese as "Legislação imigratória e dissimulação racista no Brasil (1920-1934)." *Arché* 3:8 (1994), 79-98.

———. "Immigration and Shifting Concepts of National Identity in Brazil During the Vargas-Era." *Luso-Brazilian Review* 31:2 (Winter 1994), 27-48. Published in Portuguese as "Imigração e mutações conceituais da identidade nacional no Brasil durante a era Vargas." *Revista Brasileira de História* (São Paulo) 14:28 (1994), 121-150.

———. "Asians in South America." In *Encyclopedia of World Cultures.* Vol. 7, *South America,* edited by Johannes Wilbert, pp. 58-61. New York: G. K. Hall/Macmillan, 1995.

———. " 'O judeu é o turco de prestação': Etnicidade, assimilação e imagens das elites sobre árabes e judeus no Brasil." *Estudos Afro-Asiáticos* (Rio de Janeiro) 27 (April 1995), 65-85.

———. "Neither Slave nor Free, Neither Black nor White: The Chinese in Early Nineteenth Century Brazil." *Estudios Interdisciplinarios de América Latina y el Caribe* 5:2 (July-December, 1995), 23-34.

———. *Welcoming the Undesirables: Brazil and the Jewish Question.* Berkeley: University of California Press, 1995.

Levine, Robert. *The Vargas Regime: The Critical Years, 1934-1938.* New York: Columbia University Press, 1970.

————. *Race and Ethnic Relations in Latin America and the Caribbean: An Historical Dictionary and Bibliography.* Metuchen, NJ: Scarecrow Press, 1980.

Levy, Herbert V. *Problemas actuais da economia brasileira.* São Paulo: Empresa Gráfica da Revista dos Tribunaes. 1934.

Levy, Maria Stella Ferreira. "O papel da migração internacional na evolução da população brasileira (1872 à 1972)." *Revista de Saúde Pública* supp., 8 (1974), 49–90.

Lewin, Linda. *Politics and Parentela in Paraíba: A Case Study of Family-Based Oligarchy in Brazil.* Princeton: Princeton University Press, 1987.

Lian, George. "Aspectos e particularidades da imigração árabe." *Digesto Econômico* 2:13 (December 1945), 74–77.

Light, Ivan, and Edna Bonacich. *Immigrant Entrepreneurs: Koreans in Los Angeles, 1965–1982.* Berkeley: University of California Press, 1988.

Lima, Areobaldo E. de Oliveira. *A imigração japonesa para o estado de Paraíba do Norte.* São Paulo: Empresa Gráfica Revista dos Tribunais, 1936.

Lima, Manuel de Oliveira. *No Japão: Impressões da terra e da gente.* 2nd ed. Rio de Janeiro: Laemmert, 1905.

Linger, Daniel. "Brazil Displaced: Restaurante 51 in Nagoya, Japan." *Horizontes Antropológicos* (Pôrto Alegre) 5 (1997), 181–203.

————. "The Identity Path of Eduardo Mori." In *History in Person: Enduring Struggles and Identities in Practice,* edited by Jean Lave and Dorothy Holland. Santa Fe, NM: School of American Research Press (forthcoming). Used with permission of the author.

Lisboa, Henrique C. R. *Os chins do Tetartos.* Rio de Janeiro: Typografia da Empresa Democrática Editora, 1894.

Lobo, Bruno. *Japonezes no Japão-No Brasil.* Rio de Janeiro: Imprensa Nacional, 1926.

————. *De japonez à brasileiro—Adaptação e nacionalisação do imigrante.* Rio de Janeiro: Typ. do Dep. Nacional de Estatística, 1932.

————. *Esquecendo os antepassados: Combatendo os estrangeiros.* São Paulo: Editorial Alba, 1935.

Lopez, David, and Yen Espiritu. "Panethnicity in the United States: A Theoretical Framework." *Ethnic and Racial Studies* 13:2 (1990), 198–223.

Love, Joseph L. *São Paulo in the Brazilian Federation, 1889–1937.* Stanford: Stanford University Press, 1980.

Luccock, John. *Notes on Rio de Janeiro and the Southern Parts of Brazil: Taken During a Residence of Ten years in That Country from 1808 to 1818.* London: Samuel Leigh, in the Strand, 1820. Published in Portuguese as *Notas sobre o Rio de Janeiro e partes meridionais do Brasil.* Translated by Milton da Silva Rodrigues. Foreword by Mário Guimarães Ferri. Belo Horizonte: Editora Itatiaia; São Paulo: Editora da Universidade de São Paulo, 1975.

Ludwig, Armin K. *Brazil: A Handbook of Historical Statistics.* Boston: G. K. Hall, 1985.

Luizetto, Flávio V. "Os constituintes em face da imigração (estudo sobre o preconceito e a discriminação racial e étnica na Constituinte de 1934)." M.A. thesis. Universidade de São Paulo, 1975.

Lustoza, Vicente. *Viagem ao Japão: Circunavegando o globo.* Rio de Janeiro and Paris: H. Garnier, 1909.

Macaulay, Neill. *Dom Pedro: The Struggle for Liberty in Brazil and Portugal, 1798-1834.* Durham, NC: Duke University Press, 1986.

MacDonald, John, and Leatrice MacDonald. "Chain Migration, Ethnic Neighborhood Formation and Social Networks." *Milbank Memorial Fund Quarterly* 13:42 (1964), 82-95.

MacKay, Angus. *Spain in the Middle Ages: From Frontier to Empire, 1000-1500.* London: Macmillan Press, 1977.

MacNair, Harley Farnsworth. *The Chinese Abroad: Their Position and Protection. A Study in International Law and Relations.* Shanghai: Commercial Press, 1924.

Maeyama, Takashi. "O imigrante e a religião: Estudo de uma seita religiosa japonesa em São Paulo." M.A. thesis. Fundação Escola de Sociologia e Política de São Paulo, 1967.

——. "Ethnicity, Secret Societies, and Associations: The Japanese in Brazil." *Comparative Studies in Society and History* 21:4 (April 1979), 589-610.

——. "Japanese Religions in Southern Brazil: Change and Syncretism." *Latin America Studies* (Tsukuba, Japan) 6 (1983), 181-238.

Magalhaens, Cezar. *Pela brazilidade (discursos e conferências).* Rio de Janeiro: Typ. A. Pernambucana Hermes Poffes, 1925.

Magalhães, Pero de. *The Histories of Brasil.* Translated by John B. Stetson. 2 vols. New York: Cortés Society, 1922.

Maio, Marcos Chor, and Ricardo Ventura Santos, eds. *Raça, ciência e sociedade.* Rio de Janeiro: FIOCRUZ/CCBB, 1996.

Makiko, Nakano. *Makiko's Diary: A Merchant Wife in 1910 Kyoto.* Translated, with an introduction and notes, by Kazuko Smith. Stanford: Stanford University Press, 1995.

Malheiro, Agostinho Marques Perdigão. *A escravidão no Brasil: Ensaio histórico-jurídico-social,* Parte 3, *Africanos.* Rio de Janeiro: Typ. Nacional, 1867.

Marcus, Greil. *Lipstick Traces: A Secret History of the Twentieth Century.* Cambridge, MA: Harvard University Press, 1989.

Marques, Xavier. "Imigrantismo e brasilidade." *Revista da Academia Brasileira de Letras* 41:63 (January-June 1942), 11-17.

Marr, Phebe. *The Modern History of Iraq.* Boulder, CO: Westview Press, 1985.

Marson, Adalberto. *A ideologia nacionalista em Alberto Torres.* São Paulo: Duas Cidades, 1979.

Martins, Alfredo Romario. *Quanto somos e quem somos: Dados para a história e a estatística do povoamento de Paraná.* Curitiba: Empresa Gráfica Paranaense, 1941.

Martins, Joaquim Pedro Oliveira. *O Brazil e as colônias portuguezas* [1880]. 4th ed. Lisbon: Parceria Antonio Maria Pereira, 1904.

Martins, Wilson. *História da inteligência brasileira.* 7 vols. São Paulo: Cultrix, 1978.

Mauá, Visconde de. *Autobiografia ("Exposição aos credores e ao público") seguida de "O meio circulante do Brasil."* 2nd ed. Preface and notes by Claudio Ganns. Rio de Janeiro:

Editora Zelio Valverde, 1943. Originally published as *Exposição do visconde de Mauá aos credores de Mauá e Cia. e ao público*. Rio de Janeiro: Typ. Imp. e Const. de J. Villeneuve, 1879.

McAlister, Lyle N. *Spain and Portugal in the New World, 1492–1700*. Minneapolis: University of Minnesota Press, 1984.

McCann, Frank D., Jr. *The Brazilian-American Alliance, 1937–1945*. Princeton: Princeton University Press, 1973.

McLain, Douglas, Jr. "Alberto Torres, Ad Hoc Nationalist." *Luso-Brazilian Review* 4 (December 1967), 17–34.

Meade, Teresa A. *"Civilizing Rio": Reform and Resistance in a Brazilian City, 1889–1930*. University Park: Pennsylvania State University Press, 1997.

Mello, Astrogildo Rodrigues de. "Immigração e colonização." *Geografia* 1:4 (1935), 25–49.

Mello Franco, Affonso Arinos de. *Conceito de civilização brasileira*. Serie Brasiliana 70. São Paulo: Companhia Editora Nacional, 1936.

Mendes, Armando. *O Japão que avança: Apectos econômicos, estudos e impressões de viagem ao Japão*. São Paulo: Editora Record, 1937.

Mendonça, Salvador de. *Trabalhadores aziaticos, por Salvador de Mendonça, consul geral do Brazil nos Estados-Unidos. Obra mandada publicar pelo exm. conselheiro João Lins Vieira Cansansão de Sinimbú, presidente do Conselho de ministros e ministro e secretário de estado dos negócios de agricultura, commércio e obras públicas*. New York: Typ. do Novo Mundo. 1879.

Mérian, Jean-Yves. *Aluísio Azevedo: Vida e obra (1857–1913). O verdadeiro Brasil do século XIX*. Rio de Janeiro: Editora Espaço e Tempo, 1988.

Miller, Stuart C. *The Unwelcome Immigrant: The American Image of the Chinese, 1785–1882*. Berkeley: University of California Press, 1969.

Millones, Luis. *Minorías étnicas en el Perú*. Lima: Pontificia Universidad Católica del Perú, 1973.

Miranda, Mário Botelho de. *Um brasileiro no Japão em guerra*. São Paulo: Companhia Editora Nacional, 1944.

———. *Shindo Renmei: Terrorismo e extorsão*. São Paulo: Editora Saraiva, 1948.

Mita, Chiyoko. "Ochenta años de inmigración japonesa en el Brasil." *Estudios migratorios latinoamericanos* 10:30 (August 1995), 431–452.

Miyajima, Mikinosuke. "L'abus de l'opium et sa répression au Japon." In *La vie sociale au Japon publié par Mikinosuke Miyajima*, edited by Kakichi Mitsukuri, pp. 1–57. Paris: Société Franco-Japonaise de Paris, 1922.

Miyao, Susumu, and José Yamashiro. "A comunidade nipônica no período da guerra." In *Uma Epopéia Moderna: 80 Anos da Imigração Japonesa no Brasil*, edited by Comissão de Elaboração da História dos 80 Anos da Imigração Japonesa no Brasil, pp. 247–265. São Paulo: Editora Hucitec, 1992.

Monteleone, Pedro. *Os 5 problemas da eugenia brasileira*. São Paulo: Faculdade de Medicina de São Paulo, 1929.

Montrose, Louis. "The World of Gender in the Discourse of Discovery." In *New World*

Encounters, edited by Stephen Greenblatt, pp. 177–217. Berkeley: University of California Press, 1993.

Moraes, Carlos de Souza. *A ofensiva japonesa no Brasil: Aspecto social, econômico e político da colonização nipônica*. 2nd ed. Pôrto Alegre: Edição da Livraria do Globo, 1942.

Moreira, Augusta Peick. "No Oriente (impressões de viagem)." In Juliano Moreira, *Impressões de uma viagem ao Japão em 1928*, pp. 119–145. N.p.: Biblioteca Juliano Moreira, 1935.

Moreira, Gastão. *Colonização japoneza por Gastão Moreira, engenheiro fiscal do governo do estado de São Paulo junto a Kaigai Kogyo Kabuskiki Kaisha*. Rio de Janeiro: Pimenta de Mello, 1923.

Moreira, Juliano. *Impressões de uma viagem ao Japão em 1928*. N.p.: Biblioteca Juliano Moreira, 1935.

Moreira, Nicolão Joaquim. *Relatório sobre a imigração nos Estados Unidos da América apresentado ao exm. sr. ministro da agricultura, commércio e obras públicas*. Rio de Janeiro: Typografia Nacional, 1877.

Mori, Koichi. "Mundo dos brasileiros mestiços descendentes de japoneses." Unpublished paper (1994) used by permission of the author.

———. "Buraziru Karano Nikkei-Jin Dekassedgui no Tokucho to Suii" [Evolução e situação vigente dos dekasseguis brasileiros no Japão]. In *Os dekasseguis brasileiros de origem japonesa—Coletânea de teses*, edited by Masako Watanabe, pp. 491–546. Tokyo: Editora Fukutake, 1995.

———. "Nikkei-Shudanchi Ni Totteno 'Dekassegui' no Motsu Imi" [O significado do fenômeno dekassegui na comunidade nipo-brasileira]. In *Os dekasseguis brasileiros de origem japonesa—Coletânea de teses*, edited by Masako Watanabe, pp. 547–584. Tokyo: Editora Fukutake, 1995.

———. "Por que os brasileiros começaram a apreciar a culinária japonesa? As condições de accitação da culinária japonesa na cidade de São Paulo." Unpublished paper (1997) used by permission of the author.

Moriyama, Alan Takeo. *Imingaisha: Japanese Emigration Companies and Hawaii, 1894–1908*. Honolulu: University of Hawaii Press, 1985.

Mörner, Magnus. *Adventurers and Proletarians: The Story of Migrants in Latin America*. Pittsburgh: University of Pittsburgh Press, 1985.

———, ed. *Race and Class in Latin America*. New York: Columbia University Press, 1970.

Morse, Richard B. *From Community to Metropolis: A Biography of São Paulo, Brazil*. Gainesville: University of Florida Press, 1958.

Moses, John G. *The Lebanese in America*. Utica, NY: J. G. Moses, 1987.

Mota, Carlos Guilherme, ed. *Brasil em perspectiva*. 5th ed. São Paulo: Difel, 1985.

Moura, Paulo Cursino de. *São Paulo de outrora: Evocações da metrópole*. [1932]. Belo Horizonte: Editora Itatiaia; [São Paulo]: Editora da Universidade de São Paulo, 1980.

Müller, Friedrich Max. *Introduction to the Science of Religion*. [1873]. New York: Arno Press, 1978.

Mulvey, Christopher. *Anglo-American Landscapes: A Study of Nineteenth-Century Anglo-American Travel Literature*. Cambridge: Cambridge University Press, 1983.

Nabhan, Neuza Neif. *O imigrante libanês em São Paulo: Estudo de fala.* São Paulo: FFLCH/ Universidade de São Paulo, 1989.

Nakadate, Jouji. "O Japão venceu os aliados na Segunda guerra mundial? O movimento Shindo Renmei em São Paulo (1945/1949)." M.A. thesis. Pontifícia Universidade Católica, 1988.

Nakasumi, Tetsuo, and José Yamashiro. "O fim da era de imigração e a consolidação da nova colônia nikkei." In *Uma epopéia moderna: 80 anos da imigração japonesa no Brasil,* edited by Comissão de Elaboração da História dos 80 Anos da Imigração Japonesa no Brasil, pp. 417–458. São Paulo: Editora Hucitec, 1992.

Needell, Jeffrey D. *A Tropical Belle Epoque: Elite Culture and Society in Turn-of-the-Century Rio de Janeiro.* Cambridge: Cambridge University Press, 1987.

———. "History, Race and the State in the Thought of Oliveira Vianna." *Hispanic American Historical Review* 75:1 (February 1995), 1–30.

Neiva, Arthur Hehl. "Estudos sobre a imigração semita no Brasil." *Revista de Imigração e Colonização* 5:2 (June 1944), 215–422.

———. *Deslocados de guerra: A verdade sobre sua seleção.* Rio de Janeiro: n.p., 1949.

Neiva, Arthur Hehl, and Manuel Diégues. "The Cultural Assimilation of Immigrants in Brazil." In *The Cultural Integration of Immigrants: A Survey Based upon the Papers and Proceeding of the UNESCO Conference Held in Havana, April 1956,* edited by W. D. Borrie, pp. 181–233. New York: UNESCO, 1957.

Nerval, Gerard de. *Voyage en Orient.* [1851]. Paris: Garnier-Flammarion, 1980.

Neves, Herculano. *O processo da "Shindo-Renmei" e demais associações secretas japonesas.* São Paulo: n.p., 1960.

Niemeyer, Waldyr. *O japonez no Brasil (um face de nosso problema imigratório).* Rio de Janeiro: Editora Brasileira Lux, 1925.

Nijland, C. "A 'New Andalusian' Poem." *Journal of Arabic Literature* 17 (1987), 102–120.

———. "The Fatherland in Arab Emigrant Poetry." *Journal of Arabic Literature* 20 (March 1989), 57–68.

Ninomia, Masato, ed. *Dekassegui: Palestras e exposições do simpósio sobre o fenômeno chamado dekassegui.* São Paulo: Estação Liberdade/Sociedade Brasileira de Cultura Japonesa, 1992.

Nogueira, Arlinda Rocha. *A imigração japonesa para a lavoura cafeeira paulista, 1908–1922.* São Paulo: Instituto de Estudos Brasileiros, 1973.

———. *Companhias interessadas na introdução de asiáticos em São Paulo nos primeiros anos de República.* São Paulo: Centro de Estudos Nipo-Brasileiros, 1979.

———. *Imigração japonesa na história contemporânea do Brasil.* São Paulo: Centro de Estudos Nipo-Brasileiros, 1983.

Nolte, Sharon H., and Sally Ann Hastings. "The Meiji State's Policy Toward Women, 1890–1910." In *Recreating Japanese Women, 1600–1945,* edited by Gail Lee Bernstein, pp. 151–174. Berkeley: University of California Press, 1991.

Nomura, Tania, ed. *Universo em segredo: A mulher nikkei no Brasil.* São Paulo: Aliança Cultural Brasil-Japão/Editora Nova Stella, 1991.

Normano, J. F., and Antonello Gerbi. *The Japanese in South America: An Introductory Survey with Special Reference to Peru.* New York: John Day, 1943.

Novinsky, Anita. *Cristãos novos na Bahia*. São Paulo: Editora Perspectiva, 1972.

O'Brien, Jay, and William Roseberry, eds. *Golden Ages, Dark Ages: Imagining the Past in Anthropology and History*. Berkeley: University of California Press, 1991.

O'Callaghan, Joseph F. *A History of Medieval Spain*. Ithaca, NY: Cornell University Press, 1975.

O'Neil, Charles F. "The Search for Order and Progress: Brazilian Mass Education, 1915–1933." Ph.D. thesis. University of Texas at Austin, 1975.

Ohinata, Den, director. *E a paz volta a reinar na época do "Shindo Renmei."* São Paulo: Produção Cinematográfica Liberdade, 1956.

Ohno, Massao, ed. *O nikkei e sua americanidade: Temas apresentados na III convenção panamericana nikkei*. São Paulo: Massao Ohno, 1986.

Okada, John. *No-No Boy*. Seattle and San Francisco: Combined Asian American Resources Project, 1976.

Oliveira, Antônio Xavier de. *O problema imigratório na América Latina: O sentido político-militar da colonisação japonesa nos paises do novo mundo*. Rio de Janeiro: A. Coelho Branco, 1942.

———. "Três heróis da campanha anti-nipônica." *Revista de Imigração e Colonização* 6:2–3 (May–September 1945), 235–254.

Oliveira, Lúcia Lippi, Eduardo Rodrígues Gomes, and Maria Celina Whately. *Elite intelectual e debate político nos anos 30: Uma bibliografia comentada da Revolução de 1930*. Rio de Janeiro: Fundação Getúlio Vargas/Instituto Nacional do Livro, 1980.

Onffroy de Thoron, Enrique. *Voyages des flottes de Salomon et d'Hiram en Amérique: Position géographique de Parvaim, Ophir & Tarschisch*. Paris: Imp. G. Towne, 1868.

Ornellas, Manoelito de. *Gaúchos e beduinos: A origem étnica e a formação social do Rio Grande do Sul*. Rio de Janeiro: José Olympio, 1948.

Ostle, Robin, ed. *Modern Literature in the Near and Middle East, 1850–1970*. London: Routledge, 1991.

Pacheco, Renato José Costa, ed. *Antologia do jogo do bicho*. São Paulo: Simões Ed., 1957.

Pacheco, Renato José Costa. "O imigrante na literatura brasileira de ficção." *Sociologia* 18:3 (August 1956), 201–232.

Padilha, Dráuzio Leme. *CAC: Cooperativismo que deu certo*. São Paulo: Cooperativa Agrícola de Cotia, Cooperativa Central, 1989.

Padilha, Leão. *O Brasil a posse de si mesmo*. Rio de Janeiro: Gráfica Olímpica, 1941.

Pagden, Anthony. "The Effacement of Difference: Colonialism and the Origins of Nationalism in Diderot and Herder." In *After Colonialism: Imperial Histories and Postcolonial Displacements*, edited by Gyan Prakash, pp. 129–152. Princeton: Princeton University Press, 1995.

Pann, Lynn. *Sons of the Yellow Emperor: A History of the Chinese Diaspora*. Boston: Little, Brown, 1990.

Parker, Richard G. *Bodies, Pleasures and Passions: Sexual Culture in Contemporary Brazil*. Boston: Beacon Press, 1991.

Patai, Daphne. "Minority Status and the Stigma of 'Surplus Visibility.'" *Chronicle of Higher Education* 38:10 (30 October 1991), A52.

Paula, Eurípides Simões de, ed. *O japonês em São Paulo e no Brasil.* São Paulo: Centro de Estudos Nipo-Brasileiros, 1971.

Peixoto, Afrânio. *Viagem sentimental.* Rio de Janeiro: Editora Americana, 1931.

Penna, Gustavo. *Immigração chineza para o estado de Minas Gerais.* Juiz de Fora: Typ. Pereira, 1892.

Pereira, Antônio Baptista. *O Brasil e a raça: Conferência feita na Faculdade de direito de São Paulo a 19 de junho de 1928.* São Paulo: Empresa Gráfica Rossetti, 1928.

Pereira, Antonio Coutinho Gomes. *Viagem de circunavegação do navio-escola "Benjamin Constant" (de 22 de janeiro à 16 de dezembro de 1908).* Rio de Janeiro: Imprensa Nacional, 1909.

Pereira, Jõao Baptista Borges. "Os estudos sobre imigração na antropologia brasileira." *Iberoamericana* (Tokyo) 14:1 (1992), 37–41.

Pereira, Luiz Carlos Bresser. "Origens étnicas e sociais do empresário paulista." *Revista de Administração e Empresas* 4:1 (June 1964), 83–106.

Pessôa, Lindolpho. "A missão dos brasileiros." In *Anuário contendo os fatos de maior relevância da sua atividade no ano social do 1934 principalmente a campanha contra a imigração dos assírios,* organized by Instituto da Ordem de Advogados do Paraná, pp. 93–94. Curitiba: n.p., 1936.

Petrone, Pasquale, organizer. *Pinheiros: Estudo geográfico de um bairro paulistano.* São Paulo: Editora da Universidade de São Paulo, 1963.

Phipps, E. Constantine. *Report by Mr. Phipps on Emigration to Brazil. Presented to Both Houses of Parliament by Command of Her Majesty, June 1872.* London: Harrison and Sons, 1872.

Pinheiro, José Pedro Xavier. *Importação de trabalhadores chins: Memória apresentada ao ministério da agricultura, comércio e obras públicas e imprensa por sua ordem.* Rio de Janeiro, Typ. de João Ignacio da Silva, 1869.

Pinto, Regina Pahim. "Movimento negro e etnicidade." *Estudos afro-asiáticos* 19 (1990), 190–224.

Pontes, Carlos. *Tavares Bastos (Aureliano Candido), 1839–1875.* Serie Brasiliana 136. São Paulo: Companhia Editora Nacional, 1939.

Poppino, Rollie E. *Brazil: The Land and People.* New York: Oxford University Press, 1973.

Prado, Ambrósio Fernandes. *Dialogues of the Great Things of Brazil* [*Diálogos das grandezas do Brasil*]. Albuquerque: University of New Mexico Press, 1987.

Prado, Eduardo. *Viagens: A Sicilia, Malta e o Egypto.* 2nd ed. São Paulo: Escola Typográfica Salesiana, 1902.

Prassad, Ram Chandra. *Early English Travellers in India: A Study in the Travel Literature of the Elizabethan and Jacobean Periods with Particular Reference to India.* 2nd ed. Delhi: Motilal Banarsidass, 1980.

Pratt, Mary Louise. *Imperial Eyes: Travel Writing and Transculturation.* London and New York: Routledge, 1992.

Primeiro Congresso Brasileiro de Eugenia. *Actas e trabalhos.* Vol. 1. Rio de Janeiro: n.p. 1929.

Produção Cinematográfica Liberdade. *E a Paz Volta a Reinar na época do "Shindo Renmei."* São Paulo: Produção Cinematográfica Liberdade, 1956.

Putnam, Samuel. *Marvelous Journey: A Survey of Four Centuries of Brazilian Writing.* New York: Alfred A. Knopf, 1948.

Queiroz, Antonio de. "O problema immigratório e o futuro do Brasil." *Boletim de eugenia* 11 (November 1929), 3.

Queiroz, Eça de. *O Egipto: Notas de viagem.* [1926]. 5th ed. Pôrto: Lello e Irmão, 1946.

———. *O Mandarim.* Pôrto: Lello e Irmão, n.d. Translated by Richard Franko Goldman as *The Mandarin and Other Stories.* Athens: Ohio University Press, 1964.

Queiroz, Maria Isaura Pereira de. "Assimilação de três famílias em São Paulo." *Sociologia* 12:1 (March 1950), 22-32.

R. C. P. "Um perigo para a nacionalidade: A immigração japoneza." *Mensário do "Jornal do Comércio"* 1:1 (January 1938), 119-124.

Ramos, Jair de Souza. "Dos males que vêm com o sangue: As representações raciais e a categoria do imigrante indesejável nas concepções sobre imigração da década de 20." In *Raça, ciência e sociedade,* edited by Marcos Chor Maio and Ricardo Ventura Santos, pp. 59-84. Rio de Janeiro: FIOCRUZ/CCBB, 1996.

Rego Filho, José Pereira. *O Brazil e os Estados Unidos na questão da immigração—Conferência effectuada na augusta presença de sua magestade o imperador em o dia 16 de dezembro de 1880 pelo dr. José Pereira Rego Filho.* Rio de Janeiro: Typografia Nacional, 1884.

Reichl, Christopher A. "Stages in the Historical Process of Ethnicity: The Japanese in Brazil, 1908-1988." *Ethnohistory* 42:1 (Winter 1995), 31-62.

Reis, Fidelis. *Paiz a organizar.* Rio de Janeiro: A. Coelho Branco, 1931.

Reis, Fidelis, and João de Faria. *O problema immigratório e seus aspectos éthnicos: Na Câmara e fora de câmara.* Rio de Janeiro: Typ. Revista dos Tribunaes, 1924.

Reis, João José. *A morte e uma festa: Ritos fúnebres e revolta popular no Brasil do século XIX.* São Paulo: Companhia das Letras, 1991.

———. *Slave Rebellion in Brazil: The Muslim Uprising of 1835 in Bahia.* Translated by Arthur Brakel. Baltimore: Johns Hopkins University Press, 1993.

Reis, P. Pereira dos. "A miscegenação e a etnia brasileira." *Revista de História* 12:48 (October-December 1961), 323-336.

Revorêdo, Julio de. *Immigração.* São Paulo: Empresa Gráfica Revista dos Tribunaes, 1934.

Rezende, Tereza Hatue de. *Ryu Mizuno: Saga japonesa em terras brasileiras.* Curitiba: Secretaria de Estado da Cultura, 1991.

Ribeiro, Francisco Luís. "O japonês como deliqüente político." *Investigações: Revista do Departamento de Investigações* (São Paulo) 1:8 (August 1949), 51-61.

Ricard, Robert. "L'émigration des juifs marocains en Amérique du sud." *Revue de Géographie Marocaine* 7:8 (2nd and 3rd trimesters 1928), 1-6.

———. "Notes sur l'émigration de israélites marocains en Amérique espagnole et au Brésil." *Revue Africaine* 88 (1944), 11-17.

Richmond, Anthony H. *Immigration and Ethnic Conflict.* New York: St. Martin's Press, 1988.

Ridings, Eugene. *Business Interest Groups in Nineteenth-Century Brazil.* Cambridge: Cambridge University Press, 1994.

Rio, João do (Paulo Barreto). *A alma encantadora das ruas.* [1908]. Rio de Janeiro: Edição da Organização Simões, 1951.

Rocha, Joaquim da Silva. *História da colonização do Brasil.* 3 vols. Rio de Janeiro: Imprensa Nacional, 1919.

Rodd, Laurel Rasplica. "Yosano Akiko and the Taishō Debate over the New Woman." In *Recreating Japanese Women, 1600–1945,* edited by Gail Lee Bernstein, pp. 175–198. Berkeley: University of California Press, 1991.

Rodrigues, Francisca Pereira. *O braço estrangeiro.* São Paulo: Imprensa Oficial do Estado, 1938.

Rodrigues, Hildebrando, ed. *Album do Pará: Organizado sob os auspícios do governo do estado e com o apoio da Associação commercial do Pará, sendo interventor federal senhor excellencia o sr. dr. José Carnerio da Gama Malcher.* Belém: Typ. Novidades, 1939.

Rodrigues, José Honório. "Nota liminar." In *Registro de estrangeiros, 1808–1822,* edited by Ministério da Justiça e Negócios Interiores, pp. 5–10. Rio de Janeiro: Arquivo Nacional, 1960.

———. "Brasil e Extremo Oriente." *Política Externa Independente* 2 (August 1965), 57–94.

Rodrigues, Nelson. *O melhor do romance, contos e crônicas.* São Paulo: Companhia das Letras, 1993.

Rodrigues, Nina. *As raças humanas e a responsibilidade penal no Brasil.* [1894]. 3rd ed. Serie Brasiliana 110. São Paulo: Companhia Editora Nacional, 1938.

Romero, Sílvio. *História da literatura brasileira.* [1888]. 2nd ed. 2 vols. Rio de Janeiro: H. Garnier, 1902–1903.

———. *A pátria portugueza. O território e a raça. Apreciação do livro de igual título de Theóphilo Braga.* Lisbon: Livraria Clássica Editora de A. M. Teixeira, 1905.

———. *O allemanismo no sul do Brasil, seus perigos e meios de os conjurar.* Rio de Janeiro: H. Ribeiro, 1906.

Rondón, Frederico A. *Pelo Brasil central.* São Paulo: Companhia Editora Nacional, 1934.

Rondon, José Arouche de Toledo. "Pequena memória de plantação e cultura do chá." *Auxiliador da indústria nacional* 2 (May 1834), 145–152, and (June 1834), 179–184.

Roquette-Pinto, Edgard. *Rondonia.* [1917]. 3rd ed. Serie Brasiliana 30. São Paulo: Companhia Editora Nacional, 1935.

———. *Ensaios de antropologia brasiliana.* [1933]. 2nd ed. Serie Brasiliana 30. São Paulo: Companhia Editora Nacional, 1978.

Rose, Gillian. *Feminism and Geography: The Limits of Geographical Knowledge.* Minneapolis: University of Minnesota Press, 1993.

Rugendas, Johann Moritz. *Malerische Reise in Brasilien von Moritz Rugendas.* Paris: Engelmann, 1835. In Portuguese as João Maurício Rugendas, *Viagem pitoresca através do Brasil.* Translated by Sérgio Milliet. São Paulo: Livraria Martins Editora, 1976.

Ruppin, A. "Migration from and to Syria, 1860–1914." In *The Economic History of the Middle East, 1800–1914,* edited by Charles Issawi, pp. 269–273. Chicago: University of Chicago Press, 1966.

Safa, Elie. *L'Émigration libanaise.* Beirut: Université Saint-Joseph, 1960.

Safady, Jamil. *O Café e O Mascate.* São Paulo: Editora Safady, 1973.

Safady, Jorge. *Antologia Árabe do Brasil.* São Paulo: Editora Comercial Safady, Ltda., no date.

Safady, Wadih. *Cenas e cenários dos camninhos de minha vida.* Belo Horizonte: Estabelecimentos Gráficos Santa Maria, 1966.

Said, Edward W. *Orientalism.* New York: Random House, 1978.

Saito, Hiroshi. "O suicídio entre os imigrantes japonêses e seus descendentes." *Sociologia* 15:2 (May 1953), 109-130.

——. *O japonês no Brasil: Estudo de mobilidade e fixação.* São Paulo: Editora Sociologia e
Política, 1961.

——. *O cooperativismo e a comunidade: Caso da cooperativa agrícola de Cotia.* São Paulo:
Editora Sociologia e Política, 1964.

Saito, Hiroshi, and Takashi Maeyama, eds. *Assimilação e integração dos japoneses no Brasil.* São Paulo: Vozes/EDUSP, 1973.

Sakurai, Célia. *Romanceiro da imigração japonesa.* São Paulo: IDESP/Editora Sumaré, 1993.

——. "La inmigración japonesa en el Brasil: Una historia de ascenso social." *Estudios
migratorios latinoamericanos* 10:29 (April 1995), 149-168.

Sales, Herberto. *Para conhecer melhor Aluísio Azevedo.* Rio de Janeiro: Bloch Editores, 1973.

Salgado, Plínio. *O estrangeiro (crônica da vida paulista).* [1926]. 4th ed. São Paulo: Edições
Panorama, 1948.

——. *Obras completas.* São Paulo: Editora das Américas, 1954-1956.

Salgado dos Santos, Labienne. *Visões da China.* Rio de Janeiro: Editora Zelio Valverde,
1944.

Sampaio Ferraz, Mario de. *Cruzar e nacionalizar.* [1937]. 2nd ed. São Paulo: Typ. Brasil
Rothschild Loureiro, 1939.

Saxton, Alexander. *The Indispensable Enemy: Labor and the Anti-Chinese Movement in
California.* Berkeley: University of California Press, 1971.

Schaefer, Richard T. *Racial and Ethnic Groups.* 4th ed. Glenview, IL: Scott, Foresman/
Little, Brown Higher Education, 1990.

Schneider, Arnd. "The Transcontinental Construction of European Identities: A View
from Argentina." *Anthropological Journal on European Cultures* 5:1 (1996), 95-105.

Schwarcz, Lilia Moritz. *Retrato em branco e negro: Jornais, escravos e cidadãos em São Paulo
no final do século XIX.* São Paulo: Companhia das Letras, 1987.

——. *O espetáculo das raças: Cientistas, instituições e questão racial no Brasil, 1870-1930.*
São Paulo: Companhia das Letras, 1993.

Schwarcz, Lilia Moritz, and Renato da Silva Queiroz. *Raça e diversidade.* São Paulo:
EDUSP/Estação Ciência, 1996.

Schwartzman, Simon, Helena Maria Bousquet Bomeny, and Vanda Maria Ribeiro Costa.
Tempos de Capanema. Rio de Janeiro: Paz e Terra, 1984.

Schwarz, Roberto. "Brazilian Culture: Nationalism by Elimination." *New Left Review* 167
(January/February 1988), 77-90.

Scott, James C. *Weapons of the Weak: Everyday Forms of Peasant Resistance.* New Haven:
Yale University Press, 1985.

——. *Domination and the Arts of Resistance: Hidden Transcripts.* New Haven: Yale University Press, 1990.

Sellek, Yoko. "Nikkeijin: The Phenomenon of Return Migration." In *Japan's Minorities:*

The Illusion of Homogeneity, edited by Michael Weiner, pp. 178-210. London: Routledge, 1997.

Serebrenick, Salamão, and Elias Lipiner. *Breve história dos judeus no Brasil.* Rio de Janeiro: Edições Biblos, 1962.

Sevcenko, Nicolau. *Orfeu extático na metrópole: São Paulo sociedade e cultura nos frementes anos 20.* São Paulo: Companhia das Letras, 1992.

Shibata, Hiromi. "As escolas japonesas paulistas (1915-1945): A afirmação de uma identidade étnica." Ph.D. dissertation. University of São Paulo, 1997.

Silva, Adalberto Prado e, ed. *Novo dicionário brasileiro melhoramentos illustrado.* Vol. 2. São Paulo: Companhia Melhoramentos, 1971.

Silva, Hélio. *1932: A guerra paulista.* Rio de Janeiro: Editora Civilização Brasileira, 1967.

———. *1934—A Constituinte.* Rio de Janeiro: Editora Civilização Brasileira, 1969.

Silva Rocha, Joaquim da. *História da colonisação do Brasil, organizado por Joaquim da Silva Rocha, chefe de secção da directoria do serviço de povoamento.* 3 vols. Rio de Janeiro: Imprensa Nacional, 1919.

Silverblatt, Irene. "Becoming Indian in the Central Andes of Seventeenth-Century Peru." In *After Colonialism: Imperial Histories and Postcolonial Displacements*, edited by Gyan Prakash, pp. 279-298. Princeton: Princeton University Press, 1995.

Simonsen, Roberto. "Aspectos da história econômica do café." In *Anais do Terceiro congresso da história nacional*, edited by Instituto Histórico e Geográfico Brasileiro, pp. 261-276. Rio de Janeiro: Imprensa Nacional, 1941.

Sims, Harold D. "Japanese Postwar Migration to Brazil: An Analysis of the Data Presently Available." *International Migration Review* 6:3 (Fall 1972), 246-266.

———. *Japanese Postwar Migration to Brazil: An Analysis of Data Presently Available.* Pittsburgh: University of Pittsburgh, Center for Latin American Studies, 1973.

Siqueira, Jacy. "A presença sírio-libanesa em Goiás." Goiânia, 1993. Mimeograph.

Skidmore, Thomas E. *Politics in Brazil, 1930-1964: An Experiment in Democracy.* New York: Oxford University Press, 1967.

———. *Black into White: Race and Nationality in Brazilian Thought.* New York: Oxford University Press, 1974.

———. "Racial Ideas and Social Policy in Brazil, 1870-1940." In *The Idea of Race in Latin America, 1870-1940*, edited by Richard Graham, pp. 7-36. Austin: University of Texas Press, 1990.

Sociedade Auxiliadora da Indústria Nacional. *Discurso pronunciado pelo dr. I. J. Galvão na sessão de 3 de outubro de 1870 (questão dos chins).* Rio de Janeiro: Typ. Universal de Laemmert, 1870.

———. *Discurso pronunciado por Joaquim Antonio d'Azevedo em sessão do Conselho administrativo de 3 de outubro de 1870.* Rio de Janeiro: Typ. Universal de Laemmert, 1870.

———. *Discurso pronunciado por José Ricardo Moniz na sessão de 30 de dezembro de 1870 (questão dos chins).* Rio de Janeiro: Typ. Universal de Laemmert, 1871.

———. *Discurso pronunciado por Miguel Calmon Menezes de Macedo na sessão de 30 de dezembro de 1870 (questão dos chins).* Rio de Janeiro: Typ. Universal de Laemmert, 1871.

Sociedade Importadora de Trabalhadores Asiáticos de Procedencia Chineze. *Demonstra-*

ção das conveniências e vantagens à lavoura do Brasil pela introdução dos trabalhadores asiáticos (da China). Rio de Janeiro: Typ. de P. Braga, 1877.

Sociedade Nacional de Agricultura. Immigração: Inquérito promovido pela Sociedade nacional de agricultura. Rio de Janeiro: Villani e Barbero, 1926.

Sodré, Nelson Werneck. História da imprensa no Brasil. Rio de Janeiro: Editora Civilização Brasileira, 1966.

Solberg, Carl. Immigration and Nationalism: Argentina and Chile, 1890-1914. Austin: University of Texas Press, 1970.

Sommer, Doris. Foundational Fictions: The National Romances of Latin America. Berkeley: University of California Press, 1991.

Sorkin, David. The Transformation of German Jewry, 1780-1840. New York: Oxford University Press, 1987.

Souza, Collatino. O trabalho dos chins no norte do Brazil, na Amazônia, nos estados do Rio de Janeiro e de Minas Gerais. Rio de Janeiro: Typ. do Jornal do Brasil, 1892.

Souza, João Cardoso de Menezes e. Theses sobre colonização do Brazil: Projecto de solução as questões sociaes, que se prendem à este difícil problema. Rio de Janeiro: Typografia Nacional, 1875.

Souza, R. Paulo. "Contribuição à etnologia paulista." Revista do Arquivo Municipal de São Paulo 6:35 (January 1937), 96.

Spector, Stanley. Li Hung-chang and the Huai Army: A Study in Nineteenth-Century Chinese Regionalism. Seattle: University of Washington Press, 1964.

Spitzer, Leo. Lives in Between: Assimilation and Marginality in Austria, Brazil, West Africa, 1780-1945. Cambridge: Cambridge University Press, 1989.

Spurr, David. The Rhetoric of Empire: Colonial Discourse in Journalism, Travel Writing, and Imperial Administration. Durham, NC: Duke University Press, 1993.

Stam, Robert. Tropical Multiculturalism: A Comparative History of Race in Brazilian Cinema and Culture. Durham, NC: Duke University Press, 1998.

Staniford, Philip. "Competição e conflito em Tomé-Açu, Pará." In Assimilação e integração dos japoneses no Brasil, edited by Hiroshi Saito and Takashi Maeyama, pp. 346-360. São Paulo: Vozes/EDUSP, 1973.

———. Pioneers in the Tropics: The Political Organization of Japanese in an Immigrant Community in Brazil. New York: Humanities Press, 1973.

Stepan, Nancy Leys. "The Hour of Eugenics": Race, Gender and Nation in Latin America. Ithaca, NY: Cornell University Press, 1991.

Stephan, John J. Hawaii Under the Rising Sun: Japan's Plans for Conquest After Pearl Harbor. Honolulu: University of Hawaii Press, 1984.

Stillman, Norman A. The Jews of Arab Lands in Modern Times. Philadelphia: Jewish Publication Society, 1991.

Stolcke, Verena. "Sexo está para gênero assim como raça para etnicidade?" Estudos Afro-Asiáticos 20 (June 1991), 101-119.

Suleiman, Michael W. "Los árabes en América Latina: Bibliografía preliminar." Estudios Migratorios Latinoamericanos (Buenos Aires) 9:26 (April 1994), 165-188.

Süssekind, Flora. O Brasil não é longe daqui: O narrador, a viagem. São Paulo: Companhia das Letras, 1990.

Suzigan, Wilson. *Indústria brasileira: Origem e desenvolvimento*. São Paulo: Brasiliense, 1986.

Tabajara de Oliveira, Nelson. *Japão: Reportagens do Oriente*. Coleção Viagens, vol. 4. São Paulo: Companhia Editora Nacional, 1934.

———. *Shanghai: Reportagens do Oriente*. Coleção Viagens, vol. 2. São Paulo: Companhia Editora Nacional, 1934.

———. *O roteiro do Oriente*. Coleção Viagens, vol. 8. 2nd ed. São Paulo: Companhia Editora Nacional, 1935.

Tamura, Naomi. *The Japanese Bride*. New York: Harper & Brothers, 1893.

Tannous, Afif I. "Emigration, a Force of Social Change in an Arab Village." *Rural Sociology* 7:1 (March 1942), 62–74.

Tarrazi, Philippe de. *Ta'rikh al-Sihafah al-'Arabiyah* [History of the Arab Press]. Beirut[?]: Al-Matba'ah al-'Adabiyyah, 1913–1933.

Tavares Bastos, Aureliano Candido. *Cartas do Solitário ao redactor do Correio mercantil: Liberdade de cabotagem-abertura do Amazonas. Communicações com os Estados Unidos*. Rio de Janeiro: Typ. do Correio Mercantil, 1862.

———. *Os males do presente e as esperanças do futuro (estudos brasileiros)*. Brasiliana 151. São Paulo: Companhia Editora Nacional, 1939.

———. *Os males do presente e esperanças do futuro*. Typ. de Quirino e Irmão, 1861.

———. *A província: Estudo sobre a descentralisação no Brasil*. [1870]. 2nd ed. Serie Brasiliana 105. São Paulo: Companhia Editora Nacional, 1937.

———. *O valle do Amazonas: A livre navegação do Amazonas, estatística, producções, Commércio, questões fiscaes do valle do Amazonas*. [1866]. 2nd ed. Serie Brasiliana 106. São Paulo: Companhia Editora Nacional, 1937.

Tcheng Ki-tong. *Meu paiz: A China contemporânea*. Rio de Janeiro: Imprensa Nacional, 1892.

Tenório, Oscar. *Immigração*. Rio de Janeiro: Pimenta de Mello, 1936.

———. "As idéais de Tavares Bastos sôbre a imigração." *Revista de Imigração e Colonização* 4:3 (September 1943), 395–404.

Thomas, Nicholas. *Colonialism's Culture: Anthropology, Travel and Government*. Princeton: Princeton University Press, 1994.

Tibawi, A. L. *A Modern History of Syria Including Lebanon and Palestine*. London: Macmillan, 1969.

Tigner, James L. *The Okinawans in Latin America*. Scientific Investigations in the Ryuku Island (SIRI) Report #7. Washington, DC: Pacific Science Board, National Research Council/Department of the Army, 1954.

———. "Shindo Remmei: Japanese Nationalism in Brazil." *Hispanic American Historical Review* 41:4 (November 1961), 515–532.

Tooker, Elisabeth. "Lewis H. Morgan and His Contemporaries." *American Anthropologist* 94:2 (June 1992), 357–375.

Torres, Alberto. *A organização nacional. Primeira parte, a constituição*. Rio de Janeiro: Imprensa Nacional, 1914.

Trindade, Hélgio. *Integralismo: O fascismo brasileiro na década de 30*. 2nd ed. São Paulo: DIFEL, 1979.

Truzzi, Oswaldo M. S. *De mascates a doutores: Sírios e libaneses em São Paulo.* São Paulo: Editora Sumaré, 1991.

———. "Etnicidade e diferenciação entre imigrantes síriolibaneses em São Paulo." *Estudios Migratorios Latinoamericanos* 9:26 (April 1994), 7–46.

Tsuchida, Nobuya. "History of Japanese Emigration to Brazil: 1908–1925." Ph.D. thesis. University of California, Los Angeles, 1971.

Tsurumi, E. Patricia. *Factory Girls: Women in the Thread Mills of Meiji Japan.* Princeton: Princeton University Press, 1990.

Turner, Patricia A. *I Heard It Through the Grapevine: Rumor in African-American Culture.* Berkeley: University of California Press, 1993.

Valle, J. Rodrigues. *Pátria vindoura (em defesa do Brasil).* São Paulo: Gráfica Editora Monteiro-Lobato, 1926.

Varnhagen, Francisco Adolfo de. *História geral do Brasil antes da sua separação e independência de Portugal.* 3rd ed. 5 vols. São Paulo: Companhia Melhoramentos, 1936.

Vasconcellos, F. de B. Accioli de. *Guia do emigrante para o império do Brazil pelo inspector geral das terras e colonização.* Rio de Janeiro: Typ. Nacional, 1884.

Vasconcellos, José. *The Cosmic Race: A Bilingual Edition.* [1925]. Translated and annotated by Didier T. Jaén. Baltimore: Johns Hopkins University Press, 1997.

Ventura, Roberto. *Estilo tropical: História cultural e polêmicas literárias no Brasil, 1870–1914.* São Paulo: Companhia das Letras, 1991.

Vianna, Oliveira. *Raça e assimilação.* São Paulo: Companhia Editora Nacional, 1932.

———. *Populações meridonais do Brasil.* 5th ed. Vol. 1. Rio de Janeiro: José Olympio, 1952.

Vieira, Antóvila Rodrigues Mourao. *O perigo amarelo na Amazônia brasileira: Discursos pronunciados, em 1936, na extinta Assembléia legislativa do Amazonas, pelo então deputado Antóvila R. M. Vieira, contra a concessão de terras amazonenses.* Manaus: Secção de Publicidade da Interventoria do Estado do Amazonas, 1942.

Vieira, Francisca Isabel Schurig. *O japonês na frente de expansão paulista: O processo de absorção do japonês em Marília.* São Paulo: Pioneira/Ed. da Universidade de São Paulo, 1973.

Wagley, Charles, and Marvin Harris. *Minorities in the New World.* London: Oxford University Press, 1958.

Wainer, Samuel. *Minha razão de viver: Memórias de um repórter.* Rio de Janeiro: Record, 1988.

Watanabe, Masako, ed. *Kyōdōkenkyū Dekassegui-Nikkei-Baurajiru-jin: Shiryō-hen* [Group Study—Brazilian Dekaseguis]. Vol. 2. Tokyo: Akashi Shoten, 1995.

Weiner, Michael, ed. *Japan's Minorities: The Illusion of Homogeneity.* London: Routledge, 1997.

Weinstein, Barbara. *The Amazon Rubber Boom, 1850–1920.* Stanford: Stanford University Press, 1983.

Weissman, Albert. " 'Race-Ethnicity': A Dubious Scientific Concept." *Public Health Reports* 105:1 (January–February 1990), 102–103.

Werneck, Luiz Peixoto de Lacerda. *Idéias sobre colonização precedidas de uma succinta exposição dos princípios geraes que regem a população.* Rio de Janeiro: Eduardo e Henrique Laemmert, 1855.

White, Paul, and Robert Woods, eds. *The Geographical Impact of Migration.* New York: Longman Press, 1980.

Willems, Emílio. "Recreação e assimilação entre imigrantes alemães e japonese e seus descendentes." *Sociologia* 3:4 (October 1941), 302–310.

———. "Aspectos da aculturação dos japoneses no estado de São Paulo." *Boletim da Faculdade de Filosofia, Ciências e Letras da USP* 3:82 (1948).

Willems, Emílio, and Hiroshi Saito. "Shindo Renmei: Um problema de aculturação." *Sociologia* 9 (1947), 133–152.

Wilson, Sandra. "The 'New Paradise': Japanese Emigration to Manchuria in the 1930's and 1940's." *International History Review* 17:2 (May 1995), 249–286.

Witter, José Sebastião. "A política imigratória no Brasil." In *Inmigración y política inmigrante en el Cono sur de América.* Vol. 3, edited by Hernán Asdrúbal Silva, pp. 253–260. Washington, DC: CPDP-CAS-PAIGH, 1990.

Wiznitzer, Arnold. *Jews in Colonial Brazil.* New York: Columbia University Press, 1960.

Wolfe, Joel. *Working Women, Working Men: São Paulo and the Rise of Brazil's Industrial Working Class, 1900–1955.* Durham, NC: Duke University Press, 1993.

Wray, Leonard. *The Practical Sugar Planter. A Complete Account of the Cultivation and Manufacture of the Sugar-Cane, According to the Latest and Most Improved Processes, Describing and Comparing the Different Systems Pursued in the East and West Indies and the Straits of Malacca, and the Relative Expenses and Advantages Attendant upon Each: Being the Result of Sixteen Years' Experience as a Sugar Planter in Those Countries.* London: Smith, Elder, 1848.

Yamak, Labib Zuwiyya. *The Syrian Social Nationalist Party: An Ideological Analysis.* Cambridge, MA: Center for Middle Eastern Studies/Harvard University Press, 1966.

Yamanaka, Keiko. "Factory Workers and Convalescent Attendants: Japanese-Brazilian Migrant Women and Their Families in Japan." In *International Female Migration and Japan: Networking, Settlement and Human Rights,* pp. 87–116. Tokyo: International Peace Research Institute, Meiji Gakuin University, 1996.

———. "Return Migration of Japanese Brazilians to Japan: The *Nikkeijin* as Ethnic Minority and Political Construct." *Diaspora* 5:1 (Spring 1996), 65–97.

Yamashiro, José. "Os niseis entre dois penhascos." In *Uma epopéia moderna: 80 Anos da imigração japonesa no Brasil,* edited by Comissão de Elaboração da História dos 80 Anos da Imigração Japonesa no Brasil, pp. 170–188. São Paulo: Editora Hucitec, 1992.

———. *Trajetória de duas vidas: Uma história de imigração e integração.* São Paulo: Aliança Cultural Brasil-Japão/Centro de Estudos Nipo-Brasileiros, 1996.

Yokoyama, Toshio. *Japan in the Victorian Mind: A Study of Stereotyped Images of a Nation, 1850–80.* London: Macmillan, 1987.

Zamir, Meir. *The Formation of Modern Lebanon.* London: Croom Helm, 1985.

Jeffrey Lesser is associate professor, Department of History,
Connecticut College. He is the author of *Welcoming the
Undesirables: Brazil and the Jewish Question* and coeditor of *Arab
and Jewish Immigrants in Latin America: Images and Realities.*

Library of Congress Cataloging-in-Publication Data
Lesser, Jeffrey.
Negotiating national identity : immigrants, minorities, and the
struggle for ethnicity in Brazil / Jeffrey Lesser.
p.   cm.
Includes bibliographical references and index.
ISBN 0-8223-2260-9 (cloth : alk. paper). — ISBN 0-8223-2292-7
(pbk. : alk. paper)
1. Brazil—Ethnic relations.   2. Ethnicity—Brazil.
3. Immigrants—Brazil.   4. Minorities—Brazil.   5. National
characteristics, Brazilian.   6. Asians—Brazil—Ethnic identity.
7. Elite (Social sciences)—Brazil—Attitudes.   I. Title.
F2659.A1L47   1999
305.8'00981—dc21   98-38238   CIP